Digital Convergence:
The Information Revolution

KU-200-914

Springer

London
Berlin
Heidelberg
New York
Barcelona
Hong Kong
Milan
Paris
Santa Clara
Singapore
Tokyo

John Vince and Rae Earnshaw (Eds)

Digital Convergence: The Information Revolution

With 161 figures

UNIVERSITY OF WOLVERHAMPTON
LEARNING RESOURCES

2236575

CLASS 523

CONTROL
1852331402

303.
4833

DATE
18 MAY 2001

SITE
WV

DIG

Springer

John A. Vince, MTech, PhD, FBCS, CEng
School of Media, Arts and Communication, University of
Bournemouth, Talbot Campus, Poole BH12 5BB, UK

Rae Earnshaw, BSc, MSc, PhD, FBCS, CEng
University of Bradford, Bradford BD7 1DP, UK

Cover Illustrations: ActiveX visualization components developed with AVS/Express (see Chapter 12, "Thin" vs. "Fat" Visualization Clients, by Mikael Jern)

ISBN 1-85233-140-2 Springer-Verlag London Berlin Heidelberg

British Library Cataloguing in Publication Data
Digital convergence : the information revolution
    1.Digital communications 2.Information technology
    3.Broadband communication systems 4.Internet (Computer
    network)
    I.Vince, John, 1941- II.Earnshaw, R. A. (Rae A.)
    384.3
    ISBN 1852331402

Library of Congress Cataloging-in-Publication Data
Digital convergence : the information revolution / John Vince and Rae
Earnshaw (eds.).
    p.   cm.
    ISBN 1-85233-140-2 (alk. paper)
    1. Internet (Computer network) 2. World Wide Web (Information
retrieval system) I. Vince, John (John A.) II. Earnshaw, Rae A.,
1944- .
TK5105.875.I57D54 1999   99-18267
303.48'33--dc21   CIP

Apart from any fair dealing for the purposes of research or private study, or criticism or review, as permitted under the Copyright, Designs and Patents Act 1988, this publication may only be reproduced, stored or transmitted, in any form or by any means, with the prior permission in writing of the publishers, or in the case of reprographic reproduction in accordance with the terms of licences issued by the Copyright Licensing Agency. Enquiries concerning reproduction outside those terms should be sent to the publishers.

© Springer-Verlag London Limited 1999
Printed in Great Britain

The use of registered names, trademarks etc. in this publication does not imply, even in the absence of a specific statement, that such names are exempt from the relevant laws and regulations and therefore free for general use.

The publisher makes no representation, express or implied, with regard to the accuracy of the information contained in this book and cannot accept any legal responsibility or liability for any errors or omissions that may be made.

Typesetting: Ian Kingston Editorial Services, Nottingham UK
Printed and bound by MPG Books Ltd, Bodmin, Cornwall
34/3830-543210 Printed on acid-free paper SPIN 10707816

Contents

3 Technological Issues

List of Contributors

Ali Al-Qayedi
VASE Laboratory
Electronic Systems Engineering
University of Essex
Wivenhoe Park
Colchester
CO4 3SQ
UK
Email:
amsmal@essex.ac.uk
Home page:
http://vasewww.essex.ac.uk/

Giuliano Barsanti
FINSIEL
Via Matteucci 34/B
56124 Pisa
Italy
Email:
g.barsanti@finsiel.it
Home page:
http://www.finsiel.it/

Marc Cavazza
EIMC Department
University of Bradford
Bradford BD7 1DP
UK
Email:
M.Cavazza@bradford.ac.uk
Home Page:
http://www.eimc.brad.ac.uk/

Adrian F. Clark
VASE Laboratory
Electronic Systems Engineering
University of Essex
Wivenhoe Park
Colchester
CO4 3SQ
UK
Email:
alien@essex.ac.uk
Home page:
http://esewww.essex.ac.uk/~alien/

Karin Coninx
Limburg University Centre
Expertise Centre for Digital
Media
Wetenschapspark 2
B-3590 Diepenbeek
Belgium
Email:
kconinx@luc.ac.be
Home page:
http://www.edm.luc.ac.be/

G. Constable
Department of Computer Science
University of Wales
Aberystwyth
UK
Email:
dap@aber.ac.uk
Home page:
http://www.aber.ac.uk/

Anton Eliëns
Vrije Universiteit
Dep. of Mathematics and
Computer Science
De Boelelaan 1081, 1081 HV
Amsterdam
The Netherlands
Email:
eliens@cs.vu.nl
Home page:
http://www.cs.vu.nl/

J.L. Encarnação
Fraunhofer-Institute for
Computer Graphics
Rundeturmstr. 6
64 283 Darmstadt
Germany
Email:
jle@igd.fhg.de
Home page:
http://www.igd.fhg.de/

Eddy Flerackers
Limburg University Centre
Expertise Centre for Digital
Media
Wetenschapspark 2
B-3590 Diepenbeek
Belgium
Email:
eflerack@luc.ac.be
Home page:
http://www.edm.luc.ac.be/

Marc Flerackers
ANDROME NV
Wetenschapspark 1
B-3590 Diepenbeek
Belgium
Email:
mflerackers@androme.be
Home page:
http://www.androme.com/

P.R. Giaccone
School of Computer Science and
Electronic Systems
Kingston University
Kingston upon Thames
Surrey
KT1 2EE
UK
Email:
p.giaccone@kingston.ac.uk
Home page:
http://techweb.king.ac.uk/cses/
people/PaulG/

D. Greenhill
School of Computer Science and
Electronic Systems
Kingston University
Kingston upon Thames
Surrey
KT1 2EE
UK
Email:
d.greenhill@kingston.ac.uk
Home page:
http://techweb.king.ac.uk/cses/
people/

Jill A. Hewitt
Department of Computer Science
Faculty of Engineering and
Information Science
University of Hertfordshire
UK
Email:
J.A.Hewitt@herts.ac.uk
Home page:
http://www.cs.herts.ac.uk/

Avon Huxor
Centre for Electronic Arts
Middlesex University
Cat Hill
London
EN4 8HT
UK

Email:
a.huxor@mdx.ac.uk

Home page:
http://www.mdx.ac.uk/

Mikael Jern
Advanced Visual Systems
15 Blokken
DK 3460
Birkeroed
Denmark
Email
mikael@avs.dk

Home page:
http://www.avs.dk/

J. Jiang
School of Computing
University of Glamorgan
Pontypridd
CF37 1DL
UK
Email:
jjiang@glam.ac.uk

Home page:
http://www.glam.ac.uk/

G.A. Jones
School of Computer Science and
Electronic Systems
Kingston University
Kingston upon Thames
Surrey
KT1 2EE
UK
Email:
g.jones@kingston.ac.uk

Home page:
http://techweb.king.ac.uk/cses/
people/

C. Knöpfle
Fraunhofer-Institute for
Computer Graphics
Rundeturmstr. 6
64 283 Darmstadt
Germany

Email:
knoepfle@igd.fhg.de

Home page:
http://www.igd.fhg.de/

Nikolaos Kotsis
26 Richmond Street
Glasgow
G1 1XH
UK
Email:
nick@cs.strath.ac.uk

Home page:
http://www.cs.strath.ac.uk/
~nick/

Robert B. Lambert
26 Richmond Street
Glasgow
G1 1XH
UK
Email:
robert@cs.strath.ac.uk

Home page:
http://www.cs.strath.ac.uk/

D.R. Lawrence
School of Computing and IT
University of Wolverhampton
UK
Email:
cm1994@wlv.ac.uk

Home page:
http://www.wlv.ac.uk/~cm/1950/
contact/index.html

David Leevers
VERS Associates
UK
Email:
DavidLeevers@compuserve.com

Home page:
http://www.vers.co.uk/
dleevers.htm

Douglas R. McGregor
26 Richmond Street
Glasgow
G1 1XH
UK
Email:
douglas@cs.strath.ac.uk
Home page:
http://www.cs.strath.ac.uk/

M.D.J. McNeill
School of Computing and
Mathematics
Faculty of Informatics
University of Ulster
Magee Campus
Northland Road
Londonderry
Northern Ireland
BT48 7JL
UK
Email
mdj.mcneill@ulst.ac.uk
Home page:
http://www.ulst.ac.uk/

James A. Malcolm
Department of Computer Science
Faculty of Engineering and
Information Science
University of Hertfordshire
UK
Email:
J.A.Malcolm@herts.ac.uk
Home page:
http://www.cs.herts.ac.uk/
~comqjam/

Steve Molyneux
IBM Professor of Interactive
Communication Technology
Interactive Communication
Technology Research Centre
University of Wolverhampton
Wolverhampton
UK

Email:
s.molyneux@wlv.ac.uk
Home page:
http://www.wlv.ac.uk/~le1812/

Mariapia Monaldi
FINSIEL
Via Matteucci 34/B
56124 Pisa
Italy
Email:
m.monaldi@finsiel.it
Home page:
http://www.finsiel.it/

S. Müller
Fraunhofer-Institute for
Computer Graphics
Rundeturmstr. 6
64 283 Darmstadt
Germany
Email:
stefanm@igd.fhg.de
Home page:
http://www.igd.fhg.de/

Kieran O'Hea
Techserv
Email:
kohea@ip.lu
Home page:
http://www.techserv.org/

A. Osman
Computing Department
University of Bradford
Bradford
BD7 1DP
UK
Email:
a.osman@brad.ac.uk
Home page:
http://www.eimc.brad.ac.uk/

Ian Palmer
Electronic Imaging and Media
Communications Department
University of Bradford
Bradford
BD7 1DP
UK
Email:
i.j.palmer@brad.ac.uk
Home page:
http://www.eimc.brad.ac.uk/

Jane L. Perrone
Discipline of Sociology
Faculty of Social Science
Open University
Walton Hall
Milton Keynes
MK7 6AA
UK
Email:
jlperrone@yahoo.com
Home page:
http://socsci.open.ac.uk/

D.E. Price
Department of Computer Science
University of Wales
Aberystwyth
UK
Email:
dap@aber.ac.uk
Home page:
http://www.aber.ac.uk/

Michele Re
FINSIEL
Via Matteucci 34/B
56124 Pisa
Italy
Email:
m.re@finsiel.it
Home page:
http://www.finsiel.it/

Carlton Reeve
Electronic Imaging and Media
Communications Department
University of Bradford
Bradford
BD7 1DP
UK
Email:
c.reeve@brad.ac.uk
Home page:
http://www.eimc.brad.ac.uk/

Bastiaan Schönhage
Vrije Universiteit
Department of Mathematics and
Computer Science
De Boelelaan 1081, 1081 HV
Amsterdam
The Netherlands
Email:
bastiaan@cs.vu.nl
Home page:
http://www.vu.nl/english/

and

ASZ Research & Development
Postbus 8300, 1005 CA
Amsterdam
The Netherlands
Email:
schonhage@gak.nl
Home page:
http://www.asz.nl/

A. Sloane
School of Computing and IT
University of Wolverhampton
UK
Email:
Andy.Sloane@computer.org
Home page:
http://www.wlv.ac.uk/~cm1950/

W. Tang
Electronic Imaging and Media
Communications Department
University of Bradford
Bradford
BD7 1DP
UK
Email:
w.tang@brad.ac.uk
Home page:
http://www.eimc.brad.ac.uk/

A.L. Thomas
School of Engineering
University of Sussex
UK
Email:
A.Thomas@sussex.ac.uk
Home page:
http://www.sussex.ac.uk/

M. Unbescheiden
Fraunhofer-Institute for
Computer Graphics
Rundeturmstr. 6
64 283 Darmstadt
Germany
Email:
unbesche@igd.fhg.de
Home page:
http://www.igd.fhg.de/

Frank Van Reeth
Limburg University Centre
Expertise Centre for Digital
Media
Wetenschapspark 2
B-3590 Diepenbeek
Belgium
Email:
fvreeth@luc.ac.be
Home page:
http://www.edm.luc.ac.be/

Jeremy Walton
The Numerical Algorithms
Group, Ltd
Wilkinson House
Jordan Hill Road
Oxford
OX2 8DR
UK
Email:
jeremyw@nag.co.uk
Home page:
http://www.nag.co.uk/

Simeon J. Yates
Discipline of Sociology
Faculty of Social Science
Open University
Walton Hall
Milton Keynes
MK7 6AA
UK
Email:
s.j.yates@open.ac.uk
Home page:
http://socsci.open.ac.uk/simeon/
simeonyates.html

Massimo Zallocco
FINSIEL
Via Matteucci 34/B
56124 Pisa
Italy
Email:
m.zallocco@finsiel.it
Home page:
http://www.finsiel.it/

Introduction

1

Broadband Internet: Future Applications and Challenges

Steve Molyneux

1.1 Introduction

> This is a revolution in communication technology unsurpassed since the invention of the printing press.
>
> *Al Gore, Vice-President of the USA*

There is widespread agreement that convergence is occurring at both the media and technological levels. That is to say, digital technology allows for both traditional and new communication services – voice, data, sound and pictures – to be delivered over many different network infrastructures.

Current market activities suggest that operators from the sectors affected by convergence are acting on the opportunities provided by technological advances to enhance their traditional services and to branch out into new activities. The telecommunications, media and information technology sectors are currently involved in cross-product, cross-platform and cross-sector shareholding to grasp the opportunities that convergence offers. Examples of this include:

- home banking and home shopping over the Internet
- voice over the Internet
- email, data and World Wide Web access over mobile phone networks, and the use of wireless links to homes and businesses to connect them to the fixed telecommunications networks
- data services over digital broadcasting platforms
- online services combined with television via systems such as Web-TV, as well as delivery via digital satellites and cable modems
- Webcasting of news, sports, concerts and of other audio-visual services

Such developments represent concrete examples of a move towards a "Networked Economy" and "Information Society." They show its potential to touch the lives of every citizen and highlight a significant change in the range and diversity of traditional telecommunications and media services.

One of the most significant factors is the increasing use by different sectors of the same technologies. Evidence of such convergence has been mounting in recent years with the emergence of the Internet and with the increasing capability of existing networks to carry both telecommunications and broadcasting services. The phenomenon of convergence is relatively new and a range of different views exists on what its implications are for society. There is broad agreement that developments in digital electronics and software are creating the technological potential for a new approach to the delivery and consumption of information services. Some consider that convergence will lead to the complete and rapid transformation of existing telecommunications, media and information technology services in such a way that these currently separate groups of services will merge into one another, substantially blurring the previously clear distinctions between them.

It is nevertheless clear that the implications of these developments are potentially far-reaching. The emergence of new services and the development of existing services is expected to expand the overall information market. At the same time, the new communication services environment will provide opportunities to enhance the quality of lives by increasing consumer choice, facilitating access to the benefits of the Information Society and promoting cultural diversity. How will this convergence shape the future of our society?

1.2 Digital Technologies Underpin Convergence

The term "convergence" eludes precise definition, but it is most commonly expressed as:

• the ability of different platforms to carry similar kinds of services
• the coming together of once-individual consumer devices such as the telephone, TV and personal computer

The latter definition is the one most often cited. It is easily understood by consumers and has the added interest of reflecting a wider struggle between differing industries. However, in some aspects the convergence of media and devices is much less real than the convergence of networks. Telecommunications operators are already offering audio-visual programming over their networks and have become major players in the provision of Internet access as well as backbone infrastructure. Broadcasters have provided data services over their networks for some years and these services will be enhanced by digital transmission of both radio and television and by the addition of interactivity. Cable operators are providing a range of telecommunications services, including voice telephony, and in some areas they are starting to deploy cable modems to offer high-speed Internet access in addition to their traditional business of television programming distribution.

The underlying trend is the common adoption of digital technologies by the relevant sectors. Digital technologies cover a range of disciplines generally associated with the computer and telecommunications industries. Fragmented within each of the relevant sectors, these technologies have already demonstrated their greater efficiency, flexibility and cost-effectiveness, and have shown how they can enhance creative potential and promote innovation. Computer technology now plays a key role in content creation and production in both cinema and broadcasting worlds. The ways in which audio-visual material is produced, delivered and consumed are evolving. Content is becoming "scalable" so that it can be used in different environments and delivered via different network infrastructures.

As alternative telecommunications infrastructures become more widespread, high-speed networks based on optical fibers will soon be capable, in combination with modern server technology, of operating cost-effectively in a virtual broadcast mode. The high data rates achievable through digital transmission open up the possibility of delivering high-quality audio/video signals over a variety of different network infrastructures. Transmission technologies such as ISDN, xDSL and ATM will ensure that both existing and new infrastructures can play a role in carrying the new services. The capabilities of existing networks are also enhanced by a variety of compression techniques, allowing networks of limited transmission capacity to carry services previously considered possible only on sophisticated and more costly wideband infrastructures. ATM is of considerable interest as a multimedia transport technology. It is a high-speed network technology, capable of transporting telecommunications traffic of different characteristics (voice, data, video) over the same network. This continuing competition between different technologies can change the fortunes of one approach or another, making it difficult to be prescriptive about tomorrow's network architectures. This may be a relatively minor problem given that today's applications and services are becoming increasingly independent of the underlying infrastructure that carries them.

1.3 "Haves" and "Have nots" in the "Information Revolution"

We are drowning in information and starved for knowledge.
John Naisbitt and Patricia Aburdene, MegaTrends

The convergence of media and technology has brought about an "Information Revolution." This poses a question. Who is benefiting most from the developments made in this area? Let us take this opportunity to compare this "revolution" with its forebear, the "Industrial Revolution."

A century ago, on the eve of the Industrial Revolution, the Western world was truly a civilization of "haves" and "have nots." Without the benefit of a large middle class, society was divided between an elite few who enjoyed a life of ease and leisure and the vast majority who toiled in fields and factories. Nowhere was the contrast between citizens more dramatic than in their homes. While the rich had dozens of servants to perform the tedious, backbreaking chores of daily cleaning, ironing and cooking, the masses had no such help, and, as a result, often lived in squalor.

With the Industrial Revolution came the first home appliances. These slowly began to close this gap in living conditions. Large industrial devices used to dye and press bolts of fabric in textile mills were "downsized" into washing machines and clothing irons for people's homes. Cooling pumps used by food processing companies eventually became kitchen refrigerators. The trickle of home appliances instrumental in the foundation of the Industrial Revolution became a torrent by the end of the Second World War, when a typical household owned a dozen or more modern labor-saving devices.

Home appliances helped speed the democratization of society. They provided the lower and newly emerging middle classes with the benefits of the rich – cleanliness and leisure time. Appliances – "mechanical servants" – in many ways helped equalize society and simplify people's lives.

Has the convergence of media and technology led to the development of a new gap between members of the information society, an information gap? For many, the answer is "yes." There is a widening gap between the technical elite, capable of accessing this vast amount of rich online information in their homes, offices and schools, and the rest of society. While those with significant financial resources and technical skills "surf the Web," correspond via electronic mail, conduct online banking and file their tax returns using their personal computers and modems, the ordinary consumer of average means and limited technical knowledge sees the world of electronic information as a distant mirage.

With the expansion of the Internet and the resulting explosion of media-rich electronic information, this gap between the technology "haves" and "have-nots" will continue to widen. This is especially true in countries outside the United Kingdom, where personal computers in the home, and even in many businesses, are a rarity. Moreover, study after study demonstrates that this gap will continue to grow as long as the personal computer remains the only vehicle for accessing materials on the Information Superhighway.

However, a solution to this problem is at hand. Nearly a century after the emergence of the first consumer appliances, a new class of computing devices, aptly dubbed Information Appliances, stands poised to address this information gap. By delivering simple, easy access to information in the same way that original appliances provided simple and easy automation of common household chores, the Information Appliance promises to democratize information access, narrowing the gap between today's technology "haves" and "have nots."

1.4 Simplicity: the Key to the Fountain of Knowledge

> Put simply, the power of the "World-Wide Web" is and will continue to be the simplicity with which you can make information globally available and the simplicity with which that information can be accessed.
>
> *Nicholas Petreley, InfoWorld*

Wherever someone has a question, there is a need for information. "How many cups of sugar in a lemon cake?" "How many units do we have in inventory?" "What was that stock's closing price last night?" "What is the capital of Guatemala?"

Finding the answers to these questions quickly and accurately can make a world of difference. The difference between a lemon cake and a lemon tart. The difference between satisfying a customer and sending them to the competition. The difference between profiting by £5000 on a stock and losing money. The difference between receiving an "A" and an "F" on an examination paper. In short, the difference between success and failure.

Today, finding the answers to these questions entails wading through massive amounts of often useless, unnecessary information contained in a variety of "old media" sources: newspapers, magazines, books, catalogues, broadcast TV and radio. The average consumer is barraged with thousands of commercial and informational messages a day from these traditional media sources. Making sense of all this information, this "Infoglut," and immediately finding the important nuggets people need to perform the task is nearly impossible.

But even as consumers valiantly wade through piles of junk mail and catalogues, the producers of all this information are headed in a fundamentally different direction: into the world of electronic information dissemination. By focusing on the ability to keep information timely and up-to-date, as well as the ability to deliver massive amounts of information without the high costs of traditional printing and distribution, content providers intend to increase their reach and influence through electronic means. Eventually, these providers, ranging from banks and businesses to universities and retailers, hope to leverage the ultimate capability of the electronic age: interactivity.

Unfortunately, these content providers have been unable to bring the mainstream public into the electronic Information Age. The fact is, that while enormous effort has gone into building huge databases of electronic information, millions of CD-ROM titles, and tens of millions of Web pages, as well as massive private and public network infrastructures, including the Internet, to deliver all this content to the masses, comparatively little attention has been paid to how ordinary people will interface with all of this new electronic data. Like the working class of old, who had no access to household help until the arrival of irons, washing machines and vacuum cleaners, today's consumers have no devices that will let them easily and affordably access this wealth of electronic information.

By all measures, the PC is, and will remain, a complex tool for the technical elite and well-heeled few. Today, only 4% of European homes own a computer. Among these, less than 1% use their PCs to access the Internet or other online services. Throughout the rest of the world, personal computer penetration of the home market is little better overall: 17% in Japan, 33% in the USA, and practically zero in Eastern Europe, Africa, Latin America and China.

Even in those countries where home PC penetration is highest, sales of these systems are largely concentrated in the upper income brackets. For example, in the USA, 66% of households earning more than $100,000 annually own home PCs, while only 12% of households earning less than $30,000 do.

So why has the PC been so remarkably unsuccessful as a mass market device? Primarily, it is because PCs are designed for complex use in business environments with large technical support staffs rather than the less demanding and unsupported home and education environments. Just as it makes little sense for most home kitchens to contain oversized, highly engineered refrigerators designed for restaurants or hotels, PCs are the wrong information access devices for average consumers. Consumers confirm this discrepancy between what PCs offer and their needs.

According to studies, consumers consistently say that PCs are:

- too confusing to buy
- too hard to set up and maintain
- bloated with too many unnecessary features; don't accommodate unique needs with their "one size fits all" approach
- too expensive for the value they provide
- inconvenient; too big, too heavy, too ugly

With all of these barriers, it is no wonder that a recent survey found that consumers today rate the utility of their hairdryers higher than their personal computer. Despite 15 years of development, advances in graphical user interface technology, new devices like mice, and help systems, computers still don't provide a convenient interface to the vast stores of electronic information ordinary people would like, or want, to access. While it provides all the capabilities and features that technophiles wholeheartedly enjoy, the personal computer as a device for the masses has failed.

In fact, much as the Industrial Revolution left the home lives of the average citizen untouched until the advent of the appliance, the Information Revolution has left roughly 91% of the public out of touch with online electronic information. Technologists and information providers have myopically focused on laying the concrete, building the entrance ramps, and populating the highway with interesting attractions to encourage everyone onto the Information Superhighway. But they forgot to ask if anyone had a car.

What's needed is a new model for giving people access to the Information Superhighway, a model that takes into account consumers' real needs and desires for information access. A device following this new model will approach the problem of electronic information access from scratch. It will deliver simplified data access, giving consumers the ability to locate and interact with information without the need to understand hardware, software or peripherals. It will give consumers all this at an inexpensive price point. It will be an Information Appliance.

1.5 The Information Appliance: Simple, Inexpensive and Fun

> In three years or less, it should take as much technical skill to buy, finance and register a car – on-line – as it takes today to buy a Pepsi from a vending machine.
> *Michael Fitzpatrick, President, Pacific Telesis*

Fortunately, the model for a successful solution to mass information access exists in the consumer electronics and appliance industry. Today, 98% of US households own a color TV, 88% own a toaster, 87% a microwave and 85% a VCR. The widespread popularity of consumer appliances can be traced not only to their affordable cost but also to their ease of use and convenience, and their ability to perform a single or narrow range of tasks very well. When evaluating the success of the appliance model, it's important to note that consumers have overwhelmingly accepted appliances when they provide a single, easily understood function at an affordable price. For example, combination kitchen appliances – such as the Cuisinart – have had limited success because average consumers (those who don't cook elaborate meals on a daily basis) usually find single-purpose devices like handheld beaters, slicers and graters more convenient, simpler to use and more affordable. Similarly, universal remote controls, while seemingly a good solution to an array of remotes for TV, VCR and stereo, are attractive only to a technical subset of consumers. The required complexity of a universal remote makes them too confusing for the average consumer. When appliances perform a single function, and perform it well, consumers overwhelmingly embrace them.

The single-purpose approach benefits both consumer electronics and appliance providers. Because each device performs one function they can focus on form factors, ergonomics, ease of use and low cost, rather than on delivering an array of complex features. For example, rather than adding new features and functions to a device many people considered too complex already, VCR manufacturers recently focused on bringing down costs while simplifying functions and options.

Clearly, today's consumer appliance manufacturers have defined a model for success in reaching the mass consumer market place: provide the ordinary person with a limited-purpose, low-cost device that is approachable and fun to use. Their success can be seen in the typical household, which has appliances located in nearly every room. In the Information Age, the answer is to adopt this model with respect to computing, to deliver a true Information Appliance.

1.6 Information Access for All

> The primary application for an Information Appliance is to seek, select, and exchange information. It is less a machine for those who hate or fear computers than a simplified, one- or two-function device for those who don't need something more – a consumer electronics product, as non-threatening as a CD player.
>
> *Jack Wilson, Computer Letter*

Information Appliances will deliver exactly the functionality implied by their name. By marrying a consumer electronics approach to the processing power needed to access and manipulate information, they will provide a simple, friendly, and inexpensive interface to electronic information for the millions of people who find personal computers too difficult and expensive.

Like the consumer appliance, the Information Appliance is optimized to perform a single task, simply, easily and inexpensively. For example, a kitchen information device would provide cooks with instant access to recipes and ingredients, while a sports Information Appliance would give armchair soccer players all the latest scores and statistics at the touch of a button.

The chief advantage of these devices for consumers is that by simplifying the functionality they operate like today's home appliances. Because each Information Appliance is optimized for a single or limited range of tasks, its functions can be easily incorporated into the plastic interface: multi-colored buttons for example. Operating an Information Appliance is no more difficult than using a blender.

Space efficiency is another benefit. Because they perform a limited set of functions, Information Appliances don't consume valuable space with a large CPU, disk drives, keyboard and monitor. Indeed, most devices will be delivered to the market as TV accessories, enhanced phones or hard plastic-encased, CD player-sized gadgets, capable of fitting snugly into the kitchen, living room, school desk or office cubicle.

Finally, these digital electronic appliances carry attractive price tags, comparable to today's popular consumer electronics products. Typically priced between £80 and £150, most devices will be marketed similarly to today's cellular phones or cable television boxes, whereby information service providers, telephone companies, cable systems and Internet service providers will supply devices for a nominal amount, or even for free, and then charge a fee for the related information services. As a result, consumers will pay for just the functionality they need, eliminating what so many personal computers in the home have become: £1500 word processors or email terminals. Simple, easy to use and inexpensive, these information devices will be the information interface for the rest of us.

1.7 Is There an Information Appliance Market?

> The steady escalation of desktop capabilities has, in many cases, reached the point of overkill. Information Strategy managers are beginning to wonder if an Intel Pentium-based PC running Windows 95 might be like using a sledgehammer to swat flies. The latest industry buzz indicates a growing interest in more appropriately scaled technology. We're hearing terms such as "thin clients," "shell PCs" and "information appliances" to describe a variety of simple, low-cost devices that will meet the needs of many users.
>
> *Max D. Hopper, Former CIO, American Airlines*

Although the Information Appliance market is in its infancy, most industry analysts agree that the opportunity is tremendous. Optimistic pundits predict that the US market could eventually reach the size of the $65 billion US consumer electronic market. Others believe that, at the very least, the market for these information devices should approach the $12 billion US PC market. In the USA alone, there are almost 24 million televisions sold each year. Last year, telephone sales exceeded 52 million units. These figures demonstrate an extraordinarily vital market for consumer electronics and appliances.

What about PCs and other recently announced computer devices? Although PCs have proved to be the wrong device for average people looking to access electronic information easily and affordably, they will continue to provide a specialized segment of consumers (primarily technical users and well-supported business users) with a powerful multi-purpose platform. Average consumers in their homes, schools or small businesses, though, will instead rely on Information Appliances for accessing the electronic Information Age. Some consumers may find that they will need both in their home. In this case, the PC will continue to be relegated to the den while the rest of the home will be populated with Information Appliances.

Some computer companies have recently announced plans for network computers, Internet terminals and combination PC/television devices. While these devices sound deceptively like Information Appliances and promise to be somewhat less expensive than today's PCs, they suffer from the same drawbacks as their PC forebears. Namely, they are overly complex and difficult to use. Like the PC, these devices suffer because of their general-purpose approach. They must account for a broader variety of users and an ever-wider array of contingencies. In doing so they must inevitably add more features and functions to their devices, thereby making them harder to use and maintain and less affordable. These general-purpose "stripped down" PCs stand in marked contrast to consumer appliance-like information devices. Providing a clean, simple interface to a single function, Information Appliances answer the fundamental consumer need for ease of use.

1.8 Conclusion

> I felt like I was back in the dark ages until I got my first washing machine.
> *Housewife, Life Magazine, 1951*

Convergence is not just about technology. It is about services and about new ways of doing business and of interacting with society. The emergence of new services and the development of existing services are expected to expand the overall information market. The global nature of communications platforms today, particularly, the Internet, together with the lowering cost of establishing a presence on the World Wide Web, is making it possible for businesses of all sizes to develop a regional and global reach. Convergence heralds the "Information Revolution."

When many people think of the Industrial Revolution, they think of steam trains, automated printing presses and automobile factories. But the Industrial Revolution didn't truly change most people's home lives until the advent of the appliance. It was the appliance that freed most people from backbreaking housecleaning and laundry chores to pursue new activities and recreation. It was the appliance that finally brought the benefits of the Industrial Revolution home.

In the same way, the Information Appliance can bring the benefits of the Information Revolution home to people from all walks of life, all over the world. By eliminating the need for technical knowledge and deep pockets, these appliances can become an equalizer for information access and use. Consumers will not only be able to get on the Information Superhighway, they'll be able to choose their perfect vehicle – their Information Appliance – to drive on it.

About the Author

Professor Molyneux currently holds the IBM Chair in Interactive Communication Technologies at the University of Wolverhampton and is a Fellow of ICL.

His responsibilities include monitoring technological advances which would benefit the wider student population as well as reviewing the strategic implications of Communication and Information Technology. He is Chief Architect of the ERDF-funded BROADNET project, a joint project between ICL, IBM,

Telewest and the University of Wolverhampton aimed at providing University for Industry services to businesses across the West Midlands.

Professor Molyneux holds a number of consultation posts across Europe. He is Scientific Advisor to the Europe Commission, has written numerous reports under contract to the European Parliament and is Scientific Evaluator to the Swedish Foundation for Strategic Research. He is also a member of the UK Parliamentary University Group and is frequently asked to provide briefing documents to a number of government bodies. He is a member of the Government Office (West Midlands) Information & Communication Technology Strategy Group and provides advice on the strategic use of C&IT to the Court Service department of the Lord Chancellor's Department and the Department for Education and Employment.

During his time in industry he was a consultant, at board level, to Siemens, IBM Europe, BMW and Deutsche Telekom and was Scientific Adviser to the German Ministry of Science and Education.

He is Scientist in Residence at the BBC's "Tomorrow's World" program and has given many TV and radio interviews. He is a well-respected member of the European Academic Community and is a frequent keynote speaker at industrial and academic conferences within the UK and abroad.

In the past, he has acted as scientific adviser to the DG XIII-F of the European Commission and the European Parliament on matters relating to interactive technologies and their uses in training and education. He was Chairman of the Technical Evaluation Panel of project DELTA, a 40 million ECU research and development initiative.

He is a Fellow of The Royal Society of Arts and member of the Interactive Multimedia Association of America (IMA), British Interactive Multimedia Association (BIMA) and the Forum for Training Technologies.

2

The Future of Content: Towards a 5th Framework Programme in Multimedia Content & Tools

Kieran O'Hea

2.1 Introduction

This chapter presents an overview of the development of Electronic Publishing applications by the European Commission (EC), from exploratory actions in multimedia publishing in 1994 up to the present day and its plans to establish a research and development program in Multimedia Content & Tools. The chapter focuses heavily on the emergence of creativity as a key factor in the Commission's plans for the development of a user-friendly information society. It looks at the challenges and opportunities that lie ahead for the various actors and suggests where some of the research and development activity, particularly in the area of creative content generation, might be focused.

2.2 The Story so Far: 4th Framework Programme Experiences

The home of European Commission Electronic Publishing applications for the past four years has been inside the Telematics Applications Programme. Under the sector name "Information Engineering" [1], the Commission has supported 66 individual projects since 1994 and has followed an evolutionary path that has brought it to the verge of completing its first framework cycle and sees it poised to enter its second.

The original community of traditional information users and publishers has grown to include participants from the arts, broadcasting, advertising and new media

---

Author's note: this chapter does not necessarily represent the views of the European Commission.

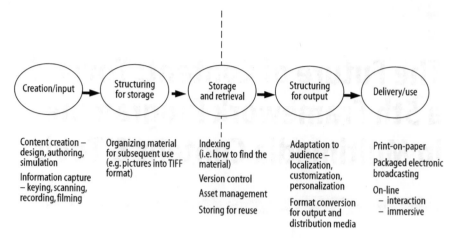

Figure 2.1 The content chain (© ELPUB2003 Interactive Digital Media).

sectors. The descriptive model of the information chain has expanded in both directions to encompass creativity at the one end and user satisfaction at the other (Figure 2.1). So what started as a very process-based model has matured to include two very human influences – creation and consumption.

All of this leads us to anticipate the future of European electronic publishing with great optimism. The accelerating development of a user-friendly information society by its very nature demands a change of focus from the technologies that will enable it to the content that will sustain it. And this is where EU efforts are likely to lie in the years ahead – in helping both European citizens and European enterprises realize their potential through the creation, management and delivery of compelling multimedia content.

2.3 The 5th Framework Programme: Content Finds Its Place

The 5th Framework Programme [2], launched in December 1998 and running until 2002, presents the European Commission with its biggest opportunity for change in 15 years – and perhaps its biggest challenge. Now is the time for the Commission to come bang up to date by implementing better structures and systems that will enable it to more effectively meet the needs of its constituents. The Commission must practice what it preaches by ensuring that the contents of its work programs are themselves compelling, accessible and relevant to the targeted communities.

The changes in the content world around us – rapidly developing markets, new business strategies, the emergence of new players – require a new approach to ensure that the opportunities presented by the program are exploited. Specific programs of awareness and targeting are needed to ensure that all would-be constituents are well informed about the possibilities. Particularly in the area of Creative Content Generation, where participation is essential, steps must be taken

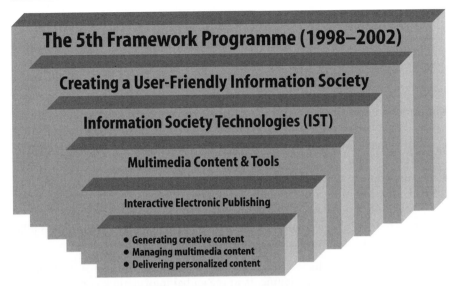

Figure 2.2 The 5th Framework Programme.

to inform members of that community that there is now a European research action catering specifically for them.

The 5th Framework Programme will be structured as follows:

- Four "thematic" programs:
  1. Improving the quality of life and management of living resources
  2. Creating a user-friendly information society
  3. Promoting competitive and sustainable growth
  4. Energy, environment and sustainable development
- Three "horizontal" programs:
  1. Confirming the international role of Community research
  2. Promotion of innovation and encouragement of SME participation
  3. Improving human research potential and the socio-economic knowledge base

Figure 2.2 follows the thread from Thematic program 2: "Creating a user-friendly information society" through to the new research areas of content creation, management and delivery. More information about the 5th Framework Programme is available at http://www.cordis.lu/fifth/home.html.

2.3.1 Creating a User-Friendly Information Society

Commissioner Bangemann has stated that "the Information Society will be driven by creative people, who are highly selective about where they live. The deciding factor when choosing where to locate new businesses will not be economic factors but the simple question of where people want to live and work. [It is] changing the balance of advantage and disadvantage between different regions and countries within Europe."

In moving towards a user-friendly information society, the EU is faced with some important challenges.

- Improving the business environment through secure transactions, digital signatures, content, electronic commerce, media ownership, copyright, standards, etc.
- Investing in the future, by supporting activities principally in the areas of research and development, education and training.
- Putting people at the center by addressing issues such as consumer protection, illegal and harmful content, universal service, access, public procurement, personal data and privacy protection.
- Meeting the global challenge through ongoing campaigns of promotion, public awareness and consensus building.

In facing up to these challenges, the EU must also take into consideration the factors that are shaping developments in the global information, communication and telecommunication (ICT) industries, and their consequences for Europe, namely:

- skills (new combinations, "skill rot," life-long learning, learner-centric)
- media (convergence, new markets, new needs, new formats, new business models)
- technologies (digitization, processing, cost, new services, new uncertainties)
- regulations (liberalization, ownership, IPR, privacy, encryption, Internet)
- demographics (unemployment, aging, women, lifestyles, literacy, "rich and poor")

For these efforts to be effective, it must be recognized from the outset that the development of a user-friendly information society demands a change of focus from the technologies that will enable it to the content that will sustain it.

2.3.2 The Information Society Technologies (IST) Programme

The research and development agenda corresponding to Theme 2: "Creating a user-friendly information society" will be addressed through a new specific program called "Information Society Technologies (IST)." Details about the program are available at `http://www.cordis.lu/esprit/src/eitcist.htm`.

> The strategic objective of the IST program would be to realize the benefits of the information society for Europe both by accelerating its emergence and by ensuring that the needs of individuals and citizens are met.

The work will be addressed via four key actions, namely:

- *Key Action I: Systems and services for the citizen*: Meeting the needs and expectation of European citizens for high-quality, affordable general-interest services.

- *Key Action II: New methods of work and electronic commerce*: Addressing the requirements and concerns of Europe's enterprises, workers and consumers, the objective would be to enable both individuals and organizations to innovate and be more effective and efficient in their work and business.
- *Key Action III: Multimedia content and tools*: Multimedia content is central to the information society; the objective here would be to confirm Europe as a leading force in this field and enable it to realize the potential of its creativity and culture.
- *Key Action IV: Essential technologies and infrastructures*: Drive their development, enhance their applicability and accelerate their take-up in Europe.

There will also be a series of generic actions addressing activities for generic research and development of technologies and support for research infrastructures.

It is worth noting that one of the more encouraging signs that the European Commission is serious about its commitment to change is the way in which new words are appearing in its work programs, words like:

- creativity
- entertainment
- talent
- enable
- empower
- unleash
- enrich
- compel

One thing is certain. A combination of shorter business strategies, even by big companies, the dynamic rate of change in the ICT industry and the increasingly sophisticated demands of users means that a fundamental change is necessary in the way the European Commission structures, operates and promotes the IST program.

2.3.3 Key Action III: Multimedia Content and Tools

The focus here will be on the development and application of technologies, systems and methods for creating, processing, managing, accessing and exploiting content. To appreciate the rationale behind the new (and timely) initiative in content, perhaps it is best to review the appropriate passage from "Working document on the Information Society Technologies (IST) Programme" [3]:

> Content is a key asset in the global information society. Technological advances have provided ever-improving information processing and communications infrastructures. Increased research is now needed to address digital content, so that it can be produced effectively, given attractive functionalities, exchanged or traded securely, retrieved confidently and used or re-used in a variety of digital ways. European research and development is needed to ensure that future technologies and tools

enable content, together with its creation and use, properly reflect the EU's cultural diversity and many languages, in order that the full potential of the EU's creativity can be realized in both social and industrial contexts.

The current turnover of Europe's content industries is estimated by the OECD at around 178 billion ECU. Digital information products (both on-line and off-line) are growing at an exponential pace, for example the number of registered world-wide-web sites increased from 50 in 1992 to seventy thousand at the end of 1995 and 650,000 in Autumn 1997. As we make the transition to the information society, work is needed to promote European excellence in advanced multimedia content systems, services and technologies. In particular it is critical to improve the functionality and usability of digital content for international business and social applications, promote new education and training systems, and enable cultural and language diversity.

Key Action III, Multimedia content and tools, has four main objectives:

- to facilitate life-long education and training
- to stimulate creativity
- to promote linguistic and cultural diversity
- to improve the user-friendliness of future information products and services

It will focus on four action lines:

- Interactive Electronic Publishing, including libraries, archives and museums
- education and training
- new language technologies
- advanced technologies for accessing, filtering and analyzing information.

Clearly content has found its place!

2.3.4 Interactive Electronic Publishing

While publishing remains a very broad area, and digital content has yet to establish itself as a tangible entity in most people's minds, there is a need to be particularly focused in this area. Events have proved that, in the area of publishing, the EU cannot lead or change the world. The objectives for Interactive Electronic Publishing must therefore be realistic and concentrated on areas of publishing where research and development on a pan-European scale can make a difference. The last four years has been a period of unprecedented development in publishing. While this development coincided with the period of the 4th Framework Programme, ironically there is no reference to the World Wide Web in the work program of Information Engineering! The sector was, however, able to adapt, but the experience has proved that flexible work programs are essential.

The 5th Framework Programme gives a good opportunity to reflect and build on the developments in recent years by:

- Stimulating and harnessing creativity in productive and profitable ways ("applied creativity").

- Learning from experiences in multimedia publishing during the last four years (learning from failure, building on successes).
- Taking a more business-like approach to R&D by solving real business problems that lead to improvements across the publishing process (creation, management and delivery of content).
- Integrating and addressing the needs of new communities not normally associated with framework programs (audio-visual content makers, advertisers, etc.).

An Expanding Publishing Constituency...

Newspapers – magazines – catalogues – business information – software – film – TV – music – games – art – photography – design – animation – advertising – information for the citizen – etc.

Interactive Electronic Publishing will address how to develop innovative and compelling content by:

- Focusing on new publishing and media paradigms for both commercial and private use.
- Addressing future publishing systems for new combinations of content.
- Providing users with new levels of interactivity.
- Encouraging the development of new forms of content: virtual objects, multi-user environments, and immersive, animated content, etc.

It will focus on Corporate Media, Knowledge Media and Consumer Media in areas including:

- Magazines
- Newspapers
- TV
- Entertainment
- Knowledge
- Digital libraries
- Business
- Catalogs/technical documentation
- STM
- Creativity
- Business models
- Research/standards

The research agenda will cover the following areas, as defined in the IST working document:

- *Generating creative content*
  Advanced authoring and design systems (including networked cooperation) and skills development (for example for 3D and virtual reality design and

conceptional modeling), systems for generation and reuse of content from existing sources, and collaborative publishing

- *Managing multimedia content*
  Managing digital media, through supporting distributed and networked content, developing management approaches for processing large sets of data in innovative ways (visualization, scenario development, spatial analysis) and devising new metrics for valuing information assets
- *Delivering personalized content*
  Personalizing content delivery, whether through "pull technologies," cost-effective content packaging, advertising and transactions, customer profiling or individualized design and presentation.

The work program will also include appropriate socio-economic research and a suitable range of horizontal actions.

2.4 Trends/Priorities in Creative Content Generation

The Future of Content [4] states that "interactive electronic publishing calls for intelligent publishing platforms with which to acquire, create and integrate content resources of all sorts. Not just books, magazines, CD-ROMs and Web sites, but films, music, 3D animated models and immersive environments, simulations, visualizations, virtual presence environments, broadcast programmes, multi-player games and worlds, cultural presentations, tours, performances, maps and much more. It demands tools and environments that enable productivity and workflow among the creative content generator – the author, artist, editor, peer reviewer, critic, journalist, producer, director, inventor, designer, or curator. Tele-collaborating, regardless of location, in the co-creative process of making composite content works, regardless of the format of the component information resources."

To do this, EU projects and actions should help to:

- Mix creative groups from the digital culture with technical groups building support systems (workflow, asset repositories, integrators, distribution management, interoperability designers) and "publishers" with a need to communicate information, in order to generate skill (culture) transfer and improved tools for team working.
- Transfer state-of-the-art knowledge between working groups.
- Boost demand for the new content skills among publishers/distributors – end users already demand high quality, but intermediaries are unfocused and there is a skill shortage in the high-quality end of the creative market. The take-up of these skills by the advertising market and the impact on consumers shows where we are going.
- Create real demand for content creation from many small companies. There is a significant threat of a drift of creative talent to the USA if there is not a market for the skills and encouragement of innovative ideas.

- Coordinate open standards that enable content creators to maximize their market potential (platform independence).
- Reveal patterns in consumer preferences in interactivity and related psycho-social issues such as user-centered design.
- Develop entirely new content creation skills and related tools, such as content design/creation over long distances from within immersive VR environments.

There is a clearly a need to create a higher profile for creativity, leading to more compelling, affordable and accessible content for the consumer. Developing more efficient cost-effective content production methods (in animation for example) can be achieved by addressing capacity problems (devising faster ways to create digital content and prepare it for publication), providing better authoring tools (see below) and by confronting bandwidth problems and production bottlenecks. The result should be to reinforce European creative strengths in the digital world (animation, design, story-telling, interpreting, etc.) and to help preserve the identity and ownership of European content in a global market.

2.4.1 Example of Focused Research: Authoring Issues

Among the key areas where research is needed, authoring quickly emerges as a priority issue. The main considerations here are:

- Authors need affordable sophisticated content generation tools.
- The availability of good tools unleashes the creativity Europe needs to compete in the global market.
- Tools must match the working practices of the experts who will use them.
- Common needs must be translated into common tools that result in applications based on common frameworks.
- There is a need for simplified customizable and powerful authoring environments that inherently place an emphasis on content rather than technology.
- We must encourage the creation, implementation and use of user-centric authoring tools that significantly ease the process of content creation.
- We need tools that facilitate distributed collaborative authoring.

Other issues that should be looked at include authoring capacity in emerging areas such as DVD and the need for infrastructure to support the training and reskilling of authors.

2.4.2 Focus on Creativity

One of the most refreshing features of the forthcoming 5th Framework Programme is its emphasis on creativity. To deliver on this, the Commission must attract the participation of the creative community. The Commission cannot afford to adopt an attitude of "here we are, come and find us." These companies will not take the time. They are moving ahead anyway and it will be Europe's loss if their expertise is not harnessed in a coordinated way for the benefit of the continent as a whole. They will find empathy with foreign business cultures and markets that are more in tune with their needs and capabilities. To sell anything, you must be prepared to make your customer comfortable in your environment. Familiarity breeds buy-in. The Commission must "sell" its content program to the content community. To attract this community, the Commission's work program must reach out and grab its audience, it must hold targeted awareness events that can compete with the best media events, it must have Web sites which are eye-catching and compelling, and it must have terms of participation which make good business sense. In short, it must create "the buzz."

Once it has done this, there are in fact several ways in which creativity can be integrated into the projects:

- *Creativity in content*: there will be a particular attempt to encourage new approaches to content creation and to the delivery of content.
- *Creative applications*: the Commission will continue to establish innovative pilot applications that typify best practice and reach wider user groups.
- *Innovative business models*: integrating creativity and innovation into business practices is a serious challenge that must not be underestimated.
- *Problem solving*: in general, more creative approaches are needed to solve known problems in publishing processes.

It is important that the concept of "applied creativity" is established. This in effect means harnessing creativity in practical and profitable ways without stifling in any way the creative source. Creativity must become recognized as a valid component of the business mix, together with technology, planning, marketing, etc.

The Commission's Luxembourg directorate DGXIII/E has long been associated with developments in the content and information industries. It has already started some practical initiatives aimed at stimulating creativity in its programs.

- Students have been given the opportunity to contribute their views through the publication "Student Perspectives on the Future of Content," published in conjunction with the Forum of the European Masters in Interactive Multimedia [5].
- For the new media professionals, the Commission is sponsoring the Europrix Multimedia Art Competition, which is intended to attract statements in creativity from across the EU.
- At the project level, dynamic creative companies are starting to appear. It is imperative that their interest is cultivated and they are not allowed to become marginalized.

2.5 The Actors in the Chain

The emerging information society brings with it challenges for the different actors, a diverse collection of problems which must be addressed and needs which must be fulfilled. It is a time of transition and convergence, but at the end of the journey lie

Table 2.1. Opportunities in interactive electronic publishing (© *The Future of Content*, Techserv, Luxembourg, 1997).

Authors	Publishers	Collection holders	Professional users	Consumers and citizens
Wider range of channels of publication, more opportunities to exploit works	Speeding up peer review, editorial and production work and distribution	Making a larger percentage of cultural artefacts accessible to the public	Delivering multimedia information to the desktop that can be easily integrated into local activities	Receiving information from diverse sources in a personalized format and in a language familiar to the user
Opportunities to learn new skills and new ways to express creativity	Presenting scientific information in more simplified ways for non-specialized audience	Finding new ways to make searching in large volumes of multimedia data less daunting for users	Learning and working in stimulating cooperative and interactive environments	Receiving information in a form that matches the user's technical capabilities
Opportunities to present content in new forms not derived from other media	Exploiting volatile content as a competitive tool	Abolition of local constraint for access through decentralized electronic access	Informing management thinking through effective decision support systems	Using virtual reality to travel and to live out cultural and entertainment experiences
Generation of content that is more appealing to basic human needs (more visual, interactive)	Expanding into global and virtual market-places and accessing a globally dispersed user community	Scope for integrating separate collections with common content (grouping by interest area)	Extracting benefit from business knowledge that is of a tacit nature	Accessing reliable information, which facilitates a better informed choice
Better opportunities for collaborative working	Capitalizing on the growing installed base of multimedia delivery platforms	Possibility of enriching the cultural experience through multimedia interaction	More effective ways for SMEs to access and integrate information in their local language	Gaining the confidence to buy and sell over networks in a secure and protected environment
Better integration with technical and publishing processes	Choice of media for different markets and publications	Possibilities to buy, exchange, loan, sell or duplicate individual assets or entire collections	Better integration of business processes such as design, documentation and training	Taking knowledge and pleasure from compelling applications, which are cost effective and easy to use
Liberating creativity	More personalized publishing and better user profiling (e.g. lifestyle publishing)	Improved management and control of business through data warehousing	Increased interactivity with suppliers and customers leading to better designed and more desirable products	
	Creating a profitable new trading environment			

many opportunities for those who can adapt. Table 2.1 presents a summary of these opportunities for the main actors in the content chain.

Success in this area will be indicated by increased competitiveness in the European content industry and by a better-informed citizenry. Electronic publishing R&D will address many of the challenges that will have an impact on this target.

We are rapidly approaching a situation where any person, at his or her discretion, may be reachable or present at any place or time through a combination of wireless communication and virtual environments.

Such developments have brought with them changes in information practice in industry, government and everyday life. There are now new ways to learn, to receive news, to buy and to sell goods and services, and to work. New market players and "infopreneurs" are helping to foster a "digital culture."

There is a need to take account of the issues affecting the main actors as they strive to adapt and capitalize. On the surface, the scale is huge and the breadth of issues which must be addressed immense. Breaking the big picture down into cells that isolate the particular concerns of the different communities is the first step to establishing a realistic research agenda for European electronic publishing.

2.6 Conclusions

The success of European Commission research and development projects is measured by high levels of participation and by the take-up of the results achieved. By actively soliciting the views of key constituents at an early stage, there is more likelihood of these objectives being met. Close collaboration with researchers, developers and users will lead to a work program that is more in touch with real world needs. Making that work program an evolving one, with the capacity for frequent revision, means that it is far less likely to lose relevance in the overall scheme of things and more likely to make a difference in the long run. Active solicitation and integration of key constituents, such as publishers, creators, broadcasters and advertisers, has already taken place and bears testimony to the commitment to content.

The participants at this conference are themselves an important source of contributions and eventual participation in the content program. How can you contribute in the short term? By helping us over the coming months to determine the overall direction, key challenges and projects that the European Commission should entertain in the area of Interactive Electronic Publishing.

- *Overall direction*: what should be the overall direction of EC policy and project funding initiatives in these areas?
- *Key challenges*: what are the key challenges that will be encountered in pursuing the key directions?
- *Projects*: what projects the EC should think about/consider funding.

These are the types of question that need to be answered now if there is to be a relevant program of work to participate in. Delegates and others reading the conference proceedings are therefore encouraged to put their views forward to the author.

References

[1]   Information Engineering: Projects and Perspectives, *IT World*, UK, 1998.
[2]   European Commission Proposal for the 5th Framework Programme, COM(97), 142.
[3]   Working document on the Information Society Technologies (IST) Programme (excerpted from COM(97), 553).
[4]   *The Future of Content*, Techserv, Luxembourg, 1997.
[5]   *Student Perspectives on the Future of Content*, UIB, Spain, 1998.

About the Author

Kieran O'Hea (BE Elec.) has worked in Luxembourg since 1992 as a technical advisor to the European Commission in the area of information industry, multimedia content and electronic publishing. He has recently co-authored a comprehensive discussion document, *The Future of Content* and is currently contributing to the development of the 5th Framework Programme in the area of Information Society Technologies (IST). He is an Electrical Engineer (UCC, 1983) and a qualified video editor, and has been a member of the Board of Advisors of the European Multimedia Forum and of the Strategic Panel of the Telematics Applications Programme.

Cultural Issues

3

Digital Convergence at the User Interface

European Research on Shared Virtual Experiences Across Networks

David Leevers

Abstract

Over the last decade a series of European projects have been building shared digital environments for manufacturing and construction applications. The first stage was extending the Macintosh metaphor from the flat desktop to support specific multimedia activities such as video conferences with construction site staff. This helped to define a family of metaphors that cover all communications modes. These metaphors have now been recognized as a comprehensive reflection of reality that can be seamlessly linked into it. However, such linking requires a far more explicit understanding of the social nature of human beings, how we use the full repertoire of implicit as well as direct communications channels, and how we actually go about our daily lives, continually switching between different communication modes.

Perhaps the most speculative part of this chapter is the attempt to show that there are fundamental constraints on the number and mixture of communications channels that can be handled by the human users of the future Global Information Infrastructure.

We have been identifying the constraints at the micro level through ethnographic studies and at the macro level by drawing on the evolutionary roots of humans. At the transition from the service orientation of the European 4th Framework R&D Programme to the social emphasis of the 5th Framework we hope that these ideas will prove a stimulating starting point for further work.

3.1 Why Telepresence and Shared Virtual Environments?

If Information and Communications Technologies (ICT) are treated as no more than a way to optimize existing products and systems there is no hope of reaching a sustainable world. Every advance encourages a rebound effect: increasing the efficiency of automobiles by "factor 4" simply increases the market by "factor 16" – and CO^2 emissions by a corresponding factor 4. However the introduction of a complete range of rich communication modes offers a sustainable alternative to material usage. There will be no need to drive to a movie theater in a factor 4 efficient automobile, no need to fly halfway round the world to establish trust with a trading partner and no need for the surgeon to be present at a telerobot operation.

A group of projects within the EC ACTS program known as the "Telepresence and Shared Virtual Environments" chain have been exploring the scope for augmenting the real with the telepresent and the virtual. The services included within these projects can be regarded as the most complex and integrated manifestations of the four key communications modes:

- *one to one*: rapport and fact transfer, supported by the telephone and email
- *one to many*: dissemination, supported by broadcasting technologies
- *many to one*: information retrieval, supported by data communications
- *small group*: collaborative, supported by audio and video conferences

Although the delivery mechanisms and the low-level architectures for the four modes are likely to remain an *ad hoc* mixture of copper, glass fiber and radio, there is a true convergence at the user interface, primarily in the Web browser. Before the appearance of the browser the four modes were separate industries, each having its own distinct and part-time interface to the individual; perhaps 1 hour per day in front of the PC screen, 2 hours on the telephone, 3 hours in front of the television set and an occasional 1 hour video conference session.

Because the universal Web interface provides the ability to glide seamlessly from one communications mode to another it can provide a persistent portal to remote information via all four communication modes. This portal becomes a universal "Community–Network Interface" that could contribute the social glue to link the whole of humanity in a rich integration of many distinct local cultures and a single synchronized global culture.

Any ICT architecture must now focus on the one thing that will not be swept away in the accelerating rate of technology change – the social nature of the human animal and our irrepressible urge to communicate. This is reflected in the timely change from "Information and Communications Technologies" to "Information Society Technologies" in the transition from 4th Framework to 5th Framework programs.

3.2 The Challenge

The sustainability implications of this work are being explored by a new ACTS project, ASIS: Alliance for a Sustainable Information Society. ASIS is building a strategic alliance of all the players required to convey the optimistic message that IST offers a path towards a sustainable planet. This is a path that need not degrade the quality of life for any of its potentially 10 billion inhabitants and which can support a world that is fair and fulfilling, prosperous and sustainable.

There is a growing recognition that the current material-oriented model for a prosperous society cannot be sustained as an increasing fraction of the world aspires to the Western middle class lifestyle. Responses to this challenge include:

- The prophets of doom, who say that there is no hope of sustaining the current population and so we will have to live through cataclysmic solutions – war, pestilence and plague.
- Restricting the use of unsustainable resources. This traditional environmental approach includes strong elements of returning to a supposed past golden age. In fact it was an age when life was nasty, brutish and short except for those who had the time and money to write the poetry!
- Use of the new Information Society Technologies to reduce the need for energy and resources. In many cases this means augmenting a limited amount of physical reality with an increasing fraction of virtual and telepresent experience. A timely example is the German Green Party proposal that tourists should only be allowed one long-distance flight every five years. The intervening years would have to be filled with virtual reality replacements of the real Bali.

The IST approach is vulnerable in that it depends on as-yet unproved hypotheses about the "humanity" of telepresence technologies and their ability to be truly "better than being there" for most of the time. The track record of the ICT industry is not good. It has grown from nothing over the last 50 years, making many mistakes along the way, and has alienated many of the more mature members of the population. Credible demonstrations of the cultural richness of networked experiences are desperately needed in order to remove associations with the IT disasters of the past.

Manufacturing broke away from a stultifying vision of the assembly line only when a post-Fordist vision was formulated. Perhaps now is the time to formulate a "post-Gatesist" vision of the Global Information Society!

3.3 A Sustainable Information Society?

This chapter proposes an architecture for the interface between the community and the network that biases social development towards a fulfilling and sustainable balance of the real, the virtual and the telepresent. There appear to have been remarkably few attempts to identify the wider significance of these technologies and indicate how they might affect society as a whole – plenty of science fiction, but little that would impress the economist or politician. However, it is hoped that the scenario and modeling activities of ASIS will explore these implications more fully (Figure 3.1).

The major challenges for this ASIS vision are:

- to demonstrate that digital augmentation of reality does not diminish that reality
- to show that the synchronized global network culture complements but does not drive out physically grounded local cultures

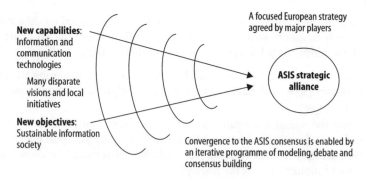

New capabilities:
Information and
communication
technologies

Many disparate
visions and local
initiatives

New objectives:
Sustainable information
society

A focused European strategy
agreed by major players

**ASIS strategic
alliance**

Convergence to the ASIS consensus is enabled by
an iterative programme of modeling, debate and
consensus building

Figure 3.1 The ASIS spiral of convergence.

By definition, any virtual experience cannot be complete. There is always some disjunction between those senses supported by the virtual, usually sight and hearing, and those that remain within the real. For instance: stereo images produce headaches because the eyes must not refocus when they converge on close objects, and the virtual battlefield produces nausea because the body is not being thrown around (or apart) in the way indicated by the visual experience. Virtual reality cannot be an end in itself. What is needed is a seamless and sympathetic augmentation of local reality with vivid and meaningful network experiences.

3.4 Cognition and Sensation

It is important to distinguish between the cognitive and sensory aspects of tele- and virtual presence. Most academic research is focused on the sensory experience. Such experiences can only last for a short period of time before the audience have had enough – the few minutes of the average rollercoaster or virtual reality ride. In cognitive experiences it is the power of the narrative flow that leads the audience forward, not the immediate sensory impact. The "virtual reality" of a novel is often far more powerful than that of a movie.

The opportunity offered by the new technologies is to use the richness of the sensory experience to ensure that all members of the audience are drawn into much the same cognitive experience. As such, the shared visualization of the computer screen is an extremely powerful tool for establishing common ground, avoiding misunderstanding, encouraging collaboration and defusing conflict.

In the traditional village the words of the storyteller were sufficient to evoke images of the same familiar landmarks in the listening children. Without the virtual reality of global television the mental imagery would be profoundly different from equator to tundra, from prairie to mountain. We are at last finding a visual *lingua franca* that can establish rapport without requiring physical co-presence. This language is no more than a pidgin tongue at present, made up as it is of fragments of pop videos, Coca-Cola adverts and McDonald's experiences. However, the next generation of interactive imagery will give the next generation of people the ability to build the deep structure of a Creole. A further generation may well use a fully mature animated and interactive environment as their first cultural language.

3.5 The Universal Human

The "Universal Human" is considered to be the genetic repertoire that *Homo Sapiens* was left with at the end of the Ice Age, just before the population explosion of the agricultural revolution. However much the user interface changes it must be bound by the capabilities and the limitations of that survivor.

The first interface between user and computer was the GUI of each application. This is very much a sensory interface, so the science of ergonomics has concentrated on what can be expected of the sensory and motor skills of the Universal Human.

As the computer supports an increasing fraction of our waking life and as we start to experience other people through the network, so the cognitive level becomes more important. This cognitive level includes each individual's belief system and social standards. Thus it has a long-term stability that complements the persistent presence of the network portal.

This report is an attempt to provide a starting point for discussing this cognitive relationship between the community and the network. It is expected that we will always remain firmly attached to the sensory panorama of our immediate physical and social surroundings, but that the new technology will give everyone the added value that only emperors enjoyed in the past. Many of these components will be implemented as intelligent agents, e.g. the maid agent inside the washing machine and the troubadour agent inside the compact disc. In a world of ubiquitous computing very few of these agents will be presented on conventional computer screens.

3.6 Geographic and Digital Cultures

Our physical surroundings are now being enhanced by multimedia information streams that transcend barriers of time, space and culture. The traditional geographic cultures are no longer strong enough to provide a moral resilience that can stand up to intrusions from outside. They are being challenged by a complementary global culture that changes as rapidly from year to year as traditional cultures vary from country to country. The interaction between the two is a vast opportunity to create a sustainable cultural richness that need never run dry (Figure 3.2).

The definition of culture that is being used here is that deep structure of individual behavior that is acquired during early childhood. This basic culture is absorbed in much the same way as a first language. Later cultural experiences do not become part of the personality in the same way. In the past this deep culture could only be acquired from immediate family, friends and community. Children in advanced

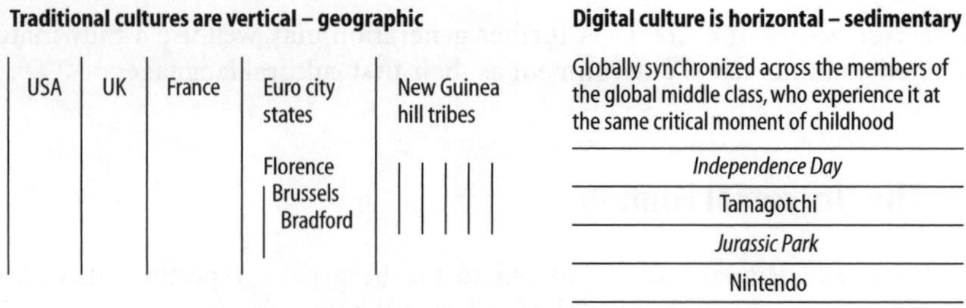

Traditional cultures are vertical – geographic					Digital culture is horizontal – sedimentary
USA	UK	France	Euro city states	New Guinea hill tribes	Globally synchronized across the members of the global middle class, who experience it at the same critical moment of childhood
			Florence Brussels Bradford	| | | | |	*Independence Day*
					Tamagotchi
					Jurassic Park
					Nintendo

Figure 3.2 Geographic and digital cultures.

countries now spend so much time in front of the television, listening to global music and playing computer games that a significant fraction of their early cultural experience is synchronized with other children of the same age world-wide.

3.7 The Community–Network Framework

The importance of the Shared Virtual Environment (SVE) was only recognized when it was found that videoconferencing was strangely lacking in many of the implicit aspects of interpersonal communication. Text-based MUDS and Internet Relay Chat (IRC) indicated that long-term awareness of a group could be supported by the minimal amounts of information transferred in typed messages. A number of SVE projects have been trying to combine the effectiveness of MUD with the visual appeal of a shared virtual reality environment seen by all participants on their own screens.

We have suddenly been presented with a profusion of new combinations of presence, telepresence and virtual presence. Technology developers have responded to the intellectual challenge of making the tele- and virtual present indistinguishable from the present. There are sound commercial reasons for this. The leading edge applications, surgery and tasks in dangerous or inaccessible environments, do require maximum realism. In addition, there are many specific remote control and monitoring applications in which a feeling of telepresence would reduce the cognitive load.

In many cases reality is not the ultimate goal. We are now looking towards an augmented reality where the important parts of the real are enhanced and those that are irrelevant are underplayed.

Over the last decade multimedia communications research has been working towards a definition of a persistent portal between the community and the network. Progress can most easily be observed in the 3D activities of manufacture and construction.

3.8 The CICC Project

CICC "Collaborative Integrated Communications in Construction" is an ACTS project that has focused on social networks, using as its starting point the construction sector. This comprises 10% of the workforce of any European country and includes a complete cross-section of society, from the prima donna architect to the casual laborer, and a comparable range of activities from the most creative to the most physical.

Particular issues addressed in CICC include the use of multimedia networking to build virtual organizations that include many office locations plus the mobile workers on the construction site. The main objective of CICC has been to demonstrate that Internet technologies do far more than place "information at our fingertips." They are equally effective in placing remote people at our fingertips: "fingertips at our fingertips!"

CICC started with the objective of using 3D shared virtual environments to support negotiation across the network. It was building on the promise of US military programs in battlefield simulation and European activities such as the Esprit Comic project. These had indicated that some of the quality of a real meeting can be captured if participants interact with avatars representing others on their screen. Construction was seen as a particularly fruitful sector in which to introduce 3D virtual environments, since the use of 3D CAD tools was just beginning to take off. The paradigm was of walking around a virtual building and discussing it with avatars of the architect and others who are visible within this virtual building.

Over the last three years there has been a complete reversal of roles. The 2D interfaces that were unsatisfactory for building design have been found to be a familiar reference point for supporting social interaction across the network, whereas the 3D interfaces that were expected to host the community have proved of far greater use in acting as a shared 3D whiteboard. This has helped to identify the following guidelines for building the persistent information and communications environments for virtual organizations.

3.9 Design Guidelines for Shared Virtual Environments

Current Telepresence and Shared Virtual Environment projects are helping to identify a number of design guidelines such as:

1. Treat the virtual environment as a window within the real world, not an alternative to the real world (immersive VR is most relevant to game and simulation applications).
2. Recognize that humans have a predator brain structure which uses stereo vision to focus on the prey rather than 360° vision to detect other predators. We only feel safe enough to think constructively when the action is taking place in front of us. This is why any group, not just Arthur's Knights of the Round Table, tend to form a circle, and why bigger groups that have to sit in rows need a chairperson. This also indicates that the screen is a more acceptable interface than the immersive headset or CAVE.
3. Recognize the power of humans to establish rapport and trust across any sort of communication link provided it is two-way and has predictable characteristics.

The handshake, the shared meal and the golf game are all real-world examples. A shared visualization is not required to establish rapport across the network. Latency is not a big issue. It simply determines the rate at which trust builds: a few seconds in the case of a handshake, several days for email exchanges.

4. Recognize that collaboration, and even competition, requires that all parties see the subject from a shared point of view as well as from their private specialist points of view. Once this can be achieved, conflict of personalities and ideals usually dissipates into clarification of facts rather than arguments over principles. This may explain the difficulty of placing participants in primitive shared virtual environments: they would have to get intimately close to each other's virtual bodies in order to see the same view on the screen (people do not enjoy the experience of walking through other bodies in a virtual environment that has no collision detector).

5. Recognize that individuals need to share two distinct spaces, a "mind space" in which they see the other and the dialog takes place, and a "problem space" in which they see the common artefacts. This problem space is often a 2D electronic whiteboard, but it might be a shared 3D visualization of a future building.

These guidelines are encapsulated in four tools for supporting persistent multimodal communication across the community–network interface.

- Hyperbola of Synchronization
- Four Information Sources
- People and Information Finder
- Cycle of Collaboration

The Hyperbola of Synchronization was the historical starting point. The process of two people making contact, building rapport and then reaching a common understanding is characterized by a sequence of one-way messages that become more frequent and shorter as time goes on. If this process takes place across the network then the relevant services need to offer appropriate bandwidth and latency characteristics at each stage and need to transfer seamlessly from one to another as the individuals move down their own shared hyperbola.

However, the hyperbola is just the interactive highlight of a total dynamic that starts with a need to interact and ends with some self-contained activity. This is a cyclic communication process in which the new technologies must provide a way of seamlessly gliding from one communications mode to another. For this reason it has been given the name "Cycle of Collaboration," or CyColl for short.

The Cycle of Collaboration is described first, and its manifestation in the Hyperbola of Synchronization follows. The "People and Information Finder," a knowledge management infrastructure that support the changes of communication mode, is then described. Finally, a hint of how these classifications can be related to human social groups is given.

This framework is showing considerable promise as a way of relating information processes in the home and workplace (presence) with those that can be transmitted across the network (telepresence at a distance), and those that would not be possible without the computer (virtual presence in visualizations of abstract data).

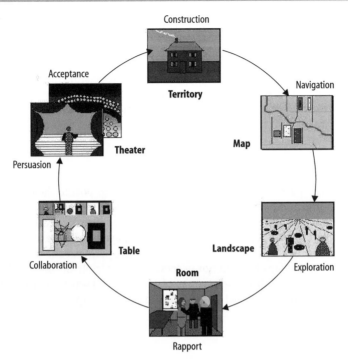

Figure 3.3 The Cycle of Collaboration.

3.10 The Cycle of Collaboration

The Cycle of Collaboration is the temporal framework for transitions between the different communications modes. By focusing on the most likely transitions from one mode to another this cycle provides a way of relating the diversity of human activities to the variety of voice data and video services.

The stages of the cycle (Territory, Map, Landscape, Room, Table and Theater) cover a typical route through different services. Each stage can be real, metaphoric or a mixture of both. The advantage of thinking in terms of the cycle is that it can be used to suggest effective ways of relating the different services that make up the individual's persistent communications environment (Figure 3.3).

3.10.1 Territory

The word *Territory* is used to indicate the non-communicating stage, when the individual is working, relaxing or asleep. Every workplace has some area within which the individual's tasks are performed: the wall the bricklayer has been asked to build, or the office where a paper is written. It is usual for others to respect this area and not interrupt unless invited. At home this territory is that quiet corner where ideas are formulated and plans are made.

There is an equivalent mental territory, that part of the unconscious mind that sleeps on what we have recently learnt and adjusts the existing mental model of the world to fit in with new experiences. We rehearse the implications of new ideas, perhaps in dreams or in play, and start to formulate what we want to do next.

3.10.2 Map

The Map is any passive material that is effectively a signpost to the next stage, to a real place or to real information. When we start to venture out from the security of our own home we are not immediately ready to confront colleagues. The Map might be the morning paper, Yellow Pages, Web pages or database information – anything that provides an easy and reliable starting point for the tasks of the day. The map is usually familiar and not necessarily completely up-to-date, but that is an assurance of its stability. Use of a map can be a mental warming-up exercise that prepares the mind for the brief interactions in the landscape

3.10.3 Landscape

As the next task becomes clearer it becomes necessary to track down the most up-to-date information in a landscape made up of people and the documents and data-bases that they are working with. The Landscape can be a real space, such as an open plan office or a building site where actions are visible and conversations over-heard, or it can be a shared virtual environment in which remote people are repre-sented as avatars and data as icons. When two or three members of a virtual team get into conversation they can be shown in video by cameras on their PCs in windows in the virtual landscape, thus simulating the casual three-way conversa-tions that are one of the main justifications for team offices

3.10.4 Room

Contentious or unresolved issues need a more committed discussion than is possible in the more public open plan landscape. The Room supports the essential building of rapport before starting a meeting. It is where the real or metaphorical handshake takes place. In real life it is often the reception area, not the meeting room itself. Similarly, the virtual Room requires different resources from the meeting itself – a high-quality video link rather than a shared whiteboard.

The walls of a real room manifest a complete security and privacy barrier that encourages occupants to share confidences. Similarly, the walls of a shared Virtual Room that are displayed on each participant's screen remain dominant until the group have established mutual trust and an appreciation of each other's points of view. Then they feel confident enough to look down at the shared Table.

3.10.5 Table

The Table is the space where the common artefact required for collaboration are displayed. In real life it obviously includes the workplace and the building site. Unlike real life, the shared window of a Virtual Table can display identical material to all participants. However, each person still has their private area, their real life notebook or a private part of their own screen.

In trials the Virtual Table has occupied the lower part of the computer screen. Across the top are video windows of the other participants together with miniature copies of their own screens. These miniatures serve the same function as looking across a real table to see what the others are doing. As in real life, the miniatures are not clear enough to read what they are writing. The video windows indicate the extent to which the others are focusing on the shared task. These views maintain rapport and trust, even when their occupant is not contributing to the conversation.

3.10.6 Theater

The Theater is that place where the results of collaborative activities are conveyed to others. A meeting is only of use if the results are accepted by the relevant audience: customers, colleagues or students. A representative from the meeting has to take on a story-telling role to convey the conclusions as a narrative. In such a performance the narrative flow is usually decided in advance, but the emotional emphasis can depend on the mood of the audience. Members of a live audience are prepared to accept the narrative if they know that the specialists have already reached agreement and, perhaps more significantly, if they sense that the rest of the audience is also accepting the message.

In project work the theater metaphor applies to any material that conveys results to a wider audience: minutes of meetings, a project database, multimedia presentations or giving instructions to staff at the start of the day.

Any effective performance changes the way members of the audience will think in future. The performance can be said to have killed the previous personality and given birth to a slightly different one. This is one reason for the rituals of trust associated with becoming a member of an audience: checking reviews before buying a ticket, studying the mood of others in the foyer and being aware of their presence during the performance. It was the loss of these rituals on the early Internet that led to such scepticism about the quality of the information found on it.

TV has taken over many of the functions of the physical theater while adding the new element of a global shared experience. What it cannot do is recreate the atmosphere of excitement and the sense of togetherness experienced by an audience when they share the real physical space of an auditorium. There are promising signs that some of the new digital television services will convey this feeling of being part of a vast and responsive audience.

3.11 Scope of the Cycle of Collaboration

The Cycle of Collaboration can be seen as reflecting daily life: waking at home, setting off using a map, actively browsing the office landscape in the morning, negotiating over the midday meal and collaborating in the hazy glow of the afternoon, then taking a seat in the theater as the sun sets to surrender the mind to the persuasive powers of playwright and actor, finally going home with new ideas teeming inside the head, ideas that will have slightly altered us. Similarly, the cycle can be seen to reflect our journey through life: emerging from the home of the womb, spending a few months in a map of poorly understood sensations, then learning from the social landscape of other children and adults. Adolescence is spent working towards a rapport with the rest of society in a constantly changing meeting room of contrasting personalities. Then the individual settles down to more focused activities round the Tables or common artefacts of career and family. Finally, the respect of the community is gained and cultural memes are passed on to the next generation.

Table 3.1 summarizes the characteristics of each stage of the Cycle of Collaboration.

3.12 Fractal Communications

Participants in a meeting room or round a table will individually go through a complete cycle in reacting to what someone else has said and then presenting a response. Thus the Cycle of Collaboration can be applied to an enormous range of time-scales, from the formulation and presentation of a single statement to the life cycle of a civilization. The longer cycles include many levels of smaller cycles, which are enmeshed with each other as the complementary components of each collaboration event.

3.13 The Hyperbola of Synchronization

The Hyperbola of Synchronization (Figure 3.4) is an alternative way of looking at the dynamics of moving through the stages of the cycle from the Map via the Landscape and Room to the Table and Theater. The hyperbola brings out the way in which the state of mind of a pair of individuals gets closer as messages between them get more frequent and shorter.

Early exchanges always take longest: letters, emails, telephone calls intercepted by an assistant. As common ground is built up, the messages get shorter, more codified and more intense until sufficient rapport and trust has been established for sharing information, collaborative problem-solving and joint decision-making.

Through the use of common social protocols the exchange of fragments gradually changes into a shared activity where all individuals make relevant contributions from their own background. Eventually the result of the combined contributions is captured in some way, perhaps as an agreed document or a diagram; the

Table 3.1. The Cycle of Collaboration – characteristics of each stage

Stage	Key feature	Typical time	Bandwidth	Topology	Number of people	User interface	Objective	Comments
Construction (mental)	An individual, thinking typing and writing	Hours	Zero	None	One individual	The pencil or keyboard	Consolidating and expressing a concept triggered by the theatre	Building new concepts or mental models in the private territory of the mind
Construction (physical)	An individual aware of the environment	Hours	Zero	None	One	The workplace	Apply behaviour learnt in the "theatre" of instructions	Constructing something in the temporary territory of the workplace
Map	Static, validated, consolidated documents	Minutes	Low	one to one, one way, e.g. HTML	Historic information from 1000s of others	Static images	Navigate to the relevant area	
Landscape	Brief interactions with trusted others	Minutes for each interaction	Medium	Star, two way	150 to 1 Community	Brief exchanges Q & A, email, people at shouting distances	Explore the relevant area	
Room	A group or community; others are excluded	10 min	High	Mesh, few to few	4 Group	High realism, people at whispering distances	Rapport with others with complementary potential	This negotiating is intended to equalize status in order to encourage collaboration
Table	Distributed creativity	1 hour	Medium	Mesh, few to few	4 Group	Manipulable artefacts in a 3D arm's length "playfield"	Distributed Cognition	
Theater to Presenter			Low	Many to one	25	Performer and audience have focused primary awareness of material, panoramic secondary awareness of audience	Convey the results agreed at the meeting	
to Audience	Narrative thread	30 min	High	One to many	Crowd or team	Rectangular 2.5D frame for the performance, plus awareness of other spectators	Learn a new behaviour	

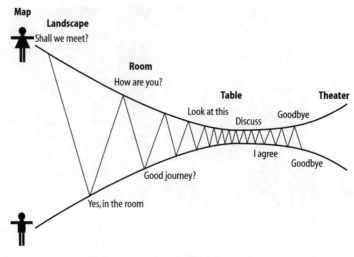

Figure 3.4 The hyperbola of synchronization.

meeting can then be said to have achieved its objective and the Theater stage is entered.

3.14 The Four Information Sources

The major activity in the Map and Landscape is seeking facts. We have found it useful to divide these facts into the following four categories, depending on their source (Figure 3.5).

- *Information in people's heads.* When this information is emotionally neutral and there is trust a direct question can be asked. However, the more relevant the information is to the task in hand the less likely it is to be neutral. Extracting this information from inside another person's head can then become an enormously complex activity, which is highly dependent on the degree of understanding and commitment between the giver and receiver.
- *Information in documents.* Both paper and electronic documents are included. These raw facts are usually easier to get hold of than information in the structured database but may be more difficult to use. The statements are in the email, but their true significance may be hidden in the database.
- *Structured database.* A database holds and manages a vast amount of information in an accurate and accessible form. However, it can be difficult to link its structure to the subtleties of the real world. A move to object orientation has improved flexibility and allowed data to reflect these subtleties as they are discovered. However, the range of facilities known as the People and Information Finder are still needed to ensure that such links are made and that this database does not dominate the wider decision-making perspective.
- *Physical reality.* Most of the information inside our heads comes from the physical world and, after passing through the document and database stages, is usually

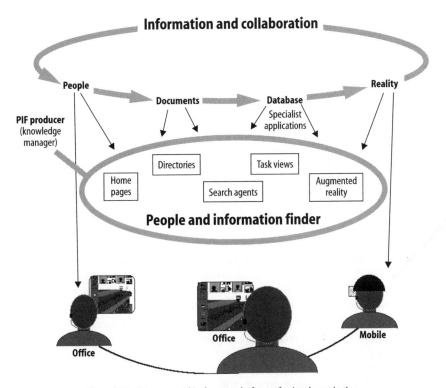

Figure 3.5 Collaboration within the network of trust of a virtual organization.

returned to the physical world in terms of structure and content. This process is particularly clear in the case of construction and manufacturing.

3.15 People and Information Finder

The four information sources are accessed using a wide range of tools that may have been considered to be of minor importance in the past. However, it is becoming increasingly clear that it is the quality of these tools as much as the raw data that determines whether a project as a whole can be successful. As this is recognized so the new role of Knowledge Manager or PIF producer is expected to become of increasing importance. This role is as much an extension of the information officer or Webmaster as of the database manager. The PIF implemented in the CICC project includes a range of information finding tools, including:

1. *Home pages.* Individuals' home pages include awareness of their position in the organization and their availability. This encourages the user to choose the best balance between troubling other people, working with documents or accessing the database objects.

2. *Task view.* This is the primary common artefact for initiating any collaborative activity. In construction and manufacturing this is usually a fixed image rather

than anything dynamic. A top-level consensus task view is implicit in any group activity. This structure can take many years to discover fully. By making it explicit it may prove to be easier to bring new team members up to speed. In construction projects a visualization of the current state of the building is already proving to be a powerful way of building this task view.

3. *Augmented reality.* The real world in its immense variety, as experienced by every member of an organization, is a grossly under-utilized source of information. Far more of this information can be used if material from the database could be linked more directly with the real world. This is the promise of augmented reality. On the one hand it can integrate what should be with what is, while on the other hand it can annotate the real world via a see-through head-mounted display. The earliest applications will be to support inherently spatial activities such as manufacturing and construction.

4. *Directories.* These directories are well established both in paper systems and in the Windows filing system. A remarkable step towards universal compatibility has been taken recently in presenting the Web in the same format as local and networked files on the Windows operating system. It would be interesting to explore what might happen if this hierarchical filing system interface was extended to the physical world of the workplace and the mental worlds of colleagues.

5. *Search agents.* These are one of the newcomers. Every time someone makes their way through the PIF to reach some nugget of information they leave new information on their pattern of work and recent requirements. The search agent can use this information, together with many other types of analysis, to provide a fast way of getting to information and of presenting it in the most convenient form.

The importance of the PIF is that it provides the access routes to support the communications mode changes indicated by the Cycle of Collaboration. Whereas the Cycle of Collaboration can be regarded as the ultimate generalization of a task life cycle, the PIF is an expression of all the access methods required to support that task. The Cycle of Collaboration reflects the sequential nature of task analysis and the PIF reflects the networked complexity of activity analysis.

3.16 Reference Social Groups

The collaborating social groups of the cycle can be divided into four categories of distinct characteristic sizes:

- 2 people – practical fact transfer
- 4 people – meeting
- 25 people – team
- 150 people – organization

Clearly there is an enormous range around these characteristic sizes. However, there is a tendency for the metaphors for meetings, teams and organizations to be associated with groups of these sizes and they appear to be well founded in the traditional societies in which humans evolved (Figure 3.6).

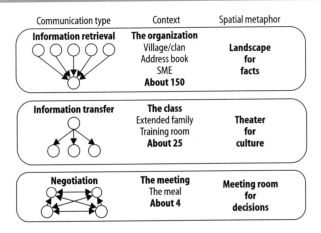

Figure 3.6 Fundamental social groups.

The new technologies do not replace the existing social structures but augment them. The group of two is increasingly implemented as a quick telephone call. A distributed discussion group can be more effective than a meeting because it may be easier to achieve the necessary equalizing of status necessary for distributed cognition when the trappings of physical locations are removed.

The size of a team is very variable. The characteristic size comes from the size of an extended family and typical school class.

3.17 The Community

The nature of an organization or tribal group changes profoundly once communication can transcend the limitations of distance. In a 150 member tribe everyone knows everyone else and it is easy to label all outsiders as alien. In a modern society to some extent, and in cyberspace to an even greater extent, it is possible for one person to belong to a number of organizations with complementary loyalties and obligations. Because these affiliations are not always visible an apparent outsider has to be treated as a potential friend because there may always be a hidden shared community. Only when the probability of this is low can conventional battle lines be maintained.

Occasionally a new type of communication between people does emerge. Early computer systems introduced a range of bizarre environments, such as "chatting" to people using text. Such chat was adopted because of limitations of the medium, not because it was better than the traditional voice and body language. However, text chat has now been recognized as having its own unique advantages: when conversations take place in parallel with other activities, when it is useful to look back at what has been said in the past and when there is a need to document what has been said.

3.18 Privacy and the Network of Trust

Anthropologists have made many studies of the rituals such as handshaking or bowing that are used to establish rapport. Zoologists have even found such behavior among other animals such as dogs, though the rituals are obviously different. The accepted reason for the behavior in both animals and humans is to build trust: offering an open hand to shake, thereby proving there is no weapon in it; or bowing one's head to present a vulnerable neck.

3.19 Related Areas

Many implementers have assumed that the sizes of the social groups are dictated by the peculiar constraints of 3D space and that cyberspace could release us from these constraints. However, there are indications that, even when gravity is removed and the space is altered, the group sizes will remain roughly the same. For instance, meetings often consist of a series of dialogues between pairs of members, with the third and fourth members of the group.playing an essential refereeing role.

3.20 Conclusions

The Cycle of Collaboration is only of use if it has predictive power in helping to design the future communications and information environment. Perhaps the greatest challenge is to ensure that a day spent in such an environment is as satisfying as a day navigating an embodied mind through a real life community of family, friends and colleagues.

References

JH Barkow, L Cosmides and J Tooby (1995) *The Adapted Mind: Evolutionary Psychology and the Generation of Culture.*
DE Brown (1991) *Human Universals.*
K Devlin and D Rosenberg (1997) *Language at Work.*
RIM Dunbar (1997) *Grooming, Gossip, and the Evolution of Language.*
AJ Kim (1999) *Community Building on the Web: Secret Stategies for Successful Online Communities.*
G Lakoff and M Johnson (1983) *Metaphors We Live By.*
D Leevers (1993) A virtual environment to support multimedia networking, Unicom Seminar on Collaborative Work, July.
S Turkle (1997) *Life on the Screen: Identity in the Age of the Internet.*

4

Cultural Objects in Digital Convergence

Marc Cavazza

Abstract

This chapter addresses digital convergence from the standpoint of the cultural objects that populate information networks. After reviewing current trends in digital media, we discuss the nature of cultural objects within different paradigms of interactivity. Taking as a starting point the opposition between interactive experience and document-based cultural objects, we introduce a possible alternative scenario based on the development of intelligent multimedia.

4.1 Introduction

Convergence of digital media is defined as a progressive fusion of telecommunications, broadcasting, information technology and consumer electronics. It is often discussed in terms of interactive services, new markets and the emergence of an information society [1]. Yet it is rarely assessed from the perspective of the *cultural objects* that essentially constitute the content of digital media.

Cultural objects are the empirical substrate supporting the transmission of information between humans. In this sense, novels, essays, songs, operas, movies and plays are all cultural objects. Most of them are also artistic productions, which have been authored for transmission of information and emotion to end-readers.

In the context of digital convergence, the notion of a cultural object is likely to undergo significant changes. One obvious aspect is the emergence of new forms of cultural objects. While, in the early days, traditional cultural objects were simply ported to a new digital support, this has soon led to the development of entirely new forms of cultural objects, like interactive CD-ROMs, Web pages and video games. In a few years, these new productions have numbered in millions. Other are still to come, as outlined in the techno-prophecies of Myron Kruger [2] and David Gelernter [3], moving towards digital experiences as implemented in telepresence, virtual and augmented environments.

In this chapter we discuss the impact of digital convergence on the nature of cultural objects, by reviewing possible evolutions for digital media. After introducing some fundamental concepts, we comment on current trends such as virtual environments and hypermedia documents, concluding with a possible alternative scenario bringing back "intelligence" into multimedia documents.

4.2 The Nature of Cultural Objects

The specific nature of cultural objects has been described by Sir Karl Popper in his classic paper about the Three Worlds [4]. To summarize his argument, *World One* is that of physically tangible objects, *World Two* is the psychological world of individual subjective experience, and *World Three* is the world of inter-subjective cultural productions such as books and theater plays. From a content theory perspective, this cultural world has also been termed the "Semiotic Sphere" by Rastier [5]. This reflects the specific structure of the relations between content units, which account for the cohesion of cultural objects and the relations between different cultural objects within a given culture. The existence of an autonomous semiotic sphere has important consequences for the theoretical foundations of content description. It means that cultural objects can be described through a systematic empirical approach, while early artificial intelligence (AI) research has aimed at reconstructing them from cognitive "first principles." This debate is likely to be reactivated by the various ontological enterprises related to emerging multimedia standards, like MPEG-7 [6] and FIPA (Foundation for Intelligent Physical Agents). It is poised to have significant consequences for the content description of multimedia documents, which is a strong demand from multimedia information retrieval applications.

The recognition of an autonomous existence for cultural objects is an essential step for their proper description. However, to further discuss the properties of cultural objects in the digital age we should also introduce additional dimensions along which these objects could be assessed. Let us call these dimensions "appropriation," "persistence" and "authoring."

Appropriation reflects the relations between the "reader" and the cultural object; traditional cultural objects follow an *interpretive* mode, while the user tends to appropriate new interactive media through experience. The interpretive mode consists in attributing meaning to the information conveyed from a global perspective. Conversely, *experience* is concerned with those interactive environments physically involving the user, like virtual environments.

Persistence reflects the temporal status of cultural objects. Traditional cultural objects tend to be persistent, while certain interactive media, like virtual reality, develop into ephemeral experiences which cannot be reproduced.

Authoring describes the creation process associated with cultural objects. Traditional single authoring of cultural objects is the basis for their identity and cultural value, and this applied to all traditional material. Broadcast material has variable authoring; for instance, TV shows or sporting events are not authored, although they can be recorded and become to some extent cultural objects as well. But authoring is not absent from the new cultural objects coming with digital media. Hyperdocuments are authored in terms of content, physical structure and logical structure. Interactive virtual environments or games are authored in terms of plot, though the number of user experiences actually instantiating that plot is not limited by its initial description.

In the next sections, we will discuss prospects for different kinds of cultural objects in the digital age. A recurring theme will be the opposition of experience to interpretation, which reflects the traditional division, *in our culture*, between concrete experience and abstract knowledge.

4.3 Virtual Environments and the Concept of Experience

One particular evolution for cultural objects is towards total spectator involvement through interaction and immersion, as realized by virtual environments. The notion of a virtual environment encompasses various implementations, such as telepresence, augmented reality and virtual reality. While all of these variants are likely to play a role in digital media, it is not yet clear which will result in the emergence of new sorts of cultural objects.

Telepresence (Figure 4.1) implements real-time, human-centered perception and sensing of remote environments. As such, it is more a communication technique without specific creative content and cannot be considered as a specific vehicle for

a   b

Figure 4.1 a A telepresence human-like device (courtesy of Prof. Jean-Guy Fontaine, CRIIF and Comme Evenements). **b** A telepresence head-like remote camera (courtesy of Prof. Gordon Mair, University of Strathclyde).

cultural objects, though traditional cultural information can be accessed through this kind of channel (e.g. virtual museums, virtual tourism). Strictly speaking, telepresence would thus appear as "pure experience" and cannot be related to any kind of cultural object.

3D television would constitute another possible paradigm for digital media, which would naturally convey *authored* cultural objects. However, broadcasting to a large audience is faced with an inherent limit to the level of interactivity that can be implemented, although feedback from a massive audience could in principle be achieved for some TV games and/or shows. In the short term, a balance is to be found between authoring and interaction; as an example, strongly authored 3D movies could offer a variety of perspectives for enjoying the action but little interaction with the plot itself.

Finally, immersive virtual environments would represent the ultimate form of interactivity but are still in search of an identity as cultural objects. So far, only 3D games have entered the marketplace, but have developed without connection to other broadcast material, like movies or TV shows, although the potential connections are great. According to a model due to Altman and Nakatsu [7] (Figure 4.2), the advent of interactivity would actually lead to a convergence of digital cultural objects themselves, through a progressive fusion of movies, broadcasts and video games. However, there could be very different approaches to interactivity in this context. The minimal level of interactivity could consist in user-defined visualization and exploration. An extreme implementation would be real-time interaction with the movie plot, for instance through spoken interaction with artificial actors. These implementations raise other issues, such as the level of implication of the audience, which can be currently illustrated by the opposition between video games and movies or TV dramas.

Currently, the VR paradigm is still based on experience, and, by essence, private experience is not a cultural object. Authoring of VR is still limited to the definition of possible interactions, and persistence of VR is low, making VR mainly an ephemeral experience. However, in the recent past many have advocated the cultural value of ephemeral performance. Will digital convergence and interactivity revive the artistic controversies from the 1960s about total shows, happenings and creation, on the basis of spectator involvement? Various forms of cultural performance could be implemented through distributed virtual environments (Figure 4.3), which would rely on a shared space for human interaction. This would constitute a

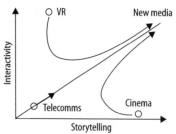

Figure 4.2 A scheme for digital convergence (adapted from Altman and Nakatsu [7]).

Figure 4.3 A distributed virtual environment (developed with the DIVE and Marilyn software).

further step, as it would implement multi-user interactivity, i.e. simultaneous interaction between the users and the environment and between the users themselves.

4.4 The Document Paradigm

Though interactivity and experience are widely recognized as the likely future of broadcasting [7], the Web has taken a step in the opposite direction by revisiting the notion of a "document," which was the basis for traditional cultural objects. The advent of the Web has even reintroduced *reading* into the digital age, even though it has both softened and enhanced it with new features, such as nonlinear reading, browsing and annotation. These new features cannot be charged with deconstructing cultural objects, as distinguished scholars have advocated browsing years before it could be digitally implemented; Roland Barthes, for instance, was fascinated by the fact that in reading the classics one was never *skipping* the same sections! Umberto Eco used to argue in favor of writing on the books themselves (a rather primitive form of annotation), on the argument that "the best way to respect books is by using them."

But further evolutions of hyperdocuments are expected which are related to their specific structure and content. For instance, an underlying homogenous content representation is needed which would be the basis for content-based retrieval of multimedia documents. A proper representation of multimedia document content is in fact required for the proper indexing and retrieval of the growing mass of documents; with the increase in digital material available, content-based access is becoming a major preoccupation. Manual tagging, besides being a gigantic task, has other limitations, such as the completeness, coherence and time-validity of handcrafted indexes.

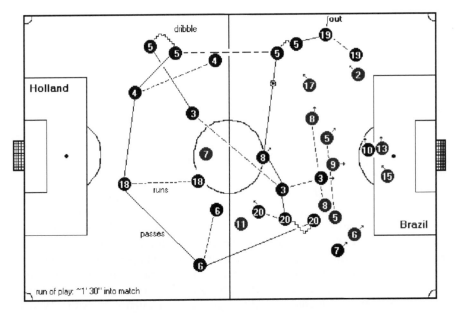

Figure 4.4 A football tactical scheme (courtesy of Ric Miller).

From the standpoint of cultural objects, the rationale for visible knowledge stands in the need and appetite for explanations, which are both visual and symbolic. Such explanations tend to be part of many cultural objects, even from popular culture. Figure 4.4 is a perfect illustration of this fact: it depicts a tactical analysis of a football game that retains a visual appearance while displaying symbolic information (temporal, causal and domain-dependent). Of course, this diagram is a static one, and whenever a complex action has to be explained this is done through a series of static images. Explanations would greatly benefit from the availability of interactive versions of these images, with an appropriate underlying knowledge representation. Depending on such a representation, it could be possible to implement self-contained knowledge units, which unlike previous knowledge interchange initiatives will be attached to a proper visualization of the application concepts. Such knowledge objects could then be exchanged as part of online documents, which would deserve the appellation of *knowlets*.

The development of software agents on networks has brought back to life a certain number of AI research themes, although some agent-related work sometimes overlooks the fact that important technical issues still have to find an appropriate solution. Among these themes is the notion of knowledge interchange and human surveyability of agent knowledge. The idea of knowledge sharing can be tracked back to the Arden Syntax [8], which is a standard defined for the description of diagnostic rules in medical expert systems. The original goal of the Arden Syntax was to provide a unified representation for the development of medical expert systems rules, which would have ensured reusability from one system to another as well as knowledge surveyability. Research in knowledge interchange formats has been boosted by the ARPA knowledge sharing initiative, which contributed to developments such as KIF (Knowledge Interchange Format) and KQML (Knowledge Query and Manipulation Language). While KQML essentially aims at modeling agent–agent interaction or interaction between agents and knowledge bases, there would be a need at some further step for the knowledge units traded by agents to be human-readable. This would not only enable human supervision of some agent processes, but would constitute a primary source of situated knowledge for the users themselves. They would have direct access to a large amount of knowledge ported to the Internet for the purpose of interactive services development (such as financial or legal transactions, online shopping services and catalogues or citizen services). However, it is not yet clear whether research in software agents is properly addressing the surveyability of agent knowledge.

Visible knowledge would then consist of a human-readable representation, with direct mapping to a knowledge representation layer, which would be the basis for interactive explanations in response to user manipulation of some "animated diagram." In the case of our football example introduced above, this would for instance take the form of an interactive map with underlying knowledge for tactical schemes. This could be possibly implemented through Qualitative Simulation (QS), a set of artificial intelligence techniques which have precisely been developed for self-explanatory systems. (Although some similarities with "Visual Programming" could be found, Qualitative Reasoning is entirely based on an existing underlying model which determines the user interaction, and does not involve induction from examples.)

QS is the branch of artificial intelligence which investigates the description of the real world in terms of high-level, user-accessible concepts. The origins of Qualitative Reasoning are to be found in at least three different sources:

- "Naïve physics," an attempt to describe the cognitive understanding of the physical phenomena in the real world (unlike folk psychology, naïve physics is supposed to retain correct approximations only) [9].
- Qualitative physics, in order to enable AI systems to reason about physical systems without having to use numerical equations. The rationale was to simplify and make reasoning interoperable with other reasoning steps [10].
- "Deep knowledge" in expert systems, which were supposed to provide a basis for reasoning from first principles, thus facilitating interactive explanations [11].

Qualitative Simulation has developed a set of techniques for the representation of behavioral concepts and their application to automatic deduction and explanation of device behavior. These techniques can be applied to a wide range of situations, provided the behavior of individual components can be described, together with rules for aggregating local behavior into a global simulation.

Visible knowledge would better appear as "intelligent diagrams": it requires a strong visual component, but explicit representations for semantic relations as well, thus being more a representational language than just another iconic language. This would assume a proper mapping of QS techniques to the interface part (in our football example, the terrain map as an interface). Interactivity would take different forms, such as rearrangements and re-descriptions depending on the particular user perspective. A good starting point for the design of such visible knowledge would be the many explanatory pictures that illustrate newspapers and magazines to explain football matches, principles of economics, mechanisms for various diseases, geopolitics or the hypothesized causes of an airplane crash.

4.6 Conclusion

Aside from market considerations, the perspectives for the cultural objects that would populate the networks of the information society still appear quite open.

The main trend is certainly towards convergence of broadcast material and interactive systems, though it is yet not clear whether this would be under a "push" or a "pull" paradigm for content transmission.

However, from a very different perspective, "richer media" or "explanatory media" could be part of digital convergence as well. Explanatory media have additional relevance in the context of the information society, as they would bring new ways to diffuse complex information, such as legal and medical information, which is currently not passed to the citizen.

References

[1]   European Commission (1997). Green paper on the Convergence of the Telecommunications, Media and Information Technology Sectors, and the Implications for Regulation, COM(97)623.

[2]   M Kruger (1989) *Artificial Reality*, Addison-Wesley, Reading MA.

[3]   D Gelernter (1992) *Mirror Worlds or the Day Software Puts the Universe in a Shoebox*, Oxford University Press, Oxford.

[4]   K Popper (1979) Three worlds, *Michigan Quarterly Review*, 18(1), 1–23.

[5]   F Rastier (1997) *Meaning and Textuality*, Toronto University Press.

[6]   B Bachimont (1998) MPEG-7 and ontologies: an editorial perspective, *Proceedings of the VSMM '98 Conference*, Gifu, Japan, IOS Press.

[7]   EJ Altman and R Nakatsu (1997) Interactive Movies: Techniques, Technology and Content. *Course Notes n. 16*, ACM SIGGRAPH '97.

[8]   G Hripcsak (1994) The Arden Syntax for medical logic modules: introduction, *Computers in Biology and Medicine*, 24(5), 329–30.

[9]   P Hayes (1978) The naïve physics manifesto, in *Expert Systems in the Micro-Electronic Age* (ed. D Michie), Edinburgh University Press.

[10] DS Weld and J De Kleer (1990) *Readings in Qualitative Reasoning about Physical Systems*. Morgan Kaufmann.

[11] B Chandrasekaran, JW Smith and J Sticklen (1989) "Deep" models and their relation to diagnosis, *Artificial Intelligence in Medicine*, 1, 29–40.

5

The Role of 3D Shared Worlds in Support of Chance Encounters in CSCW

Avon Huxor

Abstract

There is currently a great deal of interest in the use of multi-user 3D spaces to support collaborative working. These, however, are typically used for prearranged meetings and do not assist in the "chance meeting" of one person with colleagues or visitors typical of the workplace. Emerging forms of working such as telecommuting and virtual organizations threaten many of these aspects by reducing the number of such encounters, as people are not present in the same physical space at the same time.

Tools for assisting mutual awareness that allow the user to identify others have been developed for the Internet, thus increasing the chances of encounter. For example, ICQ will notify that other registered users are currently online and facilitate communication, and Virtual Places allows registered users looking at the same Web page to chat, on the assumption of a shared interest. But the conventional workplace operates in a subtler manner than these systems. While at work, it is our colleagues that we can access most easily, and the relationships of offices and studios act to bring people of related interest within the same region of a building. But we also have chance encounters with others in the workplace that may not be directly working on one's own project.

The emerging Internet-based 3D worlds might address this problem by bringing together users who are related but working on a separate tasks. Through the nature of spatial worlds and the relationships between rooms within these spaces, a user can be aware of other users, and vice versa, in a manner that reflects aspects of the conventional office building.

The ideas are illustrated through an example in which a 3D world technology, Active Worlds, is being employed as a multi-user interface to a Web-based CSCW tool called BSCW. This example is being developed as part of an ongoing experiment to develop online collaboration tools to support distance learning and collaborative research within the Centre for Electronic Arts. The design of the spaces allows for users to have a natural view of both shared content and the presence of colleagues, and an awareness of others' current interests and activities.

5.1 Introduction

Recent years have seen the emergence of easily available shared 3D world technologies on the Internet, such as those from Active Worlds (http://www.activeworlds.com/), Blaxxun (http://www.blaxxun.com/) [1] and Sony (http://vs.spiw.com/vs/). Being new, there is still some uncertainty as to what the technology can offer above and beyond existing 2D applications, and various possibilities are being explored. For example, in the area of entertainment there are a number of shared online games, such as Funtopia (http://www.funtopia.com/), in which users engage in a game with others within a "medieval world." A number of conventional computer games are also looking towards creating Internet-based multi-user versions.

Television has also provided the source of other experiments, such as *The Mirror* [2], in which a shared world was set up to run during the period of a television series devoted to the Internet – a place for viewers to meet those involved in the program and other viewers. More ambitious still was *Heaven and Hell*, in which a live TV broadcast took place from within a shared world for an hour in August of 1997. Based on a typical television game format, some 150 users logged into the world and became part of the program, which could be seen on Channel 4 from various viewpoints by the conventional television audience.

However, this chapter concerns itself with worlds in which the primary aim of the world is to support collaborative working. The Centre for Electronic Arts (CEA) is currently investigating ways in which the technology can be used to support distance learning and research collaborations, concentrating on utilizing easily available and emerging Internet tools. The current work is an extension of earlier work [21], in which a number of tutorials and committee meetings were undertaken by distributed participants within a shared world, supported by the Cybergate browser from Black Sun (now Blaxxun). It was found that in most cases very little use was made of the spatial aspects of the world. Once users had entered the world, they would engage in text-chat, often without the avatars even being within view of each other. The world model became more of an inconvenience, putting an additional load on the machine, and it is notable that Blaxxun created an alternative client to the same worlds which solely dealt with the chat aspects.

It was unclear from these informal experiences what the role of a 3D spatial representation might be for CSCW, although it became clear that the provision of content – content that made the world worth visiting – was important. Such content needs to be locatable, and a spatial approach seems an appropriate metaphor. But this view may be over-simplistic. Henderson and Card [3] seemed to find that a spatial metaphor was not readily used within their *BigScreen* system, in which (task-related) virtual desktops were laid out in a large single virtual workspace. Users would jump from one desktop to another, rather than navigating through the 2D space over the virtual workspace to get to the desktops. As they state: "task switching seemed to have a non-spatial representation in the user's mind: tasks were easy to name ('read the mail'), but hard to locate in space ('Is mail north or south of here?')." They do, however, observe that there may be situations in which spatial proximity and analogies might be used to advantage.

One view is that the physical world offers many metaphors that can be employed by 3D interfaces to make access to underlying functions simpler, an extension of the desktop metaphor. Hence many current research systems take a very literal view of the office, with tables and chairs populating the space; DIVE [4], for example. The Advanced Multimedia Interface (AMI) went further, including a photocopier and videocassettes as a means to access copying and video-playing features [5]. This chapter hopes to go further, and to ask what the role of the office is in the working environment. In addition to being a place where events and resources are located, as seen in the virtual office, there is a wider view which looks at the role of such spaces in coordinating encounters between people. Thus the relationship between spaces is as important as the design of an individual space. I suspect that the effect described by Henderson and Card [3] might be due to the fact the system was employed in a single-user situation. The argument, to be outlined below, is that awareness of other users, rather more than representing complex applications, might be a better use of a spatial interface. This is especially true as many people are looking to work away from their traditional office: working at either home, or at a client.

5.2 Emerging Forms of Working

One of the major motivations underlying this research is the change occurring within CEA. Increasing numbers of part-time students are coming onto the MA courses, and many of these and other full-time students work either at home or in another workplace. Equally, the various research activities in the Centre involve collaborations with colleagues in other, often far-flung, institutions.

These developments at the CEA reflect general trends in industry. There is an expectation of an increase in both teleworking and emergent forms of virtual organization. In addition to telecommuting as conventionally understood, increasingly we see employees who spend much time on the road, at client or customer sites. Although there are difficulties associated with the management of distributed or distance working, a variety of drivers are leading to its implementation. For example, Lewis [6] reported that the consulting firm Booze-Allen and Hamilton is investigating teleworking as part of its program to meet the US Clean Air Act Amendments of 1990, which require employers in certain areas to discourage unnecessary car use. Similarly, Line and Syvertsen [7] report on a medium-sized Norwegian company which is using the technology to create "virtual engineering teams," spread across 16 regional offices, to support a more project-based style of management in which specific skills are required to be brought together to undertake a particular project for a limited period.

5.2.1 Problems of Telecommuting

However, these new forms of working introduce new problems, especially in the maintenance of collaboration and team building. If members of a workgroup are not co-present, there is a lack of community feeling. There are many technologies to facilitate the formal meetings (such as Microsoft's NetMeeting) that make up much of the traditional workplace, but these seem to miss many of the informal aspects that are crucial to working life.

Lewis [6], from interviews with teleworkers, found that of all the problems discussed, the major concerns seemed to be the feelings of isolation and the impact on promotion prospects. I suspect that the issue of promotion is a political one in many respects, in that it draws upon the close personal loyalties created by informal social interaction. Tom Erickson [8], who works in a distributed manner, reports that when he does visit the office he will catch up on the informal aspects of the workplace and "wander the hallways on purpose so I can bump into people." Many of us know from our own personal experience the value of informal meetings that occur by the coffee machine, in the canteen and in the corridors.

Empirical evidence suggests that these so-called "chance encounters," are very important in the workplace and on its effectiveness [9]. For example, Whittaker *et al.* [10] found that 92% of workplace interactions were not prearranged (although some were intended), and were both frequent and short, lasting an average of only two minutes. These interactions have been shown to be very important: they account for much of the information flow in an organization, and the more a group engages in unplanned interactions the more likely that a project will succeed. They are not just "gossip." Furthermore, work has shown the importance of "weak ties" [11, 12], the connections and conversations with people outside of one's own work team, as they can provide an alternative view of problems and new resources to solve them.

This is not to say, however, that teleworking is invariably associated with negative consequences. Watson *et al.* [13] undertook an empirical study that seemed to challenge this view. The teleworkers in the study found that their satisfaction for informal social interaction was not reduced. The problems that they did report came surprisingly from the telephone. The authors of the study proposed that this may be due to the fact that it is an unscheduled synchronous form of communication. It interrupted them in their work when unwarranted. The face-to-face and email communication modes could be managed and scheduled. This may be a general result, or as the authors suggest, it could be due to the nature of the people in the first wave of telecommuters, who often choose to work remotely to gain control over their work-life.

This apparent contradiction is partially resolved by Bellotti [8], who has distinguished between *teleporters* and *telepaths*. Teleporters work at home to avoid interruptions in the office, to catch up on unfinished tasks. The telepaths, on the other hand, who are away from the main office for a great deal of time, have contradictory concerns. They require the technology to provide access to people and allow informal contact as if they were meeting face-to-face. It is with these users that this chapter is concerned. How can distributed employers within an organization, and beyond it, retain opportunities to engage in informal and spontaneous, communication? Clearly, such encounters can only occur if the various distributed users are aware of each other's presence online, and can then initiate communication.

5.3 Awareness in CSCW

Awareness has become an emerging and important issue in the research at present [14], as CSCW (Computer-Supported Collaborative Working) systems move into actual use. This interest has been matched recently by the appearance of a number of Internet-based tools to allow users to know of other users who are also online, be they friends, colleagues or others. For example:

- ICQ (`http://www.mirabilis.com/`) will give notification that other regis-tered persons, nominated by any specific user, are currently online, and includes tools that facilitate communication, including chat, message leaving and file transfer. It currently claims to already have some seven million registered members, indicating the potential market for these tools.
- PAL (`http://talk.excite.com/communities/excite/pal/home.html`) operates in a similar manner to ICQ.
- Virtual Places (`http://www.vplaces.com/`) allows a user visiting a Web page to encounter others also on the same page and chat, on the assumption of a shared interest. One can also set up a tour as a "guide," and lead other users around from URL to URL: the others on the tour will have their Web browsers updated to match the location of the guide.
- ProRata (`http://www.prorata.com/prorata.html`) is a video glimps-ing system which takes a video snapshot of participants every few minutes. These are displayed on each team member's monitor as thumbnail images. It is, however, not a video conferencing system, its aim instead to be an awareness tool in which team members get a sense of who is around, how busy they are and so forth.

But these tools have the potential to introduce a new set of problems. Thus ICQ could lead to disturbance of work as all colleagues and friends try to communicate when one logs on. The chance of encounters, especially if the technology becomes widespread, is almost too large. Virtual Places, on the other hand, only makes awareness possible if exactly the same URL is being viewed. Given the amount of time that most users spend on a Web page, and the number of Web pages, the chances of an encounter with someone interested in the same content are thus rather low. The problem then becomes one of managing the nature of the awareness to generate the right degree of chance for the appropriate type of encounter depending on the users' goals at any particular time. PAL, for instance, avoids many of the problems in the current version of ICQ by allowing users to create different groups of users who can be allowed to made aware or not. Thus one can ask that only work colleagues be made aware, to prevent unwanted disturbance.

The issue of awareness management can be understood by adopting an architec-tural or urban metaphor. Thus ICQ has the impression of being in a public arena, in which all one's contacts, both personal and professional, might turn up. It is as if one were sitting down to work in the market square of a small town, in which a variety of contacts might pass through during the day. Virtual Places, on the other hand, has the feel of entering a room with very few others, if any, within it. There are no corridors or foyers in which people might assemble. The nearest analogy, curiously, is with a certain form of Brazilian motel, in which this is a design goal. The couples who visit them seek to reduce any chance encounters with other guests or the motel staff, and the layout of the buildings reduces this opportunity.

For real collaborative applications, it is likely that the desired degree of encounter will be a variety of options between, and including, these two extremes. As Clement and Wagner [15] note, the growing data in CSCW indicates the need to distinguish between those interactions that aim to facilitate sharing and those that aim to maintain boundaries and privacy. Thus regionalization of communication spaces helps participants to get focused and protect their view. This notion of protected spaces is not unique to computing. Samarajiva [16] argues that the use of answering machines and caller identification in particular can be understood in a spatial way. This offers the opportunity to apply the approach to the increasing convergence between computing and existing communications media, such as telephony.

The spatial, architectural, approach also suggests that we should look to physical built environments for an understanding of how workplace awareness is managed.

5.4 Use of Space in the Workplace

For such chance encounters to occur in real life we rely on the coordination in time and space of human activities.

- In time: through regular availability. That is, the frequency of chance encounters increases if participants are in the space for more than just prearranged meetings. The standard working day creates this regularity, and even within the day one frequently finds smaller subsets. Thus in my department, if one comes in very early, one finds a totally different "place," as the building is occupied by cleaning staff who depart the offices before our "normal" day begins.
- In space: through the spatial layout of both personal and task spaces. The offices of our close colleagues are usually close to us in the building. As we move through the building, we encounter other colleagues who have more or less relevance to aspects of our work.

The fact is that the "chance encounters" are not really totally chance, but managed through the idea of regionalization introduced above. If that were not the case we would have an equal chance of encountering anyone from the planet wherever we are. The chance encounters we experience are with people we half expect to meet, even if not at that time: colleagues, friends or whatever. We work in the same buildings, visit the same parts of town and go the same bars. These social relations, which make chance encounters more valuable than the purely random ones, are both expressed and affected by the architecture (among other things).

While at work, it is our colleagues that we can access most easily, and the relationships of offices and studios acts to bring people of related interest within the same region of a building. But equally, we have chance encounters with others in the workplace who may not be directly working on one's own project, but on another that may be, in some way, related by the nature of the organization. These effects have been researched in some detail, and in a variety of building types, including

Figure 5.1 The CEA laser printer.

offices, research laboratories, universities and prisons [17], and are more generally discussed in Hillier [11]. However, many of the influences can be identified informally.

Such space-related mechanisms can be found in the physical building that houses the Centre for Electronic Arts. One of the most important features of the CEA, in terms of its role in chance encounters, is the laser printer. This machine, which is used by all the staff and students, is located in the hallway at the junction of three corridors, one of which leads to the area used by the electronic music students and staff, one to the areas occupied by the Digital Arts and Multimedia students and staff, and one to the rest of the building, the toilets and the exits (see Figure 5.1). One often finds people standing by the machine, waiting for a print job to go through, which can takes some minutes (it is a rather old machine). While waiting, many opportunities for "chance encounters" with colleagues or their visitors occurs, as they go from area to area through the limited number of corridors available.

In addition, the printer also acts as a source of conversational material for many of these encounters. Often I have discovered a new interest (both research and personal) of a colleague or student by the contents of the Web pages and other documents that appear from the printer. The printer itself is not only sited below the noticeboard, but almost acts as an extension to it. Indeed, I suspect that the machine is so crucial to assisting in the social aspects of the CEA that the possibility for many printers to be bought and placed around the various rooms is one that should be carefully considered.

On a wider scale, the members of the CEA are part of the School of Art and Design. An important place in the management of encounters within the school is the coffee and snack bar, known colloquially as the "Airport Lounge" (see Figure 5.2). It is situated next to one of the major routes from the main building entrance to other parts of the building. Through the use of low, slatted, partitions, those sitting in the area and those walking past can see each other and initiate conversations. The

Figure 5.2 The "Airport Lounge."

encounters made here are often of a very different nature from those at the laser printer. Members of staff from other subject areas, administrative staff, and visitors to the building will come through, enhancing the "weak ties."

The importance of the larger scale, of the civic nature of communication, was illustrated by Tollmar, Sandor and Schomer [18] whose experimental awareness system, called @Work, was initially used by its subjects, but this interest dropped until its used stopped. A few reasons were found for this, one of which was that the system was "closed." That is, no one external to the experimental trial could use it. But our connections to people outside our immediate colleagues are large and important; thus we need a simple and open system.

This is an important issue. Much of the research work in awareness has concentrated on the individual users and the small groups in which they work, aiming to improve their communicative efficacy. This paper is concerned with widening the area of concern into those of the larger organization and community. The weak ties and virtual communities that are not task-determined often bind these. The work of Backhouse and Drew [19] shows the importance of contacts between people within and around an organization who would normally not meet. Hillier [11] points out that these contacts seem to improve the working of the organization, as new ways of looking at problems are brought to bear when one group talks to another from a very different field. He goes further and considers an imaginary building, one which is designed with "efficiency" in mind, such that the formal structure of the organization is reflected in the spatial layout of the workspaces, making these connections difficult if not impossible. The effect, however, would be that the lack of weak ties would stifle innovation, as well as the wider social interactions that make for a rewarding working environment.

These considerations suggest a possible role for 3D environments to support CSCW. The corridor that contain the printer, and that which the "Airport Lounge" straddles, point to the importance of movement from place to place as a mechanism. These places, in the context of CSCW, are the locales [20] that contain the material that users require for tasks: the tools, documents and so forth. It is the sense of movement, and hence encounter of the avatars of those users in the world, which is one of the characteristics of shared 3D worlds.

5.5 Linking Active Worlds and BSCW

From the considerations discussed above, it was decided to undertake a further small-scale, and informal, experiment to apply 3D shared world technologies as a means of assisting chance encounters. Because of the need for the systems to eventually be easily accessible to many users, including students at home, it is important that the technology be cheap and available on inexpensive platforms. The two components were a CSCW tool to manage many of the materials required for work (BSCW), and a shared world technology (Active Worlds) in which users can meet and talk to others.

5.5.1 BSCW

BSCW (Basic Support for Collaborative Working; `http://bscw.gmd.de/`) is an Internet-based shared workspace system, based on the conventional desktop metaphor. It is a Web-based collaboration tool in which users can access "workspaces," which coordinate activity and objects. Users create workspaces that can be made available to nominated team members or interested parties, and, importantly, BSCW also manages user authentication, ensuring that documents are reasonably secure. This latter aspect proved crucial, as most of the shared world technologies do not deal with this issue to any significant extent.

The current version allows for files of various types to be stored (with version control) and accessed, and has a simple workspace-specific threaded discussion system, links to URLs, and the ability to help schedule meetings using a system such as NetMeeting. Also, many issues in workspace awareness are implemented in BSCW. Objects within the workspace have event notification, such as indicating that an object is new, has been changed, has been moved from one folder to another, or has been read or downloaded. BSCW can be used by anyone with Internet access, requiring no more than a standard Web browser, and this is important for the ongoing development, as the aim is to support the collaboration with many external collaborators without the need for specific systems.

BSCW is a popular shared workspace for collaboration, and is the basis for the "Virtual Workplace" (`http://vw.sisu.se/`), a commercial enterprise in which users pay "rent" on virtual workspace. The author also employs the basic BSCW system in a number of collaborations with other researchers and colleagues, having proved its value in a number of smaller tasks, especially in the writing of joint papers. It is currently being used by the author as a component of an experimental collaboration between multimedia students at the CEA and students at the Department of Architecture at Edinburgh University.

However, one of the features that makes BSCW so interesting is its use of the workspace metaphor, as do many other emerging Internet-based collaboration tools – *eRoom* (http://www.instinctive.com/) and *TeamWave* (http://www.teamwave.com/), for example. One motivation for the designs outlined below was to investigate whether the workspaces might be usefully represented in a more fully spatial 3D environment, within and between "spaces." The technology selected for this component was Active Worlds.

5.5.2 Active Worlds

Active Worlds (http://www.activeworlds.com/) is a shared 3D world technology that is also readily available over the Internet and is typical of many of these technologies. A figure, or avatar, which indicates the user's location and the direction of attention, represents each user; each user sees the world through the "eyes" of this avatar. The avatars are moved through the world through the arrow cursor keys, although there are also teleport and warp facilities to get to distant areas very quickly. Participants can communicate with each other through text-chat, in the frame below the main 3D world display, and there are various tools to help locate particular characters and to control others access to yourself. There are many different worlds that the client browser can access, often themed on cultural or fictional "worlds." The oldest and most popular, however, is AlphaWorld, and it is within this world that the spaces described are constructed.

Active Worlds has a number of advantages over other systems, such as those from Blaxxun and Sony, in that there is an existing kit of components which can be taken and employed to construct a building in the world. One can either copy and move objects already found in the world, or select from a library of components, including floors, walls, roofs and panels (interior walls). The speed of construction that this facilitates allows for very rapid prototyping of design ideas. There is, of course, an associated disadvantage in that the potential for the visual design of the spaces is reduced, but this is less important at the conceptual design stage that is my present concern.

Active Worlds also have many features required to link effectively to BSCW. Each Active Worlds object can also be linked to existing Web material, which appears in the associated Web browser. Certain objects in the catalogue also allow for audio and video to be fed into them, and thus can be used to integrate awareness tools, such as ProRata, into the world very quickly.

5.5.3 AlphaWorld as a Site for BSCW

A small "building" to host the CEA is being built in AlphaWorld. The basic idea is to link the objects in the space to appropriate BSCW workspaces. That is, the

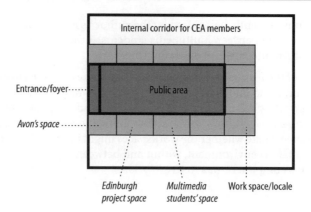

Figure 5.3 Floor plan of virtual CEA.

workspace finds representation in a 3D world. The aim is to facilitate encounters between users of BSCW, the chance of encounters between avatars, and hence users, being mediated by the spatial layout imposed upon the BSCW workspace. The building within AlphaWorld is based on the floor plan shown in Figure 5.3.

It is divided into three areas. The first (inner) area is accessed through the entrance from the outside, and is public, available to any AlphaWorld visitor. Walls and objects within this area link to Web pages and other Web content that are made available to any interested party. Beyond that is the zone containing the specific workspaces for individuals, teams or specific projects. Finally, the outer zone is an internal corridor for CEA members and guests, allowing movement from one workspace to another. The spatial layout has two roles:

1. It manages access to content. Thus, take the space designed for the Edinburgh Collaboration as an example (see Figure 5.3). This space has four "walls," each of which can have a link to BSCW workspaces, or other Web content. To the right is the space for the multimedia students, some of whom are participating in the exercise, and to the left is my personal space. Downwards is the area accessible to CEA staff and guests (the corridor), and finally upwards is the public space. By placing appropriate material into BSCW workspaces, and associating these with one of these walls, the access rights can be made clear. So finished work that can be made public is placed on the upper wall, where it can be accessed by users coming into the open area. Other documents can be made available to just CEA members and their guests, while work that is unfinished and not for wider consumption can be placed on the wall that allows for easy access to either myself and/or their fellow students.
2. The second role for the layout is that to do with the handling of chance encounters. When users enter and move through the space to access content, it is possible that they might meet other users who are present on relevant business.

The screen image in Figure 5.4 shows the external view of the CEA site, as seen through the Active Worlds browser. The entrance, lying just behind the two columns, leads into the public space. On the far side of the entrance, one of the work

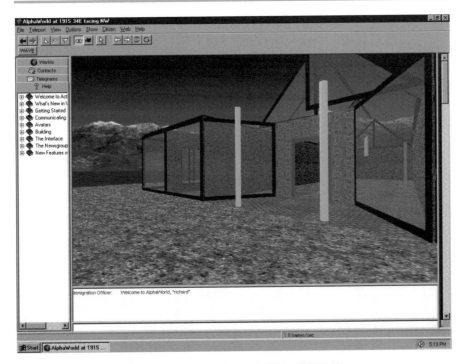

Figure 5.4 External view of the CEA building in AlphaWorld.

areas and the internal corridor are visible through glass walls. Below the main image is the chat box, in which the conversation between users within the area is displayed, as are messages from the system. Below that frame is a single line frame in which the user types text to send to others.

While in a space, such as that allocated for the Edinburgh Project (see Figure 5.5), I can see and be seen by those who enter nearby areas, while my own privacy can be protected. Active Worlds provides a number of types of "wall" that allow for a range of awareness controls. Thus there is a "solid" wall, to give visual privacy, walls with small windows that give some view into the space behind, and "glassy" walls that give a very good view, while still creating the sense of a separate space. This range of visual devices creates the permeability of experience that we find in the real world.

The motivation for any user being in that particular space is to access content within it. Thus in Figure 5.5 the user has clicked on the wall between the space and the internal corridor. This brings up the BSCW page that contains the material related to the project, which appears in the associated Web browser on the left. In this case it shows links to relevant Web sites and a text version of the project brief. Actual access to the material is, as mentioned above, controlled by the authentication system within BSCW. This is required, as Active Worlds, although having collision detection, allows users to override this feature and pass through walls. Thus security of content is maintained at the BSCW end.

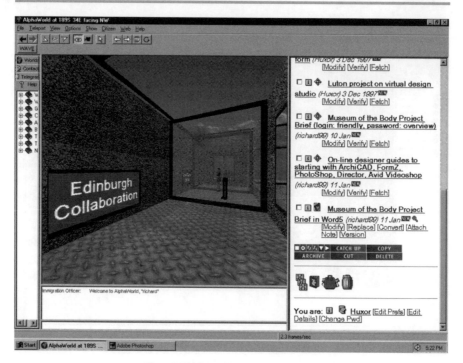

Figure 5.5 AlphaWorld site with BSCW content.

From the BSCW page, the user can now download the specific content to work upon, such as editing the project brief. The Active Worlds browser can be left running behind, and if other users enter the space, they will appear in their own spaces. In Figure 5.5 two other users (represented as avatars) are nearby, in two work areas further back (Active Worlds is designed for colour, and the avatars can only just be seen behind the "glass" walls in the monochrome image printed). Any of the users can initiate conversation through the text-chat facility.

Unlike ICQ, however, those users likely to be in the space, and with whom the chance encounter might occur, are mediated by the spaces and their contents. The user will not be bombarded by requests to chat from all the colleagues, friends and family that are currently online. And, unlike Virtual Places, the encounter is not only with a user looking at the same BSCW content. This would reduce the chance of encounter greatly. Other users could be in the area looking at their own content, or may be interested visitors looking at the CEA public Web site. This helps to ensure that weak ties are also maintained, as encounter and communication are only partially, but not fully, determined by the task content as located in BSCW.

5.5.4 Design Issues Arising

The approach being taken within my research is to construct small experiments with current technologies to determine the problems that occur, prior to the design and implementation of a fuller system. They include user movement, design flexibility and screen space usage.

5.5.4.1 Movement

One problem that arises in the majority of the shared 3D worlds is the problem of movement. It was previously noted that users eventually tire of having to control their avatar all the time, and just sit in the same place [21]. A useful feature to implement in a shared world would be ability to move in an automated manner from space to space, taking access rights into account. This must not only be a jump, as the chances for encounter are greatly reduced, but a measured motion through the space. Active Worlds has a *warp* feature, but this is for large-scale movements across the whole world, and not within smaller spaces such as the CEA building.

Movement is an issue that needs to be addressed to improve user acceptance of the technology, but it may also have an important bearing on the management of encounters. Backhouse and Drew [19] observed that in the physical workplace much recruitment into conversation occurs when people are moving between one work area and another. Possibly the same effect will translate into the virtual world, as movement will represent that the user is moving from one task to another, and hence is less likely to have a train of thought disturbed by a causal conversation.

5.5.4.2 Flexibility vs. Stability

Another issue that arose was the lack of flexibility in the design of the virtual buildings. That is, if new work or project groups form or existing ones fragmented it was difficult to change the 3D spaces quickly to account for the changes. However, this may be less of a problem, and possibly an advantage, than originally thought. One of the constant problems for shared spaces is that if the contents change too quickly, due to one user's efforts, it may then be a problem for other users to comprehend. In other words, as we move from a single-user situation to shared collaborative computing environments, the flexibility that is a goal for individual users may need to be compromised to facilitate group work.

This range of "persistence of structure" matches real-world expectations. We move into rooms those working groups that have some persistence; those groups or events that are more temporary have temporary rooms associated with them. Thus it is proposed that certain tasks, such as preparing a joint paper, might have hired spaces that they occupy for their duration. Equally, new groupings prove their persistence by occupying a hired space, whereupon it can request an extension. The greatest flexibility will be at the content level, as expressed in the files and messages within the BSCW space, which can change rapidly. The need for eventual extension of the virtual CEA to allow for organizational changes accounts for its simplistic design. The simple floor plan can be stretched to add further work area spaces with relative ease.

5.5.4.3 Awareness Space vs. Workspace

One final concern, one that can be seen in Figure 5.5, is the demand on display screen real estate. The 3D world occupies a significant area of screen space, reducing that available for actual work, be it word processing, spreadsheets, etc. Of course, this problem is one that is inherent in many of the current awareness tools based on the desktop metaphor, such as PAL and ProRata, not just to the design described above.

One solution being planned is to separate the awareness space and the workspace. The 3D world could be displayed on a projected display at some distance from the user. This would capture some of the peripheral nature of awareness rather better than at present. It seems reasonable that such a projected display would suit a 3D interface, rather than the current 2D-based solutions, which rely upon menus and text which may be less visible on the periphery.

5.5.5 Related Work

The integration of awareness tools to BSCW has been undertaken by Mansfield *et al.* [22] as part of their larger Orbit project. Orbit-Lite provided BSCW users with synchronous awareness of those who are members of a particular BSCW workspace, through live images provided by vic, the Mbone video tool. The Virtual Workplace (see above) extends BSCW through Java applets, allowing users to be aware of both the synchronous presence of members of any workspace to which they are members, and of actions that other users are making to objects within the workspaces. However, both of these systems only address awareness within a team. They do not easily support the wider community contacts, the weak ties that seem so important.

The linking of a virtual space and Web-based content has also been undertaken by Dieberger [23], whose Juggler system links a text-based MOO with a Web browser. Thus any URL typed by a user will appear in the browser, and URLs can also be associated with a room. In this case, the main aim is less to coordinate encounters between users than to provide a structure to help the navigation of the WWW through an urban metaphor. Clearly, though, these two aspects are closely related. The work described in this paper concentrates on the civic structure of awareness, although it relies upon both team awareness and content navigation to provide a more immediate rationale for the use of the worlds.

5.6 Conclusion

This chapter has been primarily concerned with addressing the question: What can 3D worlds offer CSCW, and shared computing generally? Although initially attractive and interesting, the shared worlds provided by Blaxxun and Active Worlds do seem at present to have a limited role. I have tried to argue that spatial relationships may find an important role in managing awareness between a large and diverse set of online users. The awareness tools becoming available, although valuable, seem to introduce new problems which may be best solved through an architectural, spatial, approach. The location that we found ourselves within a larger virtual world thus helps us to manage our encounters with others, be they colleagues, friends or others. Specifically, we must start to be concerned with the larger civic scale, with encounters beyond our immediate circle of contacts, not only to create more interesting virtual communities but also to support the new forms of working that are expected to appear.

The approach also suggests that virtual world design should look not only at how the lessons of real-world navigation can be applied [24, 25] to the virtual, but also how notions of private, public and semi-public space are expressed. Once we have navigated to a place in the world, we must have a sense of whose workspace it is, and what access is available. Only then will the "Interspace" proposed by Erickson come to be – a virtual space in which information spaces become social spaces and in which 3D can serve as a natural, instinctive interface.

Acknowledgments

Much of the work presented in this paper has been supported through a BT Laboratories Short-Term Fellowship. The author would like to thank members of the Shared Spaces Group, and Tim Regan in particular, for valuable discussions on the issues raised.

References

[1] R Rockwell (1996) Infrastructure and architecture for cyberspace communities, *Computer Graphics*, 19–24 November.
[2] G Walker (1997) The Mirror: reflections on inhabited TV, *British Telecommunications Engineering*, 16(1), 29–38.
[3] DA Henderson and SK Card (1996) Rooms: the use of multiple workspaces to reduce space contention in a window-based graphical user interface, *ACM Trans. Graphics*, 5(3), 211–43.
[4] C Carlsson and O Hagsand (1993) DIVE: a platform for multi-user virtual environments, *Computers & Graphics*, 17(6), 663–9.
[5] S Powers and D Sheat (1996) The advanced multimedia interface – AMI, *Proc. 3D and Multimedia on the Internet, WWW & Networks*, Bradford, UK, 16–18 April.
[6] PF Lewis (1996) A feasibility study of implementing a telecommuting program at Booz-Allen and Hamilton, in *Telecommuting '96* (eds. RT Watson and RP Bostrom), Electronic Proceedings, http://www.cba.uga.edu/tc96/proceedings.html/.
[7] L Line and TG Syvertsen (1996) Virtual engineering teams: strategy and implementation, in *Construction on the Information Highway* (ed. Z. Turk), Electronic Proceedings, http://www.fagg.uni-lj/bled96/.
[8] J Scholtz, V Bellotti, L Schirra *et al.* (1998) Telework: when your job is on the line. *Interactions*, Jan/Feb, 44–54.
[9] EA Isaacs, JC Tang and T Morris (1996) Piazza: a desktop environment supporting impromptu and planned interactions, *Proc. ACM Conf. Computer-Supported Co-operative Work*, Boston MA.
[10] S Whittaker, D Frohlich and D Jones (1994) Informal workspace communication: what is it like and how might we support it?, *Proc. Conf. Computer–Human Interaction*, Boston MA, ACM Press, pp. 260–83.
[11] B Hillier (1996) *Space is the Machine*, Cambridge University Press, Cambridge.
[12] B Hillier and J Hanson (1984) *The Social Logic of Space*, Cambridge University Press, Cambridge.

[13] MB Watson-Frith, S Narasimhan and HS Rhee (1996) The impact of remote work on informal orga- nizational communication, in *Telecommuting '96* (eds. RT Watson and RP Bostrom), Electronic Proceedings, http://www.cba.uga.edu/tc96/proceedings.html.

[14] SE McDaniel and T Brinck (1997) Awareness in Collaborative systems: a CHI97 workshop, *SIGCHI Bulletin*, 29(4), 68–71.

[15] A Clement and I Wagner (1995) Fragmented exchange: disarticulation and the need for regionalized communication spaces, *Proc. ECSCW95*, Stockholm.

[16] R Samarajiva (1994) Privacy in electronic public space: emerging issues, *Canadian Journal of Communication*, 19, 87–99.

[17] Space Syntax Laboratory (1997) Space syntax, *Proc. First International Symposium* (2 vols.), Bart- lett School of Architecture, London.

[18] K Tollmar, O Sandor and A Schomer (1996) Supporting social awareness @ work design and experi- ence, *Proc. CSCW '96*, pp. 298–307.

[19] A Backhouse and P Drew (1992) The design implications of social interaction in a workplace setting, *Environment and Planning B: Planning and Design*, 19, 573–84.

[20] SM Kaplan *et al.* (1997) MUDdling through, *Proc 13th Annual Hawaii Int. Conf. on Systems Sciences*, Vol. II, pp. 539–48.

[21] A Huxor (1997) The role of virtual world design in collaborative working, *Proc. IEEE Conf. Informa- tion Visualization*, pp. 246–51.

[22] T Mansfield *et al.* (1997) *Evolving Orbit: a progress report on building locales*, available online at http://www.dstc.edu.au/worlds/Papers/EvolvingOrbit.

[23] A Dieberger (1996) Browsing the WWW by interacting with a textual virtual environment – a framework for experimenting with navigational metaphors, *Proc. ACM Hypertext '96*, pp. 170–9.

[24] R Ingram, S Benford and J Bowers (1996) Building virtual cities: applying urban planning principles to the design of virtual environments, *Proc. ACM VRST '96*.

[25] C Boyd and R Darken (1996) Psychological issues of virtual environment interfaces, *SIGCHI Bulletin*, 28(4), 49–53.

6

Agent-Based Facial Animation

Ali Al-Qayedi and Adrian F. Clark

Abstract

Software agents are becoming an essential part of today's Internet, frequently providing elegant solutions to complex problems. In this chapter we describe a real-time facial animation algorithm based on an agent-like approach. The algorithm is part of a model-based video coding system intended for videoconferencing on the Internet. The paper describes how remotely downloaded scripts in the Tcl programming language, termed "Animation Agents," control facial synthesis from a pre-received texture map, and hence produce realistic facial expressions. Some results are shown and conclusions are drawn as to the preference of using the agent approach rather than conventional approaches to facial animation.

6.1 Introduction

The rapid growth of the Internet in recent years has initiated a great interest among the information society towards applications employing continuous media. Compression and coding for videoconferencing is one example where considerable research effort has been expended due to the large amount of data needed to represent video bit-streams and the comparatively low data rate nature of the Internet when compared with broadcast television. As a result, many schemes have been introduced for the purpose of reducing the video information rate. Almost all of them attempt to exploit redundancy between the pixels of digital images. Using such schemes one can reduce the amount of information needed to less than half without introducing gross distortions, and provide satisfactory results over 1.5 Mbps; but communicating even this amount of compressed information over the Internet is difficult, and hence even lower data rates are needed.

The quality that these compression techniques provide in very low data rate environments is normally deemed unacceptable: significant visual artefacts arise from the block-based techniques when estimating the motion of features within the data; and jerky images result from the low frame rates employed, usually less than 10 frames/sec [7, 18]. One can argue that the problems with these coding schemes arise from the attempt to compress the data *at the pixel level*, rather than exploiting any

73

higher-level information about the imagery. Moreover, in areas of visual communication, such as video-telephony and videoconferencing, a true reproduction of the original imagery is not necessary: the user only needs a reasonably faithful rendition of remote subjects. Hence conveying the same meaning with a reasonable picture quality would suffice if this is accompanied by high reduction in the data rate.

One way to achieve this goal is to employ what is known as *model-based* image coding (MBC) [13]. As generally implemented, MBC relies on having wireframe models (3D or 2D meshes of numerous vertices) of the objects to be coded at both the encoder and the decoder. In essence, MBC works as follows [18, 8]. Computer vision techniques are used at the encoder to analyze the scene contained within an image and to extract information about the shape, colour and motion of every object. This information is parameterized and transmitted to the decoder, which uses computer graphics techniques to synthesize an approximate model for each object. Improved realism can be added to objects in the decoder by projecting (texture mapping) the 2D color information from the original imagery onto the wireframe model. Tracking techniques are used to detect any changes in the geometric parameters of those objects from frame to frame. Changes are sent to the decoder, where animation techniques are used to make the model mimic the movement of its corresponding object. The requirement that models need to be available at both the transmitter and the receiver is a significant constraint in the general case; but for the types of imagery encountered in videoconferencing it is not severe, since primarily the head and shoulders only are involved.

In MBC, only a few parameters describing the results of the image analysis stage are sent; compared with conventional techniques, where a coded representation of the actual images is sent, MBC promises a vast reduction in the data rate. Indeed, data rates of well under 1 kbps have been achieved with a frame rate of 25 Hz [8] for sequences with fairly simple facial movements.

MBC can also be considered as a technique for realizing the content-based manipulation and bit-stream editing functionality of the MPEG-4 standard; this means that the user will be able to access a specific object among a number of objects within the scene or bit-stream and perhaps change some of its characteristics [14].

Two significant problems in MBC are the need to ensure the encoder and decoder have consistent models and the requirement to transmit animation parameters efficiently. These are the problems addressed herein. There are three main objectives to our work:

- To explore the possibility of achieving further reduction in the transmitted data rate by sending high-level semantic "animation agents" between the encoder and the decoder. We address this by transmitting scripts in Ousterhout's Tool Command Language (Tcl) [10, 21].
- To illustrate the benefits of using this "agent-based" approach compared with conventional schemes for facial animation.
- To consider the possibility of applying the same approach in object-oriented MBC (see below), as well as in MPEG-4 applications.

The breakdown of the chapter is as follows. Section 6.2 presents an overview of the concepts of model-based coding and describes some common approaches. Section 6.3 considers the techniques commonly used for facial animation. Section 6.4 gives an overview of agent technology and addresses its usefulness for MBC. Section 6.5 describes our approach and Section 6.6 presents some experimental results. Section 6.7 draws some conclusions.

6.2 Model-Based Coding

Two main categories of MBC systems have been identified [13]: *object-based coding* (OBC) systems (also known as *object-oriented analysis-synthesis image coding* or OOASIC); and *knowledge-based coding* (KBC) and *semantic* systems. OBC systems do not require *a priori* knowledge of the scene and are therefore applicable to a wide range of objects. KBC and semantic systems, however, assume *a priori* knowledge of the object or objects being modeled and therefore are restricted to applications such as those involving the human head and shoulders.

In a knowledge-based coding system, a 3D model of a generic human head and shoulders is designed offline and is made available at both the transmitter (encoder) and the receiver (decoder) [18]. While tracking global motion seems to be successful using the knowledge-based approach, the estimation of local motions of the eyes, nose and lips is a more difficult proposition due to the complexity of facial expressions. This results in large regions of model failure. One solution to this problem is via the use of semantic coding, a subset of the knowledge-based scheme which uses a combination of *action units* (AUs) that best describe a given facial expression. The Facial Action Coding System (FACS) [4] defines a set of more than 50 AUs that can be combined to produce different facial expressions. In semantic coding, these AUs are sent as required; once an AU is received by the decoder it is stored in a look-up table. If the same AU is encountered again, the encoder need only send an index of that AU in the look-up table – this clearly provides an effective saving in the data rate.

MBC can also be incorporated in a hybrid scheme with one of the traditional low bit rate coders, such as the H.261 or H.263, where a fallback between the two modes is achieved via a decision criterion such as the data rate or the quality of the coded sequence [3].

Most experimental work on MBC has concentrated on the knowledge-based approach through modeling of the human head and shoulders. This is due to its most probable applications being in video-telephony and videoconferencing. Few attempts have been made that consider and experiment with objects other than faces [13, 7]. It is essential that more effort is made in generalizing MBC to accommodate a variety of objects for it ultimately to be acceptable in MPEG-4-like applications.

The fastest and simplest form of model-based coding is one wherein objects are analyzed only once. Information resulting from this analysis may be used to deform the 3D model common to encoder and decoder. The encoder then encodes subsequent images in an "open-loop" manner, without re-analyzing the scene. There is another technique in which the synthesized model is incorporated in a feedback loop *within the encoder* to find compliance with the original object, and the difference between actual image and model-based reconstruction is transmitted (in addition to the model parameters, of course). Such schemes are considered to be too slow for real-time applications on current hardware, although they have the advantage of refining and adapting the synthesized model more closely to the object.

Our work on modeling human faces for videoconferencing uses the open-loop approach and is based on computer vision. We assume prior knowledge of the scene content, i.e. that it contains a human head and shoulders. The model which is used for synthesis and animation is an enhanced and extended version of the Candide face model [16].

6.3 Facial Animation

The main purpose of facial animation techniques is to manipulate the surfaces of a computer-generated 3D face model over a period of time so that one or more facial expressions is achieved. The animator's role is to provide the required control parameters that make the face "come to life." The role of the animation algorithm is to translate these parameters into expressions and finally play the sequence in real time.

6.3.1 Fundamental Animation Techniques

It can be argued that there are five basic animation techniques: interpolation, performance-driven animation, direct parameterization, pseudo-muscle-based and muscle-based animation [11].

- *Interpolation* is perhaps the most widely used technique for facial animation. The simplest example is where the two extremes of one expression are given and the animation algorithm is responsible for generating the in-between range of expressions.
- *Performance-driven animation* relies on measuring real human actions to drive synthetic expressions. Data obtained from interactive input devices such as data gloves, instrumented body suits and motion tracking systems are used to drive the animation. Performance-driven animation is extensively used in the film and video industry, where laser or video-based motion tracking systems are used to detect human actions and the resulting motion parameters are used to drive body movements or facial expressions.
- *Direct parameterization* [12] employs two sets of parameters, one to deform the facial model to match the real face and the second to control facial expressions. Facial features are then manipulated with the aid of local region interpolations, geometric transformations and texture-mapping techniques.
- *Pseudo-muscle-based animation* simulates only the muscle actions by geometric deformation operators; facial tissue dynamics are not simulated.

- *Muscle-based animation* extends the pseudo-muscle-based approach by physical modeling of the facial muscles, such as a mass and spring model [15, 20, 19].

These animation techniques are necessarily not totally distinct: one animation method may be used in conjunction with one or more other methods. An example would be the use of performance-driven animation to drive the facial expression and interpolation to define the intensity of that expression within a range of similar expressions.

6.3.2 Texture Mapping

Computer-generated three-dimensional facial surfaces lack realism, even with the aid of sophisticated shading techniques. The most practical way to increase realism and information content of synthesized faces with current modeling technology is through the use of texture-mapping techniques. Texture mapping, pioneered by Catmull [2] and refined by Blinn and Newell [1], is a technique whereby the color (texture) information of an image is projected onto a 3D surface to provide a more realistic appearance of surfaces displayed by the synthesis system. In the case of head-and-shoulders sequences, the texture information may be taken from either the first or any other frame in the sequence and mapped onto the 3D model of the human. When the model is animated, texture attached to hair and other facial features stretches according to the motion, leading to fairly realistic facial expressions. Heckbert [6] provides a detailed survey of texture-mapping techniques.

Textures can also be used in generating *codebooks* of different facial expressions, which are made available at the decoder. When the tracking system at the encoder detects a certain facial expression, an index to that expression in the codebook is sent to the decoder, which maps it onto the required place on the human model.

6.4 Agent-Based Animation

Software agents are currently being explored in many different application areas, including the management of electronic mail, business schedules and information retrieval on the Internet. An agent basically refers to a component of software and/ or hardware which is capable of accomplishing tasks autonomously on behalf of its user [9] and can vary in complexity from a simple program to a very sophisticated software suite. There are many categories under which agents may be classified, depending on the role or the task that they perform: for example, agents that exploit Internet search engines are often known as World Wide Web information agents.

In the context of the work presented in this chapter, the most important categorization of agents is into *static* and *mobile*: a static agent executes on a single computer, while a mobile agent is able to gather together executable code and data and migrate from machine to machine, providing of course that all machines involved provide appropriate software support for nomadic software.

Our agent-based animation work uses Ousterhout's *Tool Command Language* (Tcl), a simple and eoeective interpreted scripting language [10, 21]. Tcl and its associated graphical toolkit, Tk, enable the programmer to write complex applications with few lines of code. This is because the high-level Tcl commands are built on top of C library functions. Most important in the context of mobile agents, though, is the excellent portability of the Tcl and Tk interpreters, running on all flavors of Unix, Windows and the Macintosh OS. Moreover, carefully-written Tcl scripts may be executed on all these platforms *without change*.

Tcl is not, of course, the only language that claims platform independence: the best-known language that falls into this category is Java. It is illuminating to consider briefly why the authors have based their work on one language rather than the other. The authors (as, indeed, does the author of Tcl) contend that Java is best considered as a replacement for C and C++ whose compiled code is platform-independent. Conversely, Tcl is a *scripting language*, most analogous to a platform-independent Unix shell (with all the resulting advantages and disadvantages).

Security is a major concern when talking about scripts that are passed over a network and executed. A "safe" interpreter can be created in recent versions of Tcl which enables the recipient to execute the downloaded Tcl script safely without worry of viruses or other attacks. This is achieved by having two Tcl interpreters in the application: a parent *trusted* interpreter used for the main application, and within it another child *untrusted* or *safe* interpreter, used to execute untrusted scripts. So when the main application receives an untrusted script, it passes that script to the safe interpreter for evaluation. This restricted nature of the untrusted interpreter ensures that the application is safe from attack [21].

It is principally the lack of any requirement for compilation that makes Tcl attractive for this work: as we shall see, short scripts can be generated at the encoder on the fly and transmitted to the decoder to perform animations. Moreover, as Tcl is a reasonably high-level language, few lines of code are needed to represent any particular animation. The additional security offered by Safe-Tcl ameliorates the security issues that would otherwise be a major headache.

Although Tcl is attractive for the reasons outlined above, it lacks an intrinsic ability to synthesize images from 3D models. Fortunately, there are many user-contributed extensions to the Tcl core and we have made use of one of these, Togl, in our work. Togl allows one to create and manage a Tk/OpenGL widget with Tcl and render into it. All the underlying rendering and graphics manipulation functions are written in C using OpenGL, but these functions are accessed via Togl commands. Hence a typical Togl program will have Tcl code for managing the user interface and interpretation of high-level commands, and C code for computation and OpenGL rendering.

6.5 Our Approach to Model-Based Coding

We are trying to build a model-based image codec capable of real-time operation. At the encoder, we have used image analysis techniques derived from those used in

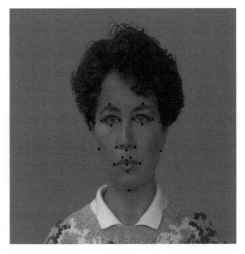

Figure 6.1 Positions of features obtained from feature extraction.

the computer vision field to extract the facial features of the subject from the first frame of an image sequence. This is achieved by searching for the positions of the feature points shown in Figure 6.1, extracting from these the facial features (eyes, nose, lips, etc.) of the subject. These features are transmitted to the decoder, where they are used to reproduce something closely approximating the facial image using image synthesis ("computer graphics") techniques. This procedure involves first deforming a general 3D head-and-shoulders model, derived from Linköping University's Candide [16], so that it resembles the subject; and secondly, texture-mapping the luminance and/or chrominance information of the original image onto the deformed model.

Tracking algorithms then estimate any 3D motion of the subject within the image sequences. The tracking results are translated into a number of invokable "agents," which are sent to the decoder and invoked by the decoder to make the model reproduce the movements.

The various stages of the process are described further in the following subsections.

6.5.1 Feature Extraction

The system extracts the facial features shown in Figure 6.1 from strong edges and corners in the gray-scale image. We have used the SUSAN edge and corner detector developed at Oxford [17]: our experiments demonstrate that it is more robust in performing this function compared with other algorithms, even though its results are, like many other edge detectors, dependent on the contrast threshold. The edge and corner output from SUSAN are shown in Figure 6.2.

In order to find the required facial features from the output of SUSAN, given a head-and-shoulders image with plain background, the analysis algorithm performs the following steps:

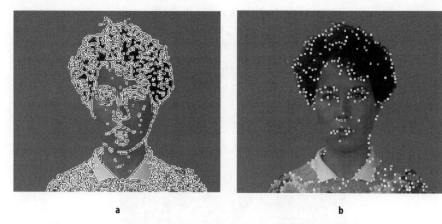

a   b

Figure 6.2 Output of the SUSAN detector with the brightness threshold set to 10: **a** edges; **b** corners.

1. Find the top of the face by searching from the top of the image downwards.
2. Find initial left and right sides of the face by looking for the first edge from either side of the image searching towards the center of the image.
3. Find an estimated bottom of the head by assuming that the overall aspect ratio of the head is approximately 5/3:4. This figure is drawn from a short experiment carried out to find the aspect ratio of the heads of 20 subjects. This assumption was found to be useful in two aspects: firstly, to confine the search region when looking for the facial features; and secondly, it supports a multi-scale search in which the algorithm can find features for people very close to the camera as well as those far away from it.
4. Find the local features (eyes, nose and mouth regions) by searching from top of the head downwards. The eyes, for example, are found by searching for a window with the maximum cluster of corners within a given search region. The rest of the features are found similarly, each time starting the search from the bottom of the previously found feature. The chin is found by searching for the darkest region below the mouth, based on the assumption that light always comes from above the speaker.
5. Find the exact sides of the face by searching for a bright/dark (face/hair) contrast change along either side of the eyes.

Two examples of the final result of the multi-scale search algorithm are shown in Figure 6.3, where the left subject is close to the camera and the right subject further away from it.

6.5.2 Deformation of the 3D Model

Figure 6.4 shows front and side views of the extended Candide model we have used in our work. The system derives a suitable model for a specific subject by performing global and local deformations of Candide. Global deformations include

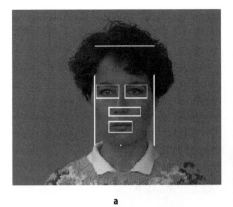 

    a   b

Figure 6.3 Face feature locations extracted by our multi-scale algorithm: **a** subject near to camera; **b** subject far away from camera.

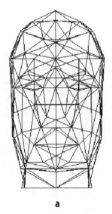 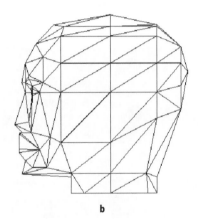

    a   b

Figure 6.4 Our 3D head model, derived from Candide [16]: **a** front view; **b** side view.

matching the aspect ratio of the model's head to that of the subject's head, while local deformations are used to ensure that the facial features of the Candide model coincide with those of the subject. The latter involve modifying the coordinates of all other vertices by interpolating feature and non-feature vertices vertically and horizontally. Figure 6.5 shows a deformed Candide model superimposed on a subject's face.

6.5.3 Facial Image Synthesis

Texture mapping, projecting 2D texture information from the first image of a subject in a sequence onto the deformed 3D model, is used to synthesize realistic-looking images; Figure 6.6 illustrates how realistic this process can be made to

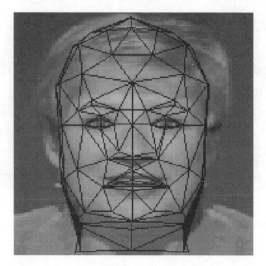

Figure 6.5 Deformed 3D head model superimposed on subject's face.

a   b

Figure 6.6 a Original image and **b** synthesized image.

appear. Because the system is intended for videoconferencing environments, where images represent mainly the head and shoulders of speakers, the system adds to the synthesized image the hair and shoulders retrieved from the original scene.

In previous work in the authors' group (e.g. [8]), the hair and shoulders have been incorporated into the 3D model and animated accordingly. This has not been done in the system described here for the following reasons:

- They make little contribution in terms of facial animation (though the shoulders might convey expression in cases like shrugging the shoulders to convey "I don't know").
- Adding them only as a background improves the real-time performance of the analysis stages because it does not need to search for their locations. This is

important, as the analysis currently takes significantly longer to perform than the synthesis.

- It improves the subjective quality of the synthesized images as it reduces the discontinuity between different parts of the imagery. A model that treated the head and shoulders as separate objects [8] would circumvent this problem, but that involves increased rendering times and can introduce problems at the join of the head-and-shoulders models.

6.5.4 Agent-Based Animation

In the context of our work, an agent is a section of executable Tcl code which is used to represent a person's movement or expression and which can be uploaded from the encoder to the decoder. Upon receiving some Tcl code, the decoder invokes it (within a safe interpreter, as discussed above) to have the model "act out" the movements, thereby reproducing the subject's motion. This differs from the conventional way of animating facial features in model-based coding, where a series of "action units" (AUs) [4] parameters are transmitted.

Table 6.1 shows how an AU that instructs the eyelids of the Candide model to drop can be achieved using the Togl extension to Tcl. The AU requires displacing the x-, y- and z-values of more than one vertex of the neutral wireframe model. An equivalent Tcl script to the above AU would be:

```
proc lids_drop {} {
    change_vertex 21 0 -14 4
    change_vertex 54 0 -14 4
    change_vertex 67 0 -11 0
    change_vertex 69 0 -11 0
    change_vertex 71 0 -11 0
    change_vertex 73 0 -11 0
}
lids_drop
```

the last line being an invocation of the procedure defined immediately above. The command `change_vertex` invokes a Togl C function that changes the x-, y- and z-values of the vertex number given in the first argument to the new values passed in arguments 2 to 4. The process is repeated for all relevant vertices, and when all

Table 6.1. Action unit (AU) for dropping both eyelids of Candide model

Vertex No.	x	y	z
21	0	-14	4
54	0	-14	4
67	0	-11	0
69	0	-11	0
71	0	-11	0
73	0	-11	0

vertices have been assigned their new values the algorithm calls another Togl C function that redisplays the modified texture-mapped 3D model, with the result that the eyelids will drop.

Although not illustrated in this example, both the AU-based and agent-based approaches allow intermediate expressions to be produced by interpolating the action over a number of frames. With the agent approach, a Tcl procedure is defined the first time a particular expression is encountered; when the expression recurs subsequently, only an invocation of the procedure need be transmitted.

6.6 Experimental Results

In our experiments, the analysis of original images, computation and rendering of synthesized images were all performed on SGI Indy workstations. We have found there that the performance penalty in using interpreted code to control facial animations is imperceptible in practice: animation is in real time, even though the machines involved lack hardware support for rendering. Indeed, although animation is real-time, image analysis – which is far more difficult than synthesis – is currently somewhat slower. As hardware performance continues to increase (and especially with the increased interest in video processing on all types of computer platform), we anticipate shortly being able to carry out analysis in real time too.

The most significant question concerns how movements of facial features are translated into agents. The information that results from face feature location and tracking concerns the trajectories of individual points on a face in the two dimensions of an image sequence. To extract global movements (e.g. head rotations) a simple rule-based system is used [8]. Movements of individual facial features are currently described in a low-level manner, at the level of vertex motions as discussed in Section 6.4. Agents are reused by matching the motions of vertices with previous trajectories; although this works, it does not make best use of the information – see Section 6.7 for a consideration of how the approach could be improved.

We have modelled the six universal expressions by means of animation agents: sadness, anger, joy, fear, disgust and surprise. Figure 6.7 shows four examples of these expressions. The animation agents mainly introduce changes to vertices within the most expressive regions of the face: the eyebrows, the eyes themselves and the mouth. We found that realistic expressions using the eyebrows and eyes can be achieved easily using our approach; however, obtaining realistic mouth expression was found to be more difficult due to the fact that the mouth of the Candide model is represented by only seven vertices, providing too few control points to animate the mouth realistically. There are several solutions to this problem: one may simply revise the model to increase the number of polygons in and around the mouth; or one may use the tessellation support in OpenGL to break down groups of polygons into groups of smaller polygons; or one may produce a "codebook" of different mouth shapes and texture map them separately on the synthesized image. Indeed, the latter approach can be used with our eye and eyebrow animating agents in a hybrid technique.

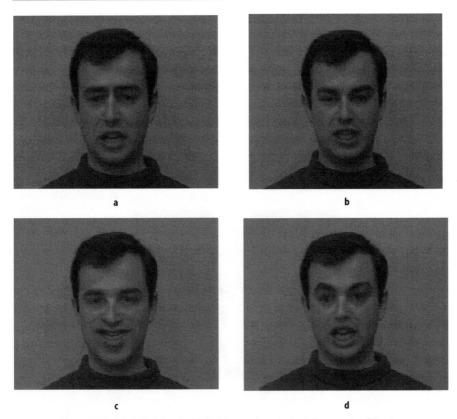

Figure 6.7 Four examples of synthesized facial expressions: **a** sadness; **b** anger; **c** joy; **d** surprise.

We have also produced other facial postures, including eye closure, pursing of the lips and wide mouth opening, as illustrated in Figure 6.8.

6.7 Concluding Remarks

In this chapter we have suggested that "animation agents" are an interesting approach to the animation of remote 3D models, with particular relevance to model-based image coding of human subjects for applications such as video-telephony. Our experiments show that employing agent-based animations of a human face produces expressions commensurate with conventional AU-based techniques, and that both result in roughly equivalent data rates. The authors have found, however, the agent approach to be somewhat more flexible, for a number of reasons:

- Agents enable animation of actions and expressions other than those supported by typical sets of AUs, such as those in in FACS [4]. In particular, subjects tend to have idiosyncratic facial gestures (e.g. arching of an eyebrow, unusual mouth

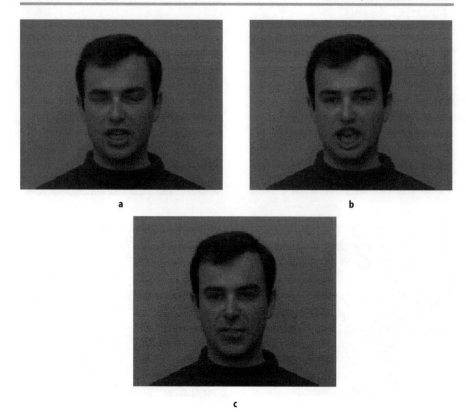

Figure 6.8 Three facial postures: **a** eyes closed; **b** mouth opened; **c** mouth closed.

movements) and these are difficult to convey with AU-based approaches. With animation agents, these are no more difficult than any other facial expressions.

- Agents are more general, as they can be used to animate parts of the body other than the face: for example animating the shoulders and the arms if they are parts of the 3D model – or, indeed, animating an entire human body model. This concept can be extended to accommodate several objects within the scene if they are also represented by 3D models.
- Agents are composed of short text scripts only, so further compression can be achieved through lossless text compression algorithms such as that in `gzip`.

Indeed, with the agent-based approach, there is no real need for any 3D models to reside permanently within the decoder: an agent may transfer a simple representation at the beginning of a connection, say, and refine that over the conversation. One may even conceive of a video-telephony situation in which a person's optimized 3D model resides on a smartcard, and this is transferred to the receiver as a call is set up.

Model-based coding is, of course, usually associated with MPEG-4. The output stage of MPEG-4 as of November 1997 [5] is essentially VRML 2 (itself now standardized as VRML 97), though using the BIFS transport rather than something based around the World Wide Web. As currently specified, MPEG-4 appears to provide facilities for only the animation of 3D objects within scenes, which would preclude the agent-based approach expounded here. However, VRML 2 includes facilities for scripting and provides an "external authoring interface." The authors believe that by exploiting these facilities it may be possible to bring agent-based animation within the capabilities of MPEG-4 systems.

Animation agents provide a novel and effective way in which visual information may be represented, transmitted and reproduced. As applied here, they provide a more flexible way of animating a 3D model of a human head than conventional approaches, which transmit only data. However, what can be achieved is limited by what information can be extracted from the image sequence in question. As the analysis of the semantic content of image sequences improves, it will be possible to generate agents that invoke agents already derived from that image sequence: a "grimace" procedure might involve screwing up the eyes and mouth, for example. In effect, one would be building a description of the sequence in increasingly high-level terms, which means that it will be possible to transmit it more and more efficiently. The authors believe that this is where the use of agents in image coding will really pay off.

References

[1] JF Blinn and ME Newell (1976) Texture and reflection in computer generated images, *Communications of the ACM*, 19(10), 542–7.
[2] E Catmull (1974) A subdivision algorithm for computer display of curved surfaces, *PhD Thesis*, Computer Science Department, University of Utah, Salt Lake City UT, UTEC-CSc-74-133.
[3] MF Chowdury, AF Clark, AC Downton, E Morimatsu and DE Pearson (1994) A switched model-based coder for video signals, *IEEE Transactions on Circuits and Systems for Video Technology*, 4(3), 216–27.
[4] P Ekman and WV Friesen (1978) *Manual for the Facial Action Coding System*, Consulting Psychologist Press, Inc., Palo Alto CA.
[5] A Eleftheriadis, C Herpel, G Rajan and L Ward (1997) MPEG-4 committee draft, *Technical Report N1901*, ISO, November.
[6] PS Heckbert (1986) Survey of texture mapping, *Computer Graphics and Applications*, 6(11), 56–67.
[7] C Jongeneel (1996) Videotelephony simplified through the use of wireframe models, *Technical report*, Delft University of Technology.
[8] M Köküer and AF Clark (1994) A model-based codec suitable for deaf communication, in *Proc. International Symposium on Very-Low Bit-rate Video*, paper 4.2, April.
[9] HS Nwana *Software Agents: an Overview*, http://www.sce.carleton.ca/netmanage/docs/AgentsOverview/ao.html.
[10] JK Ousterhout (1994) *Tcl and the Tk Toolkit*, Addison-Wesley, Reading MA.
[11] FI Parke (1991) Techniques for facial animation, in *New Trends in Animation and Visualisation* (eds. N Magnenat-Thalman and D Thalmann), John Wiley, Chichester, pp. 229–41.
[12] FI Parke (1974) A parametric model for human faces, *PhD Thesis*, University of Utah, Salt Lake City UT, UTEC-CSc-75-047.
[13] DE Pearson (1995) Developments in model-based video coding, *Proceedings of the IEEE*, 83(6).
[14] F Pereira *MPEG-4: a new challenge for the representation of audio-visual information*, http://amalia.ist.utl.pt/fp/artigo54.htm.
[15] SM Platt and NI Badler (1981) Animating facial expressions, *Computer Graphics*, 15(3), 245–52.
[16] M Rydfalk (1987) Candide, a parameterised face, *Technical report*, Department of Electrical Engineering, Linköping University, Sweden.

[17] SM Smith (1996) *SUSAN low-level image processing*, http://www.fmrib.ox.ac.uk/ steve/susan/index.html.

[18] A Murat Tekalp (1995) *Digital Video Processing*, Prentice Hall, Englewood Cliffs NJ.

[19] D Terzopoulos and K Waters (1990) Physically-based facial modeling, analysis and animation, *Journal of Visualisation and Computer Animation*, 1(4), 73–80.

[20] K Waters (1987) A muscle model for animating three-dimensional facial expression, *Computer Graphics (SIGGRAPH '87)*, 21(4), 17–24.

[21] BB Welch (1997) *Practical Programming in Tcl and Tk*, 2nd edn, Prentice Hall, Upper Saddle River NJ.

7

The Use of Dynamic Behaviors in a Network-Based Animation System

W. Tang, A. Osman and I. Palmer

Abstract

This chapter describes an animation system that allows the dynamic selection, instantiation and execution of behaviors for animated objects. The system supports name-based searches and searches based on a behavioral specification. To match behaviors to specifications, a database is used to store behavior–specification pairs. When the database is searched, the matches may be on all criteria (an exact match) or only on a subset of the complete behavior (a partial match). Objects can reconfigure their behavior during their lifetime by loading new classes from the database.

This approach allows users to define behavioral characteristics at a high level and allows objects to adapt their behavior to their environment. For example, an object may currently use one class to define its behavior but is constantly searching for a more efficient mechanism to reach its goal. If such a behavior mechanism is located it replaces its currently active one with the new behavior. The provision of behavior descriptions in a standard database format offers great opportunities for reuse of classes within both Intranet and Internet environments.

The use of Java and VRML for the implementation provides a mechanism for dynamically loading the classes. The system is therefore Internet-based, since the use of Java allows searching for and loading of remote classes from the database in a transparent way. Behavior libraries can be stored on one site and used remotely by another. This offers great advantages for collaboration and reuse of work within and between organizations. Because of the use of VRML, the end results can also be displayed and viewed over the Web. The use of Java for the behavioral mechanism provides (through the `javadoc` utility) the ability to semi-automatically generate the behavior class specifications which are then used to construct the database.

7.1 Introduction

The system described in this chapter is based on a previous animation system that used simple rules to build behaviors for animated objects. The original system,

REALISM, was implemented in C++ and made extensive use of the object-oriented features of the language to provide abstract data models for both the animated objects and the rules themselves. The system supported extension of the animated objects and rules through the usual inheritance mechanism, and through the use of repeated method calls tried to ease the process of incorporating new functionality.

However, due to the compiled nature of C++ any new code added to the system resulted in the need for recompilation and redistribution of the code. This of course required access to the original source code. While this allows the owner of the code to retain control over development, in the research context this was seen as undesirable and was never felt satisfactory. Firstly, editing the main body of source code can introduce bugs. Secondly, end users do not generally have access to the original source code. The development of the Java language presented a new opportunity to develop this work further with the dynamic extensibility to allow objects to reconfigure their behavior during their lifetime. Java allows new code to be loaded through a `ClassLoader` object while the system is running. This allows additional functionality to be incorporated without recompilation or terminating the current invocation of the system. Moreover, Java provides a common interface for network communications and for connecting to standard database systems, providing an easy route to scaling the system up to Internet-based multi-user collaborations. With this aim, the animation system was reimplemented in Java.

The rest of this chapter describes the new system and discusses its various features. Section 7.2 describes previous related work. Section 7.3 describes the system itself, how the behavior mechanism works, how the behaviors are specified and the searching process to locate new behaviors for the animated objects to use. Section 7.4 draws conclusions and describes future work.

7.2 Background and Previous Work

Traditional animation movies are created primarily by hand. They require a frame-by-frame precision-level script for each character of the animation. A few key frames are created as the first level of automation. An interpolation procedure is then applied to generate the missing frames required for a smooth animation. Historically, trainee animators carried out this process.

By using computers, the generation of the script can be automated by using automated procedures. Object-oriented languages seem to be the perfect answer to the requirements of animation programming. An object is specified by a local state (a set of state variables) and a set of procedures (the object's methods). The object's local state is processed by its methods, resulting in a new state that can represent the object at the next time frame. A wide range of behaviors can be obtained by varying the content of the object's local states and its methods.

Object-oriented animation has long been a popular research topic since it allows a natural abstraction of real-world entities. Many different research projects have shown that the object-oriented paradigm is a natural choice for animation systems. The most obvious direct ancestor to this work was the *REALISM* animation system

[1]. This defined the basic object-oriented method of control for animated objects. The system supported a library of simple behavioral rules that could be combined and applied to objects. It also supported a method of distributed collision detection, but this feature is not relevant to the current work and is yet to be implemented in the new system.

Although many of these object-oriented systems offered flexible (and sometimes interactive) control mechanisms, all the systems depended on the existence of the control code at run-time. For animation production in the traditional sense (i.e. created and rendered for use in a linear medium such as film or television) this approach is generally acceptable. However, for emerging systems using interactive computer animation (such as virtual environments, computer games and collaborative visualization) [2–5] the need to restart the system when adding functionality is proving undesirable. The distinction between behavioral work for animation and that carried out in the virtual environment (VE) community is no longer obvious. The two fields share common goals and techniques, the only real differentiation being that VEs obviously have the requirement for real-time performance. Therefore, behavioral animation continues to be an important research area, especially for the large-scale virtual environment applications that support a large number of concurrent dynamic entities or players simultaneously and a variety of information objects [2]. In such environments, objects or agents are expected to be able to exhibit some form of intelligence that responds to users, the environment and each other.

Adaptive behavioral systems have some important properties that have been identified by previous research. In the area of interaction control and animation there is large body of work that has been carried out on producing autonomous actors by implementing the techniques founded in AI (artificial intelligence) [6–9]. Most approaches are based on the classical symbolic AI paradigm in which an AI planning system is the central component of the object. The object acts via explicit logical reasoning [10, 11]. In contrast, an alternative approach to the traditional symbolic AI paradigm is that the object responds dynamically to changes in the environment without an explicit reasoning system [12]. However, in many applications, such as a multi-user virtual environment that supports user interaction, it is desired that the object's behavior is consistent with the user's vision and intentions to ensure a well-controlled environment. Therefore hybrid approaches are suitable, in which objects react to certain stimuli as well as responding intelligently to their environment.

7.3 The System

This section describes the animation system's components and how the various parts interact to achieve the desired operation.

Java was chosen over any other object-oriented language such as C++ because Java supports a feature that is crucial for this project. In order to allow dynamic behaviors to be assigned to an object, it must be possible to load and instantiate classes at run-time. Java allows classes, specifically behavior classes, to be loaded and instantiated even while a program is running. This feature is needed since behavior classes that are loaded over the network will be applied to the object dynamically.

Since, at the time of writing, Java3D was still under development, the three-dimensional environment of VRML is used to display the result of the implementation stage. To enable Java and VRML to interact together, a special VRML toolkit, known as Liquid Reality [13, 14] is used. Liquid Reality, from Microsoft Corporation (acquired from Dimension X), combines the power and extensibility of Java with VRML for creating and viewing complex and highly interactive 3D environments. It is based on the scripting methods defined in the VRML 2.0 specification.

VRML 1.0 let us build objects and place them into simple scenes. You could use the camera viewpoint to "fly" around the VRML 1.0 scene, but nothing in the scene could change or move. With VRML 2.0, an object can be made to change color, to move around and to communicate with other objects. Using script nodes in VRML 2.0 we can use Java classes to control the VRML world. We actually create a new node with associated fields and events. These fields are special because events sent to these fields will be automatically passed from the script node to an associated piece of programming code. The ROUTE statement in VRML 2.0, which is central to dynamic objects in VRML, provides a mechanism for one object to send messages to or receive them from one or more other objects.

7.3.2 Structure

Two features of REALISM are directly implemented within the current system: allowing objects to define their behavior through references to external behavior objects and promoting easy extensibility through the use of the object-oriented techniques. Incorporating the object-oriented paradigm in a computer animation system allows the separation of objects from the controlling mechanism, with message-passing providing the communication mechanism between objects. The object-oriented design of the system and the separation of objects and controllers lead to a more flexible implementation.

A simple and flexible framework is proposed to facilitate the construction of complex behaviors from simple sets of rules by the use of Java and VRML2.0. The control scheme of the work is capable of introducing a wide variety of object behaviors in an object-orientated manner. Two search mechanisms within the system allow the generation of the behaviors, which either exactly match the user's intentions or exhibit a loose match to a specification. The architecture of the behavior model consists of three engines: Animation Engine, Behavior Engine, and Search Engine.

Animated object behavior is modeled as a form of "PROTO" node which can be connected to the object within the VRML scene. Each animated object behavior stores an array of these objects that control its various attributes. The Animation Engine receives messages through the "EventOut" of the VRML and passes the relevant parameters in turn to be modified and returned to VRML via the "EventIn" node. The Behavior Engine consists of a set of basic evaluator classes that take an array of values of a particular and return an array of the same type values. The evaluators are defined as a Java interface. This means that any classes that implement the interface can be used as a behavior by an object. The Search Engine is a set of user interfaces that provide users with a means to select and access behaviors. Users can access an object behavior by explicitly naming the evaluators. Automatic selection uses a search algorithm to select behaviors from a loose specification for the evaluator to produce behaviors without the user's explicit specification.

The control system is centered on assigning behaviors to objects for them to react to. Information such as the position of an object in the VRML world would be passed to the controlling behavior object. As an example of a simple motion-controlling behavior a common interface class has been defined. This interface class acts as an evaluator interface for processing a set of four floating-point values. The first floating-point value in the set represents the position of the object in the VRML world and velocity is represented by the second floating-point value. The other two floating point values act as storage areas in case any extra values need to be used (such as acceleration for a more complete physical model).

The class that will act as an interface for processing four floating-point values is called Evaluator4f. It is defined as follows:

```
class Evaluator4f {
    Data:
        Four floating-point values
    Methods:
        evaluate - constructor for processing the four
        floating-point values
        info - constructor for printing information about
        the class
}
```

We can take one of the behavior classes that use the interface class as an example. This particular behavior class, which is called Static, will cause the object in the VRML world to stop moving. Simply setting the velocity to the value of zero does this. The class is defined as below:

```
class Static {
    Data:
        Position - object position in an axis
        Velocity - velocity value for the object
    Methods:
        evaluate - updates the velocity value by setting
        it to 0
        new velocity value = 0
        info - prints information about the class
}
```

Figure 7.1 shows a class diagram of the system following the notation as described by Booch [17]. In the example shown, the controlling object supports up to four simultaneous behaviors, and the system contains four pre-defined behaviors:

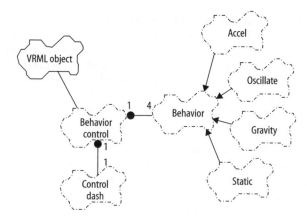

Figure 7.1 Example class diagram.

1. *accelerate* – the object will accelerate at a constant rate in a given direction.
2. *static* – will cause the object to stop moving. This particular behavior has precedence over any other possible movements and also any other behaviors.
3. *oscillates* – will cause the object to oscillate after a pre-set number of steps it has taken.
4. *gravity* – will simulate the gravitational pull downwards.

7.3.3 The Behavior Mechanism

To describe the way in which the behavior mechanism operates we will consider a simple demonstration system. We begin with the creation of a VRML world which consists of two spheres. The spheres are placed in a cube whose walls signify the boundaries that limit the movement of the object inside it (Figure 7.2).

The parameters denote the x-, y- and z-values that represent the initial coordinates of the ball in the world and are passed to the controlling program (written entirely in Java). The controlling program provides a user interface that allows manipulation of these parameters depending on the movement that is chosen by the user. The basic movements allow the object to be moved following the compass directions (North, South, East, West, Northeast, Northwest, Southeast and Southwest), with one additional facility to stop. Figure 7.3 shows this early version of the interface running on an SGI workstation.

To initiate any kind of movement, velocity value(s) need to be "added" to the object's position. For an object to move in a particular direction as selected by the user, velocity value(s) need to be assigned to the object. For example, to move the object in the Northwest direction, assuming the object is currently in a static position, requires two positive values of velocity assigned to it. One velocity value needs to be given to the x-axis and another velocity value given to the y-axis. A combination of these two velocity values would result in the movement of the Northwest direction.

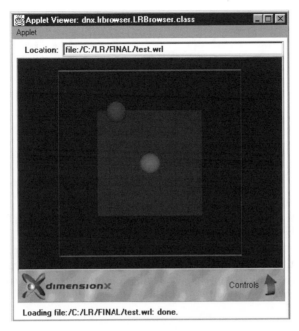

Figure 7.2 The example system running under Windows 95.

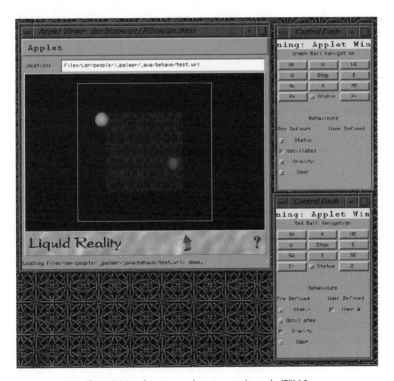

Figure 7.3 Interface to example system running under IRIX 6.2.

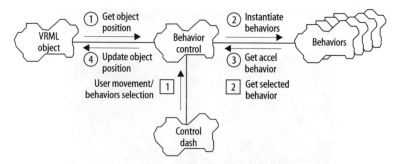

Figure 7.4 Example object diagram.

Any movement or behavior chosen by the user will cause changes in the velocity values of the object. The object's position will then be constantly updated according to the changes in velocity values by a class called `accel`. The controlling program will then pass these changes in the parameters back to the VRML world so that the changes can drive the graphics display. Figure 7.4 shows an example object diagram of the animation system.

7.3.4 The Behavior Specification

To enable searching by behavior rather than by specific class names we need a specification method. The nature of this specification will depend upon the range of behaviors that we wish to specify: a high-level specification may support abstract goals (such as "find an exit from the room"); a low-level specification may support finer grained goals (such as "move left"). In general, higher level goals may be broken down into lower levels, shorter priority ones whose appropriateness may change during the object's life to achieve the high-level goal.

In principle, as long as a standard syntax and semantics are used to specify both our goals and our behaviors, then we can store a descriptive element with each behavior in our database and search for those that match our goal. In general, it is expected that the database will consist of relatively low-level behaviors (such as motion engines and sensors). In such a system, the object searches for low-level behaviors that help it achieve its high-level goal. For example, if the object wants to "leave the room" and can sense where the exit is, it then has a goal of moving towards the exit. Assuming it has no built-in motion capabilities, it then needs to find a low-level behavior that results in it moving towards the exit. This may be something as simple as acceleration in a particular direction, or it may consist of some path-planning algorithm to avoid obstacles.

In the example system previously discussed, the low-level behaviors consist primarily of motion-based operations. The goals are then simple motion goals, such as "move left". This is specified using a simple mathematical syntax, e.g. $X(N + 1) < X(N)$ specifies that the behavior results in the x coordinate being reduced. Such goals will generally result in finding more than one match in the database, and unless some performance criteria (such as that $X(N + 1)$ and $X(N)$

should differ by the largest amount possible) are met then the first match is used. If performance criteria are used, it is then possible to continue searching for "better" matches while the system is operating. This again exploits the dynamic class-loading capabilities and allows the object to evolve into a higher performance object.

Obviously, the limited expressiveness of these example specifications means that the system can only support relatively uninteresting behaviors and goals, but it does serve as a proof of concept for the model.

7.3.5 The Database

A central server database management system is introduced to maintain and organize the object behavior specifications. This implementation scales the system into a network-oriented one by taking advantage of Java's portability and security to allow multi-user collaboration over the Internet. The integrated database system is in a standard format and integrates with Java via the JDBC (Java Database Connectivity) package [15]. The system allows searching for and loading of remote classes from the database in a transparent way. Behavior libraries can be stored on one site and used by another. This offers great advantages for collaboration and reuse of work within and between organizations. Each individual site is able to execute SQL (Structured Query Language) statements to turn the local message data structure into a distributed one, and this distributed data structure is therefore shared by all clients.

Liquid Reality, the VRML toolkit used by the system for Java and VRML interaction, works with JDK 1.0.2. JDBC was not included as an integral part of the distribution until JDK 1.1, so we employed a three-tier model to develop a JDBC communication layer that talks to a MySQL Server database [16], and then built the layer into the server for behavior specification. The JDBC-based middleware layer acts as behavior specification library that communicates with the client side. This approach enables future development of more advanced clients who use JDK 1.1, while JDK 1.0.2 clients can be migrated in the future to JDK 1.1 clients. The middleware layer therefore supports JDK 1.0.2 and JDK 1.1 clients simultaneously.

In the three-tier model, as shown in Figure 7.5, the user's commands are delivered to the middle layer of the server, which then sends SQL statements to the database. The database processes the SQL statements and sends the results back to the middle layer, which then sends them to the user.

On client side, a TCP port is firstly defined for the interchange service. The communication library on the client side contains a number of methods that implement client-side networking calls. These methods are essentially instances of traditional hashtable and vector classes. For example, the LoadAllClassNames method returns a hashtable that contains matching behavior class names from the server database as keys. This client communication library also defines a set of protocol requests. When a request is made by the client to the server, the respective method tries to set up a socket to the server's TCP port and gets the

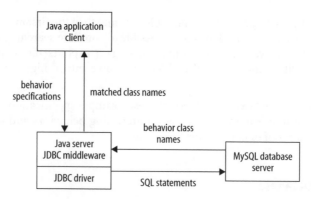

Figure 7.5 Network server middleware configuration.

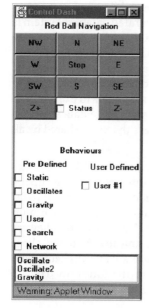

Figure 7.6 User interface under Windows 95, showing the list of found behaviors.

InputStream and OutputStream associated with the socket and then attaches a DataInputStream to the respective buffered I/O streams. The protocol requests are then written to the DataOutputStream. The server gets the request and executes the JDBC driver interface and sends the SQL statement to the database. The server then replies with class names matching the user-defined object behavior specifications. A Java list user interface maintains the updated name list of class names for behavior class loading.

The new version of the interface that supports this is shown in Figure 7.6. The list box at the bottom of the window shows the result of a search for behaviors. Using this manual interface, the user can then choose which of the matching behaviors to apply to the object.

7.4 Conclusions and Future Work

The system described here allows the definition of an animated object's behavior from libraries of external classes. These classes can be added to the object's list of behaviors during its lifetime, allowing dynamic refinement. The use of standard database technology to store the behavioral classes allows automated searching of them by specific criteria, and the network support of Java allows the database to be stored in remote networked locations.

The behavioral classes do not need to exist or be in the database when the system is initialized, and these may be created and added while the object is still active. The behaviors can then be found as soon as they are added to the database. The object goal specifications define the search criteria.

This approach provides a flexible, dynamic environment for use in interactive and evolving animated environments. The current limitations are primarily due to the simplistic goal and behavior specification. The next stage of the work will be to adopt more sophisticated rule models from AI research. This will allow higher-level goals to be defined and more interesting problems to be incorporated into the objects.

References

[1] IJ Palmer (1994) The REALISM System, *PhD Dissertation*, Chapter 3.
[2] MR Macedonia, DP Brutzman, M Zyda *et al.* (1995) NPSET: a multi-player 3D virtual environment over the Internet, *Proc. Symp. Interactive 3D Graphics*, Monterey, California, April.
[3] K Perlin and A Goldberg (1996) Improv: a system for scripting interactive actors in virtual worlds, *IEEE Computer Graphics Proceedings*, Annual Conference Series, pp. 205–16.
[4] D Kurlander, T Skelly and D Salesin (1996) Comic chat, *IEEE Computer Graphics Proceedings*, Annual Conference Series.
[5] RA Earnshaw, W Lamotte, B Champness *et al.* (1997) *Telepresence and Shared Virtual Environments (CHAINS)*, Report series, Department of Electronic Imaging & Media Communications, School of Electronics and Media, University of Bradford, Report No. EIMC 12.
[6] T Calvert, R Ovans and S Mah (1994) Towards the autonomous animation of multiple human figures, *Proc. Computer Animation '94*, IEEE Computer Society Press, pp. 69–75.
[7] P Bourgine (1994) Autonomy, abduction, adaption, *Proc. Computer Animation '94*, IEEE Computer Society Press, pp. 104–11.
[8] A Guillot and J-A Meyer (1994) Computer simulations of adaptive behavior in Animats, *Proc. Computer Animation '94*, IEEE Computer Society Press, pp. 122–31.
[9] N Magnenat-Thalmann and D Thalmann (1995) Virtual actors living in the real world, *Proc. Computer Animation '95*, IEEE Computer Society Press, pp. 19–29.
[10] S Vere and B Tickmore (1990) A basic agent, *Computational Intelligence*, 6, 41–60.
[11] S Wood (1993) *Planning and Decision Making in Dynamic Domains*, Ellis Horwood.
[12] RA Brooks (1991) Intelligence without reason, *Technical Report AI. Memo 1293*, Artificial Intelligence Laboratory, MIT.
[13] *Hermetica: Interfacing Java and VRML*, http://www.co.umist.ac.uk/~xtian/VRML/vrml.html UK Java Developer's Conference Paper, Alligator Descartes, November 1996.
[14] Liquid Reality[TM], http://www.dimensionx.com/products/lr/, Dimension X, 1997.
[15] http://java.sun.com/products/jdbc/.
[16] http://mysql.turbolift.com/testing/.
[17] G Booch (1994) *Object-Oriented Analysis and Design with Applications*, 2nd edn, Benjamin/Cummings.

[18] M Gervautz and D Schamalstieg (1994) *Integrating a Scripting Language into an Interactive Animation System*, IEEE.

[19] S Mealing (1992) *The Art and Science of Computer Animation*, Intellect Ltd.

8

Virtual Rehearsal Over Networks

Carlton Reeve and Ian Palmer

Abstract

Traditional rehearsals require all the necessary participants, actors, director and some technical crew to be present in a single location at the same time. With the advent of new technology, the rehearsal process can be more flexible. The system described in this chapter acts as a complement to existing rehearsal methods. More often than not, rehearsals take place without a constructed set. In a virtual rehearsal environment, the set can exist from the start of the process. With the ability to see each other and by interacting in a virtual space, the cast gets an idea of what the final performance will look like much sooner than before. This offers significant benefits for the characterization and blocking process.

As virtual reality technologies expand over the Internet, so participants in theater can use the new opportunities to create virtual interactive performance spaces. The cast and crew of a piece can "meet" in a computer-based model regardless of their geographic location and experience the proposed environment throughout the whole process, making any necessary changes as they progress. Users not only "exist" within the space, but also have the ability to manipulate it. With additional third-party software, participants can see and communicate with other avatars.

The research is based around a model of the Theatre in the Mill. The Mill is a small-scale regional venue based on the campus of Bradford University. It is home for an active community theater group as well as regular host to touring companies. As with many similar theaters, there is a high turnover of shows and the availability of the performance area for rehearsal is severely restricted as shows come and go. Although this is a problem for the resident group, it is even more problematic for touring companies, who until now have often not seen the venue until their actual performance dates.

Once a virtual theater is in place, it becomes an area available for rehearsal as well as performance. The virtual rehearsal trial worked in conjunction with the recent production of *The Comedy of Errors* and proved that, in concept at least, theatrical productions have much to gain from the application of the new technologies.

8.1 Introduction

This chapter explores the background and possibilities offered by new technologies and their application in the rehearsal process of the performing arts. To realize the possibilities, it is important to understand the underlying principles of rehearsal theory and multi-user VRML avatar-based systems that constitute the basic building blocks of virtual rehearsals.

The rehearsal process performs a number of roles. It is the means of refining and developing the writer's and director's ideas on the piece; it is the easiest way of learning lines, positions and movement cues; and it forms a key plank in the actor's characterization.

Although a script may include some stage directions they are usually quite vague:

> Give me your hands, if we be friends,
> And Robin shall restore amends.
> > [Exit]
> > > *A Midsummer Night's Dream, Act V, Scene i.*

Actors cannot really appreciate their characters, their emotions or their role within a story until they actually read the parts aloud and interact with other performers or properties. It is this background that makes the play believable. As well as the artistic benefits of the rehearsal process, such as identifying the role and "breathing life into the character"; there are good practical reasons for the process. Without the physical realization of the script the writer's and director's ideas are lost – not least in the fact that the performers will not know where they should be at a particular instance or what they should be saying!

The use of models for the pre-production stages of theater is not a particularly new idea: Bertolt Brecht, one of the foremost thinkers on theater practice, expounded the usefulness of such devices as a rehearsal aid in the first half of the 20th century (Willet. 1965, p. 216):

> One does not learn much by reading that a character moves in a particular direction after a given sentence, even if the tone of speech, the way of walking and a convincing reason can all be supplied (which is very difficult).... The use of models is a particular kind of art, and just so much can be learnt from it.

The nature of VRML facilitates the placing of particular sets within an existing model and actor avatars within that virtual environment. This ability greatly increases the efficiency of the rehearsals by reducing the familiarization time for a space, identifying potential problems with positioning or movement and offering the performers time to practice outside normal rehearsal hours.

The nature of the Web allows actors to rehearse in these virtual environments from geographically separate locations, removing the need to travel and offering rehearsals at unsociable hours.

8.2 Background

8.2.1 Virtual Theater Space

Bradford's Theatre in the Mill (Figure 8.1) is a typical small-scale regional theater. Each season the theater hosts visiting performance companies and three

Figure 8.1 The Theatre in the Mill.

productions by the resident drama group. With a different show every week, rehearsal time within the theater space is severely restricted, and rehearsals with the set are usually only possible in the production week itself.

The Internet, and its associated technologies of WWW and VRML, enables set designers to create fully working models (Reeve and Palmer, 1997). These virtual environments are accessible from anywhere on the computer network, and VRML 2.0 scripting enables the switching between scenes and the direct manipulation of properties and practicals. Not only does this allow different lighting states, it also offers the opportunity to view scene changes in context. Once constructed, these designs enable a cast to appreciate their scenery before its physical construction, thereby aiding characterization and confidence.

The Mill as a virtual environment allows maximum interaction with other performers and the space, and the ability to visualize the play before it is performed. VRML 2.0 (`http://vrml.sgi.com/moving-worlds/`) provides virtual environments over the Web and its VRMLScript (`http://vrml.sgi.com/moving-worlds/spec/vrmlscript.html`) permits a high level of interactivity.

8.2.2 Software

The 3D model of the theater was created in the Silicon Graphics application *Cosmo Worlds* (`http://vrml.sgi.com/cosmoplayer/`). Cosmo Worlds produces VRML 2.0 files directly and it was used to add VRMLScript for the interaction.

Figure 8.2 The Passport interface.

The specific software base for this research is a suite of programs from Blaxxun Interactive. The software allows a fully interactive virtual environment suitable for dramatic applications.

Blaxxun's Passport browser plug-in is an application with which users can see and interact with others in 2D and 3D worlds. As users explore the environment, they see other people move and can "chat" with them in real time (Figure 8.2).

Passport works with Web browsers and a VRML plug-in. Passport works in either passive VRML 1.0 or active VRML 2.0 worlds. The VRML plug-in (Cosmo Player in this case) is primarily an observational tool; with it alone users cannot see or interact with others in the same 3D space.

The Blaxxun Community Server is an interactive server offering real-time communication and collaboration through the Passport VRML plug-in, which acts as a client. Together they provide a scalable infrastructure for a virtual community. The server manages the operation, administration and use of a multi-user interactive world. It has the capability to track hundreds of users simultaneously within a single environment.

For this research the model of Theatre in the Mill and the set associated with the recent production of *The Comedy of Errors* were linked to a demonstration version of the Community Server located on an internal server within the EIMC Department, Bradford.

8.2.3 Rehearsal Theory

There are a number of recognized "phases of production" (Willett, 1965, p. 240), of which the rehearsal process forms a major part. Rehearsals begin after the preliminary stages of play analysis, discussions of setting and casting.

The first rehearsal is a simple read through for the actors to acquaint themselves with the play. After this stage, the main "episodes" of the play are translated into positions and movements with a rough indication of emphases, attitudes and gestures. It is usually at this stage that the characters start emerging from the performers.

Once this basic "blocking" finishes, the cast starts methodically working through the details and using "practicals," that is working doors, tables, chairs and so on. It is during this stage that the actors build up their characters' attitudes to the others and get to know what their characters are like. The run-throughs that follow tighten the overall continuity and balance of the piece, until close to the production when the tempo is clarified and the performances polished.

One particular challenge the director faces is how to use the available space effectively. In the past, dramatists wrote plays for a specific theater, respecting its limitations and exploiting its strengths. Modern directors often struggle in redefining a classic play on a contemporary stage. In the past it was a difficult task to determine whether or not a desired setting would work within the actual physical location. Not only do directors consider the actual neutral space of the stage; they also consider the virtual characterized space of the setting of the play and they can convert one into the other by imagination and the use of the performers. However, the development of theater spaces has opened the doors to new interpretations of texts and freed the directors and set designers from the naturalistic. Set designers no longer need to create the illusion of a room or a locality, but can make statements of greater historical or social interest.

Obviously the style of the interpretation affects not only the set but also the performances themselves. In a naturalistic set, that is a real setting, the actor must "be": on a surreal or un-naturalistic stage, the actor "acts."

8.3 Previous Work

There are a number of projects exploring the use of new technology in theatrical contexts, most notably in the USA. These range from complete virtual theater productions to VR-enhanced performances.

8.3.1 A Virtual Theater for Children at Stanford University

In this testbed application (`http://www-ksl.stanford.edu/projects/cait/index.html`), children direct improvisational routines by computer characters. The characters move as the result of choices made by the children in situated behavior menus at particular points within the "game." According to the choices, the characters respond with designated actions.

The children work together to create a shared story.

8.3.2 Raymond Interactive Theater, Renton WA

Carmilla's Kiss was the first in a series of ongoing interactive productions from Raymond Interactive Theater (http://www.rit.com/). The audience becomes the drama's leading characters in a world comprised of real people and virtual objects by direct input into a virtual theater.

8.3.3 The Institute for the Exploration of Virtual Realities (i.e.VR), University of Kansas

Mark Reaney leads a team working on many aspects of virtual reality and its use in theater at the University of Kansas (http://ukanaix.cc.ukans.edu:80/~mreaney/).

The Adding Machine was the first project that combined live theater and virtual reality in a complete dramatic production. Audiences joined live and computer generated actors in projected three-dimensional environments within which the drama unfolded. The paths taken within these "virtual worlds" were not pre-recorded, but improvised by the crew.

i.e.VR created virtual worlds through a combination of real-time computer graphics and video projection equipment. The audience watched through polarized glasses.

The production of *The Adding Machine* attempted to "demonstrate ways in which virtual reality technology can be used to illuminate an existing dramatic text. Used not merely as spectacle for its own sake, but as a new and exciting scenographic medium in the service of the script, virtual reality becomes another component of the collaborative theater art."

Wings, the most recent project at i.e.VR, was to advance the technology and techniques discovered during production of *The Adding Machine*. As well as the live action on stage and the projected backgrounds used in *The Adding Machine*, *Wings* used head-mounted displays through which the audience saw further computer-generated and live video images.

8.3.4 The Oz Project at Carnegie Mellon University

Oz (http://www.cs.cmu.edu/afs/cs.cmu.edu/project/oz/web/oz.html) is a computer system that allows authors to create and present interactive dramas. The system includes a virtual environment, autonomous avatars, an environmental paradigm, a dramatic director and a user.

Oz has three primary research foci: characters, presentation and drama. The research looks at how to create computer-controlled agents that appear reactive, goal-directed, emotional, moderately intelligent and capable of using natural language.

The Oz projects has created two worlds for this work: the animated "Edge of Intention" and the text-based "Lyotard".

8.3.5 The Gertrude Stein Repertory Theater, NY

At this small New York City venue (`http://www.ibm.com/sfasp/theater.htm`), productions are created by teleconferencing. The director, Cheryl Faver, uses collaborative computing in the form of IBM's Person to Person software to support their virtual theater projects.

Actors on stage interact live with other actors projected via teleconference from remote locations. Wireframe 3D animated figures dance next to physical performers.

8.3.6 The Virtual Theatre Group, University of Bradford

Work in this area includes Web-based collaborative design systems that exploit VRML 2.0 interactivity and multimedia performance environments.

The theater set design work offers a single theater model to multiple users across the Internet. Not only is this a tool for in-house designers preparing for forthcoming productions, but also for touring companies wanting to know whether their set will fit inside the available space.

The multimedia performance environment is a project in conjunction with a Yorkshire theater company, Twisting Yarn. It is producing a reactive sensory environment for children with special needs.

8.4 Practice

There are a number of elements that constitute the rehearsal process. Actors within virtual spaces can perform these tasks with varying degrees of success.

8.4.1 Characterization

Characterization is a key element of the rehearsal process and it manifests itself in speech and movement. As the actors become familiar with the "routine" of the play, so they can develop the characters of their parts.

> I could comprehend with my mind the process of planting and training within myself the elements necessary to create a character, but it was still unclear to me how to

achieve the building of that character in physical terms. Because, if you do not use your body, your voice, a manner of speaking, walking, moving, if you do not find a form of characterization which corresponds to the image, you probably cannot convey to others its inner, living spirit.

Stanislavski (1968), p. 5

Not only does this characterization come from the script and the blocking, actors "feed" off each other when defining their roles.

All the manifestations of the rehearsal process are aimed at producing a believable characterization. It is a process of continual refinement.

In the beginning of the process of physical embodiment an actor is immoderate and extravagant in using anything and everything to convey his creative emotions – words, voice, gesture, movement, action, facial expression. At this point the actor spares no means if only he can somehow externalize all that he feels inside him. It seems to him that the more ways and means he uses In putting each individual moment into physical form, the greater the choice, the more substantial and stuffed out will be the physical embodiment itself.

Stanislavski (1984), p. 96

8.4.2 Movement

The actors' movements are the embodiment of their roles, but they do not need to be perfectly life-like for theater performances. Indeed, one of the inherent qualities of the theater is its "heightened reality," its reflection of life through a special mirror.

For choreography too there are once again tasks of a realistic kind. It is a relatively recent error to suppose that it has nothing to do with the representation of "people as they really are." If art reflects life it does so with special mirrors. Art does not become unrealistic by changing the proportions but by changing them in such a way that if the audience took its representations as a practical guide to insights and impulses it would go astray in real life. It is of course essential that stylization should not remove the natural element but should heighten it. Anyhow, a theater where everything depends on the guest cannot do without choreography. Elegant movement and graceful grouping, for a start, can alienate, and inventive miming greatly helps the story.

Brecht (1949)

The World frame within the Passport interface contains the standard VRML scene information. It represents the user's window onto the VRML world, in this case the actor's view of the stage. In this window, other performers within the world are visible. Depending on which VRML plug-in the browser uses, the user can navigate around the space by walking, flying, sliding or pointing at objects. This is the means of travel within the VRML worlds. Using the Cosmo Player plug-in, users navigate by moving the mouse according to which way they wish to travel. The traveling itself feels akin to sliding gently across glass. The only "feedback" or friction that the interface offers is the fairly clumsy collision detection, but for the purposes of simple blocking within the rehearsals this is adequate.

Unless it is his intention to show a character with a physical defect, in which case he should be able to display it in just the proper degree, he should move in an easy manner, which adds to rather then, distracts from the impression he creates.

Stanislavski (1968), p. 38

The collision detection allows the user fairly realistic navigation of the set. He must move around tables and chairs, for example, rather than through them. However, the nature of the movement is severely restricted. While the system gives an acceptable feeling of walking, it does not offer the actor the opportunity to climb or be in any way gymnastic. The ability to clamber onto, into, under or through practical set furniture is restricted by the technical constraints of the VRML language and its browser plug-in. In addition, when the avatars "walk" they are not animated accordingly, thereby giving the impression of ghost-like gliding to the other actors within the space.

Included within the environment are the required properties for the performance. These "props" have VRMLScript functions associated with them, such as proximity or touch sensors, so that actors can use them. The actors can manipulate these "props," but the interaction is clumsy and only really useful for larger bulky objects (open doors, switch on lights, for example), rather then delicate items such as pens. Figure 8.3 shows two actors' avatars in the rehearsal space.

A key component of characterization is the actor's ability to perform appropriate gestures. In reality, these could include anything postural to any sort of nervous twitch.

An actor [should not] forget that the typical gesture helps to bring him closer to the character he is portraying while the intrusion of personal motions separates him from it and pushes him in the direction of his purely personal emotions. This can scarcely serve the purpose either of the play or part since what are needed are analogous, not personal emotions.

Stanislavski (1968), p. 76

Figure 8.3 Avatars in the rehearsal space.

In our virtual world these gestures are limited to the constraints of the Passport software. In Passport, avatars can make a small number of recognizable physical gestures, although the default choices have little obvious connection to the sentiment expressed. Whether the avatar and viewer use VRML 1.0 or 2.0 determines the level of realism in the movement. VRML 1.0 gives a rough approximation to the action. The available gestures are:

- Hello
- Hey!
- Yes
- Like
- Dislike
- No
- Not!
- Bye

When a user performs one of these gestures, the whole avatar reacts with VRML 1.0 models. For example, the movement associated with "Yes" is a forward and back rocking motion for the whole figure. With VRML 2.0 avatars it is possible refine the level of animation using a skeletal model, but the complexity of this and the possible range of reactions limit the number of gestures that are reasonably available.

Users can direct gestures at individuals or the whole group. The physical movement is complemented by a simple text message displayed in the Chat frame. For example:

```
Dromio says "Hello" to everyone
```

Actors should not over employ gestures during their portrayal of a part. Too many gestures clutter the performance and detract from the character. Actors need discipline to suppress even their natural day-to-day mannerisms.

> An actor's performance which is cluttered up with a multiplicity of gestures will be like that messy sheet of paper. Therefore before he undertakes the external creation of his character, the physical interpretation, the transfer of the inner life of a part of its concrete image, he must rid himself of all superfluous gestures. Only under those conditions can he achieve the necessary sharpness of outline for its physical embodiment. Unrestrained movements, natural though they may be to the actor himself, only blur the design of his part, make his performance unclear, monotonous and uncontrolled.
>
> *Stanislavski (1968), p. 73*

While drama theory says that an actor's use of gestures should be tightly controlled, reducing the repertoire to eight or so movements is too Draconian to be of much use after the initial stages of production.

By developing gestures and facial expressions for the avatars the level of realism can increase, but it is impractical to try to create an animation for every conceivable response or action; thus inevitably there must be a finite pool of reactions. The limited range of gestures is a major hindrance to the use of virtual rehearsal systems for anything more than a simple and complementary device for traditional techniques.

> It is with the help of the eyes, face, mimetics that a role most easily finds physical expression. Then what the eyes cannot spell out the voice takes up and expresses by words, intonations, speech. To reinforce and explain one's feeling and thought, gestures and movement add vivid illustration.
>
> *Stanislavski (1984), p. 101*

8.4.3 Communication

The basic method of communication within Passport is the Chat frame. The Chat frame displays text communication between users. The display depends on the "People" to whom the user is talking: it may be a two-way conversation or a group discussion. Public Chat is open and unstructured conversation within a world or scene. Anyone within those areas can participate. The entire available group is listed in the People list. Each message has the avatar's name preceding it, in same way as a drama script is written.

Textual communication presents a number of problems to rehearsing actors. The most immediately obvious of these is its lack of spontaneity. With actors forced to painstakingly type in lines it destroys any sense of pace or tempo in the piece, since the dialog takes so much more time that if it were spoken. Performers cannot gain any real sense of timing for reactions. It also has the effect of stripping the lines of any intonation, emphasis or accent, thereby making it a purely mechanical exercise. It is difficult to express irony or sarcasm, for example, with a line of straight dialogue.

However, text-based "talk" does have some advantages. It is an active memory enforcer. Methodically typing text greatly helps actors with the hateful line learning. It is also intolerant to errors, since mistakes cannot easily be hidden or covered by "ad libbing." This prevents actors from "writing their own scripts" and it stops those alterations from permanently slipping into the routine. The other benefit of text dialog is that it is relatively straightforward to track or detect key phrases automatically. This has the potential to integrate AI-driven avatars into the rehearsal process, as discussed later.

Audio communication is possible with the current system, but requires a "webphone" or similar application to run alongside Passport.

8.4.4 Use of the System for *The Comedy of Errors*

The complete system went on trial with the Bradford production of Shakespeare's *The Comedy of Errors* (Theatre in the Mill, Bradford, 24–29 November 1997).

The actors had mixed feelings about its usefulness. Some, from non-technical backgrounds, had problems initially with both the concept and the installation, not least the user interface, which they found clumsy and unnatural. Those performers more familiar with the technology adapted the system quickly.

In practice, the weakness described above became quite obvious. The slow speed of use and the potential for disorientation caused frequent hold-ups. The awkwardness of the movement and the lack of gestures meant that it did not perform particularly well in developing characters.

However, where the actors found it extremely useful was in the learning of their blocking and lines. The manual repetition of scripts and diligence required to move around the virtual world were great reinforcers of the traditional rehearsals.

8.5 Conclusions

The whole point of theater is entertainment, and this entertainment rests largely on the "believability" of the characters. Of course there are a few "natural" actors, but all performers will benefit from a comprehensive rehearsal process. The application of virtual environments to this business provides a complementary means of developing characters and aiding those concerned in the production.

The ability to view the completed set in context is extremely useful to actors who might otherwise not see it *in situ* until the week of production. With a clear idea of the setting and their positioning within it, they can concentrate on their characterization, sure in the knowledge that their ultimate performance will fit the space, not only physically but emotionally too. Having been in the space before, albeit in a virtual world, actors are not so disorientated when the rehearsal moves from bare rooms to the actual setting.

The virtual rehearsal gives the actors the opportunity to explore and get the feel of their ultimate environment. Even with the fairly rudimentary system in place at present, users can brush up on blocking and entrances and exits outside "normal hours." The collaborative nature of the system means that actors can rehearse, albeit with some heavy gesticular and communicatory constraints, more or less whenever they want. And it allows the director to watch a version of the action in the proposed setting well before the actual production.

Not only is this system an aid for actors learning their lines and movements, it could be an invaluable tool for directors as they develop their ideas and identify any potential problems with the blocking, such as using devices too many times or obscuring the view of the audience.

The current problems of the system are mainly interface-related. The system suffers from an unfriendly navigation and communication methodology. It slows down the pace of the drama unacceptably so that users lose all sense of pace and tempo, and the mode of interaction and movement is a distraction from the main task in hand: developing believable characters.

The obvious next development of this work will be the introduction of AI-driven avatars. These avatars could be programmed to play any character's role, thereby allowing individual users to benefit from the system whenever they wanted. They would not need the participation of others, but could practice lines and blocking at will.

The Blaxxun suite has a mechanism for automated avatars called HuBBots. These are programmable avatars that can inhabit virtual worlds. They can be programmed to perform set tasks or react to specific events, such as particular lines of text.

With all applications of virtual theater that include artificial intelligence characters, the greatest challenge is the behavior of those avatars. Within the virtual worlds the autonomous actors must behave as realistically as possible within the constraints of their character. For this realism the actors need initial data from the author or director. This information includes:

- a set specification of the character's personality
- its moods and relationships to other characters, which can be changed later by certain actions or events
- a hierarchy of responses based on character traits and possible sequences or combinations of events
- a clear map of the setting and its occupants
- the prompt or trigger lines

When the autonomous avatars react "transparently" and create a wholly believable (virtual) world, there are enormous opportunities for these techniques. In the same way that a successful film suspends the disbelief of the audience, a successful virtual theater application will transport participants to entirely new worlds in which they can explore their environment and themselves.

8.5.1 Future Work

8.5.1.1 Interactive Drama

One obvious future implementation of the virtual theater technology is an open interactive drama. Participants could come to a particular virtual world, take on an individual character and "perform" accordingly. There is no real need for scheduling, as the drama could be an ongoing story with characters coming and going when they wanted. These worlds could include disguised "robots" that interact freely and anonymously with other visitors. These avatars could reveal clues about the scenario and act as "guides."

8.5.1.2 Hyper-drama

Hyper-drama is very similar in spirit to interactive drama in that the ending of the performance is not set. However, with hyper-drama the audience chooses to follow various characters and plots at specific points in the drama – changing how they perceive the story from performance to performance instead of a complete improvisation. In the hyper-drama, the audience is not involved personally; rather they are "Gods" directing the course of events from pre-defined alternatives. The performance possibilities are finite because they are still "script-driven;" the characters still perform written lines.

8.5.1.3 Psychotherapy

Psychodrama is a form of therapy where participants enact certain traumatic situations to gain an understanding of the trauma and thereby gain healing. Its whole purpose is cathartic rather than entertainment. Otherwise psychodrama shares many elements with interactive drama – there are no passive participants, the scenarios are brief and there are loose improvisational rules.

8.5.1.4 Games

Perhaps the most exciting aspect of virtual theater technologies is not related to performance but to game play. Those who participate in interactive drama do so predominantly because they consider it to be a social game – not because they consider it to be a new and exciting form of theater. However, serious actors could find usefulness in the improvisational opportunities, not only during the rehearsal process but also in unstructured open sessions with strangers.

In terms of pure entertainment, however, there are significant commercial opportunities in virtual reality Web-based games. The challenges here are the quality of interaction needed for collaborative and competitive puzzles and the maintenance of the player database.

8.5.1.5 Virtual Training

The virtual interactive world offers unprecedented opportunity for an experience-based learning environment. Virtual Reality training has existed for some time. It usually exists for military or extremely high-technology applications. This is due to the high costs involved in dedicated VR equipment. However, there is a significant amount of work training that requires access to specific equipment or situations that currently require physical realization. This is most expensive when employees must travel to the training location. The principles of the virtual theater could be extended to provide a common classroom where users, regardless of actual location, interact in problem-solving or simulation exercises.

8.5.1.6 Museum Exhibitions

The technology and application of virtual theater performance could extend to re-enactments of historical events for installation in museums. These could consist of free-running performances, in which viewers could "roam" around the virtual world, or interactive dramas of the particular events. For the interactive dramas, these could be directed to follow the true course of history or completely unrestrained, giving an alternative version of the events.

References

Baker, C (1977) *Theatre Games: A New Approach to Drama Training*, Methuen, London.

Bates, J (1990) Computational drama in Oz, in *Working Notes of the AAAI-90 Workshop on Interactive Fiction and Synthetic Realities*, Boston MA.

Bates, J (1992) Virtual reality, art, and entertainment, *PRESENCE: Teleoperators and Virtual Environments*, 1(1), 133–8.

Bates, J, Loyall, AB and Reilly, WS (1992) An architecture for action, emotion, and social behavior, in *Proceedings of the Fourth European Workshop on Modelling Autonomous Agents in a Multi-Agent World*, S. Martino al Camino, Italy.

Belt, L and Stockley, R (1991) *Improvisation through Theater Sports*, Seattle Thespis Productions.

Bentley, E (1968) *The Theory of the Modern Stage*, Pelican, London.

Brecht, B (1949) *Kleines Organon für das Theater*, Sinn und From Sonderheft.

Etzioni, O and Weld, D (1994) A softbot-based interface to the Internet. *Commun. ACM*, 37.

Hayes-Roth, B and Brownston, L (1994) Multiagent Collaboration in directed improvisation, *Stanford University Report KSL 94-69*.

Hayes-Roth, B, Sincoff, E, Brownston, L, Huard, H and Lent B (1994) Directed improvisation, *Stanford University Report KSL 94-61*.

Johnstone, K (1987) *IMPRO: Improvisation in the Theatre*, Penguin Books, New York.

Kantrowitz, M (1990) Natural language text generation in the Oz interactive fiction project, *Technical Report CMU-CS-90-158*, School of Computer Science, Carnegie Mellon University, Pittsburgh PA.

Kantrowitz, M and Bates, J (1992) Natural language text generation in the Oz interactive fiction project, in *Aspects of Automated Natural Language Generation* (eds. R Dale, E Hovy, D Rosner and O Stock) Lecture Notes in Artificial Intelligence, Vol. 587, Springer-Verlag, Berlin, pp. 13–28.

Kepner, L (1997) Dance and digital media: Troika Ranch and the art of technology, *Digital Creativity*, 8(1), Intellect Books.

Laurel, B (1986) Toward the design of a computer-based interactive fantasy system, *PhD Thesis*, Drama Department, Ohio State University.

Laurel, B (1991) *Computers as Theater*, Addison-Wesley, Reading MA.

McKenna, J, Pieper, S and Zelter, D (1990) Control of the virtual actor: the roach, *Proc. Symp. Interactive 3D Graphics*.

Nachmanovitch, S (1990) *Free Play: Improvisation in Life and Art*, Jeremy P Tarcher, Inc., Los Angeles.

Ozanne, M (1997) *Virtual Theatre: Background and Content*, EIMC Report, University of Bradford, UK.

Reeve, C (1997) *Virtual Theatre*, EIMC Report, University of Bradford, UK.

Reeve, C and Palmer, I (1997) Collaborative theatre set design across networks, in *From Desktop to Webtop: Virtual Environments on the Internet, WWW and Networks*, Conference Proceedings, National Museum of Photography, Film and Television, Bradford, UK.

Rousseau, D and Moulin, B(1996) Personality in synthetic agents, *KSL 96-21*, Stanford University.

Rousseau, D and Hayes-Roth, B (1996) *Mixed Initiatives in Interactions between Software Agents*, KSL, Stanford University.

Sharples, M (1997) *Storytelling by Computer, Digital Creativity*, 8(1), Intellect Books.

Smith, S and Bates, J (1989) Toward a theory of narrative for interactive fiction. *Technical Report CMU-CS-89-121*, School of Computer Science, Carnegie Mellon University, Pittsburgh PA.

Stanislavski, C (1968) *Building a Character*, Methuen, London.

Stanislavski, C (1984) *Creating a Role*, Methuen, London.

Suchman, L (1987) *Plans and Situated Actions: The Problem of the Machine/Human Communication*, Cambridge University Press, Cambridge.

Willett, J (1965) *Brecht on Theatre*, Methuen, London.

9

WWW Television News in Context: Organizational Practices and Media Products

Simeon J. Yates and Jane L. Perrone

Abstract

WWW-based news services are fast becoming a standard feature of many broadcast television news organizations. The introduction of WWW technologies into television newsrooms raises several important issues. This chapter considers the possible changes to the following three aspects of television newsrooms which WWW technologies bring:

- Organizational structure
- Process of news gathering
- Changes to presentation of news

The discussion within this chapter is based upon two studies: a set of ethnographic studies of different types of electronic newsroom systems and news organizations, including WWW news broadcasting, and an analysis of WWW-based news coverage of a range of stories. We examine the extent to which WWW-based news broadcasting demands a structure of newsroom organization. The paper concludes with a discussion of the structure and presentation of WWW news and considers the news-gathering and production technologies needed to support different approaches to WWW-based news services.

9.1 Introduction

A number of previous ethnographic studies of broadcast television newsrooms have highlighted the complex relationship between the organization of news production and the affordances of the technology in use [1–3]. Ethnographic researchers have found that journalists develop their work routines and practices over a long period, molding them around the restraints of time, resources and technology [1, pp. 120–1], [2, 3]. In particular, studies have focused upon the ways in which technologies support the "stopwatch culture" of television news production. Over the last few years the development of computer-based technologies has further increased the ability of newsrooms to produce broadcast output more quickly and with fewer staff. The first of these technologies were the electronic newsroom systems (ENS). ENS were introduced during the 1980s and provide a text-based medium for the main writing and production processes involved in news work. In all of the following four case studies the ENS in use was BASYS, which has for a long time been the industry standard. More recently, computer-based digital recording and editing equipment has become available. These technologies afford rapid production of audio and video content by speeding up the overall process, especially the editing process. The integration of these digital production technologies with ENS is currently under way with varying degrees of success. The final goal of such developments is the ability to conduct all aspects of news production, from story writing to the editing of audio-visual content, from one workstation. Most recently the arrival of the Internet and the World Wide Web has provided a new digital medium for the broadcasting of news content. The first news broadcast medium to make use of the WWW was the press. There are now a large number of online newspapers. Many online newspapers essentially present the same or repackaged material from their print version. Television news producers were slower to develop online news services, despite being more able to exploit the multimedia potential of WWW technologies. In the USA the lead has been taken by large cable networks (e.g. CNN), sometimes in conjunction with key computing industry players (e.g. MSNBC). In the UK the 1997 general election provided the stimulus for both the British Broadcasting Corporation (BBC) and Independent Television News (ITN) to set up online news services.

This chapter uses four case studies to explore the relationship between new digital technologies, especially the WWW, and newsroom organization. The data for three of the cases were collected during ethnographic studies of the newsrooms during the production of two days of news material. In the fourth case the data were provided on the WWW by the news desk itself. The four case studies all made use of a standard ENS (BASYS in all four cases) and were:

- a "standard" analogue television newsroom
- a digital news desk using digital editing/production equipment
- a small WWW-based television news desk
- a large WWW-based television news desk

The chapter questions the extent to which the integration of news production into a single-person single-workstation activity is a product of the technology itself. We then consider the changes to television news production organization and practice that WWW-based news delivery has brought. These changes range from the organization of the news desk to the range of skills required by journalists, producers and editors. We conclude with a discussion of the implications of the findings for the development of television newsroom technologies and newsroom practice.

9.2 Organizational Structure

Though new technologies do not *determine* the new types of social and organizational structures within an institution, they provide new *affordances* [4], both technologically and organizationally. In the case of television newsrooms, digital technologies have led to a reappraisal of the roles and functions of individual members and allowed the size of production teams to be reduced. At the same time, the expanding potential for new forms of media communication which digital technologies provide, especially the WWW, has led to the development of new roles within the newsroom. This section details the organization of four different cases of news production and, through a comparative analysis, explores the relationship between the organization of the newsroom and the technologies in use.

9.2.1 Organization of a "Standard" Television News Desk

The introduction of WWW-based news broadcasting to television newsrooms required a rethinking of existing organizational structures and practices. Figure 9.1 represents the production process of a news story in a "standard" analogue newsroom. The data used to construct this diagram were collected during an ethnographic study of a large regional newsroom serving a national UK public service broadcaster.

In Figure 9.1 an event which has generated or may generate a news story is picked up by various staff in the newsroom. Early in the day (stage A in Figure 9.1), a

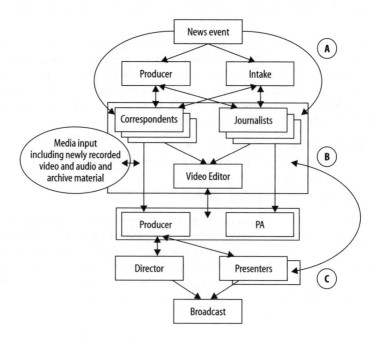

Figure 9.1 Production process in a large UK regional newsroom.

meeting chaired by the News Editor (not shown on diagram) decides on the likely running order for the broadcast and allocates staff and resources to the collection of material for the chosen stories. Some of this material will already have been flagged up by the previous day's Intake Producer, who will have been looking for relevant stories likely to arise in the next few days. The News Editor has overall managerial responsibility for the production of the program but is not involved directly in day-to-day production tasks. The running order of items will change during the day as new possible stories arise. The Producer of the day has responsibility for coordinating the various staff involved in the production of the news stories during the course of the day (stage B in Figure 9.1). This includes the collection of new primary source audio and video material used in the production of new packages. Once the items have been produced, the final broadcast is coordinated in studio by the director (stage C in Figure 9.1). Presenters will view material and possibly re-edit stories to fit personal presentation preferences. A central element of program production is the primary news-gathering activity of the journalists and correspondents, including the recording of relevant audio and video material by specialized camera and audio-tape operators.

9.2.2 Organization of a "Digital" Television News Desk

The large-scale and labor-intensive process presented in Figure 9.1 is itself changing as digital recording, editing and production technologies become more widely used in the television news broadcasting industry. A recent ethnographic study of the implementation of such technologies in a leading UK national commercial television news center discovered a very different form of organization. Figure 9.2 represents the process of news production in this case. The differences between Figure 9.1 and Figure 9.2 arise for a number of reasons. First, the digital newsroom was dedicated to the production of only one half-hour broadcast for distribution to global satellite clients. It was therefore a much smaller operation, with only four permanent staff, which relied on the main "standard" news desk for

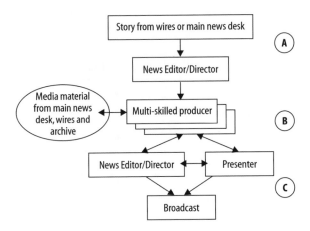

Figure 9.2 Production process on a global satellite digital news desk.

primary news intake. Second, this very small operation was made possible through employing staff trained in the use of computer-based digital production technologies. The use of these multi-skilled journalist/producer/video-editors allowed large sections of the program output to be constructed by one person.

In the case of the digital news desk, news stories are selected from the various wire services available and from the main news desk. Once again the running order is prepared by the News Editor (stage A in Figure 9.2). In this case the News Editor plays a more proactive role in the day-to-day production of the news program. Once selected, the news items are produced by one multi-skilled Journalist/Producer/Video-editor (stage B in Figure 9.2). In this case all of the tasks conducted at stage B in Figure 9.1 are being conducted by only one staff member. The video and audio material, as well as relevant information on the story, will be collected from the wire services and the main news desk. This type of production is termed "re-packaging," as the producer is taking existing material and reworking it for a new broadcast or audience. The final broadcast is directed in-studio by the News Editor – another example of multi-skilling.

9.2.3 Organization of a Small WWW News Desk

Interestingly, an ethnographic study of the WWW news desk based in the same organization found a very similar structure. Figure 9.3 describes the production process for a WWW news story. Once again this is a small-scale operation with only four fixed members of staff. In this case, all four staff were trained in the use of a set of media production technologies ranging from analog video and audio editing equipment, through digital video and audio capture and editing, to WWW authoring software.

As in the case of the digital newsroom, the News Editor selects the stories to be covered that day (stage A in Figure 9.3). Once again a set of multi-skilled online Journalist/Producers engage in the task of writing news stories. As with the digital

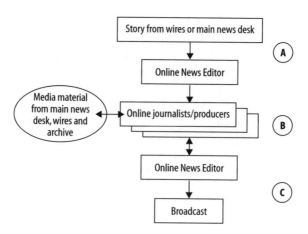

Figure 9.3 Production process on a UK national commercial WWW news site.

news desk, they are primarily engaged in repackaging existing material from the wires and the television and radio news desks into the medium of WWW pages (stage B in Figure 9.3). In this case there is no final "program" but rather the development of an existing WWW site. The Online News Editor engages in the final gatekeeping task of editorially checking the stories before they are uploaded to the WWW (stage C in Figure 9.3). The process of uploading material to the WWW is conducted by any of the members of the news desk team.

9.2.4 Organization of a Large WWW News Desk

The fourth case is a major US commercial news organization with a larger and more established WWW news service. At its launch, CNN Interactive (CNNin) had nearly 1000 pages, 3000 still images, 200 sound files and 100 QuickTime video clips [5]. Interestingly, the organizational structures and process are more complex than those in our last two cases and in some respects are akin to the "standard" news desk. Figure 9.4 presents the production process for a WWW news story at CNNin. In the previous two cases, the digital and WWW news desks were organizationally attached to a "standard" news desk; in fact, they are physically based in the same room. In the case of CNNin, the WWW news desk is organizationally viewed as a separate unit/"network" [5, p. 106] and has its own office space. This greater resourcing and larger output lead to both a larger number of staff and more clearly differentiated roles. This range of roles reflects the need to manage a larger

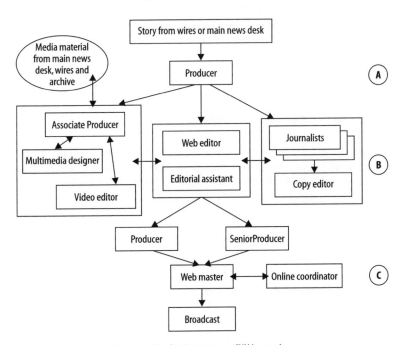

Figure 9.4 Production process at CNN Interactive.

throughput of material in an effective and rapid manner. Having said this, there still remains a higher level of multi-skilling, especially in terms of audio/video media production and editing, though in this case the journalistic role has remained separate. This approach reflects existing CNN organizational culture, as Jeff Garrard of CNNin notes [6]:

> How do you handle all the multimedia stuff? Do you hire an army of artists? Following the CNN model, we decided to hire journalists to learn Photoshop and other technical skills to handle most of the daily visual and sound elements. Instead of having everyone do everything for his or her story, we went for divide and conquer. This was the best approach for breaking news.

As with the previous two examples, stories are selected from the wires and main news desk on a regular basis. There are three shifts per day covering the full 24 hours. As with the "standard" television newsroom, a running order is selected from this material, this time by the Producer, who is in charge of the overall management of the production process. The CNNin Producer is equivalent to the News Editor in the previous three cases (stage A in Figure 9.4). The difference in terminology reflects slightly different organizational naming practices. Once the running order has been established during a meeting at the start of the shift, the responsibility for coordinating production passes to the Web Editor. The packages themselves are written by journalists with the collection and preparation of audio and video material falling to the Associate Producer in conjunction with a Video Editor and Multimedia Designer (stage B in Figure 9.4). In some cases all three media production roles are taken by one individual. This separates out the production process across a team, as in the "standard" case, whereas the digital and smaller WWW news desks allocated all of these tasks to one individual. Finally the Producer and his or her line manager, the Senior Producer, editorially check the completed packages before they are sent to a Web Master who has responsibility for maintaining the site contents (stage C in Figure 9.4).

9.3 Roles in Contemporary Newsrooms

Looking specifically at the roles of individuals within these systems, the relationship between the impacts of the technology and the organization and management of the newsroom becomes clearer. The following tables detail the type and number of staff involved in the production of one television news broadcast or WWW site. In the case of CNNin, the numbers given are approximated for one "shift" of a 24-hour service.

9.3.1 Roles in "Standard" Newsroom

Table 9.1 describes the roles of each person indicated in Figure 9.1 and the approximate number of staff employed in the production of one half-hour regional news bulletin.

Table 9.1. Roles in a "standard" non-digital newsroom

Role	Description	Number
News Editor	Manager of news desk, in charge of deciding main structure and content.	1
Producer of the day	Coordinates the structure of the program. Manages primary news gathering. Responsible for ensuring the program is complete and runs to time. Checks on editorial and technical standards.	1
Intake Producer	Plans out next day's program.	1
Correspondents	Specialized single topic journalists. Mainly involved in primary news gathering of non-day-to-day news.	approx. 5
Regional Journalist	General journalist. Mainly involved in primary news gathering of day-to-day news.	approx. 5
Production Assistant	Helps Producer in organizational aspects of program production.	approx. 3
Video/Audio Editors	Editing of video and audio material.	approx. 3
Director	In charge of the final live broadcast from studio.	1
Presenters	Reading of headlines, news items and links, interviewing of guests, and sometimes engaging in writing/re-writing of current stories. Can do small amounts of their own journalism.	2
	Total	22

Table 9.2. Roles in a "digital" newsroom

Role	Description	Number
News Editor/ Director	Manager of news desk, in charge of deciding main structure and content. Also directs the studio recording of the final broadcast. Checks on editorial and technical standards.	1
Multi-skilled: Journalist/ Producer/Digital Video Editor	Repackages news stories from main "standard" news desk as well as creating news packages from wires material. Writes, edits and produces the final output single.handed.	2
Presenter	Reads headlines and links packages in studio.	1
	Total	4

9.3.2 Roles in a Digital Newsroom

Table 9.2 describes the roles of each person indicated in Figure 9.2 and the approximate number of staff employed in the production of one half-hour global satellite news bulletin.

9.3.3 Roles in a UK Commercial WWW Newsroom

Table 9.3 describes the roles of each person indicated in Figure 9.3 and the approximate number of staff employed in the production of each day's WWW news coverage.

Table 9.3. Roles on a small WWW news desk

Role	Description	Number
Online News Editor	Manager of news desk, in charge of deciding main structure and content. Also works as one of the Online Journalist/Producers.	1
Online Journalist/Producer	Re-packages news stories from main "standard" news desk into WWW pages. Writes, edits and produces the final output single handed. Can coordinate responses to interactive elements of WWW site. Publishes material directly to WWW site.	3
	Total	4

Table 9.4. Roles in a large WWW newsroom

Role	Description	Number
Senior Producer	Overall management of news desk. Maintains organizational and management link to television news desk. Makes decisions on WWW coverage.	1
Producer	Coordinates the structure and production of the WWW news coverage. Checks on editorial and technical standards.	1
Writer	Journalist writing text or WWW news stories – can look for relevant external WWW links.	approx. 5–10
Copy Editor	Checks Journalists' text, writes headlines.	1
Web Editor	Produces HTML – finds relevant external WWW links.	1
Editorial Assistant	Supporting Writers, Web Editor and Multimedia Producer/Editor.	1
Web Master	Manages WWW site and coordinates publication of pages to site.	1
Online Coordinator	Coordinates use of material received from interactive elements of WWW site.	1
Associate Producer/Multimedia designer/ Video editor	Set of tasks conducted by one or more staff. Including multi-media design, editing of video and coordination of the media elements of a WWW news story.	approx. 3
	Total	20

9.3.4 Roles in CNNin WWW

Table 9.4 describes the roles of each person indicated in Figure 9.4 and the approximate number of staff employed in the production of WWW news material during one of three shifts as part of a 24-hour service.

It is clear that the organizational structures in WWW and digital production newsrooms are a function of a number of factors, which include:

• size of the operation
• existing structures and organizational culture
• types of technology in use
• types of trained personnel available
• types of media output

In all three of our digital technology-based examples (cases 2–4), some level of multi-skilling has taken place. This multi-skilling can be seen to take two forms. First, there is the training of journalists in the production and editing of digital media. Second, there is the integration of production skills to support the production of multimedia output. In the case of the UK commercial digital and WWW news desks (Figures 9.2 and 9.3 and Tables 9.2 and 9.3) the technology has supported news production using very small teams compared with the "standard" case. This model relies totally upon the use of the first type of multi-skilling. In the case of CNNin, though using similar technologies, the newsroom employs a larger number and wider range of staff. This reflects both a larger organizational commitment and the need to manage the more complex process of producing a large output of material.

9.3.5 Conclusion

A great emphasis has been placed in recent years on the importance of digital technologies, including the WWW, to the development of broadcast news production. One key part of this process was the development of multi-skilled journalist/media-production-editors who combine roles which have until recently been conducted by separate individuals trained in each area. Although there is evidence from a range of research, including the studies reported above, that multi-skilling is becoming more widespread, the need to manage a complex process within a large organization creates opposing pressures. Managing a large broadcast outfit, even one based on WWW technologies, requires staff with distinct roles, even if they differ from those in a "standard" television news production setting. In some cases these roles will involve forms of multi-skilling in media production. Multi-skilled news production does differ importantly from previous practices. In the following sections we consider some of the ways in which producing WWW news differs from existing television news production practices.

9.4 News Gathering

9.4.1 Primary News Gathering

Online news sites offer very little original content [7]. For example, in examining CNNin's selection of 13 stories on 23 January 1998 under their "World" and "US" sections, five were credited to CNN; on two stories, specific CNN correspondents were named as providing information; one story was credited to CNNin's sister site, AllPolitics; five stories were credited solely to the Associated Press; and Reuters were credited for three stories, and they also contributed to two other stories. From such a selection of sources it is apparent that much of CNNin's site content is repackaged from its sister networks. Some content is clearly taken directly and without substantial revision from the major news agencies, as CNNin copyrights some stories directly to wire agencies. Thus rather than gathering news directly, they draw largely upon the inventory of the traditional news branches of their firm, benefiting from their news-gathering activities by obtaining audio and video material of events, archive pictures and so on. Online journalists cull stories from the news wires, rework material written for broadcast news shows and use film shot for these other networks. In the case of the WWW journalist the technology itself provides the affordance of connecting the reader directly with source material itself.

9.4.2 Gathering News From the WWW

Online journalists use the Internet not only as a medium of communication to their audience but also as a news-gathering tool. WWW sites do exhibit one kind of news gathering by offering links to external sites. This technique of bundling links allows online journalists to deploy one of the most distinctive features of Internet technology: the ability to link effortlessly between pages. Bundled links are often indicated by visual cues, such as a change in typeface, a disclaimer or an accompanying description of the site. A television remote control can be used in a similar fashion, but news anchors urge the viewer to "stay tuned," while news sites actively encourage users to wander, by laying out suggested routes away from the original site.

At both the UK commercial WWW site and CNNin, part of the job of producing a package for WWW publishing is the search and selection of appropriate WWW links. At the former, the Online Journalist/Producer performs this task, whereas at CNNin it is shared between the Web Editor and the Writer, giving them more time to conduct an extensive search and evaluate the credibility of selected sites. This may help to explain why CNNin tends to offer more links on average per story than the UK site. For example, stories placed under the national and world categories on the UK commercial site and CNNin site on one day (23 January 1998) were compared. For 13 stories on CNNin, there were a total of 81 bundled external links. On the UK site, there were a total of 22 stories, but only 12 bundled external links. Assuming that this is a representative sample, CNNin bundles an average of six external links with each national or world story, while the UK site bundles an average of less than one link per story.

This is news gathering in its most basic form: in fact, source-gathering might provide a more apt description of the job. Once an online journalist locates a WWW site, and determines that it is credible enough to be used as a bundled link, its address is simply dumped on the page, and the reader is left to decide whether to look at its content. Nevertheless, locating links is a skilled job, requiring, as McAdams [8] has observed, the knowledge and ability of an editor, a reporter and a researcher. This task, however, is performed either as an accessory to the tasks of writing the story or tagging it with HTML, or as an optional extra if the journalist has the time to look up links. As Morris [9] noted, use of bundling places a greater onus on the readers to assess the credibility of these sources of information themselves, rather than relying on the journalist as a gatekeeper.

9.5 News Production

Another important feature of WWW broadcasting is the presentation of news via hypertext. Previous research into new media texts has highlighted the manner in which new standard formats, or genres, develop out of the interaction between existing genres of communication and the affordances provided by the technologies in use [10]. In the case of WWW news the main point of departure for those developing services has been print-based newspapers [11]. This is partly reflected in the backgrounds of those working in WWW television newsrooms (see Table 9.6) as well as some aspects of the presentation of online news. This section presents a comparative content analysis of print and WWW news coverage of the same headline story.

A comparison of the coverage of a single event on the front pages of three newspapers (the *Guardian*, the *Independent* and the *Daily Telegraph*) and two WWW online news sites (ITN Online and BBC News Online) offers a somewhat limited and yet interesting analysis of the differences between the construction and presentation of a news story in traditional print journalism and online journalism conducted by broadcast news outfits. Coverage of the results of the referendum on Scottish devolution from 13 September 1997 was collected and compared. Table 9.5 shows that the newspapers generally offered more information purely in terms of text on the front page. The news sites, meanwhile, used the affordances of the WWW medium to create a more diverse and complex presentation of the news.

The ITN site presented the most complex story structure. First came a front page featuring a large image, a short caption and a single link, which moved to the main contents page for news about the referendum. There was also a link to a story about the death of Mother Teresa at the bottom of the front page. This type of presentation could be paralleled with traditional media practices, such as the broadcast news teaser or the front page plug for a story inside a newspaper. Following the link to the next page, the reader is provided with a menu of further links to 10 stories, audio and video clips, images and accompanying captions, and bundled links to external sites such as Scottish newspapers to provide further coverage. The "main story" was difficult to categorize from this list, although one story stood out due to a larger font size. This page offered simply text with no direct quotes, and could be

Table 9.5. Analysis of news presentation of online sites and newspapers

Type	Paper/section	Words	Direct quotes	Images	Internal links	External links	Audio clips	Video clips
Online news	ITN:front page	20	0	1	0	0	0	0
	ITN:contents	50	0	5	12	8	5	1
	ITN:main story	420	0	0	0	0	0	0
	BBC:front page	30	0	1	4	0	0	0
	BBC:main story	570	3	4	14	3	1	0
Newspapers	*Guardian*	570	5	2	3			
	Independent	700	5	0	2			
	Daily Telegraph	1000	6	0	3			

classed as news analysis. Thus the initial page offered a choice of subject matter; once the user had decided to pursue a link to further information on the referendum, the second page gave a range of choices of the type of information available via links; the stories themselves were "dead ends" in that they provided no further links, but rather simple text in the traditional print journalism style.

The structure of both online news sites was such that stories tended to deal with specific aspects of the referendum, allowing the reader to choose. For example, BBC News Online's front page offered readers links to "Full story," "Reaction," "British Press Reaction" and "Results, Audio, Video." The BBC's main story also provided contextual links to maps of Scotland, results from individual areas and so on. Thus both of the online sites offered a richer text that allowed readers more control over the specific information they wanted to view, whereas choice in the newspapers was limited to a main story and two or three stories inside the front cover (called "internal links" in Table 9.5). The newspapers, meanwhile, attempted to summarize the events of the previous evening's referendum announcement in a single story, including the results, voter reaction and political reaction.

Table 9.5 also shows that the newspapers used more direct quotes than the online coverage. Instead, the WWW sites offered audio clips, and in the case of ITN Online, video clips, which in fact achieve the same goal of providing direct comments from those involved in the story. Only the *Guardian* used an image on its front page, but this is easily accounted for by the print deadlines of newspapers, which must be ready to go to press in the early hours of the morning. This did not allow sufficient time for photographs to be shot and included in the newspaper. The online sites, meanwhile, are not restricted to such deadlines and are able to update site information at any time. (For example, the CNNin site, which indicates when every story was first posted on the Internet, offered its first coverage of the referendum results at 06:27 GMT.)

It is perhaps surprising that BBC News Online did not employ more audio and video clips in its coverage of the referendum results. This may be accounted for by the fact that, at that time, the site was a prototype for a more substantial site that was launched in November 1997 in conjunction with the new BBC 24-hour news channel. At the time of writing, both sites now provide streaming video (some of it live in the case of the BBC), of their newscasts. The public service nature of the BBC, however, may also keep the emphasis on text, which is accessible to more users with lower-end computers, as Edward Briffa, the BBC's controller of online services, has noted [12].

This analysis illustrates that WWW technology offers a wider range of options for both the online journalist and for the reader. Online news sites provide more "depth', through layers of links within a story that allow multiple paths though story elements. Thus the construction of online news requires more than just the provision of a panoply of choices for the reader. These choices must be structured to provide ease of access and navigation for readers who are dealing with a new and possibly unfamiliar hypertext medium. At present care may also have to be taken to provide routes for those readers who do not have the computing power to make use of every multimedia element on offer.

This analysis also shows that conventions are being established for individual online news sites – these may be tied to constraints of the method of page production: the ITN Online site uses a frame structure, whereas the BBC News Online site does not. Online news sites are not, however, restricted to the same time and content restraints as either their digital or "standard" newsroom counterparts or print media. The flexibility of the medium is counterbalanced, however, by the same customer demands for accurate, updated content. Indeed, the need to gain a competitive edge by "being first" with breaking news coverage perhaps places even greater demands for timeliness than those faced by traditional television and print media.

9.5.1 Backgrounds of Newsroom Staff

In the four cases discussed earlier, staff were found to have varying backgrounds in terms of training and experience. Table 9.6 shows that in the "standard" newsroom there was a small percentage of staff with print experience. These individuals were mainly those in more senior management roles. Clearly, in the "standard" newsroom environment multimedia training proved unnecessary. The digital newsroom staff showed high levels of multimedia and television experience, indicating the use of multi-skilling in this environment, and the redundancy of print experience in a digital television newsroom. In the WWW newsroom, however, a range of backgrounds was necessary to cope with the multimedia possibilities of the WWW medium. Nevertheless, the two WWW newsrooms differed considerably in terms of the background of their staff. The UK WWW site's staff all had a print background, but few had multimedia training. Multimedia skills were learned either on the job or in their own time.

At CNNin, those staff whose jobs entailed use of multimedia such as digital video editing had received formal multimedia training. Those in other roles at CNNin had mainly worked in other parts of the CNN organization as video journalists or writers before moving to CNNin. When multimedia jobs are separated from the task of writing the story, it seems that they are done by those with formal multimedia training, who may not be journalistically trained. Previous experience at CNN provided not only training in television but also a clear understanding of CNN conventions and standards. The only member of CNNin staff with print journalism

Table 9.6. Backgrounds of newsroom staff (figures taken from profiles of CNNin staff members which can be found at the CNNin WWW site)

Case	Percentage with print experience[a]	Percentage with television experience	Percentage with multimedia training
"Standard" newsroom	15	100	0
Digital newsroom	0	100	71
Online newsroom	100	75	25
CNNin	9	64	27

[a]These percentages may add up to more than 100 because some staff are trained in more than one area.

experience was the Copy Editor, which is not surprising considering that this job draws largely on the practices of print journalism. The diversity of the experience and training of CNNin staff perhaps reflects the division of labor found in the organization, which negates the need for multi-skilling and thus experience or training in a variety of fields.

9.6 Conclusions

We would like to draw a number of conclusions from the data presented above. First, the use of multi-skilled staff is a product of three things:

- commercial pressures to exploit technology to the maximum and minimize staff costs
- affordances and integration provided by digital technologies
- availability of new types of staff trained in new media production – especially multimedia

Within the media industry multi-skilling is often viewed in the context of video journalism where journalism skills and audio/video recording and editing skills are combined. This view has been further reinforced by the continued development of supporting single-person single-workstation technologies. Our comparative analysis has indicated that there is in fact a range of multi-skilled roles. These roles go beyond video journalism and can range from the combination of media editing skills for the production of multimedia through to the combination of journalism with WWW use and authoring skills. Having said this, it is clear from our analysis that the main driving force behind multi-skilling arises from organizational and commercial pressures. The presence of digital technologies provides the affordances which support these organizational developments.

Second, new technologies have brought new types of overall organization to television newsrooms. All three of the digital newsrooms discussed above relied heavily on the primary news gathering taking place on a "standard" news desk, the focus of work in these cases being the repackaging of existing material. The only primary news gathering taking place in the WWW case was the selection of links to relevant external information sources. Third, although the WWW provides a new multimedia medium for news presentation, existing print media practices were often drawn upon. This includes the employment of staff with print media backgrounds and the presentation of material in newspaper story form. Having said this, television-based WWW news is able to make considerable use of the audio and video material available to add multimedia elements to these packages. This makes television-based WWW newsrooms able to truly exploit the WWW as a "fourth" news broadcast medium based upon the integration of print (newspaper), audio (radio) and video (television) elements in a multimedia format.

Staff employed in these multimedia multi-skilled news environments are therefore heavily dependent upon technology to support their work. This is not a new phenomenon, as television news has always been at the leading edge of communications technology use. In this case, though, the reliance is upon integrated digital technologies which can be delivered on one workstation. An examination of the data we have collected points to two areas where further developments might assist those working in WWW based newsrooms:

- Specially designed WWW news authoring tools – at present few WWW-based newsrooms make use of specialist software. MSNBC is the only network we know of that provides standardized HTML "shells" and supporting software allowing affiliates to set up local Web sites with a standardized look and feel which integrates with the main channel's style and site [13].

- Improved or specially adapted search engines would also help in the development of online journalism in the context of both WWW news desks and general primary news gathering [14].

Overall, we expect to see further development of WWW- and digital-based news services. During the next few years we would expect further integration of WWW news operations into the overall organizational structure of television news broadcasters, as they are uniquely placed to support the production of high-quality, high-volume multimedia output.

References

[1]   G Tuchman (1978) *Making News: a Study in the Construction of Reality*, Free Press, New York.

[2]   H Gans (1979) Deciding What's News: a Study of "CBS Evening News," "NBC Nightly News," "Newsweek" and "Time," Pantheon Books, New York.

[3]   DM White (1950) The "Gatekeeper": a case study in the selection of news, *Journalism Quarterly*, 27, 383–90.

[4]   DA Norman (1988) *The Psychology of Everyday Things*, Basic Books, New York.

[5]   DM Flournoy and RK Stewart (1997) *CNN: Making News in the Global Market*, University of Luton Press, Luton.

[6]   CNNin (1996) *The Big Launch*, (http://cnn.com/EVENTS/1996/anniversary/flash-back.machine/flashback4.html).

[7]   D Shaw (1997) Newspapers take different paths to online publishing, *Los Angeles Times*, Special report on media and the Web, 17 June (http://www.latimes.com/HOME/NEWS/REPORTS/MEDIA/3main.html).

[8]   M McAdams (1995) Inventing an online newspaper, *Interpersonal Computing and Technology: An Electronic Journal for the 21st Century*, 3, 64–90.

[9]   M Morris (1996) The Internet as mass medium, *Journal of Computer-Mediated Communication*, 1.4, (http://www.usc.edu/dept/annenberg/vol1/issue4/vol1no4.html).

[10] SJ Yates and TR Sumner (1997) Digital genres and the new burden of fixity, in *Proc. Thirtieth Hawaiian International Conference on Systems Sciences, Volume VI: Digital Documents Track* (ed. RH Sprague), IEEE Computer Society Press.

[11] CR Watters and MA Shepherd (1996) The Digital broadsheet: an evolving genre, in *Proc. Thirtieth Hawaiian International Conference on Systems Sciences, Volume VI: Digital Documents Track* (ed. RH Sprague), IEEE Computer Society Press.

[12] K McEvers (1997) Online storytelling: Are you using the medium's strengths to tell the story?, *theAntenna*, 2.12 (http://www.theantenna.com/97/dec/webmasters/kmcevers12_97.html).

[13] W Mills (1997) The advantage of an MSNBC affiliate, *theAntenna*, 2.6 (http://www.theantenna.com/97/jun/bottomline/wmills6_97.html).

[14] R Reddick and E King (1997) *The Online Journalist*, Harcourt Brace, London.

10

Live Internet Broadcasting: Some Unique Experiences

D.R. Lawrence, A. Sloane, D.E. Price and G. Constable

Abstract

This chapter gives an outline of "hands on" experiences gained when organizing and implementing a unique live-to-Internet broadcast of a rock concert performance (1 November 1996) from a remote part of rural Wales.

"State of the art" leading edge technology was utilized with all of the accompanying problems and contingency plans. A detailed account is given of the event, which involved the live broadcast (and recording) of vision and audio of the concert using Multicast, CuSeeMe, RealAudio and "video in a Web page." The background to the event is described, together with details of how the communications technology was organized and implemented. The event provided a very useful vehicle for researching into issues related to maximizing the potential of Internet live broadcasting, – and the findings are discussed here.

The main body of this chapter, and its conclusions, would be of interest to those planning similar events, and/or those interested in video conferencing and Internet broadcasting research.

10.1 Introduction

On Friday 1 November 1996, a unique musical event was broadcast live-to-Internet and received all over the world. Leading edge technology was used to transmit video and audio in several different formats as part of this experimental broadcast. A great deal of work, organizational and technical, was involved in making this event successful and effective. The event was managed and coordinated by the *WWWales project* (World Wide Welsh Arts Live Event Simulcast – a non-profit-making organization), and implemented as part of ongoing projects by research groups at the University of Wales (Aberystwyth) and the University of Wolverhampton in the UK. The success of the exercise also relied on the technical and experimental expertise of many collaborating academics and professionals around the world.

A great deal was experienced and "learnt" during the various stages of the project – both in terms of organizing such an event and also in terms of making leading edge technology and ideas actually "work." This chapter attempts to focus on describing the various experiences and on the issues relating to the technology utilized. This kind of project provides several "clues" as to how to maximize the broadcasting opportunities available to Internet users, but also leaves many existing and new questions to be addressed in future research.

10.2 Background to the Event

In July 1996 the *WWWales project* team was gathered together and formed the aim of utilizing Internet broadcasting technology to provide a broader and more effective stage for Welsh-based performing and creative artists – in particular those that do not have easy access to traditional media exposure. Planning for the inaugural event was quickly put into action – it was decided to hold the event from a venue in rural Mid-Wales in the last quarter of 1996. The main purpose of the inaugural event was to raise awareness of the effectiveness of this kind of broadcast, and to form an infra-structure of people who could produce a professional product combining traditional performing arts staging expertise with Internet technology skills.

In recent years, a great deal of work has been carried out in the areas of computer communications and telematics at the University of Wales, Aberystwyth (Telematics Research Group, Department of Computer Science) and at the University of Wolverhampton (CoNTACT Research Group, School of Computing and IT). On invitation, the two teams of researchers embarked on a collaborative project to design and implement the technology necessary to make the Internet broadcast "live" from the venue.

The concepts behind the inaugural broadcast provided a useful vehicle for research into issues such as the optimization of video and audio quality, the comparison of various broadcasting environments, the practical considerations required to accommodate the needs associated with live performances of this kind, and the technical difficulties likely to be met when simultaneously utilizing a variety of Internet broadcasting techniques.

The concert was to be performed from within a "Celtic Experience Centre" (called Celtica, in Machynlleth, Mid-Wales, UK) in what was called the "Vortex" room. This was a circular, and relatively small room resembling a "stepped pit" with floor and walls black in color, and with an impressive Celtic tree stretching from the floor to the ceiling. Visually this room was absolutely ideal for the show, but in a practical sense it meant difficulties in terms of positioning of the musicians and performers, movement of camera crew and seating of the audience.

10.3 Internet Broadcasting

There are many examples of software and networking techniques utilized to relay streams of audio and/or video onto and around the Internet [1]. There is also a great deal of contemporary research activity in this area [2–5], and although there continue to be problems with achieving consistently high levels of audio/video transmission quality, advances in the technology and the utilization of available technology are apparent. The roles of networks and communication technologies have been identified as being dominant in the application of video conferencing – especially where individuals are using the technology at or from their homes [6].

The main constraint with regard to Internet broadcasting ("netcasting") is the variable, and often limited, available bandwidth [7]. Bandwidth is limited for the end-user (particularly those home-based) on the Internet both by the need to use telephone connections and by the sharing of intermediate Internet links by a number of other users. Recent research, however, has begun to address the problem of varying video quality in netcasting by the use of "scalable" video codecs [8]. This type of codec is designed to encode video sequences only once, but depending on the bandwidth available at each particular receiver the codec server is designed to select an appropriate bit rate from the stream for that receiver.

In the case of the Celtica broadcast (i.e. the netcasting of a live music performance) it was recognized that greater emphasis needed to be placed on audio data, with relatively low video frame rates being acceptable to the viewer/listener. A slightly different situation arises with the netcasting of an academic conference – an activity which has recently become more prevalent [9, 10]. In the case of the OECD conference, held in Turku, Finland, it was found that the slides used in the seminars were difficult to interpret when viewed over a limited bandwidth stream – partly due to slow frame rates and also due to problems with audio/video synchronization. A "whiteboard" approach is often used in netcasting (particularly in multicasts), as it helps to conserve bandwidth while enhancing the effectiveness of communication.

When planning an event which involves live-to-Internet relay of audio and video it is very important to consider carefully which broadcast software is to be utilized. At present, there are no universally agreed guidelines with regard to the software format(s) and networking infrastructures to be adopted for any of the many possible event types and characteristics. It is a common aim of the research teams involved in this collaborative project work to explore and experiment with a variety of broadcasting techniques, and to utilize that experience to move towards recommending a suitable framework for netcasting design.

10.4 Design of the Celtica Netcast

10.4.1 General Strategy

The starting point in designing a netcast strategy is to identify the characteristics and needs of the target audience for the event.

The overall aim of the Celtica netcast was to make transmissions available to as wide an audience as possible. Our likely audience would have a large variety of different styles of Internet connection and the quality of those connections would be subject to large variation. Some of our audience might watch from a business location and perhaps have quite high bandwidth and high-quality connections, whereas others might be on slow modem links to equally slow and perhaps over-loaded sections of the Internet. It was decided that a variety of different ways of making the material available on the Internet should be used, thus maximizing the probability that any given interested "user" could connect and experience the concert. As a priority, it was the intention to provide video and audio at respective optimum quality levels and also to make it reasonably possible for "modem users" to be able to successfully connect to and receive the broadcast.

The utilization of a range of netcasting techniques makes an event available to a number of Internet communities – experience indicated that there are distinct communities of Internet users who tend to use particular formats for receiving live or recorded Internet broadcasts. Until there is a clearer framework for potential audiences to be aware of any available broadcasts, and be able to easily "tap" into them using familiar software, there is a necessity to "duplicate" the netcasting effort by transmitting across multiple formats/routes – in order to reduce the exclusion of particular Internet communities from the event. For totally "new" users, it should be speedy, straightforward and inexpensive to acquire relevant software and tools.

An appropriate approach is to:

1. require users to be attached to certain types of Internet subnet

and

2. provide alternative choices of readily available connection methods.

In the case of the Celtica netcast, it was decided to select broadcast formats which satisfied the above general criteria and also with which the research teams had previous experience – MBone Multicast, CuSeeMe, RealAudio, and video in a Web page (now known as WebVideo).

MBone multicasting is an established and well-managed method of Internet broad-casting, but access tends to be limited to academic institutions and some of the larger corporate organizations. CuSeeMe [11] and RealAudio [12] both had the advantages of being very widely used and providing the opportunity for people to connect to a broadcast from a variety of platforms (including PCs with only 28.8 kbps modems) and using free-download software. WebVideo [10], sometimes known as "video in a Web page," only requires the use of a suitable Web browser, with users being able to pick up video images simply by connecting to a specially constructed Web page.

10.4.2 CuSeeMe

CuSeeMe was originally developed at Cornell University [11] and is widely used (particularly in the USA and Europe) for both social and "business" videoconferencing. Audio is available, but tends not to be used – most favoring the use of a "chat-board" feature.

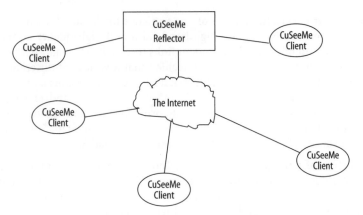

Figure 10.1 Standard CuSeeMe setup.

When transmissions are needed to reach multiple users, CuSeeMe utilizes special software (called reflectors) to enable sets of people to form a conference. The CoNTACT research group (School of Computing and IT, University of Wolverhampton, UK) had been using an experimental reflector for about two years prior to the Celtica event. This has tended to be an *ad hoc* activity with no guaranteed uptime for users but a service available for experimental purposes only. The general setup for a simple CuSeeMe conference is straightforward, with clients connecting to a central server as in Figure 10.1. This allows anyone with access to the Internet to be able to connect to the reflector. Generally all the users who connect and who transmit are seen by all the other users of the conference, but it is possible to just watch and listen to a conference (termed "lurking").

In the case of a netcast (as opposed to informal conferencing and/or socializing), there need to be some changes to this standard setup to enable CuSeeMe to be used as a broadcast medium. This is for two main reasons:

1. Too many users at one reflector site will inhibit performance – due to possible insufficient available bandwidth on its Internet connection.
2. Geographically distant users may create Internet difficulties in other places if connection is, say, via a single site only.

These potential problems can be largely solved within the reflector software by selecting appropriate configuration parameters. These parameters allow various options that are particularly useful for controlling access (and hence bandwidth usage) and for "chaining" reflectors together. The chaining together of reflectors increases the total potential audience (as each reflector can only successfully support finite numbers of people connected) and localizes groups of users to connect to reflectors in geographically proximate areas. Controlled access can be used to deny transmit access to users at the primary reflector sites (which avoids the user's video/audio being transmitted "down the line" of the chained reflectors).

The reflector software allows a number of further parameter changes that can influence the broadcast quality. These were tried in advance using a video feed from a standard VHS player. This allowed testing to be done using a setup that was replicated in the concert later. It proved easy to check the functioning of the various tie-in reflectors from a sample workstation, together with email/chatboard contact with overseas representatives.

10.4.3 MBone

Much activity has taken place over the Multicast Backbone (MBone). The MBone is an experimental interconnection of multicast-capable local networks. Most of the interconnection is made by prearranged unicast "tunnels" linking together workstations acting as multicast routers (mrouters). These mrouters are often located at commercial or academic research laboratories. A variety of encoding techniques and tools are in use. We decided to choose three tools, which at the time were in common use and known to give good quality. The tools chosen were all developed by the Network Research Group at Lawrence Berkeley National Laboratory in collaboration with the University of California [13]. We used "vic" for video encoding, "vat" for audio and "wb," a shared whiteboard. The whiteboard was used to enable viewers to provide feedback on technical quality and their general reaction to the concert/netcast.

10.4.4 RealAudio

At the time of our transmission, RealAudio software was widely used around the world and was receiving good reviews and so was selected for use for the audio component of the Web service. Although other selected formats provide video and audio transmission, it was recognized that an alternative audio-only channel was needed – to give the audience further choice and to overcome the possible problem of video streams dominating bandwidth and reducing the quality of audio received. People would be able to receive RealAudio only or choose whether or not to receive it in addition to one or more of the other formats.

10.4.5 WebVideo

The team at the University of Wales, Aberystwyth, had previously made good contacts with a group at the University of Ulm, Germany [14, 15]. The Ulm group had developed a product, then called WebVideo, which enabled the transmission of video into a small window contained within a Web page. Users therefore do not need special software, nor downloading facilities, to receive the video stream – except for a suitable Web browser. We had some prior experience of using this software, so with the permission of the originators a new version of the software was downloaded for use. It is viewed as a very useful technique (and since the time of the Celtica netcast it has become much easier to implement!) as it provides extremely ready access to video on the Internet (more recently the software now caters for audio in addition to video).

10.4.6 Celtica Netcast Encoding, Transmission and Monitoring

As may be apparent already, the Celtica netcast involved, by necessity, a fairly complex local networking and processing arrangement – especially bearing in mind the location of the concert to be broadcast – Celtica, a tourist-based Celtic Experience Centre in Machynlleth, in rural Mid-Wales (UK), some 18 miles north of Aberystwyth. First, a pragmatic way of bringing the audio and video streams to Aberystwyth needed to be found. The WWWales Project were able to arrange that a special ISDN connection was made available at the venue (sponsored by BT Research Labs (UK) [16]). Suitable ISDN lines were already in place at Aberystwyth (university campus) and added to the fact that suitable computer facilities were available, this location was chosen as the primary telecommunications channel that would be used. The next step was to decide on exactly what terminal equipment would be used to form the links between the venue and the various processors at Aberystwyth.

There were two approaches that could have been taken to address the choice of terminal equipment. The first approach would have seen us attach ISDN-based Internet routers to the link at the venue. This would have enabled the concert transmissions to be encoded at the venue in Machynlleth into the various Internet formats, but would have meant that we would have had to relocate a large amount of equipment to perform that task, and indeed find sufficient space at the venue. The second approach (which was adopted) was to attach H.320 VideoTelephony equipment to the links (at both the venue and at Aberystwyth). This approach would enable us to keep all our Internet encoding equipment in Aberystwyth, and enable a setup to be used which could be tested/simulated quite readily in advance of the event. While this approach has its technical deficiencies, as mentioned in more detail later, it was clearly going to be a pragmatic solution to our problems.

In total there was a considerable amount of communications/computer equipment involved locally in the event (for capture, transmitting, encoding, relay and monitoring). At Aberystwyth, three offices were used to house all the equipment, with temporary Internet and video/audio interconnections constructed between them. In total 13 computer systems were directly involved in the transmissions, 11 of which were located in the three interconnected offices, with the other two located in a computer room in the next building. We also had a VHS recorder available to capture the incoming video and audio for later examination.

As mentioned earlier, the signals arrived at Aberystwyth from the venue via ISDN into a videophone. In fact, the equipment we used was a PC equipped with a BT-supplied VC8000 videophone package. This product has the capability to supply video and audio to devices outside itself and it was this capability that provided the start of our operation. At the venue, the link was formed by a self-contained BT VC7000 videophone. This source of audio proved to be very adequate. The quality was good and quite suitable for the further encoding we needed to perform. The video, however, was far from ideal. Having been transmitted across the ISDN link using H.261 encoding, the video received was now full of various edges and artefacts. The output socket provided video in analog form, so, while far from perfect, it could be used. It was necessary to feed three video encoders as well as the

Figure 10.2 Two examples of the video images received at Aberystwyth.

VHS recorder, and it was decided to passively split the signal. This was achieved without problem. Experience actually showed that this imperfect video was not our major problem. The lighting at the event had been chosen to be suitable for capturing the "mood" of the concert on high-quality video camera equipment. The video feed into our VC7000 at the venue was acquired from the video camera mixer desk. This source video proved to be a little dark compared with what would have been preferred for Internet relay purposes. Figure 10.2 shows two examples of the video images received at Aberystwyth (as taken from the VHS recording).

The MBone encoding was all achieved using a Sun Unix workstation equipped with a SunVideo video capture card. This proved to be perfectly adequate for the task. The machine used was a Sparc Classic. The workstation also ran a copy of WB (a whiteboard, text-based facility) to enable us to exchange reactions with the Internet audience.

A second Sun Sparc IPX workstation was used to monitor the MBone quality that we were achieving.

The WebVideo was encoded using an Apple Macintosh LC630. The signal generated was then fed over a local Internet connection into a Sun SPARC ELC located in the computer room that was running the WebVideo server software. Audio for the web was encoded on a slow Pentium PC (75 MHz) using RealEncoder from Progressive Networks. This was then transmitted to the same Sun that also ran a RealAudio server. Three further PCs were in use, monitoring WebVideo quality, RealAudio quality and RealAudio server connections respectively.

CuSeeMe was run on a PC to encode both the video and audio transmission. The PC was equipped with a Creative Labs SoundBlaster audio card and a Creative Labs VideoBlaster SE100 video capture card. CuSeeMe requires the use of a "reflector" to which all participants connect. The reflector was run on a Sun Sparc SS10 workstation located in the computer room. Two further PCs were used to monitor the quality of the CuSeeMe transmissions and connections to the reflector respectively. In effect, this was a "secondary" route for CuSeeMe, as the main source was directly from the venue from a PC to the primary CuSeeMe reflector housed at the

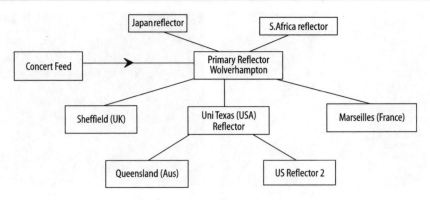

Figure 10.3 Logical reflector configuration.

University of Wolverhampton. Figure 10.3 shows the "logical design" of the reflector access for Internet users of the Celtica CuSeeMe netcast.

The maximum transmission speed was kept below 80 kbps between the CuSeeMe reflectors. This gave a variable frame rate for the video portion of the transmission of up to about 10 fps at the best of times, although it was usually lower. Sound seemed adequate if a little choppy via CuSeeMe. Pictures were in monochrome, since the primary reflector software was not a version that handles color.

A number of organizational problems occurred during the run-up to the event – these are often trivial but occasionally difficult to circumvent. Some of these are listed below:

- There have also been numerous upgrades to the CuSeeMe client and reflector software available from Cornell University [11], and not all the same versions were running; there were therefore some initial minor compatibility problems.
- There is also a commercial version of CuSeeMe available that was used by some users, causing some compatibility difficulties.
- Tying reflectors together for testing is not practical for long periods, as the individual reflector's users experience some change to their expected outcomes, i.e. users can appear in conferences that are attached to other reflectors in the chains.
- Organizational problems were the main headache – setting up the reflector chains needed numerous emails to be sent between the various reflector managers with clear instructions/requests for reflector tie-ups.
- Every change in the reflector setup requires the software to be restarted. This multiplies problems when changes need propagating down the chain.

A further PC at the venue, and several associates around the world, provided monitoring of CuSeeMe relay quality – generally the response was very good, with people being impressed with what was achieved with the technology utilized and in the context of the practical constraints. However, at one point in the proceedings the audio aspect of the CuSeeMe test transmission became very weak and extremely "choppy", so a contingency was applied, namely to send another stream of RealAudio out directly from the venue (using the "monitoring" PC), which CuSeeMe users could connect to in addition to the CuSeeMe video stream (and hence video-only sent via CuSeeMe). Messages were placed on the CuSeeMe chatboards accordingly.

10.5 Netcast Quality and Audience Reaction

An analysis of the Web logs recorded at Aberystwyth shows that there were a total of 138 accesses from 86 different sites to the Web-provided material from Celtica during the time of the transmission and the few weeks following the event. This can be regarded as either access to the RealAudio and/or WebVideo transmission. The notices and comments placed on the MBone whiteboard were very positive and indicated that there were approximately 30 people "viewing" the netcast worldwide (in addition to the 20 or so students enjoying the concert in Computer Labs at the University in Aberystwyth). A record of the CuSeeMe connections is more difficult to quantify, but 26 people applied for pre-registration on the various reflectors "advertised" on the event Web site, many more casually connecting to the netcast while casually surfing reflectors.

Our only real quality problems directly attributable to software tools came from our use of CUSeeMe. We have never had real success with this product, although to be fair, new versions have appeared since the time of the concert and in particular a "commercialized" version is now available from WhitePine. Our experience is mainly based on what now should be regarded as "early" and free "beta" versions of both the application and reflector acquired directly from Cornell.

The other tools worked well. We had an audience from around the globe. This included connections from Cisco Systems locations in the USA, some sites in Korea and a gentleman from just south of the Arctic Circle in northern Sweden. We received a large amount of positive feedback, the Arctic Circle gentleman being quite enthused not only with the quality but with the simple circumstance that enabled him to attend a concert being transmitted from the wilds of Rural Wales.

Figure 10.4 shows a screenshot, again taken from the VHS tape recording at Aberystwyth, of the musicians immediately after the concert – listening and responding to feedback from different parts of the world.

10.6 Conclusions

This event provided an excellent opportunity for the research teams to explore the technology utilized and gain experience of how a multi-platform and multi-format configuration of netcasting could be implemented successfully – even in the case of a live concert from a remote rural area.

The number of connections around the world, and the positive reactions gained, were very encouraging – especially bearing in mind the very modest marketing effort and that it was a concert performed by a band that at the time was relatively unknown.

Figure 10.4 A screen shot from the VHS tape recording at Aberystwyth.

Research in this area by the two teams continues, including the hosting of subsequent live and recorded netcasts. Experimentation with various formats and networking configurations, and the addressing of issues which specifically relate to designing the netcast implementation to cater for the needs of artists/performers and of Internet audiences remain as important features of the research program.

References

[1]   M Bogen, C Bokowski, R Rodrigues-Val *et al.* (1997) Desktop video: building large-scale services with incompatible products, in *Proc. 8th JENC (Joint European Networking Conference)*, Edinburgh, Scotland, 12–15 May, pp. 922-1/922-9.

[2]   G Sidler, A Scott and H Wolf (1997) Collaborative browsing in the World-wide Web, in *Proc. 8th JENC (Joint European Networking Conference)*, Edinburgh, Scotland, 12–15 May, pp. 122-1/122-8.

[3]   SN Bhatti and G Knight (1997) Issues in residential broadband Internet service provision, in *Proc. 8th JENC (Joint European Networking Conference)*, Edinburgh, Scotland, 12–15 May, pp. 132-1/132-10.

[4]   NF Maxemchuk (1997) Video distribution on multicast networks, *IEEE Journal on Selected Areas in Communications*, 15(3).

[5]   DR Lawrence and I Amado (1998) Live Broadcasting of an international multimedia art installation around the Internet, in *Proc. 7th IFIP ICCC Conference on Information Networks and Data Communications*, Portugal, June.

[6]   HW Agius and MC Angelides (1997) Desktop video conferencing in the organization, *Information & Management*, 31(6), 291–302.

[7]   A Sloane (1998) Infrastructure issues for Internet broadcasting to home-based users, *HCC-5, Fifth World Conference on Human Choice and Computers*, Geneva, August.

[8]   U Horn and B Girod (1997) Scalable video transmission for the Internet, in *Proc. 8th JENC (Joint European Networking Conference)*, Edinburgh, Scotland, 12–15 May, pp. 921-1/921-8.

[9]   OECD Conference: http://www.turku.eu.net/eunet.html.

[10] EC Telematics conference: http://www.aber.ac.uk/~dap/tap_barcelona.html.

[11] Cornell University CuSeeMe page: http://cu-seeme.cornell.edu/.

[12] RealAudio site: http://www.real.com/.

[13] MBone tools: http://www-nrg.ee.lbl.gov/.

[14] University of Ulm: http://rr-vs.informatik.uni-ulm.de/rr/.

[15] University of Ulm: http://www-vs.informatik.uni-ulm.de/soft/wv/.

[16] BT Research Labs, UK: http://www.labs.bt.com/.

About the Authors

Dr Dave Lawrence is a senior lecturer in the School of Computing and IT at the University of Wolverhampton, UK. He is also a member of the CoNTACT research group at the University, with a special interest in communications/networking issues regarding the live netcasting of creative and performing arts. Dave worked for a number of years in industry before moving into academia, and has published widely in the areas of "business user IS development" and Internet broadcasting/conferencing – both in academic journals and at international conferences.

David Price is currently the technical director of the Telematics Group located within the Department of Computer Science, University of Wales, Aberystwyth. Most of David's work in the last few years has been associated with new uses of the Internet, especially its use to support telepresence style applications. David is also working actively on the use of telematics to improve the business and lifestyle of rural areas. Our involvement in projects that use the Internet to bring rural arts to a global audience is an important part of our activities.

Dr Andy Sloane is currently coordinator of the CoNTACT research group in the School of Computing and IT at the University of Wolverhampton and is extensively involved in research into many different aspects of communication. He is also the author of two widely used textbooks in computer and multimedia communication, and of more than 30 academic papers. These cover areas as diverse as the use of EDI in small businesses to the infrastructure issues for Internet-based education.

11

Jogging the Memory: Dynamic Visualization Over the Web

Jeremy Walton

Abstract

The use of visualization as a technique for understanding and explaining numerical data is well established, and today's user can choose between a number of popular visualization packages. Following the
rise in popularity of the World Wide Web (WWW), traditional explanatory uses of visualization have
been complemented by *Web publication*. Here, the ability to publish 3D scenes using the Virtual Reality
Modeling Language (VRML) has led to an increase in shared understanding of visualizations of complex
datasets.

The recent standardization of VRML 97 allows the possibility of visualizing dynamically changing
datasets on the Web. In this chapter we present a number of examples of this type of visualization and
indicate their superiority over more traditional methods based on publication in a static medium. We
also give an account of some of the shortcomings that we presently perceive in VRML 97, and indicate
ways in which the language could usefully (from a visualization perspective) evolve in the future.

11.1 Introduction

The World Wide Web (WWW) has had an enormous impact on the way in which
information can be shared between disparate locations. Originally used exclusively
for the transfer of traditional media such as text and images, these data types have
been supplemented for some time by three-dimensional geometry, thanks to the
definition of a language for describing 3D scenes on the WWW. The Virtual Reality
Modeling Language (VRML) [1, 2] is a standard for the interchange of 3D data and
can be used to publish 3D Web pages – that is, pages containing information that is
best experienced in three dimensions. Examples of this include games, architecture, some educational experiences, and scientific and engineering visualizations.
In this chapter we describe some of the features of VRML and present a few examples of its use in the construction and sharing of these types of information. In
particular, we discuss several scientific visualizations that have been created in
VRML, paying attention to those that make use of the new features of the latest

version of the language. Some of these scenes have been developed at NAG, but there are others which come from elsewhere on the Web.

The chapter is arranged as follows. We give a brief survey of the origins of VRML in the following section, and describe its relationship to the Open Inventor [3] graphics library. We then (Section 11.3) present two contrasting examples of the way in which VRML has been used as a delivery mechanism for sharing visualizations on the WWW. The first of these, an *interactive polyhedron generator*, is a useful educational tool for the description of a complicated (but beautiful) branch of mathematics. The second example – more rooted in the "real" world – is an *airline planning system*. Here, several datatypes are displayed in the same space to produce a visualization of airline routes, which is then shared with remote sites (actually, the control towers of interested airports) via VRML. Section 11.4 contains a description of the new functionality that the latest version of VRML offers over the original language, followed by a number of examples of its use. Some of these have been constructed using IRIS Explorer [4, 5], a data visualization toolkit based on Open Inventor. Finally, in Section 11.5, we attempt to assess VRML as a language for scientific visualization. We discuss the parts that we have found to be useful and the parts that have received less attention, and outline ways in which it could be further enhanced in the future.

11.2 VRML – A 3D Language for 3D Visualization

11.2.1 Creating and Sharing Visualization on the Web

The generation of 3D visualizations of scientific data is a comparatively mature field, and today's user can choose between a variety of public domain and commercial packages. Examples of popular general-purpose visualization systems include IRIS Explorer [4, 5], AVS [6], Data Explorer [7] and Khoros [8].

Classically, visualization is used (a) to understand or *explore* data and then (b) to *publish* the result in order to communicate this understanding to others. Following the rise in popularity of the WWW, traditional forms of publishing such as print and video have been complemented by *Web publication* [9]. The relative merits of the traditional media vs. the Web are still under discussion, but one advantage that the Web has is the possibility of publishing and sharing data in new forms. To see this, consider for example a visualization of a complex 3D object such as an oil reservoir model consisting of an assembly of colored hexahedra.

Traditionally, the publisher has the option of choosing a fixed view of the object (by specifying the position and orientation of the camera in 3D space) and saving it as an *image*. Alternatively, if there are several views that are significant they may be specified by choosing a path for the camera to take as it moves around the object; the views are then saved as a *movie*.

Both of these forms of presentation offer only a limited number of views of the object, which – if the object is complicated – may be over-restrictive for other users. They may wish to share in the understanding of the object or explore it in ways or

Table 11.1. Some file sizes for the reservoir model, published on the Web in a variety of forms. The resolution gives the screen size (in pixels) of the image and the movie, and the duration (in frames) of the movie. Clearly this is not applicable to the 3D model, since its view in the browser can be any size desired by the user.

Type	Format	Resolution	Size (bytes)
Image	JPEG	750 × 614	62347
Movie	SGI compressed	209 × 201 × 49	51089
3D	VRML ASCII	n/a	70647
3D	VRML gzipped	n/a	29203

from positions that had not occurred to the original publisher. This leads us to consider the possibility of sharing not *views*, but a copy of the *object itself*. Here, the user can select any view of the scene, and interact with it in the same way as the publisher. Moreover, if individual views (i.e. camera locations and orientations) can be stored along with the scene, the publisher still has the ability to draw the user's attention to specific features of interest. Finally, it should be noted that the sharing of views as images or movies can take up more space on disk (and download time) than the sharing of the object, as Table 11.1 illustrates for the reservoir model. Clearly, the quantitative aspects of this comparison are model-dependent, since its complexity determines the size of the 3D file, whereas the size of the image or movie file is related to its resolution in screen space. However, we have found in practice that the trend illustrated in Table 11.1 has held for a wide range of visualizations that we have developed and used elsewhere.

11.2.2 Open Inventor and VRML 1.0

We have seen the advantages of interactivity that 3D publishing offers, although we have not yet discussed the character of the file format used to do this. The field of 3D geometry creation and storage is somewhat immature, and until comparatively recently 3D formats were usually tied to a particular CAD application. Similarly, those scientific visualization packages that allowed users to save their results as geometry (not all did) would often use a proprietary – often undocumented – format.

This situation changed with the advent of Open Inventor [3], an object-oriented 3D graphics library that defines a simple file format for the description of 3D scenes. An Open Inventor application creates and manipulates 3D scenes in a database known as a *scene graph* made up of *nodes*. Various classes of nodes implement geometry elements (primitive shapes, surfaces, text etc.) and properties (color, lighting, texturing, transformation etc.), as well as other behaviors. The ordering of the nodes in the scene graph and their relationship to one another defines the 3D scene.

Having created the scene graph in the application, *actions* can be applied to it. These include rendering the scene (Open Inventor uses the well-known OpenGL 3D graphics library [10] for rendering), calculating the scene's dimensions as a bounding box, or writing the scene to a file. The file format used by Open Inventor is rather intuitive, and relates directly to the structure of the scene graph. The simplicity of the format, and the ease of use of the write action, led to its adoption as a *de facto standard* for 3D geometry files. Thus, a number of translators between Open Inventor and other formats (such as Autodesk's DXF and the IGES format) have been developed, and it is straightforward to pass 3D data between one Inventor-based application – such as IRIS Explorer – and another. Indeed, in many cases, this can be performed using the *cut and paste* mechanism that has become ubiquitous for the transfer of more conventional data such as text.

The establishment of the Inventor file format as a *de facto* standard led to its adoption as the basis of the first version of VRML in 1994 [11]. The use of an already extant language has a number of advantages, including the possibility of leveraging existing Open Inventor data and applications in order to generate new VRML content. For example, Figure 11.1 shows the generation of VRML from an application running inside IRIS Explorer.

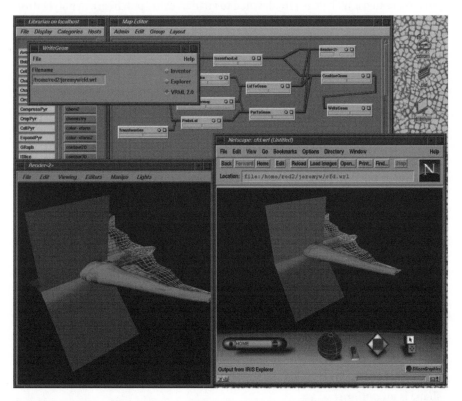

Figure 11.1 Outputting an IRIS Explorer scene as VRML 97. The IRIS Explorer application consists of a collection of *modules* connected together, and can be seen in the middle at the top of the figure. The window of the Render module at bottom left contains the visualization, which consists of a variety of geometry. In the application, these are passed to a module which outputs them as a VRML 97 file. The file is then viewed using a suitable browser (here the Cosmo Player plug-in for Netscape Navigator) in the bottom right-hand corner. Clearly, although both displays are on the same machine here, in general, the VRML could be viewed anywhere on the Web.

Following the definition of VRML 1.0, a number of browsers and authoring tools quickly appeared, and the language was enthusiastically adopted on the Web. In the following section we present some 3D applications which have been built around VRML and which highlight some of the possibilities that 3D on the Web offers in the visualization arena. Our selection of VRML scenes here complements that made in an earlier paper [12], where we discussed the Visualization Web server [13], mining a molecular database [14] and visualization benchmarking [15].

11.3 VRML as Enabling Technology – Some Examples

11.3.1 A Polyhedron Generator

Hart has created a Web page [16] devoted to virtual reality polyhedra (a polyhedron is a three-dimensional solid whose faces are polygons). The page consists of more than 1000 examples of polyhedra, sorted according to a classification scheme and their relationship to each other. Although the first entries are the familiar Platonic solids (tetrahedron, cube, octahedron, dodecahedron and icosahedron) which can be easily visualized by many people, they rapidly become more complex. This adjective applies to both their appearance, and their names (e.g. parabidiminished rhombicosidodecahedron).

Hart's page presents an excellent example of a novel way of publishing this information. Classically, a polyhedron would have been described using static diagrams on the printed page; but most of the examples presented here are clearly too complicated for this to be an effective medium. (For example, see Figure 11.2, which is a snapshot of the display of an antiprism together with its dual.) The other traditional means of presentation is as paper models. Hart argues that while the best way to understand a polyhedron is to build a model, the next best way is to play with somebody else's model – such as the ones that are assembled (as VRML files) on his page. These actually have at least one advantage over traditional paper models in that the user can fly inside them to gain perspectives that are not possible in a paper model.

Besides containing a list of polyhedra, the page also contains interactive applications such as the prism maker (see Figure 11.2). Here, the user can specify a number of options, including:

- the polygon which forms the top and bottom of the shape
- whether one of the polygons is given a twist relative to the other (in which case the shape is an *antiprism*)
- whether the *dual* of the shape (whose vertices and faces correspond to the original shape's faces and vertices) is created

The prism maker is implemented as a JavaScript application that generates VRML on the fly. The source of the VRML file is also available from the Web page.

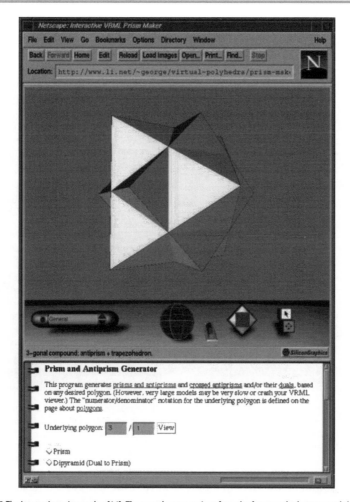

Figure 11.2 The interactive prism maker [16]. The user chooses options from the frame at the bottom, and the generated polyhedron appears in the frame at the top (this example is using the Cosmo Player VRML browser as a plug-in to Netscape Navigator). This polygon is a compound of a trigonal antiprism (i.e. a tetrahedron) and its dual trapezohedron (i.e. a cube). The "top" face of the antiprism is colored yellow, while its sides are red (in this case, all its faces are equilateral triangles) and the dual is colored blue.

11.3.2 An Airline Route Planning System

Chiba *et al.* at the IRIS Explorer Center, Japan, have developed a visualization system for Japan Airlines to enable them to display routing information in a more intuitive fashion [17]. The system (see Figure 11.3) takes physical data such as wind and tropopause information and overlays it on a terrain map, and then overlays other data such as airport locations and details of air traffic control zones. The dataset is multi-sourced, three-dimensional and time-dependent – all of which make 3D visualization essential for its understanding. The system – which in this case is built around IRIS Explorer – assembles the visualization and exports it as

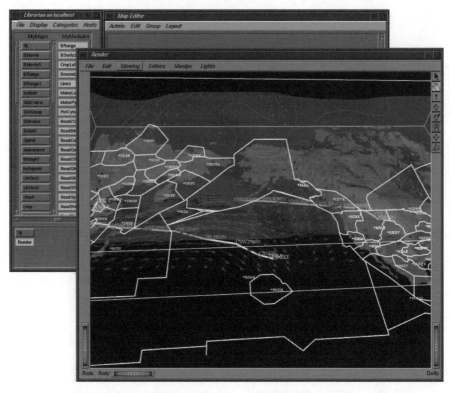

Figure 11.3 The airline route planning system in IRIS Explorer [17]. Tropopause data is rendered as contours and semi-transparent surfaces; wind data is displayed as vectors. This is overlaid on terrain data and air traffic control information. Finally, the flight path information (including location labels) is added. The whole scene is then output as VRML (see Figure 11.1) and published on the Web.

VRML for download by users in airport control towers who require access to the routing information. Here, VRML is being used as a delivery mechanism for the visualization of the complex 3D dataset. This gives the users the freedom to roam throughout the display and make the necessary decisions based on the information portrayed.

11.4   Worlds That Move – VRML 97

Although VRML 1.0 is fundamentally a 3D scene description language, it was considered by many of its adherents to be but the minimal starting point for the implementation of a much larger vision. This is the use of a collection of *inter-linked, dynamic, multi-user* 3D worlds as a means to organize information space and navigate through it.

In this section, then, we discuss some of the drawbacks of VRML 1.0 with reference to both this vision and, more prosaically, its use as a language for scientific visual-ization. We then show how these limitations and other considerations led to the definition of the second version of the language. Following a brief description of some of its features, we finish by presenting a few example worlds written in this language.

11.4.1 What Was Wrong with VRML 1.0?

One of the defining characteristics of VRML 1.0 was its *simplicity*. While this proved crucial for its widespread adoption, it led to some limitations in the types of worlds that it could describe. Apart from the lack of dynamics and multi-user support mentioned above, it had no support for curved surfaces (e.g. NURBS). A number of visualization techniques have a requirement for these – for example, ribbons are used in the display of particle traces through vector fields, and also in the display of high-order structure in large molecules such as a protein. VRML 1.0 scenes were required to mimic such structures by using trianglular strips, which is a much less compact representation than the implicit parameterization of the surface.

Another problem with VRML 1.0 was its poor support for prototyping new nodes, which is important for certain domain-specific scenes. For example, the visualization of a molecule as a set of spheres (atoms) and cylinders (bonds) is not handled efficiently in vanilla VRML, where each element (sphere or cylinder) has to be represented explicitly [18]. This is because the file format stores and manages a collection of similar pieces of geometry in a very general fashion. Some way of grouping these pieces together into (say) a set of spheres is required. The sphere set could be stored in a more compact form in the file, and knowledge about its contents could be used to minimize the overhead associated with such actions as rendering.

11.4.2 What's new in VRML 2.0?

In contrast to the simplicity of VRML 1.0, VRML 2.0 [1, 2] is a much larger and richer language. It is not a superset of the earlier language, although translators exist to upgrade from 1.0 to 2.0, and most VRML 2.0 browsers automatically invoke these when passed a scene in the older format.

The chief design objective for 2.0 was the introduction of *behavior*. Behavior and logic are incorporated into the world via the use of script nodes that contain a reference to a piece of code written in a programming language such as Java or JavaScript.

The way in which these extant languages are used within VRML deserves attention. One of the considerations in the design of VRML 2.0 was whether it would be best to add animation and interaction capabilities by rewriting it as a fully fledged programming language. This was not adopted, for the following reason [2]. Programming languages are very powerful, but they make poor file interchange formats. Thus, for example, PostScript and HTML are both used to define 2D documents and both could be used as file formats, but HTML is far more common, even though it was introduced long after PostScript and is much less powerful. One of the reasons HTML is so successful as a file interchange format is the wide variety of HTML editors that can read, modify and write any HTML file. By contrast, because PostScript is a programming language it is almost impossible to do the same for PostScript files.

The other main new features in VRML 2.0 were *animation* and *interaction*. Animation can be added to scenes using a TimeSensor node and *interpolators*. A TimeSensor provides a "stopwatch" in the scene, with user control over the starting time, duration and cycling behavior. An interpolator can be used to change the value of elements of the scene such as positions, orientations, coordinates, normals, scalars or colors. Connecting a timer to an interpolator produces dynamic variation in the element; we present some examples in Section 11.4.3.

Interaction with objects in VRML 2.0 is handled using *sensors*, which trigger events (based on options such as collision, proximity, touch or viewpoint) when an object is selected in the browser. The language also saw the addition of new geometry nodes, such as Extrusion, which can be used to define curved surfaces. Finally, the language also incorporates the ability to prototype new nodes via a mechanism that is more extensive than the offering in VRML 1.0.

The specification of VRML 2.0 was completed by the VRML community in August 1996, after which it was submitted to the International Organization for Standardization for ratification. Following minor technical revisions, this process was completed in December 1997, and the current version of VRML is known as ISO/IEC 14772, or (informally) as VRML 97 [19].

Because of the relative newness of the language (and possibly because it is more complicated) there appear to be fewer VRML 97 resources on the Web currently, although more are under development. For example, browsers such as SGI's Cosmo Player [20] and Intervista's WorldView [21] are available on the Web, together with Newfire's Torch [22], which is a VRML-based games engine which incorporates some browser functionality.

11.4.3 Jogging the memory – VRML 97 and visualization

In this section we present some examples of scientific visualizations which have been created in VRML 97 and indicate ways in which the introduction of behavior, animation and interaction have expanded the range of information that can be presented. First, we briefly describe three simple examples that have been produced by IRIS Explorer and converted to VRML 97. Extra features, such as interpolators, were then added by hand. Note that these scenes are all available for viewing on the Web.

- *Particle tracing* [23]. Here the output from a particle tracer is animated through the interpolation of *position*. A sphere travels along the trace; its speed is proportional to the local velocity of the underlying vector field. The input to the interpolator is the set of points on the trace.

- *Heat diffusion* [24]. The visualization of heat flux in a flat plate is animated through the interpolation of *coordinates* and *color*. The local temperature on the plate is mapped to displacement of the surface, and this changes dynamically. The inputs to the interpolators are the coordinates of the plate from three time steps, plus a colormap.
- *Isosurface morphing* [25]. One colored isosurface (for some threshold value) morphs into another (for a higher threshold value) which surrounds the first. The input to the interpolator is the transparency of the second isosurface.

Next, we discuss two example worlds from the Web. We reiterate our comment above regarding the comparative paucity of VRML 97 resources on the Web, but note that these two present excellent examples of the possibilities of the use of VRML 97 for scientific visualization.

Brickmann *et al.* [26] have used VRML 97 to present the normal modes of *molecular vibration* for an example molecule. Molecules, like other rigid structures, can vibrate in distinct *modes* that are related to the stretching, bending and twisting of bonds. Each mode has an associated energy, and this can be used to characterize the molecule in terms of its infrared adsorption spectrum. Since the molecule can be a complex 3D structure, the presentation of the distinct modes via static 2D media (such as paper) can be challenging. The presentation as a dynamic 3D scene is much more insightful, since each mode can be stored in a VRML 97 file, with the mode encoded as a set of interpolations of coordinates and orientations. Again, delivery via VRML has advantages over its delivery as an animation, since the molecule can be rotated and zoomed by the user while it is vibrating. Finally, the periodic nature of the vibrational motion can be easily reproduced by making the TimeSensor node repeat its cycle.

The molecular vibration page [26] is shown in Figure 11.4. The user selects an energy from the upper pane, which is displaying the adsorption spectrum, and the corresponding mode appears in the lower pane. The interplay between the two panes leads to a rapid understanding of the different modes of vibration and their corresponding energies.

Casher has constructed a dynamic visualization of the SN2 *reaction mechanism* [27]. This mechanism is exhibited by, for example, the following reaction

$$Cl^- + CH_3Br \rightarrow CH_3Cl + Br^-$$

which proceeds via a transition state whose formula is $(ClCH_3Br)^{\ddagger}$. In this reaction, the chloride ion is substituted for the bromine in methyl bromide, producing methyl chloride and a bromide ion. The mechanism (that is, the way in which the atoms in the molecules are rearranged in the course of the reaction) is, again, a complicated dynamic process in three dimensions. This can only be represented on the printed page with some difficulty (although reaction mechanisms are an important part of chemistry, and there is an extensive literature devoted to them). However, as Casher's scene illustrates (Figure 11.5), the presentation of the mechanism as a dynamic 3D scene is much more illuminating. It provides an excellent example of way in which VRML 97 can be used to add value to static scenes in the display and analysis of scientific data.

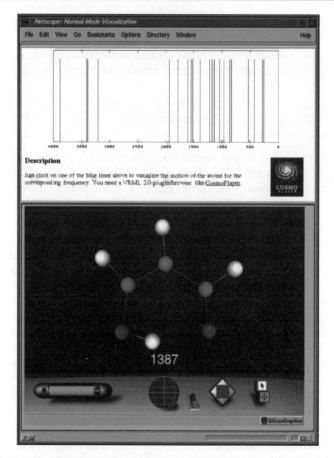

Figure 11.4 The Normal Mode Visualization page of Brickmann *et al.* [26]. The upper pane displays the vibrational spectrum of the molecule; clicking on a frequency downloads a dynamic 3D model illustrating the corresponding mode of vibration into the lower pane.

11.5 Conclusions and Further Work

In this chapter we have discussed the use of VRML as a tool in scientific visualization, paying attention to the use of some of the enhancements in the latest version of the language. However, we have not yet made use of or illustrated many of its other new features. In this final section, then, we shall briefly discuss ways in which these could be employed, before going on to describe areas in which we perceive the language could be further improved for the benefit of the scientific visualization community.

11.5.1 VRML 97 – What Else is There?

All of the dynamics that have been incorporated into our example worlds have used interpolators. These work well for simple changes to parts of the scene, but cannot

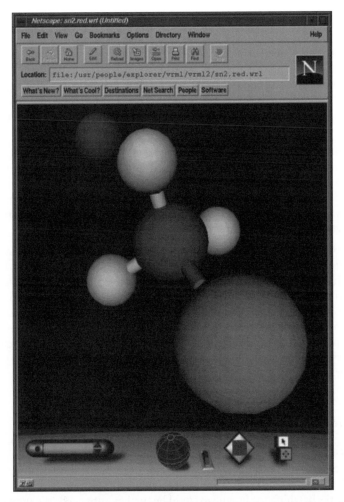

Figure 11.5 The reaction mechanism visualization of Casher [27]. The tetrahedral molecule at bottom right is methyl bromide (the large atom is bromine) while the chloride ion is at top left. This shows the manner in which the chloride ion approaches the molecule (avoiding the bromine) at the start of the substitution reaction. In the VRML scene, clicking on the molecule starts the animation of the reaction.

be used for behavior that is more complex, such as the dynamic loading of a series of scenes that represent time steps from a simulation. Such behavior could perhaps be incorporated into the scene via scripting, although this would depend on the details of the scripting language supported by the browser – for example, Java is more flexible than JavaScript, but has a longer startup time.

Another possibility would be to incorporate behavior into the scene as *visualization nodes*, which would be encoded in the scripting language. Thus it might be possible to incorporate (say) a node that generates an isosurface through a 3D scalar data set. The viewer of the scene would be able to select a threshold value and have the isosurface recalculated in the scene. This client-side calculation is to be contrasted with the server-oriented approach of Wood *et al.* [13], which is built around a CGI script that passes instructions to the server about the visualization to be created. The visualization is downloaded, as a static 3D scene, to the client machine. Each change to the visualization (e.g. a new value for an isosurface threshold) requires a round trip to the server. Downloading the scene together with instructions for modifying it (in the form of scripting nodes that would be invoked locally on the client) might lead to a more efficient use of local and network resources.

Other enhancements in VRML 97 include the new graphics nodes, such as Extrusion. As mentioned above, this is used to create curved surfaces such as ribbons and tubes that find extensive use in vector field visualization and the display of molecules. Depth-cueing can now be added to a VRML scene using the Fog node. As is well known, this can be helpful in providing an enhanced sense of 3D structure to scenes, especially when they are rendered in wireframe.

The improvements in the mechanism for prototyping and sharing new nodes could be exploited immediately. The ability to do this is important for (at least) two reasons. In the first place, it allows for more efficient organization of scenes (as illustrated by our SphereSet example above). Secondly, it suggests the possibility of reuse of other work. For example, consider the creation of a user-defined Axis node, whose characteristics are defined in terms of a small set of parameters (e.g. starting and finishing values, number of divisions and labels). Publishing this node on the Web would allow it to be incorporated into other scenes (possibly created by other users) with minimum effort.

11.5.2 VRML – What Else is Needed?

VRML 97 represents a significant increase in functionality over the earlier version of the language and presents a wider range of options for the scientific visualizer (some of which have been discussed in this paper). However, it is still possible to imagine ways in which the language could be further enhanced. We note that these suggestions – many of which arise naturally from consideration of useful features in existing visualization applications – are domain-specific, although some may turn out to be requirements for other application areas as well. The main thrust of current developments for the next version of VRML is apparently the support of multiple users – this would no doubt have a big impact on those parts of scientific visualization that have a requirement for collaborative work.

Some of our suggestions appear to be comparatively simple to implement. For example, lines and points are currently restricted to be just one pixel wide. This causes aliasing (or invisibility) in images when VRML scenes are printed, and flicker in videos when they are saved as animations. The only way to get "fat" lines and points at the moment is to use polygons (cylinders and spheres, say), which is wasteful and slows down the rendering of the scene. It would be useful to be able to specify a line or point thickness in the language.

Other enhancements would probably require a good deal of work on the part of the language developers and the browser builders. Thus, for example, it is well known that *annotation* is an indispensable part of visualization. Typical elements of this kind include titles, keys, menus and color bars, all of which should be easily visible in the scene. Some of the new features in VRML 97 are useful here. Thus, the new Billboard node implements a label that is always turned to face the viewer (see, for example, the way it is used to display the frequency of vibration in the scene shown in Figure 11.4). The prototyped HUD (head-up display) node inverts the camera rotation matrix to apparently fix an object in a position in 3D space which is unaffected by camera motion. This can be used to position annotation elements so that they apparently remain fixed in "screen space." However, this is somewhat unsatisfactory, since the matrix inversion is rather cumbersome, and – perhaps more importantly – the location of the elements (and their visibility) is dependent on the dimensions of the browser window. It would be better if there was some way to specify screen space locations explicitly. In other visualization systems, this is implemented by allowing for multiple cameras in the scene – one in each space. We note in passing that such an enhancement would be of use to other areas that make use of VRML (many of which – such as games – are more popular and receive more attention than scientific visualization). For example, locating elements of the scene in screen space would allow for the incorporation of items such as dashboard controls that indicate speed or location in the world.

The language could be extended in still further ways. One of the most useful features of Open Inventor is the way in which new nodes can be defined along with methods for displaying and outputting them. Such a mechanism has been used in the past to create new visualization nodes (such as textured smoke for flow volumes [28]) which can then be incorporated into Inventor-based applications such as IRIS Explorer. If this could be incorporated into VRML, it might lead to still greater use of this important technology for distributing and sharing 3D on the Web.

References

[1] J Hartman and J Wernecke (1996) *The VRML 2.0 Handbook: Building Moving Worlds on the Web*, Addison-Wesley, Reading MA.

[2] R Carey and G Bell (1997) *The Annotated VRML 2.0 Reference Manual*, Addison-Wesley, Reading MA, http://www.wasabisoft.com/Book/book.shtml.

[3] J Wernecke (1994) *The Inventor Mentor. Programming Object-Oriented Graphics with Open Inventor, Release 2*, Addison-Wesley, Reading MA.

[4] D Foulser (1995) *IRIS Explorer: a framework for investigation, Computer Graphics*, 29(2), 13.

[5] J Walton (1998) *Data Visualization using IRIS Explorer – An Introduction*, http://www.nag.co.uk/visual/ie/talk/stanford.980129/paper/hepvis.html

[6] C Upson T Faulhaber Jr, D Kamins *et al.* (1989) The application visualization system: a computational environment for scientific visualization, *IEEE Computer Graphics and Applications*, 9, 30.

[7] B Lucas, GD Abram, NS Collins *et al.* (1992) An architecture for a scientific visualization system, in *Proc. Visualization '92*, IEEE Computer Society Press, p. 107.

[8] J Rasure and M Young (1992) An open environment for image processing software development, in *Proc. 1992 SPIE/IS&T Symposium on Electronic Imaging*, p. 1659.

[9] I Ritchie (1997) Commercial publishing on the Internet – the birth of the post-Gutenberg society, in *The Internet in 3D: Information, Images and Interaction* (eds. RA Earnshaw and JA Vince), Academic Press, London, p. 285.

[10] J Neider, T Davis and M Woo (1997) *OpenGL Programming Guide: The Official Guide to Learning OpenGL, version 1.1*, 2nd edn, Addison-Wesley, Reading MA.

[11] See the Web page at http://www.vrml.org/Specifications/VRML1.0.html.

[12] J Walton (1997) World processing: data sharing with VRML, in *The Internet in 3D: Information, Images and Interaction* (eds. RA Earnshaw and JA Vince), Academic Press, London, p. 237.

[13] JD Wood, KW Brodlie and H Wright (1996) Visualization over the World Wide Web and its application to environmental data, in *Proc. Visualization '96*, IEEE Computer Society Press, p. 81.

[14] O Casher, C Leach, CS Page *et al.* Advanced VRML-based chemistry applications: a 3D molecular hyperglossary, in *Proc. 2nd ECC Conference,* http://www.ch.ic.ac.uk/eccc2/.

[15] J Walton (1996) Visualization benchmarking: a practical application of 3D publishing, in *Proc. Eurographics UK 1996* (eds. H Jones, R Raby and D Vicars), Vol. 2, p. 339, http://www.nag.co.uk/doc/TechRep/PS/tr9_96.ps.

[16] See the Web page at http://www.li.net/~george/virtual-polyhedra/vp.html.

[17] H Chiba in *Render, The Newsletter for IRIS Explorer Users,* issue 7, http://www.nag.co.uk/visual/IE/iecbb/Render/Issue7/IECJ.html.

[18] O Casher and HS Rzepa (1996) The Molecular Object Toolkit: a new generation of VRML visualization tools for use in electronic journals, in *Proc. Eurographics UK 1996* (eds. H Jones, R Raby and D Vicars), Vol. 1, p. 173.

[19] See the Web page at http://www.vrml.org/Specifications/VRML97.html.

[20] See the Web page at http://cosmo.sgi.com/.

[21] See the Web page at http://www.intervista.com/.

[22] See the Web page at http://www.newfire.com/.

[23] See the scene at http://www.nag.co.uk/visual/IE/iecbb/VRML2/cent4.wrl.

[24] See the scene at http://www.nag.co.uk/visual/IE/iecbb/VRML2/surfs.wrl.

[25] See the scene at http://www.nag.co.uk/visual/IE/iecbb/VRML2/isos.wrl.

[26] See the Web page at http://ws05.pc.chemie.th-darmstadt.de/vrml/vib/.

[27] See the Web page at http://chemcomm.clic.ac.uk/rxnpath/.

[28] BG Becker, DA Lane and NL Max (1995) Flow volumes for interactive vector field visualization, in *Proc. Visualization '95*, IEEE Computer Society Press, p. 19.

About the Author

Dr Jeremy Walton is leader of the Visualization Group at NAG Ltd in Oxford, UK. The main activity of his group is the development, support and porting of IRIS Explorer (a visualization toolkit), but they also work extensively with graphics libraries such as Open Inventor and OpenGL. His activities include module development, consultancy, training and user support. Before joining NAG in 1993, he performed research in data visualization and molecular modeling at BP Research. A 1980 graduate of Imperial College with a BSc (1st class Hons.) in Chemistry, he received a DPhil in Physical Chemistry from the University of Oxford in 1980.

12

"Thin" vs. "Fat" Visualization Clients

Mikael Jern

Abstract

A thin client, by definition, has the minimal software requirements necessary to function as a user interface front end for a Web-enabled application and raises the issue of client vs. server data visualization rendering. Real-time visual data manipulation does not translate well into a "thin" client. While the VRML file format allows distribution of visualization scenes to the Web, the user has no interactive control of the underlying raw data sources. The "mapping" of numerical data into geometry format (VRML) takes place on the server side.

Local data manipulation, information drill-down techniques, context-sensitive menus, object picking and other interactive user interface functions that have traditionally been available on the client are now controlled by the visualization server. In the "thin" client model, nearly all functionality is delivered from the server side of the visualization engine while the client perform very simple display and querying functions.

Web components and plug-ins are now being used to overcome some of these limitations. Java allows the creation of "applets" and "JavaBeans" and we have Windows/COM components. These components, together with data reduction methods, can significantly increase the data interaction between the client application and user and allow tasks to be executed on the client. Highly interactive user interface tasks are delivered that provide point-and-click navigation through multidimensional data structures. Visual data interfaces such as information drilling or moving a cutting plane through a volume data set can be supported.

This chapter explains and demonstrates the concepts of thin vs. Fat visualization clients with several examples. The implications of using a static VRML environment with reduced geometry are compared to sending compressed data to the client and performing interactive client data visualization on a desktop.

A detailed description for designing data visualization components based on the PC desktop standard ActiveX technology is also provided.

12.1 Introduction

The widespread popularity of Web technology has created several new interactive visualization models, such as HTTP/CGI, VRML, Java applets, ActiveX and Beans. The Web first started out as a giant URL-based file server for publishing electronic documents. The explosive growth of the Web has dramatically changed user expectations concerning the delivery of information to a client and has led to the acceptance of the three-tiers of the client–server database and/or simulation, the Web server and visualization, and the Web client.

The Common Gateway Interface (CGI) technique is used today to access most server environments. The universal Web browser, easy distribution of the application and centrally administered code solve many of the largest problems facing client–server computing and we can find amazing Web-based visualization applications. However, CGI is not perfect. HTTP with CGI is very slow and cumbersome, and represents a stateless protocol, which is not suitable for developing modern Web-based client–server applications based on object-oriented Java and ActiveX components. The main problem is that CGI-based Web applications require HTTP and the Web server to mediate between the applications running on the clients and the server. There is no way for a client object to directly invoke a server object.

The Web introduced a new user interaction model in which the client GUI, based on HTML, is less functional and relies upon the data or application servers for visualization traditionally executed on the client. The HTML user interface form submitted from the client is still the basic unit of any client–server interaction but is not suitable for highly interactive visualization with data stored in a data warehouse on the server side. This chapter will discuss the concept and benefits of "thin" vs. "fat" visualization clients.

Just as HTML, GIF and PNG allow text and 2D images to be browsed on the Web, the Virtual Reality Modeling Language (VRML) provides the same function for 3D graphics. VRML is seen as an abstract functional specification of virtual worlds providing a universal file format and Internet standard for 3D, going for a solution that can be scaled up or down to fit different implementation capabilities. VRML allows users to view and navigate though 3D data worlds and hyperlink to new worlds. VRML 97, based on the VRML 2 specification has now become a formal ISO standard. There are several VRML 2 plug-ins available such as Netscape's Live3D, SGI's Cosmo Player and Microsoft's Internet Explorer.

Java was the first step towards creating the Object Web. Java is now being used to overcome some of the limitations with HTTP/CGI. Java, a platform-independent language, allows the creation of client-side applets which are automatically downloaded from the server and executed on the client. Java applets can significantly increase the visual data interaction between the client application and user and allow tasks to be executed on the client. Java applets are interpreted on the client by the Java Virtual Machine, which is usually embedded in a Java-enabled browser such as Netscape's Navigator or Microsoft's Internet Explorer. Java applets must be downloaded every time they are used and performance depends on the available bandwidth.

In its earlier incarnations, object orientation was purely a programming discipline which delivered its benefits directly to programmers (code reuse through inheritance), but only indirectly to end-users. Unlike a C++ class library, which you must compile into a program, a component is a ready-to-run package of code. The first PC components were VBXs and OLE Controls (OCXs). The Netscape plug-ins work fine but are restricted to the Web browsers. We are now entering the world of ActiveX and JavaBeans components. These models are fast becoming the most popular way to package software. This chapter will introduce 3D desktop visualization components based on the ActiveX industry standard.

12.2 Thin Client

In the traditional Web-enabled world, the client is effectively reduced to a browser (viewer) of information supported by a server. A true Web client is not capable of program execution unless the executables are downloaded to the client as plug-ins, Java applets or ActiveX components. This client is normally referred to as the "thin" client. A thin client, by definition, has the minimal software requirements necessary to function as a user interface front end for a Web-enabled application.

Local data manipulation, information drill-down techniques, context-sensitive menus, object picking and other interactive user interface functions that have traditionally been available on the client are now controlled by the visualization server. In the "thin" client model, nearly all functionality is delivered from the server side of the visualization engine while the client performs very simple display and querying GUI functions based on HTML forms.

The most appealing aspect of the "thin" client to visualization users is that the overall cost of software and maintenance can be dramatically reduced. The "thin" client allows the application developers to eliminate the notion of software distribution at the client level (no license issue!) and also eliminates the notion of maintaining local software and supporting multiple operating systems on remote clients.

3D interactive graphics on the network requires a 3D interactive format and a navigation system that combines the 3D input and high-performance rendering capabilities. VRML is the industry standard for describing 3D virtual worlds networked via the global Internet and hyperlinked within the Web. VRML is an open platform-independent file format for 3D graphics developed by Silicon Graphics. By defining a new file format to represent 3D scenes, and by creating standalone "client" viewing programs for that file format, today's Web browsers can also handle 3D scenes on the PC platforms. VRML viewing is an example of a "thin" client scenario, providing "free" advanced 3D visualization to desktop users.

The interaction between the visualization server software and the client "Web browser" with a VRML viewer plug-in is described in Figure 12.1. The user interface is created with a standard HTML form. This form contains a number of fields to be set by the user which control not only the data to be visualized but also the visualization attributes. The user accesses the visualization server through this HTML page in a Web browser.

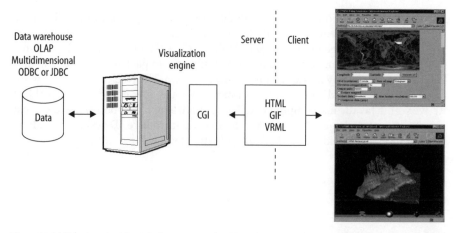

Figure 12.1 Schematic view of the Web client–server architecture showing a "thin" visualization scenario. A virtual VRML scenario is defined on the basis of a simulation or other analytical expressions are generated interactively with CGI scripts. The HTML user interface form permits the user to control the visualization method and its attributes dynamically.

On submission of the form a CGI script is executed on the server. The script contains the sophistication necessary to guide the visualization software in producing appropriately laid out graphics and the attribute information and data request specified in the form. This is then passed to the visualization engine (in this case AVS/Express), where it is used to set parameters. The requested data is accessed, the mapping instructions are executed and the geometry is created, which is finally converted into the standard VRML 97 file format. The VRML is transferred to the client and viewed by the favored VRML browser.

The effectiveness of VRML viewers for communicating information about 3D environments can be dramatically enhanced by attaching annotations and hyperlinks to the 3D scenes. Links in VRML work in precisely the same way as they do within HTML; thus pointing to an object with a link will first highlight the object using a "visual cue" and "descriptive text." By clicking on the selected object, more data attributes can be made visible, another VRML display created or a new application invoked. These hyperlinks can be used to develop "information drill-down" in a 3D space. The WWWAnchor node in VRML provides the framework to have links (interaction) to other worlds, animations, sound and documents.

While the VRML file format allows distribution of visualization scenes to the Web and links to other worlds, the user has no interactive control of the underlying raw data sources. The "mapping" of numerical data into geometry format (VRML) takes place on the server side. In the context of information visualization analysis it is clear that visualization tools need to be more than simply presentation vehicles. They need to be tightly integrated into the "*data navigation paradigm.*" The notions of "slice" and "drill-down" through data space need to be mapped to the data visualization navigation concept. Therefore the concept of a "thin" client raises the issue of where the data visualization must take place to provide maximum data exploitation. The VRML browsers are presentation tools and do not

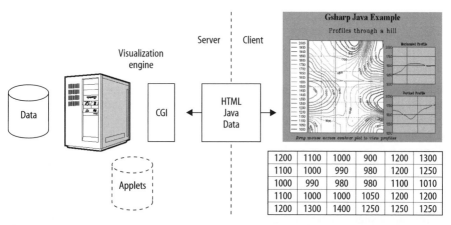

Figure 12.2 Example of a Java-based 2D visualization client. Horizontal and vertical profiles are calculated and displayed interactively as line graphs, based on the user's mouse movements. Both profile calculation and graphics rendering are done on the client side. The 2D contour isolines graphic was produced on the server side by a visualization engine using the Java2D API class library. The Java graphics primitives are embedded in an applet and are rendered on the client side. The profile calculation is written in Java and is transferred together with the underlying gridded data and is executed in the visualization client. The advantages are local data manipulation in the client and improved text quality (hardware text is a Java primitive rendered in the client – an alternative is to send GIF images across the network).

permit any visual data manipulation at the client side. The user interaction is here dependent upon the network bandwidth.

12.2.1 Java-Based "Thin" Client

Java, a platform-independent language, allows the creation of client-side applets which are automatically downloaded from the server and executed on the client. Java applets can significantly increase the visual data interaction between the client application and user, and allow tasks to be executed on the client.

Figure 12.2 shows an example of a Java-based visualization client. The 2D contour map, color legend and the two charts to the right were produced on the server side using the Java2D API embedded in a Java applet. An applet was transferred from the server and executed on the client side to perform the profile calculation and drawing of the horizontal and vertical profiles. A Java-based client represents the true "thin" client concept.

12.3 Fat Client

The Java applets that deliver locally available executables are, however, still dependent on the network bandwidth. Depending on the scope and application, applets and their data sets must be downloaded every time the application is used. Java applets are only resident during execution and are therefore removed from the local disk after the completion of the task. As the demand for larger applets and data sets grows, significant download time could be incurred and the network will become a bottleneck. Keeping commonly used applets resident on the client would significant reduce download time, although this practice is counter to the Java applet architecture.

In the "fat" client scenario, the visualization process takes place on the client side. The user performs data manipulation locally, selecting the dimension mapping and visualization paradigm. A "fat" client delivers highly graphical, highly interactive data-driven user interfaces that provide point-and-click navigation through multi-dimensional data models, such as exploring complex data warehouse trends.

A "fat" visualization client can provide local functionality through plug-ins embedded in a Web browser. However, Web components based on Microsoft's ActiveX or Sunsoft's JavaBeans architectures represent the framework for a next-generation visualization system. Visual data manipulation is provided on the client side through locally stored components. Highly interactive user interface tasks are delivered that provide point-and-click navigation and information drill-down through multidimensional data structures. Visual data interfaces such as information drilling or moving a cutting plane through a volume data set (Figures 12.3 and 12.4) can be supported. Clearly, a full-featured visual data manipulation has many advantages over the rudimentary offerings of Java applets and HTML query forms.

12.4 Viewing vs. Client Data Visualization

Despite new Web techniques, developers still cling to the standard HTML, GIF and VRML formats for a simple reason – it's practically guaranteed that the widest Internet audience possible can view the information. Real-time visual data manipulation, however, does not translate well into these standards. While the VRML file format allows distribution of visualization scenes to the Web, the user has no interactive control of the actual underlying data.

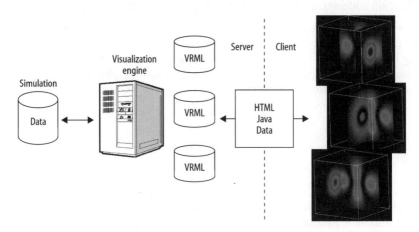

Figure 12.3 Example of a VRML scenario where a user would slice through volume data. A new VRML file is created for each slice.

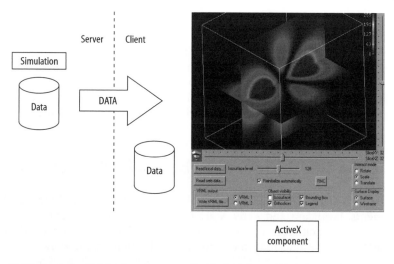

Figure 12.4 The application "fat client" component scenario. The simulation runs on the server side, producing a large amount of volume data. The mapping of numerical data into geometry and rendering is performed on the client side. The user can interactively manipulate the data. The visualization process is fully controlled by the end user. This special visualization ActiveX component was developed with AVS/Express and performs "data slicing" and isosurface generation through a volume data set.

For example, the user may want to slice through a 3D volume of data interactively. The Visualization Engine on the server side must generate a new VRML file for every new selected data slice. The user on the client side clicks on the browser's Reload button every time to get a new updated VRML display. Unfortunately, with low network bandwidth and maybe several hundred people clicking their Reload button every minute, the Web server would become overloaded, preventing anyone from getting images or data. Clearly, in some situations the wide acceptance of HTML and VRML cannot offset the inherent limitations of these formats. In these cases another option is needed.

The solution is to move the actual data rendering process (turning your data into geometry) from the server side to the client side. Any of the following techniques are available: plug-ins, Helper Applications, Java applets, ActiveX controls or JavaBeans.

The most compelling reason for the use of local tasks is the need for sophisticated user interfaces. Ease of use is the primary factor for considering a Web-based solution. However, the limitations of HTML make the implementation of complex front ends very difficult. A more sophisticated graphical user interface, written in Java, C++ or Visual Basic, can deliver highly graphical, highly interactive user interfaces that provide point-and-click navigation through complex data models and data drilling.

Java applets are still dependent on network bandwidth to deliver the executables. Depending on the scope and capability of the applets, large numbers of executables may need to be downloaded in order to accomplish the task. Executables are only resident during execution and are removed from the local disk after the completion of the task. As the demand for larger applets grows, significant download time could be incurred.

Plug-in modules are programs specifically written to run "embedded" within a particular Web browser. Netscape plug-ins have been the most popular. Visualization plug-ins can be used to let the user (client) read a script language, which controls the visualization type, attributes and the data to be visualized. The Web browser knows about the visualization plug-in and will automatically launch it and load the plug-in once the data transfer finishes. The visualization plug-in will perform the data manipulation and rendering locally on the client side.

12.5 Client-Side Behavior with Visualization Components

Ultimately, Web-based visualization capabilities will be delivered through Web components. JavaBeans and ActiveX are two competing component frameworks that allow component objects (called "Beans" and "Controls") embedded within documents to communicate with one another and with the framework.

12.5.1 Data Reduction on the Web

Real-time visual manipulation does not translate well into using large VRML geometry data sets. To improve performance and interactivity in the "thin" client scenario, the VRML geometry data should be reduced ("decimated") on the server side as part of the overall visualization process and before it is downloaded through the network to the end user.

In Figure 12.5, a CFD simulation generates large volume data. The visualization system reads volume data and the mapping process generates isosurfaces and creates a large number of triangular geometries. Decimation is implemented in the isosurface process to reduce the number of triangles and nodes. The network transfer time is reduced and the VRML viewer can render the reduced geometry data with highly interactive feeling and control.

Suitable decimation methods include the surface reduction method (Klein, 1996) and vtkDecimate (Schroeder *et al.*, 1992).

This data reduction scenario (Figure 12.6) can form the framework for an interactive Web-based isosurface application, where the end user will specify the isosurface level in an HTML form. The form is sent to the server and handled by CGI code, which sends a request to the visualization system to calculate a decimated isosurface, stored in the VRML format. The VRML file is transferred to the client and viewed by the user.

12.5.2 ActiveX Controls

The Component Object Model (COM) and its successor DCOM (Distributed COM), developed by Microsoft, are methodologies for the creation of binary software components. Thus COM allows developers to create software building blocks

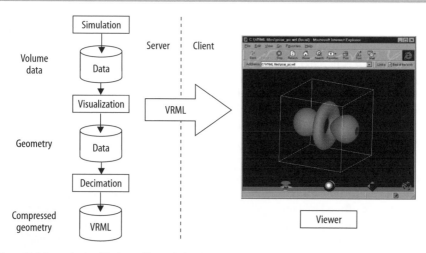

Figure 12.5 Data reduction ("decimation") is applied to the isosurface geometry before generating the industry-standard VRML format. The reduced VRML geometry is sent across the network to the viewer.

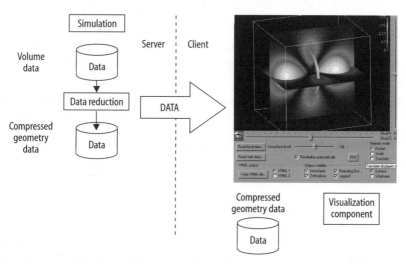

Figure 12.6 The "fat client" visualization application component scenario. Compressed volume data is transferred to the fat client for local data manipulation. The ActiveX visualization component was developed with AVS/Express (3D visualization) and Visual Basic (GUI component). The 5 Mbyte ActiveX component is stored locally on the client side.

which can be used by their clients without intimate knowledge of the component, but still lets them leverage the expertise of the developer.

DCOM also allows for network-enabled inter-process communications and so makes it feasible to let software entities running on different machines work together as if the components were located on the same machine. In fact, from the programmer's point of view it does not make a difference if the components are located on the same or on different machines. Thus DCOM can, for example, be used to let several machines connected via a network work in parallel on the same problem.

ActiveX (or OCX in older terminology) controls are components (or objects) which can be inserted into a Web page or any application capable of hosting ActiveX controls in order to reuse packaged functionality programmed by someone else. For example, the ActiveX controls introduced in this chapter allow you to enhance your Web pages and Office 97 applications with advanced 3D visualization.

ActiveX controls can be embedded within Web browsers, such as Internet Explorer, applications, such as Office 97, or programming environments, such as Visual Basic, Visual C++, Visual J++, Power Builder or Borland's Delphi. Since ActiveX controls can be written in any language, they let application developers use the performance offered by languages such as C and C++ to solve certain time-critical problems, but still allow them to use tools like Visual Basic or Delphi (or even Java using the Java–ActiveX bridges) for the overall design of their applications.

Component software development using ActiveX technology should not be confused with object-oriented programming (OOP). ActiveX is not an OOP technology in the traditional sense. There is, for example, no support for inheriting the implementation of previously programmed functionality or for enhancing or customizing this functionality to suit one's current needs (this is supposed to change when Microsoft introduces COM+ with Windows NT 5.0 or Windows 98, respectively). OOP, on the other hand, is a way to build object-based software. The difference between both approaches is that OOP requires infinitely more detailed knowledge about the existing code.

Components are used and designed as "black boxes," i.e. they usually do not depend on other software, whereas in traditional OOP, programmers need to have a deep insight into the inheritance hierarchy and the dependencies of the objects that they want to use. OOP can be used to create ActiveX controls, but not vice versa. Two examples of object-oriented programming environments used to create ActiveX controls are Microsoft Visual C++ and AVS/Express for visualization controls.

AVS/Express can be used to design and construct customized ActiveX components, which support advanced visualization techniques such as isosurfaces, cutting planes and glyphs, and interactive features such as drill-down, picking, rotating, zooming and scaling. The AVS visualization components described in this paper can be embedded in any Windows-based application capable of hosting ActiveX controls, and were designed for use with any ActiveX hosting development tools, including Visual Basic and Visual C++.

The first step in the process of creating an ActiveX control with AVS/Express is the design of the actual visualization control (data viewer). Using the AVS Network Editor and the usual visual programming techniques, you assemble the objects ("read data," "slice," "isosurface," "3D Viewer,"...) that you need for your visualization component and draw connection lines between the selected objects to indicate data references. The Network Editor shown in Figure 12.7 demonstrates the defined network for a component that can perform both vertical and horizontal slices through a volume data set. When the component is designed and tested, you can

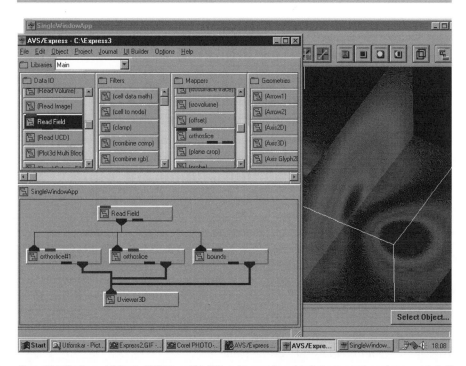

Figure 12.7 The Network Editor in AVS/Express. This OOP environment is used to design, customize and create an ActiveX visualization component. The component is exported through C++ wrapper classes imbedded in an application template (ActiveX control).

then "save and export" the result through C++ wrapper classes, which can then be embedded into a generic code template for ActiveX controls.

An important design decision in AVS/Express is to define a stable and well-defined interface for the visualization component consisting of the so-called properties of the ActiveX component. These properties can be anything from an "isolevel number," or "cutting plane section" to a "viewing attribute" (rotate, scale, translate).

Another important aspect of component creation is the ability to combine components into new components via a mechanism called COM aggregation. For example, using Visual Basic (VB), a developer can assemble an entirely new ActiveX control with a customized set of interfaces by combining VB's built-in controls (which are, in fact, also ActiveX controls) with other existing ActiveX controls (in our case, for example, an AVS/Express visualization component) and tying them together by a few lines of Visual Basic code. This task is comparatively simple and can be performed even by non-expert programmers in a few hours.

The visualization component developed in our AVS/Express example has many properties but no user interface that controls them. In order to facilitate using the controls in a Windows environment and to spare the user the effort of implementing a user interface, we have created the user interface control with VB (see Figure 12.8).

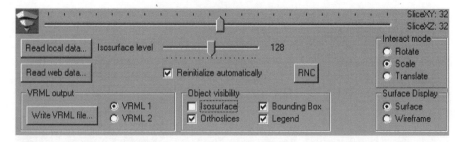

Figure 12.8 The user interface controlling the visualization component is designed and constructed with Visual Basic.

The new ActiveX component, which contains both the user interface and the AVS visualization control, is then assembled in VB.

In VB the forms and dialog boxes are created that will be the basis for the application's user interface. VB enables you to interactively assemble and test your user interface (including forms, dialogs, menu bars, labels and file selection) and persistently set the properties for the objects you have created. In VB, you will also write the code necessary to integrate the visualization control with the user interface. These event procedures contain the reference to the visualization code to be executed when the event occurs. For example, moving the "slider control" will trigger an event to redraw the cutting plane.

In the final step, we have created a new control with VB which contains the user interface as well as the "visualization viewer" control via COM aggregation (see Figure 12.8).

To embed this new assembled visualization ActiveX component into an application that can act as a container, simply register the ActiveX control. You can then import the ActiveX control into any desired container and immediately start using it. For instance, in Internet Explorer you bring the control into the ActiveX Control Pad. You don't have to write any more code.

To instantiate such a control in an Office application (such as Word 97 in Figure 12.8), move your mouse pointer over the toolbar area and press the right mouse button. A popup menu with a choice of additional toolbars will appear. Select "Control Toolbox" and move the mouse pointer to the new toolbar. Click on the "Additional controls" button and select the AVS/Express visualization control from the list of available registered components.

The customized ActiveX visualization control contains only those graphics objects used by the application, which makes the application small and more efficient compared with using AVS/Express as the visualization application on the PC's desktop.

The ActiveX visualization component (in Figure 12.6) is quite large (5 Mbyte), but it needs to be installed only once on each client's system. When the ActiveX control resides on your computer it will not need to be downloaded again.

For example, the Word 97 document shown in Figure 12.9 contains the embedded ActiveX component. When the document is transferred over the Internet, it will

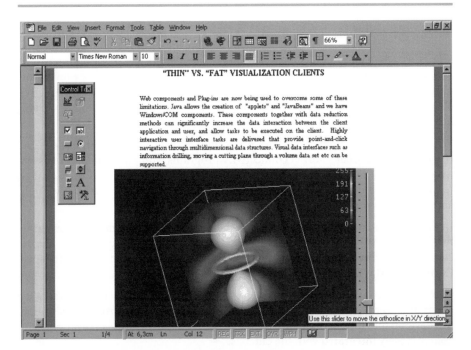

Figure 12.9 Example of a visualization ActiveX control embedded in a Word 97 document, prototyped by AVS/Express and Visual Basic to perform data slicing and isosurface generation of large volume data on the PC desktop.

only *refer* to the component, and thus the total size of the document remains small (30 kbyte). Any project can therefore exchange Word 97 documents with embedded advanced 3D visualization over the Internet using pre-installed ActiveX components on the client side. Locally stored data is accessed by a "data reader" in the component or transferred over the Internet using the "URL reader."

12.6 Conclusion and Future Trends

In this exploding world of abstract data, there is great potential for information visualization to increase the bandwidth between us and an ever-growing and ever-changing world of data.

The future trends and improvements in visualization for the Web can be summarized as follows:

- information drilling on the Web
- 3D visualization on affordable and powerful desktop PCs
- non-immersive VR navigation using "visual" user interface technology
- real-time visualization of very large data sets
- component-based development – JavaBeans and ActiveX
- data visualization components

Traditional software development has moved to a Web component-based approach using smaller, single-purpose building blocks. Technologies such as Sun's Java language with JavaBeans and Microsoft's ActiveX provide an important component of cyberspace – the ability to create an object that behaves similarly in different applications and on different computers. I can create an interactive component on my computer and distribute it to you in cyberspace, and it will still behave in the same way when you use it.

With ActiveX technology, Windows programmers will have a much easier time combining traditional Internet connectivity programs with powerful desktop software packages. For example, with ActiveX components projects can exchange "smaller" Office documents over the Internet that refer to these already available and installed components on the client side.

In the future, a component's location on the network will become as irrelevant to the developer as its source language is today. Developers will expect to be able to compose, distribute and troubleshoot solutions wherever, whenever. Distributed COM (DCOM) is one way forward.

Over the next couple of years we will see Web evolve in giant steps into interactivity and multi-user participation based on the new emerging standards. Visualization will develop into interactive data drilling on the Web, providing visualization technology closely integrated with the database.

Visualization on the Web will become even more active and dynamic, with JavaBeans and ActiveX components streaming down the Internet to the Web client.

Acknowledgments

This work was supported by the European Community in the ESPRIT Project INDEX (EP 22745). Dirk Schabe (AVS) put a lot of work into the components.

References

Abraham, R, Jas, F and Russell, W (1995) *The Web Empowerment Book*, Springer-Verlag, Berlin.
Brown, J, Earnshaw, RA, Jern, M, and Vince, JA (1995) *Visualization: Using Computer Graphics to Explore Data and Present Information*, John Wiley & Sons, New York.
December, J (1996) *Presenting Java*, Sams.net Publishing.
Earnshaw, RA and Vince, JA (1997) *The Internet in 3D – Information, Images and Interaction*, Academic Press, London.
Ernst, W (1996) *Presenting ActiveX*, Sams.net Publishing.
Ford, A (1995) *Spinning the Web: How to provide Information on the Internet*, Thomson Computer Press, London.
Gobel, M (ed.) (1995) *Virtual Environments '95*, Springer-Verlag, Vienna.
Herzner, W and Kappe, F (eds.) (1994) *Multimedia/Hypermedia in Open Distributed Environments*, Springer-Verlag, Vienna.
Klein, R (1996) Surface simplification inside a tolerance volume, *IBM Research Report RC 20440*.
Klein, R, Krämer, J and Strasse, W (1996) Mesh reduction with error control, *Visualization '96*, ACM, November.
Lefer, B and Grave, M (eds.) (1997) *Visualization in Scientific Computing '97*, Springer-Verlag, Vienna.

Marrin, C. and Campbell, B. (1997) *Teach Yourself VRML 2 in 21 days*, Sams.net Publishing, Indianapolis.

Munzner, T and Burchard, P, *Visualizing the Structure of the World Wide Web in 3D Hyperbolic Space*, Geometry Center, University of Minnesota.

Pfaffenberger, B (1995) *Publish it on the Web*, Academic Press, London.

Scateni, R, van Wijk, J and Zanarini, P (eds.) (1995) *Visualization in Scientific Computing '95*, Springer-Verlag, Vienna.

Schroeder, W, Zarge, J and Lorensen, WE (1992) Decimation of triangle meshes, *Computer Graphics SIGGRAPH 1992*.

Veltkamp, RC and Blake, EH (eds.) (1995) *Programming Paradigms in Graphics '95*, Springer-Verlag, Vienna.

13

How to Build a Pan-European Multilingual Information Distribution System

James A. Malcolm and Jill A. Hewitt

Abstract

Researchers who are involved in EC programs need to exchange and disseminate information. A system that supports such access to multimedia information from across Europe has many requirements, including the need to present the information in several natural languages, to have local variants of some parts of the data and to maintain a consistent style despite multiple sources of information.

When asked to solve such an information dissemination problem, the World Wide Web springs to mind. Certainly, these requirements can be met by suitable discipline in constructing and maintaining the collection of Web pages, but it is better to define the structure of the information in a database schema. The SPIREnet prototype Web server demonstrates the feasibility of setting up a distributed information service based on a generic data model, and of automatically generating Web pages from a relational database. The way in which information is presented is determined by the form design, a separate step from the design of the data.

A design based on a data model will also facilitate a multilingual keyword catalogue to assist browsing in different languages. Keywords and multi-language support should be addressed by enhancing the data model so that the representation of the information in natural language is held in the database along with the information itself.

It is tempting to assume that, because the Web is a distributed system, applications built using it would use the Web's distribution mechanisms. In fact, the Web should be seen simply as a local distribution mechanism, and global distribution should be addressed by distributed database technology. Since relevant information will be stored in the local copy of the database, this enables fast and consistent access. A common data model will ensure compatibility of information between the different sites, which means that users should be able to view information from different sources as if it were a single unified system.

In the future, we expect that the whole Web should become more like a database, with the structure of the information explicitly available for processing rather than being hidden inside the database which is the source of a particular set of pages.

13.1 Introduction

In this chapter we identify the requirements for a pan-European information system. We describe our motivation for this exercise and experience of similar systems, then describe how such a system should be built. We describe how we use the World Wide Web as the basis of our design, then show how the limitations of the Web for this kind of system may be overcome and how those requirements that are not met by a straightforward Web-based system may be achieved.

13.2 Motivation

Many EC-funded programs have generated an enormous amount of information that is in the public domain. Whereas access to this bulky information will be possible through paper-based dissemination mechanisms, access to the underlying knowledge will remain difficult for the intended users of such services as well as for many project participants [1, 2]. We intended to produce an information system for European projects in the area of support for the disabled which would serve the needs of researchers involved in EC programs for information dissemination and exchange. It is anticipated that user organizations, companies, end users and other researchers would also benefit from such a service. Typically, users are dispersed across the European Community and will come from many different disciplines with varying levels of IT knowledge.

The goal of the work described here was to define an information and communication framework that would facilitate information access and exchange and to implement a set of multilingual services which incorporate tools for data entry, indexing, filtering and annotating information pertinent to the knowledge domain of interest. This includes narrative material, pictures, and audio and video material, as well as more structured information.

In addition, it is our hope that the development of the system will result in consistency in information access and sharing. Inter-project communication should be improved, facilitating the achievement of consensus and the exchange of experiences. This can bring significant benefits, such as convergence of technologies and alignment of informational technical solutions adopted in different domains for end users.

In this chapter we do not address all of the issues considered by such a proposal, but we do show how each of the requirements listed in the next section may be met.

13.3 Requirements

The following are the requirements that we believe are met by our design and are necessary, or at least desirable, features of any pan-European information system.

- We want to build a system that provides access to information for users. We separate the role of information provider from that of normal user. It is expected that the volume of updates will be relatively small, and will not be made by ordinary users.

- There will be many users, so we require that the system provide simultaneous access by multiple users.
- Users will be at various geographic locations, so remote access to the information is desired.
- The performance and reliability of the system should not be compromised by the fact that information is to be distributed to remote users, probably over an unreliable public network.
- We want to provide an open information system, where anyone can gain access to the data. This means that platform independence, at least at the user end, is an important goal.
- There may be several information providers, but the information presented should not be fragmented. There should be a single image for the system, which may have multiple sources of information but should have a consistent style.
- There is a need to present information in several natural languages, with automated translation being a desirable addition.
- There should be a facility for language-independent keyword searching that will find documents on a topic whatever language they are written in. Manual translation of relevant material can be arranged once it has been identified.
- Information will be distributed across several sites.
- There will be local variants of some of the information. We require local variants of some parts of the data, but still desire to maintain a compatible appearance across sites.
- The system should accommodate multimedia where relevant, and not just text.
- The system should be open to those with disabilities and to the socially disadvantaged.

13.4 Experience

The above aims, and the design we present below, are based on our experience designing and implementing a number of information systems.

13.4.1 Modema

The Modema project [3] was a pan-European project, funded under the TIDE program to build a computer-based information system to assist with the integration of people with disabilities into paid employment. It is implemented in KnowledgePro, and utilizes multimedia technology to provide video and photographic material to enhance its information base. Versions were produced in four European languages.

A problem with Modema was that, at the time of its development, the Web was not widely enough used in industry for it to provide a viable distribution mechanism. It therefore remained a standalone application. There was also a problem of translation. There was no easy mechanism to convert the system from one natural language to another.

13.4.2 SPIREnet

Following on from Modema, we developed Spire [4], which is a system to provide information to disabled students and to the staff who support them. This was further developed to produce SPIREnet [5], a distributed multimedia information system providing information over the World Wide Web relating to the integration of students with disabilities into higher education.

The SPIREnet system differs from some other systems in that, even though it contains a large amount of text, it is based on the concept of automatic generation of Web pages from a relational database. The use of a relational database as a back end for the system has a number of advantages:

- It has allowed us to establish a generic relational data model for disability-related information and advice. This can be used by other universities and also tailored to their own specific requirements. It imposes a standard for the storage of information, which enables ease of transfer of data between local systems and the central system.
- It is easily integrated with other data management tools, thus allowing the development of a simple interface for data entry. This enables non-technical users to easily input and update data in the system, without needing any knowledge of either the underlying database or of how to create Web pages.
- A common interface presented as a series of Web pages enables the users to view the information from different sites as if it were a single unified system [6].

13.4.3 Action Cash

Our ideas on the internationalization of Web-based systems come from our experience with Action Cash, a system for credit managers to keep track of queries on invoices, which was converted to operate in three different natural languages (Spanish, Catalan and English) [7].

13.5 The Web

First we consider what the World Wide Web [8] is and what it can do. This is perhaps well known, but merits repetition.

13.5.1 Remote Access

The first point is that the Web provides remote access. There are many, many Web servers, but at any point in time a client will be communicating with at most a single server. It therefore provides distributed access to data. But to what kind of data?

13.5.2 Document-Oriented

The World Wide Web provides a document-oriented view of computing. A Web client can look at a text from any Web server on the Internet, but there are limitations of text: text has no structure. It is worth asking how many commercial systems are based on plain text. We can search through a file for a particular piece of text, but what is it? Is it part of a name, of an address, or what? Free text databases do have their place, but in general text is not amenable to automatic processing.

13.5.3 Hypertext

As regards its processing, hypertext is perhaps even worse. Hypertext links between documents and files allow information to be accessed in any manner and allows data to be transparently distributed across several machines, networks or even continents. The Web is therefore a global database of information and data that can be accessed using a variety of machines and software. This is tremendously powerful. But, this is a database with no data dictionary, no schema; a database without any explicit structure.

13.5.4 Multi-platform

Web client software is available for practically every possible client. Because the HTML in which Web documents are written describes the structure of the information rather than its appearance, it is possible for a client on a machine with limited resources to render the information in a form that can be viewed on that machine. For example, the Lynx browser will operate on a standard VT100 dumb terminal. The ability to view Web documents on any platform is an important feature of the Web, which is being lost [9]. As the inventor of the Web has said, "Anyone who slaps a 'this page is best viewed with Browser X' label on a Web page appears to be yearning for the bad old days, before the Web, when you had very little chance of reading a document written on another computer, another word processor, or another network" [10]. Too many documents are being written for the Web which depend on particular features of HTML which are not particularly standardized and which therefore will only work on a limited number of platforms. The multi-platform nature of the Web can therefore be subverted, and we must be careful to avoid doing so in any systems we design.

13.5.5 Open Access

The Web does provide a very open system, but we must be careful to ensure that our designs are accessible to all users, including the blind or partially sighted. Many Web pages are not. For example, care must be taken to add ALT keywords to all images. Obviously the word "Cat" does not convey as much as an attractive color picture of a black and white kitten playing with a ball of wool, but designers must ensure that it is not necessary to see the picture in order to navigate the site. There are, however, guidelines for making Web documents accessible to disabled users [11].

Many users find some pages hard to read, either because the text is too small or because the foreground and background colors appear too similar on their particular display screen.

If we desire an open information system, it is important that we do not make assumptions about what software client machines will be using. There are many different browsers in use. It is important not to assume that the client machine is the latest high-specification machine. Many users have much smaller machines with slow network connections. This is important even within a university, and much more so if we consider truly open public information systems. Those with fewer material resources at their disposal should not be disadvantaged in the information society.

13.5.6 Hypermedia

The Web is not in fact just a hypertext system: it is hypermedia. A major problem is that there are too many media and too many formats. It is time-consuming, confusing and sometimes expensive to maintain the ability to display every kind of document that might appear on the Web. This is exacerbating problems of platform, disadvantage etc. Every new format requires a new viewer or plug-in, but these tend not to be available for all platforms. The appropriate viewers are often distributed free of charge, but even with free viewers, those with small machines, slow links, disabilities, non-Intel processors or non-Microsoft operating systems can be disadvantaged.

There is also a danger in taking a "graphic design" approach to the production of Web pages. There can indeed be beautiful presentation of the information, but the graphics may have to be redone on every update. Such graphics may not be visible, if we have a blind user, a slow link, or a non-graphical browser.

13.5.7 Performance

Despite its many benefits and successes, people often moan that the Web is too slow to be of any practical use. Having a more local copy of the data can ameliorate the slow speed of access. Often making use of a cache does this, but if the local data has to be different in some way then a separate local copy can be maintained. The major advantage of a cache is that it is automatic. If we need local variants of pages, there should be some way of keeping them in step with the rest of the system without manual intervention.

13.5.8 Indexing and Information Provider Issues

Despite all of the above, the World Wide Web has been a huge success as a mechanism for information dissemination. Many information providers already run Web servers that can be browsed by interested parties. However, the sheer volume of information now available can be a deterrent to busy users and equally to sites that have the burden of maintaining and updating an information service. Because Web pages are simply text, it is not easy to keep the information up to date. This is a problem with any documentation, but if the Web is public then everyone sees the incorrect and/or inconsistent information. Even on a private intranet [12], it is not good to have incorrect information distributed throughout the organization.

Indexing is the only option for imposing some kind of structure on a collection of hyperlinked text files, and many such indexes have been produced [13–16]. But even with a relatively small domain, such as Computer Science Technical Reports [17–19], it is hard to produce a system that presents information from a number of sources in an integrated fashion.

13.6 Databases on the Web

As we have stated above, the Web is a huge database with no data model. Rather than process information as unstructured text, most computing applications use structured databases. There are obvious and well-known benefits in data processing applications associated with the use of database management system technology and associated techniques such as entity relationship modeling. In fact, these benefits (of databases) can be obtained in Web-based systems also.

In designing this system, the approach we have taken agrees with work done by Gorman [20]. His focus is on large businesses, but the same ideas apply to Web design. He identifies a need for interrelated models of an enterprise to be produced, with everything defined only once, and cross checks and interrelationships to maintain consistency and avoid duplication. These models should be non-redundant and complete; and systems should be generated from the models in as automatic a fashion as possible. That is, in his view, specification is the key to successful system building. In a similar way, we propose that Web pages should be generated automatically from a comprehensive model, implemented as a database.

There is an unstoppable trend towards distributed processing, but if we allow the *definition* of data and processing to be distributed along with the data and processing itself, we will have a totally fragmented and uncontrollable system. In a way, we risk going back to where we were in the 1970s (before database management systems) with multiple incompatible systems (which in those days would have been on a single machine). "Fragmented and uncontrollable" is perhaps a good description of the World Wide Web, but it should not apply to individual collections of data. Gorman's approach, like ours, gives a unified data model, despite the physical distribution of the data.

To implement such a system what we need is a facility to send information from a database to a Web client, without the user having to know that a database is involved. We also don't want special software at the client, or we would be undermining the platform-independent nature of the Web. There are a number of technologies that provide this facility, namely the ability to run a program at the server, that will generate a Web page dynamically, rather than merely retrieving it from disk. Much is made of the relative efficiency of different mechanisms, but there are few real differences.

Normally, a Web server receives a request for a page, which it satisfies by sending back to the client a file that was stored on disk. With CGI and similar technologies [21], the Web server recognizes that it is a page that will be generated by a program. The server runs the required program, which generates HTML (or possibly some other format that the browser can understand) which is sent to the client. There are therefore typically several context switches. Where database access can be done by the same operating system process that is handling the network input, the response will be faster.

There is also the problem of transactions that span more than one interaction between the user and the database. Because the Web does not maintain any state information between requests (which helps to make Web servers fast), all state has to be held at the client. This can be solved by Java applets using JDBC [22], where the applet communicates with the database directly (bypassing the Web server) once Java applet is downloaded. However, the database consequently has to maintain state for several connections.

13.7 Multi-Language Systems

Many European sites already maintain Web sites in more than one language and it would be feasible for an organization to replicate all their information in another language. The most common approach to providing multiple languages is for the pages to be translated manually into each required language. In some cases, only part of the site is translated. Separate sets of Web pages take a lot of effort to maintain, because any change in one version of the pages requires a re-translation of each other natural language version. In some cases, because of the prevalence of English language on the Internet, only two languages are used: that of the country in question and English. Some sites mix the languages quite successfully, with some pages in only one language and others mirrored in both. But it is also common to see sites where the version in one language is incomplete. This sort of problem can happen in a site that uses only a single language, but the likelihood of it occurring where there are two or more languages to be supported seems higher.

If we look at standalone applications, it is more common to see a separation between the text parts of an application, and the program proper. This in fact is the key to successful internationalization. We see this with Windows or Macintosh resource files. In Microsoft Access, where there is no resource file, we can take an approach based on an OLE DLL which reads the appropriate set of strings from a resource file [23]. But if we are using a database, why not use it to store the text on forms as well as data? In other words the database should contain all the strings that would have been in the resource file. We have tried this approach, and find that it works well, and is not unduly slow.

Every control in the system that includes any text (labels, combo-boxes, text boxes with default text, buttons with text...) needs to have a unique identifier. This unique identifier can be used as the key when looking up the actual text to be used in the database itself. Some languages are more verbose than others, so of course all forms need to be checked after each translation to ensure that all text fits in the available space on the controls. Controls should be copied rather than reimplemented in order to give a consistent appearance to the application. This also avoids duplication in the message table. For a simple system, the message table can have a row for each message, with the message id as the key. Apart from the key, the table should have one column for each language supported by the application. In every form that includes text, before the form is loaded a function that fills in the form with the correct text for the currently selected language can be called. The code itself should not contain any text [7].

The reason for the popularity of the former approach (for the pages to be translated manually into each required language) is probably that in most Web sites the pages are viewed simply as text. As we move towards a more structured view of the information that we are presenting, we can think about a separation of user interface and data.

But there is a better approach. Only part of the data in a system like Spire is stored as free text; much is names and other individual words, interrelated by the database structure. Such individual words are susceptible to machine translation.

We propose that in a Web-based system the skeletons of all the forms are translated manually. It seems reasonable that a lot of work has to be done to set the system up in a new natural language. But as the system grows, new information becomes available in all of the languages of the system with very little effort. The key is that the database itself has tables describing which pieces of information are stored in multiple languages. Translation is done by straightforward table lookup through the database. The Spire system has about 15 tables and the multilingual system will have more; but the added complexity greatly facilitates both keyword search (see below) and multiple language support.

13.7.1 Keyword Searching

Recently, keyword searching has mostly been seen as a string search problem, but many older systems rely on a fixed thesaurus of keywords. Our system will use keywords. Each keyword is represented in the underlying database as a unique identifier. The database will contain a table relating each keyword to its natural language representation. Thus a user, whose native tongue is, say, Spanish, will be offered a menu of keywords in Spanish. He or she selects the keywords on which a search is to be made, and the database will be asked to retrieve the records that are linked to that keyword. The actual records are not searched. The record may include large text fields that are in a particular language.

The distinction between local and global information could mean that only the global information would need to be translated, because local information would have been created in the correct language. A multilingual keyword dictionary could enable searches in a user's own language, which would enable the user to view information in a variety of languages, and then, if necessary, get a translation into their own language.

13.8 Multiple Site Systems

The Web is a distributed system, but it is not a fully general one. Most distributed systems are in fact client–server systems, and the Web is only notable in that there are many thousands of servers and millions of clients. But at any time, a client is only talking to one server; and even then only for as long as it takes to download the current page – then the association between them is broken.

So the Web is not the tool for this job. What possibilities exist? There is a need for a replication mechanism of some kind. It is possible to design a special-purpose replication mechanism for this particular system, for example the Domain Name System, but these are just special-purpose distributed databases. There is no reason in this case not to consider a general distributed database solution. Once the database has been designed according to the model, there is no need for it to remain a centralized service. A distributed database can implement the same data model, with local data remaining local and shared data replicated across the system.

13.8.1 Distributed Database

A distributed database provides a central shared data model, without the need to centralize the data. Actually it may be that the data is distributed, not in the sense that some of the data is at one site and some at another, but copies of most or all of the data are at each site. This of course gives us a problem whenever one of the copies is updated.

We can design the database so that a single site is responsible for the master copy of each record. Allocating some tables to specific sites can do this, which is relatively easy to manage. In other cases we need to allocate the master copy of a record to a particular site based on the value of the key. If there is always a single master copy, then the distributed database needs to lock only that copy in order to perform an update.

There are a number of approaches that can be taken to update a distributed database. The commonest is that typically used in online transaction processing systems. Here many users can update the database. To avoid conflicting updates, a two-phase commit protocol can be used. Here the update proceeds in two phases. First we ask each copy (or part) of the database to prepare to commit. They only agree to this if they can guarantee to commit on request. The second phase, which takes place if all copies agree to the requests to prepare to commit, asks each copy of the database to commit finally.

This requires all copies of the data to be available – on line – at the time of the update. Majority voting protocols minimize problems that can be caused if part of the network is unavailable. If more than half of the copies of the database can be contacted, this is sufficient to guarantee that the update will be successful. When the other copies come online the update is propagated to them.

Optimistic concurrency control avoids locking the data for a long time. The data required by a transaction is read, but is not locked until the moment of update. If it then turns out that the record has been changed by another user since the original read it is left to the user to fix problem. This approach is good if there is a low level of updates and/or few conflicts. This is likely in an information system such as we are discussing.

It may not be necessary to lock the data at all if very few users are doing updates. Microsoft's Jet Replication [24] is like optimistic concurrency control, in that it is assumed that conflicting access to data is rare. Each record in the database has a version number. Periodically changes are replicated to other copies of the database. The copies do not need to be online at all for updates to proceed. This seems like the most resilient approach for an information system where most updates will be to local information and conflicting updates to global data are unlikely, or can be managed by human intervention.

13.9 Conclusions

The SPIREnet prototype Web server demonstrates the feasibility of setting up a distributed information service based on a generic data model, and of automatically generating Web pages from a relational database. For efficiency, generated pages should be cached, although there is some evidence that on-the-fly generation gives acceptable performance [25].

We have shown how to extend these ideas to build a multilingual system. Keywords and multi-language support should be addressed by enhancing the data model.

Because the Web is a distributed system, it is tempting to assume that applications built using it would use the Web's distribution mechanisms. Our proposal is instead that the Web should be seen simply as a local distribution mechanism. Global distribution is a more complex problem, and it needs to be addressed by appropriate distributed database technology. In many cases a simple form of distributed database, like Microsoft's Jet Replication [24], may be adequate.

As far as possible one should separate:

• the structure of the information (defined in the schema)
• the information itself (stored by the database)
• the way it is presented (determined by the form design)
• the representation in each of several natural languages (also held in the database)

For collaborative projects, the development of such systems will result in consistency in information access and better communication between participants. Generalizations of these techniques apply to other information-based services, such as program schedules, weather forecasts and traffic reports.

In the future, we believe that not only will collections of Web pages be generated from database management systems, but the Web itself will become more like a database, with some kind of explicit data model. Each item of data stored should have a type indicating the values it may take and the operations permissible on it. Perhaps such a thing could be called an object-oriented Web?

References

[1] The IMPACT/PROMONET - INTRASOFT project deals with information dissemination, marketing and communications for SMEs based on INTERNET models and tools. Reference can be found at http://usnic.snic.umu.se/promonet/.

[2] The ESPRIT/AMIDE - INTRASOFT project concerns the development of an information dissemination environment on the Web which will allow electronic payments and copyright protection of online information dissemination. Reference can be found at http://amide.ip.lu/.

[3] J Hewitt, J Sapsford-Francis and P Halford (1994) MODEMA - a multimedia public information system, in *Multimedia Technologies and Future Applications*, Pentech Press.

[4] M Bearne, S Jones, J Hewitt *et al.* (1996) Providing public access to information in complex and weakly structured domains: a 3-layered model for hypermedia information systems, *The New Review of Hypermedia and Multimedia: Applications and Research*, Vol. 2.

[5] J Hewitt and M Bearne (1996) Access to higher education and disability awareness - a networked information service, *ICCHP '96*, Linz, Austria.

[6] *Welcome to SPIREnet* by Human Factors Consultancy, University of Hertfordshire, December 1995; http://orawww.cs.herts.ac.uk/Spire/.

[7] MA Ortega-Lafuente (1997) Software Internationalisation, *Final-year project report*, Universidad Autonoma de Barcelona.

[8] T Berners-Lee, R Cailliau, J-F Groff *et al.* (1992) World-wide web: the information universe, *Electronic Networking: Research, Applications and Policy* 2(1), 52–8.

[9] CD Burstein (1998) *Best Viewed With Any Browser: Campaign for a Non-Browser Specific World Wide Web*; http://server.berkeley.edu/~cdaveb/anybrowser.html.

[10] T Berners-Lee (1996) *Technology Review*, July, quoted in [9].

[11] GC Vanderheiden, WA Chisholm, R Trace *et al.* (1998) *Unified Web Site Accessibility Guidelines*. University of Wisconsin–Madison for the Web Accessibility Initiative Guidelines Working Group, January; http://www.w3.org/WAI/GL/author.htm. There is also a shorter Checklist (3 pages) at http://www.w3.org/WAI/GL/authorcl.htm.

[12] BJ Read (1995) WWW in an open office system, in *International Seminar on Client Server Computing*, IEE Digest no. 1995/184, October.

[13] E. Selberg (1997) *A Brief History of MetaCrawler*, http://www.metacrawler.com/selberg-history.html.

[14] Archiplex: for searching archives of files and software. An example can be found at http://src.doc.ic.ac.uk/archiplexform.html.

[15] Lycos: for searching indices of Web documents by title, content, headings and keywords; http://www.lycos.com/.

[16] WebCrawler: for searching indices of Web documents by title, content; http://webcrawler.com/.

[17] E Fox (1995) World Wide Web and Computer Science Reports, *Communications of the ACM*, 4, 43–4.

[18] JR Davis and C Lagoze (1994) A protocol and server for a distributed digital technical report library, *Technical Report TR94-1418*, University of Cornell, Department of Computer Science, June; http://cs-tr.cs.cornell.edu/TR/CORNELLCS:TR94-1418.

[19] MD VanHeyningen (1994) The Unified Computer Science Technical Report Index: lessons in indexing diverse resources, in *Proc. Second International WWW Conference*, Chicago, October; http://www.cs.indiana.edu/ucstri/paper/paper.html.

[20] MM Gorman (1994) *Enterprise Database in a Client Server Environment*. John Wiley, Chichester.

[21] The Common Gateway Interface, or CGI, is a standard for external gateway programs to interface with information servers such as HTTP servers; http://hoohoo.ncsa.uiuc.edu/cgi/overview.html.

[22] The JDBC™ Database Access API; http://java.sun.com/products/jdbc/.

[23] Using an OLE Server DLL for Localized Strings; http://premium.microsoft.com/msdn/library/techart/html/accatm.htm.

[24] T Poll (1996) *Database Replication in Microsoft Jet*, Microsoft Corporation, Redmond WA, November.

[25] A Fox, SD Gribble, EA Brewer *et al.* (1996) Adapting to network and client variability via on-demand dynamic distillation, in *Proc. ASPLOS VII* (also published in *ACM Operating Systems Review*).

About the Authors

Jill Hewitt is manager of the Department of Computer Science's Software Development Service. She has been active in the field of human–computer interaction since 1988, and has managed a number of research and consultancy projects funded by industry, government and the EC.

James Malcolm has teaching and research interests in the areas of networks and distributed systems and in the design and implementation of systems which make practical use of network technology.

Technological Issues

14

A Distributed Object-Based Architecture for Remote Rendering on the WWW

M.D.J. McNeill

Abstract

This chapter presents a system to support remote rendering of rich and interactive 3D graphics data across the World Wide Web. The motivation for this work is the emergence of a number of converging technologies: protocols and tools for distributed, heterogeneous application development (such as Java and CORBA), graphics languages which support distributed, object-based, virtual worlds (such as VRML), and the increasing number of consumer and business applications with a high degree of graphical content (interactive virtual shopping, visual simulation and information visualization, for example). Key technologies are identified and analyzed for their implications for the design of distributed photorealistic 3D applications, where performance (which can be critical to the success of the product) is often measured in terms of the performance delivered to the application, i.e. at the local display. Experience of implementing a CORBA-based photorealistic rendering application on a network of workstations is presented, and extensions are made to a WWW-based renderer, suitable for implementation on corporate networks (intranets and extranets) and the Internet.

14.1 Introduction

High-quality computer-generated images are frequently made by applying a combination of global illumination algorithms to a database containing mathematical definitions of physical objects (cars, buildings, etc.). The output of the algorithms is a set of frames which can be displayed on a computer screen, or written to CD-ROM, computer disk or other medium as appropriate. Applications which employ high-quality rendering include film production, lighting and architectural simulation, and medical applications. More so than many applications, owing to the visual nature of computer-generated image production, speed of generation is an issue, but few global illumination implementations can generate images in (or even near) real time. On the other hand, many desktop systems are today available with 3D accelerator cards which can produce images at the required 30 frames per second or faster in real time, but to date these contain hardware implementations of *projective* graphics algorithms. *Global* illumination algorithms, the type with which we are concerned, exhibit a higher quality of rendering, which take into account the effects of inter-object lighting and exhibit properties such as color bleeding and soft shadows, all of which add visual cues to the scene which are desirable for the accurate simulation of reality.

Owing to the demand for high-speed rendering, a variety of techniques are employed to accelerate the rendering process:

• acceleration through new and faster algorithms
• acceleration through dedicated hardware
• acceleration through exploiting networks of workstations

New and more efficient algorithms are continually being sought for more realism and faster rendering, and to support new features such as animation and new styles of interaction. Combined with the increase in complexity of the rendered environment (including, for example, participating media such as fog and smoke) implementations of rendering systems must maintain a high degree of extensibility. The number of entities in photorealistic rendering systems is large and their complexity high, which has led to the adoption of modern styles of programming such as object orientation as the *de facto* standard for implementation. Information hiding, polymorphism and inheritance all contribute to the maintainability and extensibility of rendering systems.

Dedicated hardware for the acceleration of photorealistic rendering algorithms has remained difficult for a number of reasons. There is a great deal of floating-point computation in these algorithms, which, combined with the fact that there is a large amount of interaction between data during rendering, has meant that most "hardware-oriented" solutions rely on general-purpose microprocessors for computation. This is in contrast to projective algorithms, where integer and fixed-point arithmetic are often found, and every surface (primitive) in the scene can be dealt with in a known, uniform way (typically by passing it through a hardware pipeline). However, in global illumination algorithms each primitive cannot be handled in isolation (because of the influence of inter-object lighting). Implementations of photorealistic rendering algorithms are almost exclusively in software, using either general-purpose single-processor hardware [1, 2] or multiprocessor systems [3, 4].

Some research programs have suggested the use of networks of general-purpose microprocessor-based systems for the acceleration of these algorithms [5-7], and this has obviously generated research into the efficient parallelization of the algorithms. Typical issues for research have included the granularity of tasks, communication overheads, efficiency and load balancing. Such networks have the advantage of being relatively commonplace in today's computing environment. However, a drawback has been the lack of general-purpose high-level programming tools to exploit the available hardware. Also, there have been, until recently, few tools that have integrated distributed processing with software paradigms such as object orientation, popular for large rendering systems. However, programming tools and industry-standard communication protocols to support distributed object-based processing are now emerging. These exciting developments will lead to a number of applications which use networks of workstations (including the Internet) in a variety of ways to accelerate computation-intensive applications such as computer graphics.

14.1.1 Motivation

With algorithms implemented in software, particularly the rendering algorithms described here, it has long been recognized that networks of machines are particularly attractive, since

- computational requirements for rendering algorithms, particularly global illumination algorithms are large, and
- networks of machines are now relatively common.

Further, the Internet and associated technology (object-based communication tools and protocols) have enabled application-to-application communication across distributed, heterogeneous platforms using relatively high-level tools.

The motivation is, then, that networks of workstations (such as the Internet) provide suitable platforms for distributed (i.e. remote) rendering. In most cases this is also a relatively low-cost solution, for it is often the case that desktop machines are routinely networked for purposes such as file sharing, server requirements and backup.

Distributed rendering is attractive for a number of applications where powerful computing resources are not available locally, i.e. where the pixels are required for viewing. The world of mobile computing is one such application, where local resources may be relatively limited. The end-user (client) can initiate rendering to the rendering server, which then undertakes the processing and returns the result (pixels) to the client. With appropriate compression techniques the communication between client and server can be relatively low, but the information content very high. Further, the client need not be aware of the details of the implementation of the server processes. Depending on the speed of rendering required by the client, the server can provide one of a number of services as appropriate. The services offered by the server can be updated dynamically, without the knowledge of the client, thereby ensuring that the most up-to-date services are always available. The application developer need not distribute upgrades to the client; similarly, the client has no need to install new software, thereby reducing downtime and associated risk to the client. The widespread adoption of corporate intranets and extranets makes the use of such technology for a variety of applications more likely in the future.

This chapter surveys technologies that are emerging to support network-based application development and investigates how suitable these technologies are for supporting remote rendering over the WWW. In Section 14.2 an introduction to photorealistic rendering algorithms is presented. Section 14.3 introduces an architecture for a distributed photorealistic renderer using a client–server model. Existing and emerging technologies for application development, distributed application programming and Internet communication are presented in Section 14.4. In Section 14.5 a radiosity implementation using CORBA, the emerging industry-standard object communication protocol from the Object Management Group (OMG), is presented. An architecture for an Internet-based renderer is presented in Section 14.6. Finally, some conclusions and suggestions for further work are presented.

14.2 Photorealistic Rendering

Global illumination rendering algorithms (so-called *photorealistic* rendering algorithms) model the physical characteristics of light, either by casting vectors simulating rays of light (in ray tracing), or by distributing the energy associated with all surfaces in a scene (in radiosity) or a combination of both (composite photorealistic rendering). A brief description of the radiosity algorithm follows. Readers are pointed to the literature [8, 9] for further details of the radiosity algorithm.

14.2.1 Radiosity

The radiosity algorithm, described originally by Goral *et al.* [8], is based on the principle of energy transfer. The environment (i.e. graphics database) is seen as a collection of surfaces, each of which is subdivided into smaller patches. Every patch is considered to be an emitter and/or receiver of light energy. The *radiosity* of a patch is defined as the sum of the emitted and reflected light at that patch. The amount of emitted light and the reflectivity of the patch is specified in the database. The unknown is the amount of incident light hitting the patch, which can be calculated by summing the amount of light that all other patches contribute to the patch. Central to this is the concept of the *form factor*, defined to be the fraction of energy that leaves surface j and lands on surface i. The radiosity B_i of surface i is given as:

$$B_i = E_i + \rho_i \sum_{j=1}^{n} B_j F_{ji}$$

where E_i is the light emitted by the patch, ρ_i is the reflectivity of the patch, and the summed term represents the contribution of all other surfaces to patch i. The fraction of light energy leaving surface A_i arriving at surface A_j (the form factor) is given as:

$$F_{dA_i \to A_j} = V_{ij} \int_{A_j} \frac{\cos \Theta_i \cos \Theta_j}{pr^2} dA_j$$

where V_{ij} is the visibility term, r the distance between the areas dA_j to the center of the element j, and Θ_i and Θ_j are the angles of the normals to the respective areas with the line connecting the two areas. The fraction of light energy leaving one surface and arriving at another surface is therefore a function of the distance

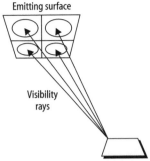

Emitting surface

Visibility rays

Receiving element   **Figure 14.1** Using ray casting to determine visibility.

between the surfaces, the relative orientation of the surfaces and the visibility of the two surfaces.

In practice, every surface in the environment is decomposed into a number of patches of unit area, across which the light emitted is deemed to be of a constant value. Patches are used either to receive light emitted from another surface or to emit light. Each receiving patch is usually decomposed into a number of smaller *elements*, which are used when receiving light from an emitter.

The most computationally demanding part of the radiosity solution is the calculation of the visibility between the receiving element and the emitting patch. Several techniques exist for determining this visibility – a popular method is the casting of rays from the vertices of receiving elements to the center of emitting patches. These rays are thus used to determine the visibility between the receiving vertex and the emitting patch (Figure 14.1).

Whether or not the patch vertex receives light energy is determined by the presence of other objects occupying space along the path of the ray between the emitting element and the receiving patch. Most surfaces will not of course lie along the path of any single ray, but inevitably in a complex environment an object will sometimes lie along a ray path and therefore block the light energy from the emitter. In a brute force approach, each visibility ray must be tested with every surface in the environment. This visibility determination has been calculated as by far the most expensive part of the radiosity algorithm, consuming some 70–85% of the total computation time [7]. As such it is the most appropriate candidate for acceleration.

14.2.2 Implementation Issues

14.2.2.1 Algorithms

Most radiosity implementations are based on the principle of *progressive refinement* [10], where the surface with the most light energy is first chosen to distribute all its light energy into the environment. Calculating the formfactors for all receiving vertices for this emitter effects this. Once the formfactors have been calculated for a single emitter, the image can be rendered, giving an approximation to the final image. The next most "energized" emitter can then be selected, and the process continues until the solution converges, that is, until only a small (predetermined) percentage of light energy remains to be distributed. In this way the image appears early in the solution, becoming gradually more refined as more emitters contribute to the image.

The progressive refinement algorithm can be summarized as:

1. Repeat until solution has converged
    2. Select the surface with highest energy (the emitter)
    3. Calculate form factors between the emitter and all receiving surfaces
    4. Update radiosities of the receiving surfaces
    5. Render and display the intermediate result

A common acceleration technique is found by directly addressing the major part of the calculation, i.e. the visibility testing between emitters and receivers. A spatial partitioning structure is built which subdivides space into smaller non-intersecting volume elements, or voxels. Each voxel contains only a subset of surfaces in the whole environment. As a ray is cast from the receiving surface to the emitter, only surfaces that lie in voxels along the ray path are tested for intersections. In this way a large number of redundant intersection tests can be avoided, as illustrated in Figure 14.2.

In Figure 14.2, a visibility ray is cast from a receiving vertex on surface A to an emitter B. Only surfaces lying in voxels along the path of the ray (i.e. surfaces G and H) are candidates for occlusion and must be tested. Other surfaces (C, D, E and F) need not be intersected. In the case shown, no surface is intersected along the path A–B, so vertex A will receive all the light energy emitted from surface B. This is an important efficiency gain, particularly for distributed rendering implementations, where surfaces may be distributed across the network and network traffic must be kept to a minimum.

14.2.2.2 Software

The object-oriented paradigm has proved popular in the design and implementation of photorealistic rendering algorithms. Object orientation is well suited to the design of complex algorithms where there are many different entities which must communicate by sharing data. Implementations can easily be of the order of hundreds of classes, comprising thousands of lines of code. Class reuse,

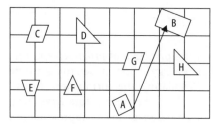

Figure 14.2 Ray–voxel crossing (2D).

inheritance, containment, information hiding and polymorphism can all be exploited in order to simplify implementations, enable extensibility, increase productivity and increase maintainability. Implementations are often in C++, where source code, although highly portable, can be compiled and optimized for the intended target operating system and architecture.

Example classes are:

- *Camera*, which provides the functionality to set up a viewing frustum and define transformation matrices for specified viewing parameters. Different camera implementations may invoke different characteristics (orthographic projection, parallel projection, etc.).
- *Geometry*, which provides the ability to store and access data to represent whole environments, identifiable objects (such as cars or buildings), surfaces (which together make up complete objects), and patches and elements.
- *Ray*, which provides the ability to store and access data to represent a generalized vector in space (for example, start point, end point, direction vector).

Libraries of classes are often designed which encapsulate particular groups of functionality.

14.3 Distributed Photorealistic Rendering

The focus of the research presented here is the efficient *distribution* of the application over a network of workstations. Issues in designing distributed systems include the identification of system entities and the efficient flow of data between these entities.

The architecture adopted here is one where the graphics database is distributed over a number of workstations. Such a scenario is one envisaged by recent industry standards for graphics environments, such as VRML [11], where parts of the virtual environment can be stored in different locations, specified by their URL. If the database resides on a single file on disk, a manager node is responsible for distributing the database across individual nodes on the network. Similarly, the manager node handles rendering of the radiosity data that is returned to it from the various nodes.

Central to the radiosity algorithm is the calculation of form factors for surfaces, and this forms the basis for the design of system objects, which operate in a client–server paradigm. A server encapsulates the geometry and material properties of an object (or number of objects) in the environment, and offers a variety of services to clients. A number of services which each server must offer have been identified:

- initialization of geometry and material data (i.e. building of internal data structures as appropriate to store geometry data – such as patch and element subdivision – and material property data)
- identification of the highest emitting surface in the local environment
- distribution of energy from a given emitting surface to all surfaces held locally
- distribution of the radiosities of locally held surfaces to a renderer

14.3.1 Implementation

A manager process initially parses the environment (i.e. the graphics database) and distributes geometry (and associated material properties) to server objects across the network. Depending on the number of available nodes on the network, some nodes in the environment may host more than one server object. When all the geometric objects have been distributed, the manager object sends a request to each server to return the energy associated with the largest emitting patch in their environment. The manager process then sorts the returns and selects the patch with the highest energy value in the whole environment. It then requests the geometry of this highest energy emitter from the appropriate server, and subsequently distributes this patch to all servers. All servers then distribute the light energy from this emitter to the geometry for which they are responsible. Since the implementation described here is a progressive refinement scheme, when the energy has been distributed the results (radiosities) of every object are returned to the manager, which can then render the scene, writing pixels to the local display. Figure 14.3 illustrates the architecture.

Note that, when calculating the form factors of surfaces, rays are cast from the receiving vertices of surfaces to the current emitting patch. When casting visibility rays, every surface lying in voxels in the path of these rays must be tested for intersection. This entails access to geometric data, which will not, in all probability, be available locally, but will reside on one or more remote nodes in the network. There are two basic approaches to solving this problem:

- the visibility ray is passed to the node where the required geometry is held and the remote node can perform the intersection test, returning the result
- the remote geometry is copied from the remote node where it is stored to the local node, where it can be tested against the visibility ray

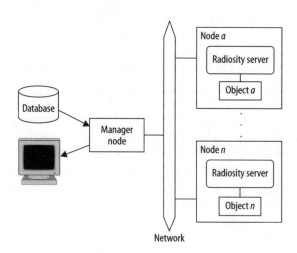

Figure 14.3 Distributed rendering architecture.

Experience shows that the latter scheme is the most efficient [5]. Strong spatial and temporal coherence can often exploited by such a system, since the likelihood is that adjacent visibility rays cast will cross the same space (over several frames), and therefore require access to the same object. By caching the remote geometry locally, network communication can be kept to a minimum and therefore the solution found more quickly. This scheme also avoids the situation where the node storing the geometry in the proximity of the emitter is swamped with requests for ray intersections from all other nodes, since a large number of rays will enter this space during each iteration of the progressive refinement loop.

14.4 WWW Technology

14.4.1 Programming Technology

Java has been adopted for WWW programming because of its ability to simplify the development of highly portable applications, and offers good support for the development of applications with graphical user interfaces. The close integration with Internet browser software and Java make it a useful language for the development of WWW applications. Java applets can be downloaded from remote servers over the WWW and run on the client platform without concerns about operating system or hardware. A run-time Java environment on the local machine executes the downloaded program, typically by interpreting the intermediate Java bytecode to the target architecture. In many cases the client application is embedded in an Internet browser. Java as a pure programming language exhibits many of the properties of popular object-oriented languages: data hiding, encapsulation and inheritance are all supported. Many elements familiar to C++ programmers have been simplified (such as memory management), which decreases development time for many applications.

One issue facing application developers is whether to redesign and implement their systems in Java. We decided not to pursue this for a number of reasons:

- Due in part to the highly visual nature of graphics, the success or failure of graphics applications is often determined by performance. Interpreted Java is not suitable for applications such as graphics, where rendering speed is often critical – even compiled Java suffers a performance penalty compared with, for example, C or C++.
- Like many software developers we faced legacy system issues when deciding whether or not to redesign and implement an existing system in a new language. Many graphics implementations are very large – the rendering system implemented here consists of more than 130 classes, for example – and the cost of redesigning such systems is very high.

The question may be not so much whether a total redesign in Java technology is warranted, but rather whether elements of the application can be developed which exploit Java's advantages for Internet programming, while leaving a large part of the application relatively untouched. In this way the advantages of high performance associated with compiled code (in C and C++) can be exploited and the cost-effectiveness of leaving existing implementations relatively untouched is achieved. By analyzing emerging distributed object technologies we can see that such a scenario is possible.

14.4.2 Application Communication Technology

In a distributed world, communication between objects can be critical to the performance of an application. Until recent advances in distributed technology, developers were forced to use proprietary or relatively low-level tools when implementing communications in a client–server environment. Sockets, for example, as endpoints for communication, proved popular for early implementations [12], but sockets are low-level mechanisms and few high-level tools were available to the developer. Most distributed applications tended to operate only in homogeneous (local) environments, where the computing resources were a known quantity and system developers could hand-tune applications for specific environments.

Following the widespread adoption of object-oriented technology for large applications there emerged a requirement for *distributed* object-based systems. Major industry players such as Microsoft and IBM are developing distributed object-based technologies, but a popular technology gaining widespread adoption in industry is the Object Management Group's Common Object Request Broker Architecture (CORBA) [13]. CORBA is an infrastructure for distributed objects, which together with Java is providing the mechanisms necessary for portable Internet-based applications which integrate with existing applications. CORBA can be thought of as the communications "glue" between existing client–server applications (written in any language) and portable Internet-aware applications implemented in Java [14].

14.4.2.1 *Common Object Request Broker Architecture (CORBA)*

CORBA can be viewed as an integration technology, not a programming technology. It provides the means for objects implemented in a number of languages (Java, C, C++, Ada etc.) to communicate across language boundaries via language-specific stubs. The advantage for the developer is that programmers can work completely within their favorite language environments. The fundamental approach taken by CORBA applications is a client–server paradigm. Client objects (*clients*) can invoke operations on server objects (*servers*) regardless of the programming language in which the server is implemented, or the host platform on which the server executes. As a result, the developer can focus on the design of the entities in the system and the specification of clear and precise interfaces for the objects – all underlying communication mechanisms are handled transparently. In order to achieve this, the services offered by each server object are defined in terms of a CORBA *interface* to the object. This interface is the only part of the object exposed to the distributed computing environment – the implementation remains hidden. Implementation of the objects can be in any one of a number of programming languages supported by the particular implementation of CORBA adopted – support for C, C++, Ada, Smalltalk and Java are available [15]. The key medium used to define the interface is the Interface Definition Language (IDL).

14.4.2.2 *The Interface Definition Language (IDL)*

The Interface Definition Language (IDL), specified by the OMG, is a standard language for defining interfaces between distributed components (objects). From IDL interface definitions, an ORB product automatically generates code in the chosen language to allow integration and distribution. In the system implemented here, each IDL interface is defined by a C++ class. This class must implement each of the functions that correspond to IDL operations and attributes. Instances of such classes (CORBA objects) are then accessible from anywhere in the distributed system. An example IDL class definition is given in Section 5.2.

14.5 Distributed Rendering Using CORBA

The CORBA application implemented consists of a set of objects, a number of client processes (*clients*) and a number of server processes (*servers*). Client objects issue requests to server objects through their exposed IDL interfaces. Note that server objects can also issue requests to other objects, in which case they become clients for the duration of the call. A server process can be manually started through an explicit call, or it can be activated dynamically at run time when a client binds to one of its objects.

The Client: a client needs only to be aware of the IDL interface of every available object in the distributed system, i.e. the operations that the object exposes. These operations are implemented (in our case) as C++ member functions. In order to call a member function of a CORBA object, a client first binds to it through the specification of a unique object identifier. A handle to the object is returned, through which the client can invoke member functions of the object.

The same handle is used to access both local and remote objects transparently. The object handle returned by the binding process is just a normal C++ pointer. When the required object is remote, the object handle refers to a *proxy* object for the remote object. A proxy is a local representative of a remote object, and its task is to forward calls to the remote object and return results to the client (Figure 14.4).

The Server: a server process can encapsulate more than one object. Each server process has a name, unique within its host machine. Objects are uniquely identified using:

- the object's name, which together with its interface name forms a unique handle within the server process
- the server process name
- the host name

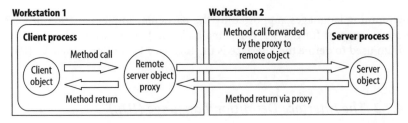

Figure 14.4 Client–server communication via proxy.

All servers in the distributed system are registered with an Implementation Repository (IR) before they can be used by clients. Registering the server with the IR involves mapping the server's name to the executable which implements that server. As a result, the program that implements the server can be dynamically loaded when a member function call is made to any of the objects managed by that particular server.

14.5.1 Creating a CORBA Object

CORBA objects can be created by defining IDL interfaces and subsequently implementing the methods specified by the interfaces. An existing C++ class can therefore be made CORBA-compliant through the addition of an IDL interface, which defines the services offered by the object. An IDL compiler creates an intermediate class from the interface definition. The CORBA class is then created by inheriting from this intermediate class and the existing C++ class. Instances of this derived class are then valid CORBA objects. The transition from an existing C++ class to a CORBA class is therefore reasonably straightforward: once the IDL interface has been defined, automatic tools are available to assist in the creation of the CORBA-compliant class.

14.5.2 Example IDL Definition of a Radiosity Server

Associated with each geometric object is a server process, which handles all interface to other objects (clients). A typical interface to such a server may be:

```
interface IDL_RadiosityServer {
    Surface IntersectRay (Ray ray);
    short GetLargestEmitter ();
    PatchGeometry GetLargestEmitter();
    void ShootEnergy (Patch emitter);
    Energies GetEnergies();
}
```

This interface is directly associated with the services identified in Section 14.3. The reader is pointed to [16] for further details of the implementation.

14.5.3 Advanced Features

14.5.3.1 Multi-threaded objects

In order to accommodate different applications, CORBA offers a number of integration hooks that the developer can use to tailor the implementation for the specific application. For example, *filters* allow the developer to specify code to be executed, for example, before or after every CORBA call. We have found filters useful to implement multi-threading and thereby increase efficiency. By default, a server process has only one thread, which handles incoming requests. As a result, a server can only handle one call at a time, which is potentially damaging to the performance of the system, as all other calls to the server will block pending completion of this call. In our case, a filter is used which creates a separate (lightweight) thread for each server request. The threading mechanism of the underlying operating system (Windows NT in this case) is used to supply the required functionality. This mechanism is particularly useful in the implementation of the server object that handles requests to intersect a ray with a geometric object. At any one time, a single server object may receive many requests for such intersections from a number of clients. Rather than queuing these requests in a single-threaded system, in our system each request spawns a separate thread of control. In this way many requests may be handled simultaneously.

14.5.3.2 Caching Remote Data Locally

The automatically generated CORBA proxy class can also be used as a base class for a more efficient kind of proxy class, called a *smart* proxy, which can provide local caching of data from a remote object. This feature is particularly useful for applications such as photorealistic graphics, where spatial and temporal coherence is often high, and local caching of remote data can have significant impact on the performance of a system [5]. This feature has been used to implement the geometry caching scheme outlined in Section 14.3.1.

14.5.3.3 Copying Data Across Process Boundaries

According to the CORBA standard (version 2.0), objects can be passed to and from hosts only by reference. This represents a barrier to efficient program design, since there are occasions when an object must be *copied* from one host to another, particularly during initialization. Copying an object requires that its internal state is passed from a source process to a target process, and a copy of the passed object is constructed in the new location. To achieve this, an extension to the CORBA 2.0 standard is adopted: a special type of object called an *opaque type*, which permits object copying across process boundaries. Special marshaling and unmarshaling functions must be provided by the user which pack the object state for transmission and unpack it at the new location, thereby creating a new instance of the object. The overhead of constructing the special functions required is relatively small, and we have found the use of opaque types useful in the design of the manager process, which initializes the system.

CORBA is therefore an appropriate technology for implementing application to application communication in a heterogeneous object-based distributed application such as photorealistic rendering. Many of the features desirable for distributed rendering (data copying, data caching, multi-threading in a client–server world) are supported by CORBA. We now look at how a complete Internet-based application can be developed which exploits the relative advantages of Java, C++ and CORBA technologies.

14.6 Remote Rendering on the WWW

We see the architecture presented as suitable in cases where there is a requirement for high-quality rendering but resources are not available locally. The graphics database may reside on the client or on the server. If it exists on the client, the database is uploaded to the remote rendering server, where all rendering takes place. Rendered frames are downloaded from the server to the client application, where they are viewed. All user interaction (such as navigating through the virtual environment) is handled by the client.

The scenario envisaged is as follows: the client application is running an Internet browser, with a Java run-time environment on the local machine. Since implementations of CORBA classes in Java are available (and future releases of Java promise a native Java ORB), this provides the ability to dynamically (and transparently) CORBA-enable Java applets on the client side.

The end-user navigates using a browser to the required URL, which identifies an HTML page containing an applet tag. The browser downloads and interprets the HTML, and subsequently the Java classes are downloaded to the local Java interpreter. As the Java interpreter processes this top-level code, it automatically downloads the IDL stubs and then the required Java classes to CORBA-enable the applet. All this is transparent to the end-user. Once CORBA-enabled, the applet can then communicate with the back-end CORBA-compliant services on the server, i.e. the remote radiosity rendering system as presented in Section 14.3. The architecture is shown in Figure 14.5.

14.6.1 Local Services

The client side of the proposed architecture deals with the initialization of the application and all subsequent user interaction. It can upload and download data to and from the remote servers. User interaction is necessary for many graphics applications today, where the user may be navigating through the virtual environment. To enable the user-side services to be fully portable they are implemented in Java. A number of services have been identified which are desirable for the client:

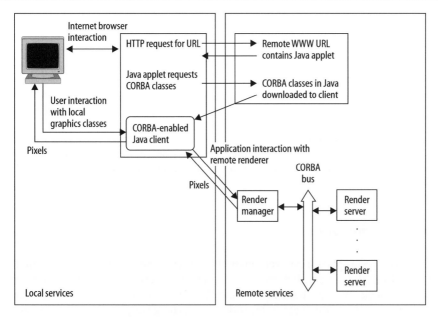

Figure 14.5 Remote rendering over the WWW.

- CORBA-enabling the local Java client, connecting to back-end services (i.e. the remote renderer)
- determine the current view in response to user navigation through mouse, keyboard etc.
- upload view parameters to the server
- upload requests for rendering to the server
- download frames from the server and display locally

The client software therefore handles user navigation through the virtual environment. This includes the ability to change camera parameters such as view position and look-at position and to accept mouse or other interaction device input. Advanced user interaction such as picking and highlighting of objects may require additional support via, for example, the ability to upload a pixel position on the screen to the server. Alternatively, the client may be better equipped to handle such services locally; in which case some of the services can migrate from the remote server to the local application.

14.6.2 Remote Services

The remote graphics server provides all the functionality necessary to render a graphics scene and download pixels to the application. Since the database can reside either at the client or on the server side, the server can also receive the geometry from the client if necessary. The addition of server-side frame compression and client-side frame decompression can aid the speed of communication of frames to the client application. In addition to the rendering functionality already described, remote services include:

- ability to receive the graphics database from the client application
- ability to receive camera parameters from the client application
- ability to receive requests for rendering from the client application
- ability to download frames (compressed) to the client application for local display

Depending on the application, some or all of the services may migrate over the WWW to the local server. For example, if the local server has a dedicated graphics engine, it may be appropriate to handle all the rendering of the radiosities locally.

14.7 Conclusions

Internet-based application development is maturing rapidly. Technologies such as Java and CORBA, integrated with existing technologies, are providing the necessary protocols and mechanisms for the development of Internet-based client–server applications which are independent of language implementation, operating system and the architecture of the underlying hardware. Application developers can concentrate on the design of system-level entities rather than focusing on lower-level object communication mechanisms.

As new and more efficient algorithms are developed using such technology, they can be (relatively) seamlessly integrated with existing implementations without regard to the client software. This benefits both the application developer and the user – the application developer can extend and optimize the algorithms without a total redesign of the system or rebuilding of large executables, and the user benefits by being able to use state-of-the-art technology. Implementations remain hidden behind the exposed interfaces.

This chapter has reported on the development of an existing object-based graphics application to a Internet-based distributed environment exploiting platform independence via Java and CORBA technologies. The work presented here shows that the necessary technologies for Internet-based distributed applications are maturing rapidly, and are suitable for complex applications such as graphics. Advantages include:

- No special hardware or software (beyond the Java run-time environment) is required.
- Users can exploit the resources of large numbers of networked computers to accelerate the application, thereby reducing computational time and cost.
- Developers can continually update components of software without the need to build and distribute large monolithic applications and distribute bug fixes etc.

Further work is needed to implement the system described here on a larger number of machines to investigate issues of scalability and load balancing. In addition, work is required on the effects of security in Internet networks (such as the existence of firewalls) on the performance of the system.

Acknowledgments

The author acknowledges the contributions of the members and former members of the Centre for VLSI and Computer Graphics, School of Engineering, University of Sussex, and in particular Antony Plataniotis. Much of the groundwork for this paper took place at the University of Sussex.

References

[1] SE Chen, K Turkowski and D Turner (1991) An object-oriented testbed for global illumination, *Eurographics Workshop on Object-Oriented Graphics*, pp. 155–66.

[2] P Slusallek and H Seidel (1995) Object-oriented design for image synthesis, in *Eurographics '95, Proceedings of the 5th Eurographics Workshop on Programming Paradigms in Graphics*, Maastricht, The Netherlands, September, pp. 285–96.

[3] M Feda and Purgathofer (1994) Progressive refinement radiosity on a transputer network, in *Photorealistic Rendering in Computer Graphics: Proceedings of the 2nd Eurographics Workshop on Rendering*, pp. 139–48.

[4] W Sturzlinger, G Schaufler and J Volkert (1995) Load balancing for a parallel radiosity algorithm, *Parallel Rendering Symposium*, Atlanta, October, pp. 39–45.

[5] D Badouel, K Bouatouch and T Priol (1994) Distributing data and control for ray tracing in parallel, *Computer Graphics & Applications*, 14(4), 69–77.

[6] P Guitton, J Roman and C Schlick (1991) Two parallel approaches for a progressive radiosity, *Proc. 2nd Eurographics Workshop on Rendering*, Barcelona, May.

[7] A Ng and M Slater (1993) A Multiprocessor implementation of radiosity, *Computer Graphics Forum*, 12(5), 29–342.

[8] CM Goral, KE Torrance, DP Greenberg *et al.* Modeling the interaction of light between diffuse surfaces, *SIGGRAPH '84 Conference Proceedings, Computer Graphics*, 18(3), 213–22.

[9] MF Cohen, DP Greenberg, DS Immel *et al.* (1986) An efficient radiosity approach for realistic image synthesis, *Computer Graphics & Applications*, 6(3), 26–35.

[10] MF Cohen, SE Chen, JR Wallace *et al.* (1988) A progressive refinement approach to fast radiosity image generation, *SIGGRAPH '88 Proceedings, Computer Graphics*, 22(4), 75–84.

[11] The Virtual Reality Modeling Language (VRML) Specification; http://vrml.sgi.com/.

[12] M-P Hébert, DJ McNeill, B Shah *et al.* (1990) MARTI – a multiprocessor architecture for ray tracing images, *Proc. Fifth Eurographics Hardware Workshop*, Lausanne, September.

[13] The Common Object Request Broker: Architecture and Specification, Revision 2.0, July 1995, OMG; http://www.omg.org/corba/corbiiop.htm.

[14] D Curtis, *Java, RMI and CORBA*, White Paper, Object Management Group; http://www.omg.org/news/wpjava.htm.

[15] Orbix, IONA Technologies Ltd; http://www.iona.ie/Products/Orbix.

[16] A Plataniotis, S Samothrakis, MDJ McNeill *et al.* (1997) Distributed, Object-based Radiosity, *Sixth Eurographics Workshop on Programming Paradigms in Graphics*, Budapest, September.

15

Multi-User Visualization: a CORBA/Web-Based Approach

Bastiaan Schönhage and Anton Eliëns

Abstract

This chapter introduces a framework for visualization in a distributed multi-user environment which builds upon two important observations. First, multiple users with different backgrounds have individual information needs and thus require multiple views of the information. Second, to allow users to experiment with the information and the visualization the visualization must be adaptable. To meet these requirements, the framework decouples the generation and presentation of information by means of an intermediate derived model, allowing users to adapt the visualization to their information needs.

As a realization of the framework, we will discuss a Web-based software architecture which deploys CORBA to allow for dynamic and interactive visualizations. The distributed visualization architecture, DIVA, consists of generic software components reflecting the conceptual framework. Using Web-based standards, such as VRML and Java, the visualization can be deployed independently of the platform used. As an example, we discuss the visualization of business process simulations where multiple users can view the generated information on-the-fly while controlling the running simulation.

15.1 Multi-User Visualization

In recent years, the quantity of available information has increased enormously due to the application of information databases and the Internet. However, although computers and networks are getting better at managing information, people have only a limited capacity to do so. To aid people in finding the right information, visualization can be deployed. Visualization abstracts from the low-level contents of data and shows graphical representations of aspects of information that are interesting to the user.

15.1.1 Visualization

Visualization is the transformation of data and information into presentable media including pictures, animation and 3D scenes. It presents data in a form that enables users to understand and manipulate it more naturally. Visualization often comes in two flavors: scientific and information visualization. McCormick *et al.* define scientific visualization as follows: "Visualization is a method of computing. It transforms the symbolic into the geometric, enabling researchers to observe their simulations and computations" [9]. Scientific visualization is used by experts to give a deeper understanding of scientific phenomena. Examples of scientific visualization are the visualization of the flow of air and a 3D volumetric visualization of an MRI scan.

Recently, a new visualization research focus has emerged, intended to visualize abstract information. Robertson *et al.* state: "Information visualization attempts to display structural relationships and context that would be more difficult to detect by individual retrieval requests" [11]. Consequently, information visualization is used by a more diverse audience whose focus is on searching for structure in the information (see also [7]).

Most of the time, visualization is used to present static information. This can be information stored in a database, information resulting from a simulation or information about the structure of a large corporate Web site. However, sometimes it is more useful to visualize dynamically changing data. For example, visualizing a running simulation model will improve the understanding of the simulation. Additionally, some relationships between information concepts are only discovered when users are able to see the dynamics of the information.

When using dynamic data as the source of visualization, new visualization primitives have to be used to present dynamic information. Instead of a static picture or a static 3D model, an animation or an animated 3D scene has to be presented to show the dynamics of the underlying simulation.

15.1.2 Example of Multi-User Visualization

To illustrate our architecture for multi-user visualization, we will first describe an application of distributed multi-user visualization. We will use this example to motivate the requirements for the system and as the basis for discussing its architecture.

Imagine an international company with offices in countries all over the world. The CEOs of the company have decided that the offices in different countries have to standardize the work process to improve the service level of the whole company. A business process redesign (BPR) project is started which must result in a standardized business process based on the different existing ones. The managers in the different countries will make the final decisions about the new work processes at a conference. However, they want to prepare and discuss some alternatives before the actual decisions are made.

We want to deploy information technology to support the managers in studying the alternatives and making the decisions. In addition to Web pages and email to exchange information, we create business process simulations to *execute* the redesign alternatives [2]. To fully exploit the potential of the business simulations we

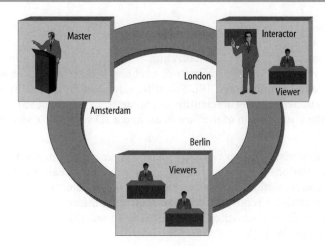

Figure 15.1 Example configuration of a multi-user visualization system.

want to allow the managers to discuss both the results of the simulation, e.g. the costs and profits, and the running simulation itself, e.g. to illustrate the activities in the redesigned alternative.

Essentially, we want to support two forms of collaboration: *synchronous distributed* and *face to face* [4, 15]. First, to help the managers prepare for the conference, we support *synchronous distributed* collaboration, where the users cooperate at the same time but at different places. Second, at the conference, where the decisions are made, the managers will discuss the selected alternatives *face to face*, i.e. same time, same place.

By taking a closer look at the example, we can discriminate some roles that the participants of the distributed visualization play. First there is the role of the *master* who demonstrates a redesign alternative to a number of *viewers*. The viewers are allowed to follow the explanation and browse through the information coming from the demonstration. They are not allowed to interact with the business simulation itself. However, to increase the interactivity of the session, a number of people may be allowed to interact with the simulation. We will call them the *interactors*.

Figure 15.1 illustrates an example configuration consisting of one master, one interactor and three listeners. The master in Amsterdam presents the results of the running simulation to the interactor in London and the three viewers (two in Berlin and one in London). How the information coming from the simulation must be presented to the users and what software architecture is needed to support this process is the subject of the rest of this chapter.

15.1.3 Requirements for Multi-User Information Visualization

Visualization is employed to equip users with the required information. However, multiple users often have different information requirements. For example, a BPR project is typically performed by a team of people with different backgrounds. A team can consist of external BPR specialists, management of the company and employees who are executing the business process. Every individual of the BPR team has his or her own information needs to evaluate the design alternatives. Consequently, when multiple users have different information requirements they need a different view (i.e. visualization) of the data. A flexible visualization system must support this by allowing multiple views of the information.

In the example described we have two levels of interaction: no interaction (viewer) and full interaction (master and interactor). In an elaborate collaboration system this will probably not be enough, and something more fine-grained is needed.

Interaction allows users to experiment with alternative situations to understand the consequences of changes to the simulation model. Instead of a number of fixed experiments, the interactor is able to play with the possible alternatives herself. By making the coupling of generating and visualizing information loosely, we allow for multiple adaptable views on the information.

To allow for synchronous distributed cooperation, it is necessary to have the information available at the desktop of the individuals. This requires a distributed system where the users are linked via a computer network. Furthermore, there is a preference to integrate the visualization architecture with the World Wide Web. The Web is an excellent medium to provide the context of the visualization, consisting of information such as text, pictures, sound and video. Additionally, by using Web-based standards such as HTML, VRML and Java the visualization can be deployed independently of the platform used.

Concluding, we have three requirements to support multiple users in visualizing information:

1. Multiple views or perspectives to support users with different information needs.
2. Adaptive visualization to allow for experimentation.
3. Networked or Web-based architecture to support visualization at the user's desktop.

15.2 A Conceptual Architecture for Distributed Visualization

As we have seen above, the process of visualization transforms data and information from the symbolic into the geometric. In other words, we create a visual representation of the available information. In a single-user/single-machine environment, a visualization program can read and process the data on the hard disk and display the visualization on the monitor. When we extend this to a distributed multi-user environment things get more complicated and we have to rethink the architecture.

We regard the process of visualization as a transition of data through a sequence of models, starting with the generation of data and ending with the presentation of a visualization [13]. To allow multiple perspectives on the data, we introduce an intermediate model between the generation and presentation of information. This

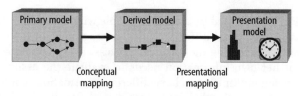

Figure 15.2 Conceptual architecture.

intermediate model contains information based on the originally generated data, adapted to the information requirements of its users.

15.2.1 Primary, Derived and Presentation Models

Figure 15.2 depicts our architecture on a conceptual level. It contains three models going from symbolic data in the primary model to a visual representation in the presentation model.

The *primary model* is the source of the visualization. It contains explicitly or implicitly all information that is available. A static primary model, for example, is the database that contains the data used in the visualization. In this case, the primary model explicitly contains the data the system is using to make a visualization. The situation is somewhat different when simulation is used to visualize dynamic data. In this case, the primary model is the simulation model that the simulation program is using to generate data. This difference draws the essential distinction between visualizing static and dynamic data: in static data visualization the primary model never changes, whereas in dynamic visualization new data is generated based on a primary model. In the rest of this chapter we will focus on the visualization of dynamic data.

The intermediate model between the generation and presentation of information is the *derived model*. It contains information derived from the primary model. The idea is that the derived model forms the information that is presented during the visualization process because it has adapted the data from the primary model to the information requirements of its users. Consequently, several derived models can be created to serve a number of users based on a single primary model.

The rightmost box in Figure 15.2 is the *presentation model*, which is used to display the visualization. What the presentation model contains is dependent on the presentation technique used, e.g. for 3D visualizations the presentation model is the 3D scene graph. By separating the derived and presentation model, users can share the derived model while their presentation is different. The information content of the visualization is the same, although the *style* can differ depending on the available platform and the user's preferences.

15.2.2 Transition from Model to Model

In addition to the three models described above, Figure 15.2 contains two transitions or mappings between the models. The *conceptual mapping* (from the primary to the derived model) gives us the flexibility to adapt the data space to our information needs. This is useful because we are only interested in information with some value for our current interest; data only becomes information when it is of use to answer the questions we have. As a consequence, data in the derived model differs from data in the primary model in two ways. First, only data that is useful for the current perspective is selected for the derived model, and second, information derived from primary data is added to the derived model.

The mapping from the derived to the presentation model allows us to specify how to present the information available in the derived model. In [3] we have demonstrated that style sheets are a powerful means to specify the presentation of hypermedia and multimedia documents. In line with this approach, we believe that a combination of (1) high-level mappings to application-specific visualization primitives and (2) style sheets to fine tune the visualization are powerful enough for most visualization applications.

15.2.3 Example

To illustrate the conceptual architecture, we will show an example of the Amsterdam–London–Berlin architecture. In our example (Figure 15.3) we have one primary model (the business simulation), two derived models and the six persons (views) in the three different cities. The arrows illustrate the flow of data and information through the system. For simplicity, we have not drawn the flow of control.

As can be seen from the figure, all but one of the users share the same derived model. They share the same information that is used for the visualization. However, although the information content is the same, the five viewers can display the information according to their preferred style. The manager in London might use moving objects to illustrate activity, whereas the master in Amsterdam employs color to visualize the same information.

One person in Berlin has her own derived model, and focuses on a different aspect of the simulation. She might, for example, be interested in the resource allocation in

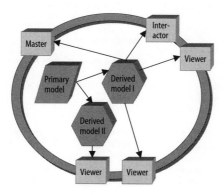

Figure 15.3 Example of conceptual architecture.

the redesign alternative and hence require completely distinct information. As said before, we can realize this because we are using derived models that stand between the primary and presentation models which users or groups of users can employ to base their visualization on.

15.3 DIVA Software Architecture

The *distributed visualization architecture*, DIVA, reflects the conceptual architecture outlined in the previous section. DIVA consists of generic software components that embody the primary, derived and presentation model. These components, written in C++ and Java, can easily be reused to create new visualization applications.

15.3.1 Software Components

Figure 15.4 illustrates the DIVA architecture, containing six components (represented by the boxes). The three large boxes at the top represent the main components containing the information models. The components represented by the three small boxes are used to control the visualization. The fat arrows in Figure 15.4 represent the flow of data and information through the architecture, while the small arrows represent the control responsibilities.

The *generator* component contains the primary model and generates all the data needed for the visualization. In our example, the generator is a simulation program which runs a business process simulation and hence generates the raw simulation output. This output is fed to the next component, the *shared concept space*. To control the simulation, i.e. the generator, a separate *generation control* component is introduced. This control may be deployed by masters and interactors, but is unavailable for viewers who are not allowed to interact with the simulation.

The component embodying the derived model must allow for an expressive and adaptive storage of information. As explained before, the users must be able to adapt the derived model in such a way that it suits their information needs. In our

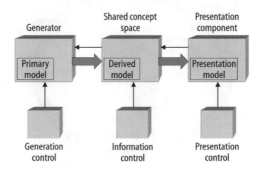

Figure 15.4 Components of the DIVA architecture.

approach we have defined the *shared concept space*, which is a software component containing hierarchical conceptual data. The hierarchical nature of the derived model enables the clustering of information in concepts and subconcepts which allows a better separation of useful and superfluous information. The data coming from the generator is stored in the *data properties* of the concepts. During the session, these concepts are updated to new values by the generator. What information is selected to appear in the concept space and what new information is derived using *computed properties* is controlled using the *information control* component. As with the generation control, this control can only be used by masters and interactors.

The *presentation component* is used to present the visualization. This component is used to execute the main part of the visualization process: transforming the information in the shared concept space to a visual representation. It does this by mapping the information concepts in the derived model to visualization primitives (*gadgets*) in the presentation model. The gadgets are generic visualization primitives which are used to present certain types of information. Examples of gadgets are rotating or moving objects to represent activity and histograms to give statistical overviews.

15.3.2 CORBA

DIVA is designed as a *distributed object-oriented* system. This implies that it is based on software components which are distributed over a network. The components provide an interface offering services to other objects.

The Object Management Group's (OMG) *Common Object Request Broker Architecture* (CORBA) is an architecture to create applications using distributed objects. The distributed objects, collected in components, can be used like local objects. The software components allow for multiple interfaces which are specified using the *interface definition language* (IDL). The communication between the components of the distributed application takes place via an *object request broker* (ORB).

CORBA abstracts from hardware, operating system and programming language. It enables, for example, the connection of C++ components on Unix machines with Java components on Windows NT/95 machines.

By combining CORBA and Web technologies such as HTML, Java and VRML, it is possible to connect server components with platform-independent Java clients. For example, the DIVA generator and shared concept space components can be hosted on heavy Unix servers, while the presentation components are run in a Web browser on Windows client machines. More information about CORBA can be found in [16]; more about the integration of CORBA and Java is in [10].

15.3.3 Web-Based Visualization

Like most Web-based visualizations (see for a number of examples [12]) we deploy the Virtual Reality Modeling Language (VRML) [8] to display the visualization.

This is because VRML has the promising features of being platform-independent, integrated in the Web and extensible with Java and JavaScript control.

Users navigate through the 3D scene by means of a VRML browser. The contents of the visualization is altered by the Java–CORBA presentation component which communicates with the VRML browser through the *external authoring interface*. This combination of CORBA, Java and VRML offers us enough flexibility to present dynamic visualizations of running simulations.

15.4 Multi-User Support in DIVA

The previous section describes how a DIVA visualization application is split up into components. However, nothing has been said about the flow of data and control between the components. When we want to use the architecture for multi-user visualization, it is important to describe how multiple users can use the same server component and, additionally, how data coming from a server can be broadcast to multiple users.

15.4.1 Patterns to Support Multiple Users

To support multiple users we have to transport the dynamic data coming from the generator via the shared concept space to the presentation component of the user. When new data or information is generated, the derived model and the presentation model might be updated depending on the conceptual and presentational mapping. To show how this can be achieved, we will discuss two design patterns. Design patterns are "descriptions of communicating objects and classes that are customized to solve a general design problem in a particular context" [5]. Patterns are a kind of best-practice solution to common problems such as updating a number of viewers.

15.4.1.1 Observer Pattern

The observer pattern, discussed in [5], describes a one-to-many dependency. As illustrated in Figure 15.5, there is one subject, which contains a state, and a number of observers, who are interested in the subject's state and consequently in updates to the subject's state. The subject contains a list of its observers and sends each observer an `update` message when its state has changed (a). Thereupon, the observers ask the subject for its new state (`getstate`) and get the new state back from the subject (`result`) (b).

In DIVA we could apply the observer pattern between the generator (subject) and the shared concept space (observer) or between the shared concept space (subject) and the presentation component (observer). When a component decides that an update is not necessary because it is of no interest to the user (based on the

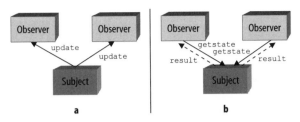

Figure 15.5 Observer pattern.

mapping between the components), it can decide not to send an `update` message (subject-side) or to ignore the `update` message (observer-side).

However, there is one major drawback when using the observer pattern for multiple users: it does not scale very well. The subject is dependent on the number of observers in the sense that upon sending an update message, it is unknown how many observers require additional action by issuing a `getstate` operation. When the number of interested observers reaches a certain limit, the subject can get overloaded.

15.4.1.2 Talker–Listener Pattern

The talker–listener pattern, sometimes called publisher–subscriber, is based on an intermediate communication channel between the talker (subject) and the listeners (observers). The talker publishes its data and information on the single channel which takes care of the distribution to the different listeners (see Figure 15.6). Instead of an `update`, `getstate` and `result` message, the talker has to publish the changed data immediately. The advantage for the talker is clear: it does not have to maintain a list of observers. Instead, it can talk to a single interface without having to worry about joining and leaving listeners.

In this pattern, the talker is completely independent of the interested listeners. Whether the number of listeners is large or small, and whether it increases or decreases is irrelevant to the involved talker. Concluding, the talker–listener scales much better than the observer pattern.

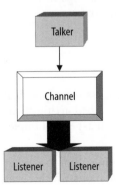

Figure 15.6 Talker–listener pattern.

As a remark, we want to add that matters are not as black and white as discussed here. Hybrid solutions integrating parts of both patterns are very well possible.

15.4.2 Multicasting in CORBA

Because of the advantages discussed above, we have decided to apply the talker–listener pattern to distribute updates in DIVA. How the pattern is implemented depends on the available services of the CORBA implementation. In a bare CORBA system, we can write a channel component ourselves which distributes the updates to the available listeners, using simple one-to-one communication.

In a more elaborate CORBA system, services are available that support the talker–listener pattern. For example, Iona's OrbixTalk (for more information see http://www.iona.com/) is such a service. OrbixTalk distributes information from talker to listener transparently using IP multicast. The channel broadcasts the incoming data to a multitude of listeners by sending it only once to an IP multicast group. The listeners, who are part of the IP multicast group, pick up the needed data and continue working with the updated information. For the distributed objects, it seems as if they are talking respectively listening to local objects. OrbixTalk also supports, in addition to a *reliable multicast protocol*, a *store-and-forward protocol* allowing listeners to join a session after it has started. The channel will bring the late listener up-to-date by sending the stored updates.

15.4.3 Multi-users in DIVA

Currently, the exchange of information between the generator and the shared concept space and between the shared concept space and the presentation is based on the talker–listener pattern. This implies that data from the running simulation is efficiently sent to some derived models. After the data has been processed, the adapted information is broadcast to a number of viewers.

Our support for more involved collaborative tasks, such as exporting viewpoints or perspectives and direct user-to-user communication, is, however, still immature, and the subject of our current research. By extending the DIVA architecture with session management and more interaction support we want to expand it from multi-user visualization to a collaborative visualization architecture.

15.5 Practical Considerations

Before ending up with the conclusions, we would like to discuss some practical considerations of implementing a prototype based on the described architecture. We will do this point by point by addressing the most important aspects of implementing DIVA.

Currently, we do not have a full-blown prototype implementing all of the issues discussed in this paper. However, we have partial implementations which cover some of the most critical parts. We are integrating these partial implementations into a more complete *proof of concept*.

15.5.1 (Business Process) Simulation

To generate data for visualization we use the discrete event simulation library SIM [1]. SIM has been written in C++ and thus can easily be wrapped into a CORBA component. An arbitrary simulation model can be programmed in C++ using the SIM library. However, event graph simulations can easily be specified using a text-based specification.

In addition to SIM, we are using BPSIM [2], which is a business process simulation library built on top of SIM. BPSIM is based on the *logistics-based modeling* method [6], offering high-level primitive entities such as *operation*, *waitqueue* and *employee*.

15.5.2 Shared Concept Space

At the moment, the shared concept space has been implemented as a (hierarchical) data dictionary. Derived properties, which base their outcome on distinct data properties, can be integrated, but have to be programmed at compile time.

To increase the flexibility, we are experimenting with knowledge base technologies that allow for dynamically adding (or removing) derived properties at runtime.

15.5.3 Visualization

Currently, we have two distinct implementations of the presentation component, one Web browser plug-in based on C++ and the visualization toolkit VTK [14]. The other one is based on VRML 2.0 and Java. Because of the promising features of VRML and Java, such as Web integration, platform independence and the possibility to create interactive, animated 3D scenes through the *external authoring interface*, we will focus on the VRML visualization in the future.

15.5.4 CORBA and Multicasting

We have implemented DIVA components in C++ and Java, on Sun Sparc Solaris and Pentium Windows NT/95. Because we are using CORBA-compliant ORBs, supporting the Internet Inter-Orb Protocol (IIOP), these components can cooperate seamlessly.

More problematic is the incorporation of a Talker–Listener service into the prototype. The discussed OrbixTalk would be a good candidate if it supported Java. However, OrbixTalk only supports C++ and thus cannot be used to broadcast updates to Java presentation components.

Implementations of the standard OMG Event Service – a service to broadcast untyped events to a number of listeners (see [16]) – exists, but is currently not implemented using IP Multicasting.

Another interesting option is to use Object Space's Voyager (for more information see http://www.objectspace.com/voyager/). Voyager is a Java-based "Agent ORB" supporting mobile Java objects and CORBA and DCOM integration. Voyager contains "Spaces," which are groups of objects. When you send a message (e.g. a data update) this message will be multicast to all members of the space. Hence, the Voyager Space architecture implements a variation of the talker–listener pattern. However, the Voyager multicast messages are not completely reliable, implying that updates might get lost when a listener is momentary unreachable.

Concluding, we state that although in theory a scalable CORBA-based multicasting architecture is possible, there is currently no practically applicable solution available.

15.6 Conclusions

This chapter presents an architecture to support multiple users in visualizing dynamic data. First, we support multiple views or perspectives by means of a number of derived models based on a single simulation. Second, we allow adaptive visualization by means of a modification of the mappings between the models, using the control components. Finally, we use distributed object technology to create networked visualization. DIVA enables the visualization of dynamic data in a Web browser by means of Web technologies such as Java and VRML.

To support multiple users in visualizing dynamic data we deploy the talker–listener pattern, which is based on a communication channel between talker and listener components. By using a channel which is implemented with IP multicast groups this solution becomes well scalable.

Currently, we are investigating the possibility of extending DIVA to collaborative visualization by means of interactive visualization and user-to-user communication.

References

[1] D Bolier and A Eliëns (1994) Sim – a C++ library for discrete event simulation, *Technical Report IR-367*, Vrije Universiteit, Amsterdam, November.
[2] A Eliëns, F Niessink, SPC Schönhage, JR van Ossenbruggen and P Nash (1996) Support for business process redesign: simulation, hypermedia and the Web, in *Euromedia 96: Telematics in a Multimedia Environment*, London, UK, December, The Society for Computer Simulation International, pp. 193–200.
[3] A Eliëns, JR van Ossenbruggen and SPC Schönhage (1997) Animating the Web – an SGML-based approach, in *The Internet in 3D – Information, Images and Interaction* (eds. R Earnshaw and J Vince), Academic Press, London.

[4]   CA Ellis, SJ Gibbs and GL Rein (1991) Groupware: some issues and experiences, Communications of the ACM, 34(1), 680–9.

[5]   E Gamma, R Helm, R Johnson and J Vlissides (1994) *Design Patterns – Elements of Reusable Object-Oriented Software*, Professional Computing Series, Addison-Wesley, Reading MA.

[6]   JWM Gerrits (1995) Towards information logistics: an exploratory study of logistics in information production, *PhD Thesis*, Faculty of Economic Sciences, Business Administration and Econometrics, Vrije Universiteit, Amsterdam.

[7]   N Gershon and SG Eick (1997) Information visualization, *IEEE Computer Graphics & Applications*, 17(4), 29–31.

[8]   International Organization for Standardization (1997) The Virtual Reality Modeling Language, *Draft International Standard ISO/IEC DIS 14772-1*.

[9]   BH McCormick, TA DeFanti and MD Brown (1987) Visualization in scientific computing, *ACM SIGGRAPH Computer Graphics*, 21(6).

[10] R Orfali and D Harkey (1997) *Client Server Programming with JAVA and CORBA*, John Wiley & Sons, Chichester.

[11] GG Robertson, SK Card and JD Mackinlay (1993) Information Visualization using 3D Interactive Animation, *Communications of the ACM*, 36(4), 57–71.

[12] RM Rohrer and E Swing (1997) Web-based Information Visualization, *IEEE Computer Graphics & Applications*, 17(4), 52–9.

[13] SPC Schönhage and A Eliëns (1997) A flexible architecture for user-adaptable visualization, in *Workshop on New Paradigms in Information Visualization and Manipulation '97, Conference on Information and Knowledge Management*, 10–14 November, Las Vegas, USA.

[14] W Schroeder, K Martin and B Lorensen (1996) *The Visualization Toolkit: an Object-Oriented Approach to 3D Graphics*, Prentice Hall, Englewood Cliffs NJ.

[15] B Shneiderman (1998) *Designing the User-Interface, Strategies for Effective Human–Computer Interaction*, 3rd edn Addison-Wesley, Reading MA.

[16] J Siegel (1996) *CORBA Fundamentals and Programming*, John Wiley & Sons, Chichester.

16

Scene Capture and Modeling for Three-Dimensional Interactive Stereo Television Broadcasting

A.L. Thomas

Abstract

A way of merging the broadcast transmission of images generated synthetically using geometric modeling systems and computer graphics with images captured by TV cameras is presented. Taking advantage of the good points of each method increases the capabilities of the whole broadcasting system by extending digital display technology into the TV industry. Digital television already exists, based on the digital frame store which by itself permits some integration between the synthesized and the captured, using common hardware and common algorithms. However, more seems to be on offer.

16.1 Introduction

Initially, the frame store-based image representation (as an array of pixel color values) presented bandwidth problems for broadcasting, owing to the volume of raw digital data which this required to be transmitted to maintain refresh video rates. The current approach employed in MPEG systems is a *bottom up* solution to this difficulty, using signal processing and image compression techniques.

Another possibility is emerging. Transmitting animated images over the Internet is not confined to video-sourced sequences. It is now possible to transmit animated synthetic sequences using scene modeling and local display-processing capabilities. This latter approach offers a different way of combating the bandwidth problem by harnessing the coherent structure and behavior of scenes captured in their mathematical models, in what can be considered as a *top down* approach to the transmission problem. If the scene structure is broadcast then only the changes in high-level component behavior need to be subsequently transmitted. What is more, the view of the scene that the receiver gets is under local control through parameters fed to the display processor.

In order to apply this second approach, it is necessary to structure the captured image sequences into the same geometric models that are used to drive a receiver's computer display system. This is a subset of the task studied under the heading of machine vision, because all that needs to be achieved is a shape capture capability that can harnesses the data compression that geometric object and scene modeling can provide. What the objects are, in a cognitive sense, is not relevant to this objective. In fact, the representation that supports this geometric task may well not be the most efficient or propitious way to link the objects in a scene to a linguistic classification scheme.

16.2 A Real-time Geometric Modeling and Display System

The starting point for this presentation is a geometric modeling scheme with which it has been found possible to drive real-time display hardware with little to no supporting software. Although this scheme predates depth buffer systems [5], it can be viewed as a form of superior depth buffer processor, providing a superset of the depth buffer's functionality and allowing parallel processing and parallel display memory access.

The simplest raster display system is the frame store, and the simplest display algorithm to support hidden area removal is the painter's algorithm [8]. The difficulty with this approach was the possibility of circularly interlocking facets, which made it impossible to define an ordering for painting the polygon's in-fill values into display memory. The solution to this problem was the depth buffer, which allowed the depth priority of each new pixel value entered into the display to be individually tested against any existing displayed values.

However, it was realized when evaluating the potential of the frame store for *real-time complex scene rendering* that, by itself, this was unlikely to represent an optimal final solution because it requires multiple serial entries to be made to much of the display store for each display refresh cycle. Since the access time to memory was and still is related to the state of the art in IC design and manufacture, the resolution of displays and the size of displays determines the access time required by serial processing, and the demand for these to increase will not be satisfied until wall size displays are commonly available, multiple accesses to the same pixel working in serial mode across the whole screen must be avoided if possible. Either preprocessing in software to select most of the front or visible surfaces must be done before scene rendering or some parallel accessing method to the display memory must be defined corresponding to the output methods developed in VRAM ICs.

Both these approaches have been developed in the solution which underpins this research project. The preprocessing requires the scene model to be subdivided into simplified sections which can be locally processed for subsections of the display screen and rendered in parallel. The parallel access to display memory required multiple processors, each linked to their own collection of memory cells. An approach was needed to make the processors as simple as possible, and also to allow the spatial subdivision to be determined for the whole screen space rather than by individual objects in the scene. The problem with processing polygons and triangles, for example, in Watkin's algorithm [21], was that comparisons between polygons could only be carried out in a pairwise manner. This inherently required an $O(n^2)$ process, whereas otherwise, using a screen subdivision algorithm such as Warnock's algorithm [20], an $O(n\log(n))$ scheme is possible.

The approach which allowed the processors to be simple (amounting to not much more than a block of combinatorial logic, and a selection switch attached to depth buffer memory) and the display area to be a rectangular subdivision of the display screen was made possible by extending the depth comparison operation used for hidden area removal in Watkin's algorithm to execute polygon facet clipping also [12].

It was noted that the display of the nearest surface to the viewing position at any pixel position solved the instability caused by object interference, by displaying the union of any overlapping volumes. Experiments displaying the furthest surface at each pixel position were shown to generate the intersection volume of overlapping objects, if a distinction was made between front facing surfaces and back facing surfaces. Combining these two operations together allowed a set of convex solids defined by a Boolean expression model (Figure 16.1) [1] to be displayed using a pixel processing unit of the form shown in Figure 16.2.

A scene can be built up from a set of convex volumes defined by a single-level Boolean expression model:

S:= V1+V2+V3...

where

V1:= A.B.C.D; V2 := E.F.G.H; V3 := I.J...; ...

S:= (A.B.C.D) + (E.F.G.H) + (...) ...

This gives a display list which can be processed serially by a pixel processing unit that uses very little local memory.

This pixel processing unit is made up from two parts: a *depth processor* and a *property processor*, which usually works as a slave to the depth processor. These two elements correspond to the depth buffer and frame store in conventional display systems. The depth processor is made up from three registers RA, RB, RC, arranged in the way shown in Figure 16.2. The data from the display list flows sequentially through register RA. When there are no changes, the data in registers RB and RC is refreshed, flowing round circularly through the switches S. This arrangement allows new values entering into RA to be compared with the current value in RB, and at the same time the value in RB to be compared with the value in RC. Once a new value has been entered into RA or RB the results of these comparisons can be used to reroute the new value into RB or RC from RA or RB respectively, replacing the previous value by setting the S switches in the required way.

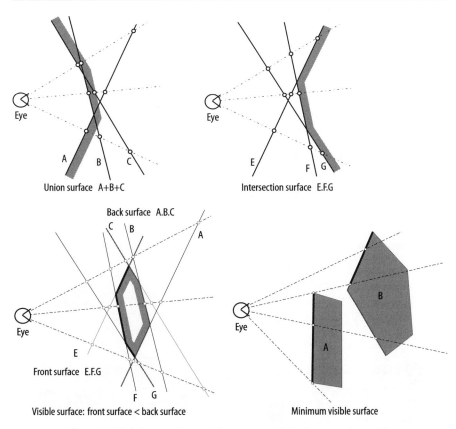

Figure 16.1 Displaying a set of convex objects represented by Boolean expression models.

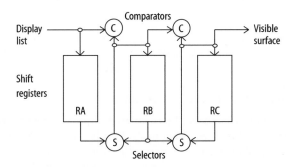

Figure 16.2 Pixel processor, depth processing unit.

For a pixel position this scheme allows registers RA and RB to select the depth values for convex objects by selecting the largest depth value for front surfaces, checking that there are no back surfaces nearer than these selected front surface values. Registers RB and RC, by selecting the smallest depth value from any convex object in the scene, carry out the conventional depth buffer hidden area removal

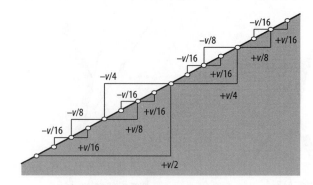

Figure 16.3 Binary incrementing tree.

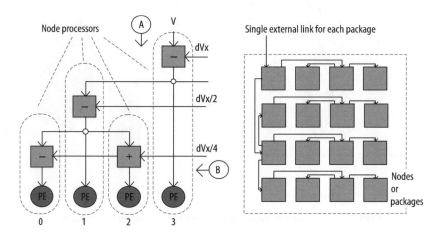

Figure 16.4 Tree-structured architecture for the display processor.

operation. Corresponding registers in the property processor allow color and texture values associated with each surface to be selected in a matching way by setting a similar set of selection switches. However, if this processor is to be duplicated and used in parallel then it must be possible to calculate the depth values for a collection of pixels in parallel at the same time.

Pixel values for plane surfaces can be calculated in parallel by the tree structured incrementing process illustrated in Figure 16.3. This can be implemented using the tree of adders shown in Figure 16.4, where each pixel processor is shown labeled PE. In practice there are a variety of architectures which can implement this parallel processing task. One layout suitable for an IC implementation because of its limited need for input output pins is shown in Figure 16.4.

A simulation of the display hardware algorithm produced the images in Figure 16.5 using the simple sequence of convex elements as a display list structure. Preprocessing the display list by subdividing the display screen and selecting only those components in a scene model relevant to each sub-panel of the display allows hierarchical occultation tests to be included that can reduce the overall computation

Figure 16.5 Objects generated as lists of convex pieces.

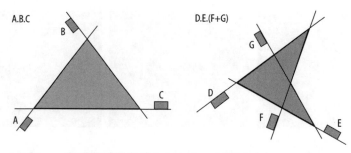

Figure 16.6 Concave surface regions.

load from O($n$log(n)) towards O(n), and allows the resulting sequence of display lists for rectangular panels to be processed in real time by the kind of processor outlined above [13].

This scheme has been tested using a hardware demonstrator [14]. However, there are limitations to the approach. The first is that once Boolean expressions are used in an input language for generating object and scene models it is natural to want to use full expressions with many levels of nesting, and to use the complement operator to subtract one shape from another. Although it is possible, algebraically, to convert a more complex expression model of this kind into an equivalent single-level expression [15], the problem is that there can be an unacceptable increase in the length of the equivalent expression as a consequence of such an expansion.

Figure 16.6 illustrates the problem. The second shape contains a concave sequence (F+G), which can considered as the complement of the convex solid element (F.G). The representation (D.E.(F+G)), which cannot be processed by the simple processor, can be multiplied out to give (D.E.F + D.E.G), which can. However, if the outer convex shape were 200 elements long and the inner concave shape were 200 elements long this multiplication process would create a display list of 40 000 elements.

In exploring this problem, an interesting and useful consequence of re-expressing complemented sub-expressions was discovered. First, it allowed the complement operator to be removed from the expression by taking it down to the terminal nodes of the tree, where it could be implemented simply by reversing the orientation of the individual surface facets. Second, this process ended up with a tree structure which could be set up so that each level was controlled by a single operator, either intersection or union, where these operators alternate from one layer in the tree to the next. The geometric interpretation of this algebraic structure is shown in Figure 16.7. Each level in the tree represents a convex element. This element is either a convex solid if the operator is an intersection operator, or a convex void or hole if the operator is the union operator. What is both interesting and also a very valuable property of this system for processing purposes is that each element is hierarchically contained within the intersection of the convex elements above it in the expression tree structure.

Another natural requirement that occurred with this method of inputting object descriptions was the need to convert this solid modeling scheme into the more

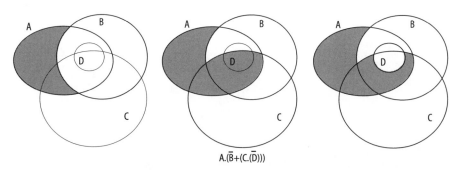

$$A.(\overline{B}+(C.(\overline{D})))$$

Figure 16.7 A Boolean model as a hierarchy of convex elements.

usual boundary representation schemes. Exploring a formal way to achieve this conversion led to the definition of a boundary operator "@". Set up initially on pragmatic grounds, it became clear on further study that it was the reinvention of the differential operator, only in a form suitable for Boolean expressions and conforming to the rules:

Boundary operator @:

$$@(V1.V2) = @V1.[V2]+@V2.[V1]$$

$$@(V1+V2) = @\overline{V1}.[V2]+@\overline{V2}.[V1]$$

$$@(V1+V2) = @V1+@V2+@(\overline{V1.V2})$$

If this operation is applied to the convex hierarchical expansion $A.(\overline{B}+(C.(\overline{D})))$ defining the object shown in Figure 16.7 the result is an expression which represents a series of convex boundary shells clipped by a standard Boolean expression representing the region in which the shell exists (Figures 16.8 and 16.9).

Combining these two algebraic operations together gave a more versatile format for the display list, allowing standard structures such as polygonized and triangulated surface models to be processed by the same scheme that handles Boolean expression solid models. This display list could still be processed using a pixel processor with the data path illustrated in Figure 16.2. Although there remains a multiplicative expansion to the display list applying this approach, the effect is minimized when the display list is preprocessed into sublists suitable for the rectangular panels in the display. The scene model is converted into the tree structure matching the hierarchy illustrated in Figure 16.7, and is then pruned for each display panel created by subdividing the screen. Only these "sub" lists need to be expanded using the boundary expansion to give a display list in a form suitable for input into the pixel processors.

One of the major advantages of adopting this overall approach is that it allows both surfaces and solids to be modeled and displayed in the same self-consistent system. It also allows surface property patterns of texture and color and illumination patterns such as shadows to be projected onto objects and surfaces using this clipping phrase structure, in the way summarized in Figure 16.10 [16]. *It is this*

Figure 16.8 Applying the boundary operator to give clipped convex shells.

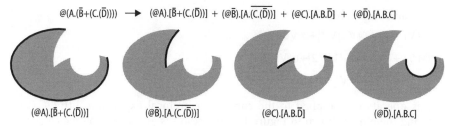

$$@(A.(\bar{B}+(C.(\bar{D})))) \longrightarrow (@A).[\bar{B}+(C.(\bar{D}))] + (@\bar{B}).[A.\overline{(C.(\bar{D}))}] + (@C).[A.B.\bar{D}] + (@\bar{D}).[A.B.C]$$

$(@A).[\bar{B}+(C.(\bar{D}))]$ $(@\bar{B}).[A.\overline{(C.(\bar{D}))}]$ $(@C).[A.B.\bar{D}]$ $(@\bar{D}).[A.B.C]$

Figure 16.9 Hierarchical convex boundary shells generated by the boundary operator.

construct, by providing a bridge to shape capture and broadcasting, that sets up the main theme of this chapter.

16.3 Transmitting Scene Descriptions

If we consider the image captured by a single camera in relationship to the scene represented in the image we have the classical projection diagram shown in Figure 16.11. The rays of light entering the eye from objects represented on the screen are from positions on the screen, arranged so that they match the path that they would have followed from real objects in the original scene. This approach allows multiple images to present different views of the same scene, but each of these views must be captured and broadcast if the viewer "is to be taken on a journey around objects in a scene." This is true even though much of the information for one view is already

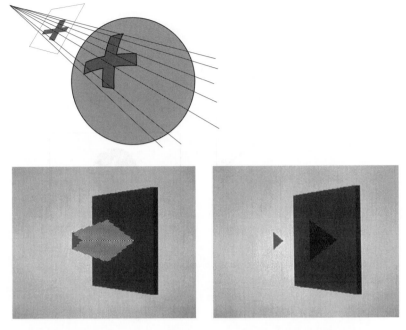

Figure 16.10 The projection of shadows and patterns using the clipping phrase structure.

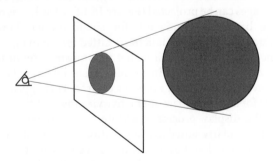

Figure 16.11 Scene projected on a plane screen.

captured in previous images. It is not possible to project the different images onto multiple screens so that common areas overlap. If the screens are flat, simple geometry dictates that the projections will not line up, an exception being a continuous panoramic view projected on the inside of a faceted drum.

However, with the emergence of synthetic computer graphics a more sophisticated possibility is emerging. It is now standard practice for surface properties to be painted or texture mapped onto geometric shapes. If the captured images of scenes could be projected on object surfaces that correspond in shape to objects in the original scene then an alignment and correct overlap would occur that would allow

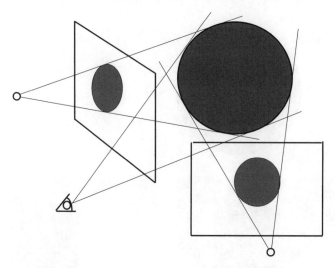

Figure 16.12 Multiple projections onto a geometrically modeled screen.

the projections to be viewed from positions different from those used to capture the original images.

These object shapes can be viewed as complex geometry screens, onto which standard broadcast images can be projected (Figure 16.12). Clearly this offers no advantage in reducing broadcast bandwidth for single frames; however, it could considerably reduce the volume of data transmitted for a moving image sequence. It also offers a new possibility, which is that the transmission of the images seen from a collection of capture stations in a studio can be integrated by the receiver to reconstruct whatever viewpoint an observer desires. This appears to provide the necessary support for a range of new interactive viewing facilities. The link between these ideas and the display processor architecture outlined above is that this display system is particularly suited to this partition in transmitted data. The task is to capture the shape model and each texture or scene projection in a compatible form for this kind of display processor. If this approach is implemented then it is only a small step to being able to integrate synthetically generated objects into a camera-captured, broadcast scene. The areas of digital television, computer graphics and animation, virtual studios, virtual reality and computer-aided program planning all become naturally integrated into one general overall scheme.

If the display system outlined in the previous section is to be used, it is necessary to find ways of projecting the TV images onto the geometrically modeled screens to implement the operation illustrated in Figure 16.12. There appear to be several ways in which this can be done. One possibility being investigated is to use an appropriate image transform. The Hadamard or Walsh transforms use simple basis functions which can be set up as geometric structures using *exclusive OR* Boolean operators acting on a set of parallel lines or a set of planes passing through the viewing position and a set of parallel lines in the image plane (Figures 16.13 and 16.14).

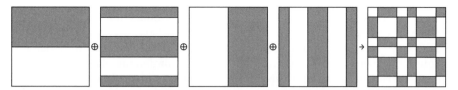

Figure 16.13 Basis functions using exclusive OR operations.

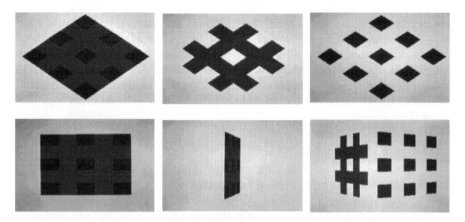

Figure 16.14 Projected patterns generated using exclusive OR operators.

Although this approach needs considerable further investigation, it appears to possess several potentially useful properties for a TV transmission system where the viewpoint might be selected at the receiver. If the transform employs a hierarchy of basis functions, then it is possible to filter out the higher frequencies by removing the higher order elements. This is a valuably simple approach for handling the loss of detail associated with increases in viewing distance. Various *wavelet* transforms also appear to have the necessary geometric properties and hierarchy to support this kind of system.

Another problem, which will need to be investigated further, is the association of texture or image projections with their correctly corresponding screen elements. In an environment with multiple capture stations some of the images could end up being projected onto surfaces that should lie behind other objects given the direction of viewing which they are captured from unless some form of tagging is implemented. A mechanism that can achieve this already exists in the property processor developed to handle multiple light sources and overlapping patterns [15].

16.4 Real-Time Shape Capture and Geometric Modeling System

The first attempt to capture shape made by the author by other means than by point by point measurement was carried out in a final year special study called "Models in

Design Procedures", undertaken in a Bachelor of Architecture degree course in Liverpool University in 1966–67. The objective of this exercise was to explore the many ways of modeling design problems, and in particular how to model and capture the complex deformations that occur in continuous plate structures. A short experiment successfully used moiré patterns to estimate the deformation and hence the strain distribution in the plate. The moiré pattern was generated by projecting a parallel grid of lines onto the non-deformed surface and then onto the loaded deformed model plate surface, photographing the two results and then overlaying the two images. Many variations of the same approach have been reported in the field of machine vision, where stripes, projected textures and laser scans have all been used to provide the triangulation measurements necessary to calculate surface distance information. However, when a method of deriving the same information using a passive non-invasive approach was sought, which would allow the Boolean expression model of shape to be built up, a different approach seemed necessary.

16.5 Shape from Silhouette Contours

If we capture the image of an object set against a highly contrasting background we can extract the edge points (using edge filtering) of the object's silhouette from any chosen point of view. These edge points when linked up with the viewing position give a pyramid volume in which the target object must lie. If this process is carried out for the same object from points of view taken all the way round it, then the intersection of these pyramid volumes will give an approximate model of the object. An experimental project [6] was set up in which an object was placed in front of a TV camera and rotated to give such a systematic set of views. These were then processed to produce the required pyramids which were then transformed into the correct overlapping spatial relationship with each other and the intersection of the pyramids used as a Boolean expression model to give the displays shown in Figure 16.17.

In order to carry out this procedure it was necessary to generate the silhouette edges of the object images as a Boolean expression model. This was done in steps in the way illustrated in Figure 16.15. The silhouette of an object from a particular point of view is given in Figure 16.15a. The first step was to extract edge points using a standard image-processing edge detection algorithm. The second step was to process these edge points and create their convex hull in the way shown in Figure 16.15b. All sequences of contiguous edge points not lying on this hull boundary were then collected together into sets which were then processed to obtain new convex hulls, as shown in Figure 16.15c. This was repeated recursively until either the size of the subset of edge points was small enough to ignore (a form of spatial filtering) or all the edge points were accounted for. Once this spatial decomposition had been carried out, each convex hull at its own level was represented by the Boolean intersection or product of the edge lines of the convex hull polygon considered as plane half-spaces. These convex elements were then combined to give the Boolean expression model for the total boundary in the form:

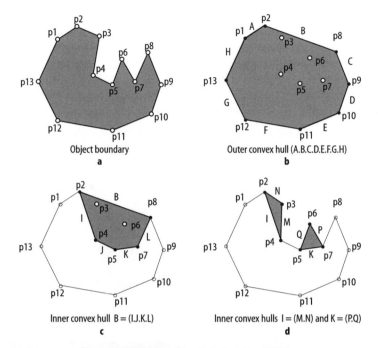

Figure 16.15 Object boundary: silhouette contour definition.

A.C.D.E.F.G.H.(J + L +(M.N) + (P.Q)))

Each of the symbols in this expression corresponds to a straight-line segment of the polygonal boundary. These lines can be converted into three-dimensional plane half-spaces by combining them with the viewing position in an appropriate way, giving a silhouette boundary pyramid with its apex at the eye, and tangent to the object being viewed.

These pyramid volumes taken from different viewing positions round the object, illustrated in plan view in Figure 16.16, can be combined by simple Boolean intersection. The advantage of using the Boolean expression modeling approach is that this operation is little more than list concatenation. The test objects and the geometric models generated from them using this approach are illustrated in Figure 16.17.

This process worked but was limited in scope and accuracy. It could be improved. It was necessary, for example, to find some way of characterizing the shape within the concave areas of an object's surface, which could never form part of a silhouette boundary. One possibility was to use the gray-scale gradient of the interior region of an object in a particular image projection to reconstruct this shape information. In order to do this, the way in which the shading values relate to the shape of the object needed to be studied. The starting point for this work was based on Lambert's Law for diffuse reflection from matte surfaces.

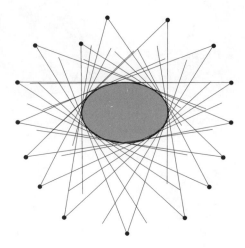

Figure 16.16 Multiple projections intersect to approximate the object.

Figure 16.17 Boolean expression shape capture.

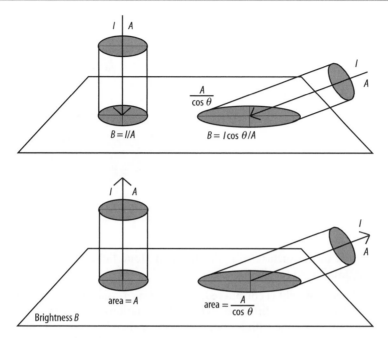

Figure 16.18 Light energy incident to and reflected from a surface.

16.6 Shape from Shading

If a surface of luminance B is viewed from different angles, and if the surface is a matte surface, then it will appear to be of the same brightness whatever the viewing angle. It can be seen by inspecting the diagrams in Figure 16.18 that a viewing tube of the same projected area A obtains its light energy from a smaller area of the surface for perpendicular directions compared to oblique directions. If this reflection property is to be met, then the amount of light coming from each unit area of the surface that is being reflected in the oblique direction must be less than that in the perpendicular direction, because the area providing the reflected light in the oblique case is larger than the projected area, but the total reflected light energy passing through it is required to be the same. In contrast, when considering the case of incident light, the same illuminating light energy is spread over a greater receiving area for oblique angle illumination than for perpendicular illumination, so the brightness of the surface will be greater for the perpendicular illumination than the oblique illumination.

To appear equally bright, irrespective of the viewing direction, a surface must obey Lambert's Law of reflection: $R = kI\cos\theta$, where R is the reflected light energy *per unit area of the surface*, I is the incident light energy *per unit area of the surface*, θ is the angle between the normal to the surface and the viewing direction, and k is a constant related to the surface's properties. The area of surface required *to give a unit projected area* will be $1/\cos\theta$, so multiplying this by R ensures that the *same*

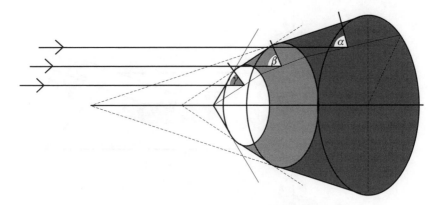

Figure 16.19 Shape reconstruction from illumination contour bands.

projected area of the surface will emit the same total light energy whatever the viewing angle adopted for the surface.

If a parallel beam of light is considered, illuminating a cone, then if the axis of the cone is parallel to the light direction then the illumination of the surface of the cone will be constant. If a cone with a shallower slope is then taken, again with its axis parallel to the lighting direction, then a new surface of even but different brightness will be obtained. If these two cones are intersected then it is clear that their relative positions can be varied in space, generating different boundaries between the two zones of brightness. This is illustrated in Figure 16.19. If it is assumed that a surface is smooth and matte, it has been shown theoretically that its shape can be derived from the illumination distribution on its surface [4]. However, the diagram in Figure 16.20 presents the practical nature of this problem. Real source data is quantized, both spatially on a grid in the case of a TV camera, and in the numerical values used in the gray-scale representation. This means that although it may be possible to construct a surface cone of the kind shown, or a more sophisticated variant of it for a particular illumination value, *if the light source direction is known,*

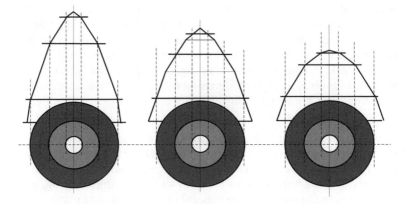

Figure 16.20 Reconstructed cross-sections using equal illumination cones.

there is a cumulative error from the piecewise approximation of the surface using cones, which is a consequence of the discrete steps in the received data.

In this visualization of the problem this is shown by the different positions in which the cones can be placed relative to each other which could still give the same gray-scale distribution in a two dimensional image. In Figure 16.20 the cross-sections through a series of illumination cones are shown where the shading bands are reconstructed using cones placed at the extreme positions which the contour boundaries make possible, and also a mid-range reconstruction. These diagrams suggest that the more contour levels there are the more tightly the reconstruction will be constrained to give a single surface.

16.7 Shape from Stereo Contours

Accurate reconstruction of three-dimensional objects was going to need more information than that provided by single gray-scale images. It was also going to be useful to find a method which would work even where there were many light sources in a scene giving complex illumination patterns on objects in the image or images being used to reconstruct the three-dimensional model of the scene.

The important consequences of Lambert's Law are firstly that the brightness of a matte surface will depend on the strength and direction of the illuminating light falling on that surface. Secondly, the brightness distribution of an illuminated object will not be changed by changing the position it is being viewed from. This means that in stereo views of the same object the same points will appear to be of the same brightness. If Lambert's Law were not being obeyed this could not be assumed. This property opens up the possibility of reconstructing an object's shape from stereo pair images. If each array of gray-scale values making up each image is contoured, then it is possible to project these contours into three dimensions in the way shown in Figure 16.21.

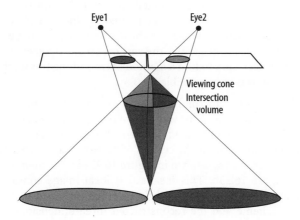

Figure 16.21 Viewing cone intersection volume for a contour ring.

The potential advantage that this has over a similar approach applied to features in a scene is that features first have to be recognized, and that secondly they have to be correlated with each other in the two separate stereo images. Although the contours come from a continuous distribution, and even though the captured image values have been quantized onto a grid, it is still possible to interpolate new values between the given data values. If both eyes are centered on the same object point in space then the centers of vision for the images seen by the two eyes should correlate automatically. If we process the contour distribution systematically out from this center we are carrying out an ordered spatial search which implicitly executes a form of cross-correlation.

Exploring this idea further, based on the idealized geometrical layout shown in Figure 16.21, where the intersection volume created by overlapping the two cones obtained by projecting matching stereo image contours is shown, the problem of defining the three-dimensional location of the original contour seems to be reasonably easy to solve. If we could get the smooth surfaces shown in Figure 16.21 then geometrically this might be so. However, even though we can contour the gray-scales in the two stereo images as finely as we like, we have the quantization effects introduced by the pixel grid to contend with.

The simplest interpolation is linear interpolation on gridlines joining the data point positions. If we assume that the location of a contour point on these gridlines can be found accurately enough for our purposes, we still have the problems generated by the straight-line segments used to link these points together to give the complete contour line loops. The simplification obtained by using straight-line segments is necessary to have a process which we can compute at a reasonable speed. By linking these edges to the viewing position we can generate a three-dimensional plane surface. The contour cones can then be made up, like the silhouette pyramids discussed above, by a sequence of plane half-spaces. The task then becomes one of intersecting these to obtain the intersection volume shown, and extracting from it its equator line which will be the required three-dimensional projection of the contour we want.

In Figure 16.22 the way that this planar approximation creates inaccuracies that can serious affect the shape of a reconstructed surface is illustrated. The two cones shown are convex; however, the line generated by their intersection can be a sawtooth or coronet structure of the form shown. The finer the angle between these intersecting cone surfaces, the greater the vertical error displacement can be from the true line. It was necessary to find a method of smoothing this intersection line if good reconstruction was to be possible.

The next study presents an exploration of a system which projects two stereo images onto a common plane in the way shown in Figure 16.23. This is being set up so that the two images, obtained from aligned TV cameras, have their raster lines parallel to the stereo axis joining the centers of the two images. This means that the images are lined up in the way shown in Figure 16.23a rather than in the unaligned way shown in Figure 16.23b. This means that local image comparisons can be carried out along corresponding raster lines. Figures 16.24 and 16.25 show a simulation of such a scheme and the reconstructed three-dimensional contour lines obtained from the input stereo gray-scale images.

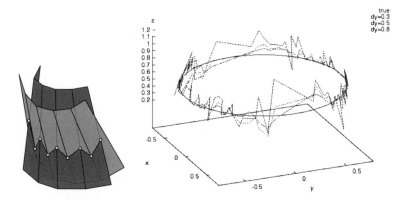

Figure 16.22 Intersecting contour cones giving a "coronet" intersection line.

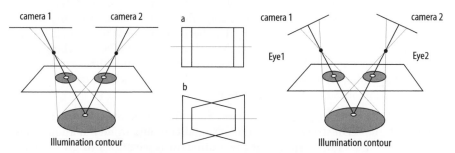

Figure 16.23 Matching image pixel values along common raster lines.

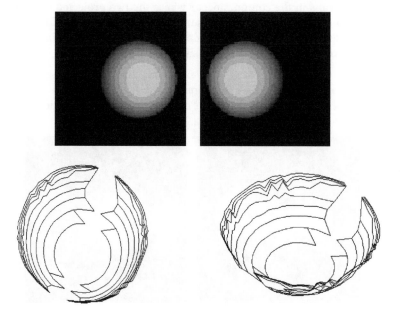

Figure 16.24 Simulated stereo pair for a sphere: diffuse reflection and viewpoint lighting.

Figure 16.25 Simulated stereo shape capture for a sphere: diffuse reflection and oblique lighting.

The advantage of this approach is that contour point interpolation along raster lines avoids the worst of the errors shown in Figure 16.22. It also allows contour lines from one image to be correlated easily with contour lines from the second image. This can be done by assuming Lambert's Law, because the highest and lowest points of each contour loop will then, theoretically, fall on matching raster lines. When this was associated with the natural way that contour lines are nested in groups, it provided a highly structured framework within which to carry out feature correlation and object-matching operations.

In Figure 16.24 the simulated stereo views of a diffuse reflecting sphere are shown, along with the reconstructed three-dimensional contours of illumination. These contour sets are shown rotated into two different orientations to give a better appreciation of the reconstructed shape. In Figure 16.25 two similar results are shown where the direction of illumination in the original simulation has been changed. The gaps in the contours occur where the two projected contour cones intersect each other almost as parallel surfaces at the highest and lowest point of each contour loop. A similar loss of definition occurs where the maximum value for the illumination occurs, and it is impossible to distinguish further internal shape differences.

Figures 16.26 and 16.27 illustrate the same approach applied to two spheres in the case where one sphere partly occludes the other in one of the stereo views. The basic

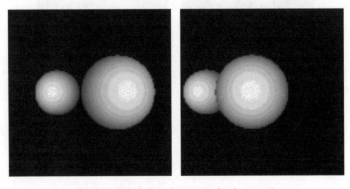

Figure 16.26 Occluding spheres: a simulated stereo pair.

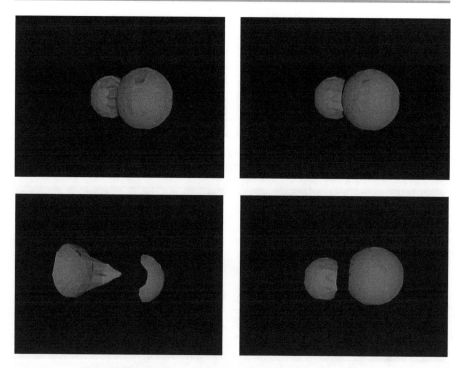

Figure 16.27 Simulated stereo shape capture removing occluded surface elements.

stereo reconstruction mechanism is not affected as the surfaces on the left of Figure 16.27 show. However, parts of this surface do not belong to any object in the scene, being projections of one of the object's silhouette. If these reconstructed surfaces are to be used as screens onto which further detail will be projected from different directions, then these virtual elements need to be removed [17].

One way of doing this is illustrated in the right half of Figure 16.25 by testing corresponding contours for their match in shape. Where a true contour in one stereo image is occluded by another object, it is not cut but merely wraps itself round the occluding object to give a complete loop. This means that it no longer matches the shape of its partner in the other stereo image. It was found possible to remove the sections of contours that did not match in this way to produce the pieces of the spheres' surfaces shown on the right of Figure 16.27.

Figure 16.27 also shows the result of triangulating the contour lines to give surface facets. This allows the objects to be rendered. It can be seen that where the stereo images were simulated assuming pure diffuse reflection, it was possible to reconstruct the original three-dimensional surfaces with results which were good enough to justify further exploration along these lines.

Figures 16.28 and 16.29 illustrate the same techniques applied to real images captured from a real object (a rubber duck) by a single small TV camera moved to capture the two images [7]. It can be seen that the results are considerably poorer. The holes over the wings are the consequence of a mismatch in corresponding

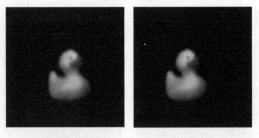

Figure 16.28 Camera-captured stereo pair for a rubber duck.

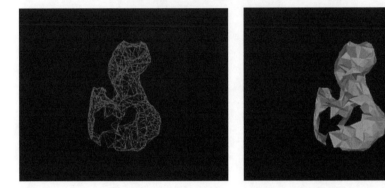

Figure 16.29 Rough stereo shape capture showing specular region pruning.

contour loop shapes. This appeared to be caused by two factors. The first was specular highlights; the second, interacting with the first, was a surface texture of small enough grain size to not be correctly captured in the input images. The assumed alignment between the images (easy to get in the simulation) was impossible to achieve with the poor capture facilities available for this initial set of experiments, and is partially to blame for the crumpled paper look of the reconstructed object.

16.8 Active Vision Stereo Capture

In Figures 16.30 and 16.31 the result of shape-capturing a face is shown using an active vision stereo system. In this system a texture pattern is projected onto the surface of the face, and this pattern is then used to correlate points on the surface of the object in the stereo reconstruction process. Figure 16.30 shows the triangulated grid generated for the face. It is relatively coarse. In practice, the method can give finer meshes; however, that is not the relevant point in this context. What is interesting is how good the rendered faces appear, even with this level of subdivision.

Figure 16.32 shows how this triangulated image improves when the texture map of the face is projected back onto the surface. The results are good enough to allow the texture-mapped model of the face to be rotated into any viewing position required.

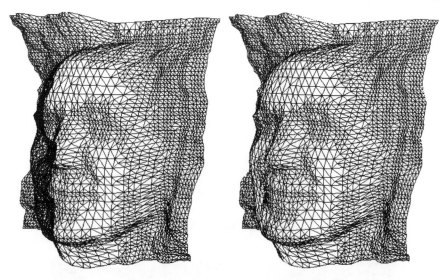

Figure 16.30 Triangulated mesh captured from stereo.

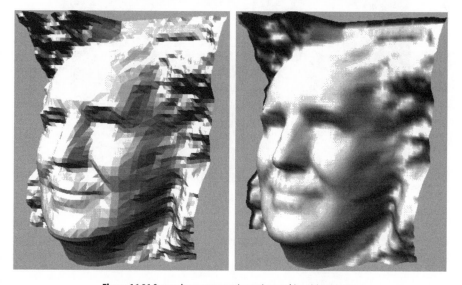

Figure 16.31 Stereo shape capture using active machine vision capture.

It is the quality of these results which supports the proposal made in Section 16.4, and which justifies further work on the passive capture of scene models in a way which corresponds to this approach. Although this invasive approach gives highly accurate results and is valid for many shape capture tasks, unless the effect of the projected texture mask can be reduced or eliminated its application to the broadcasting task would seem to be limited to offline work. On the other hand, to improve the passive capture method it appears necessary to remove specular

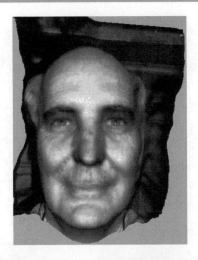

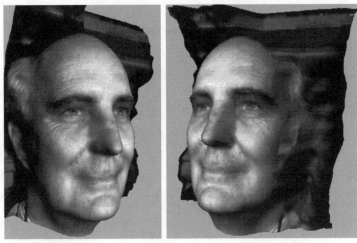

Figure 16.32 Active machine vision shape capture with a projected texture map.

effects, and current work has been exploring the possible ways in which this might be done.

16.9 Specular Reflections and Transmitted Light

It was initially thought that assuming Lambert's Law as the basis for these experiments would require special surface treatment for objects if their models were to be captured in this way, and if the problems of specular reflection were to be avoided. However, an exciting aspect of the current exploration is the observation that images in a mirror are further away than the mirror surface, so grouping and correlating contours based on Lambert's Law could produce more interesting results than was originally expected when specular reflection was ignored.

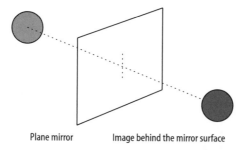

Plane mirror   Image behind the mirror surface

Figure 16.33 Reflection.

Reflection models may be set up in a variety of ways. In this context the most productive way of doing so appears to be to divide the reflected light from a surface into two components, the first giving the brightness value which a surface point possesses, irrespective of the direction of viewing, and the second component giving the rest. This definition allows the observation to be made that the minimum brightness at a point on a surface viewed from any angle can be taken as its diffuse reflection component. If the object shape is known then this value is relatively easy to estimate; where the surface shape is not known it is more difficult to establish. However, in spite of the difficulties this approach generates a variety of interesting consequences.

Considering the case of mirrors led to the following basic observations. It is possible to focus on the image in a plane mirror "behind" the surface of the mirror (Figure 16.33). If the mirror is dirty then at times two surfaces can be seen overlaying each other. The stereo reconstruction of the contours should give the structure of the reflected scene as long as there is little interference from the true mirror surface.

An accidental experiment reinforced and extended these ideas. Soldering a printed circuit board late at night in the light of a single powerful angle-poise lamp became very difficult because of the strong reflections coming from bright, new, solder joints (Figure 16.34). The highlights seemed to be floating in front of the printed circuit board. Thinking tiredness was the problem I was all set to pack up when the persistence of the perception effect struck me. Parallax tests with the soldering iron bit showed the highlights to be real images floating about half a centimeter in front of each joint. Given the curved shape of the solder joints this seemed to be possible to explain using the properties of convex and concave mirrors. If this depth effect was being generated by a stereo process then matching it in a simulation would seem to require the unmodified projected contours to be intersected, including specular illumination, to give the corresponding three-dimensional reconstruction. Such an approach would have to determine which surfaces were objects and which reflections after they had been generated.

On the other hand, one consequence of treating the specular component as an image at a different distance from the eye to a reflecting surface is that transmitted light effects and reflected light effects can be treated in a similar way. The problem with directly matching stereo iso-illumination contours for areas of the image that

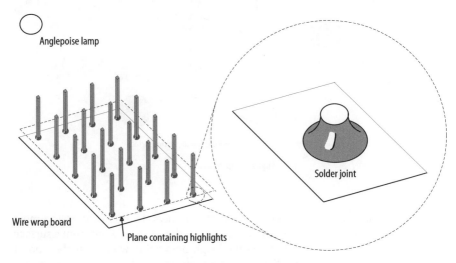

Figure 16.34 Specular stereo effects.

are larger than small local highlights is that the resulting surface distances from the eye, calculated from the contours defined by a combination of the original illumination values, could well end up being an unacceptably bad compromise, diverging wildly from the true distances.

If two images are overlaid and the two intensity maps are added together, then the result can be taken to represent both a mirror showing a reflected scene or a sheet of glass through which the same scene is being viewed. Any movement on the part of the observer will create a relative parallax motion between the two image surfaces, in the way summarized in Figure 16.35. It has been shown that time series images of two patterns A and B moving at a constant velocity relative to each other, but added together, can be separated by a Fourier transform-based image-processing operation. In other words, the separated images A and B can be regenerated by operating on four of the additive images taken in order from the time series [19]. Where the assumptions underlying this process apply, this approach provides a possible way in which the reflection maps of each of two surface illumination patterns which have been overlaid can be estimated.

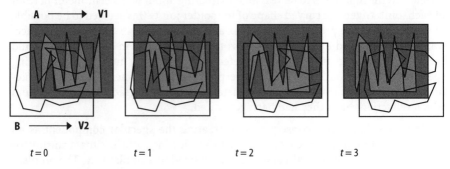

Figure 16.35 Two images added together, but moving with different velocities.

The difficulty with this approach is that square regions of the image have to be used for the Fourier-based operations. The parallax motion of many irregularly shaped objects with complex surface reflections, at different distances and moving at different speeds, may or may not fit into this framework comfortably. However, the relationship between the Fourier transform and the parallel structure of neural networks suggests that this approach could have considerable potential and is worth further investigation for the current application, particularly for plane mirrors and transparent screens such as windows.

In the simple case of diffuse reflection, processing contours along epi-polar lines allows contour lines from one image to be correlated easily with contour lines from the second image. This can be done because the highest and lowest points of each contour loop theoretically fall on matching epi-polar lines. When this is associated with the natural way that contour lines are nested in groups it provides a highly structured framework within which to carry out feature correlation and object matching operations. Another consequence of assuming diffuse reflection is the way that the movement made by the opposite edges of contour loops along epi-polar lines should match when the viewing position is changed. When this does not happen it provides an alternative indication that the reflection may not be purely diffuse in nature, and leads to another way of constructing overlaid surfaces.

16.10 Contour Motion and Parallax

Translating a viewing point with a constant velocity will, for the case of diffuse reflection, cause contour lines also to move with a constant velocity across the display screen. This case is illustrated in Figure 16.36. The surface lies at the

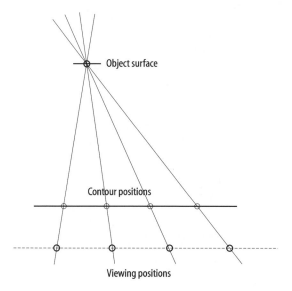

Figure 16.36 Constant velocity contour line.

crossing point where the viewing rays projected through the contour line at each time interval intersect. The geometry of this diagram shows that a unique position can only be obtained if the surface point keeps its illumination value constant and the spaces between the positions taken by the camera and the corresponding positions taken by a contour line at equal steps in time are regularly spaced.

If there is a strong surface pattern with sharp changes in color or tone then it can be seen that this reconstruction approach can be applied to the contours that lie on the edges of the change with a relatively high expectation of accuracy. If this kind of change is located by identifying steep illumination gradients then the process essentially reverts to a form of edge filtering. Where this approach does not match up with the movement of absolute contour values then again an indication of non-diffuse lighting is given.

If the contour's position is seen to accelerate when the camera is moved with constant velocity, then, given certain assumptions, it is possible to estimate the position of two surfaces whose illumination distributions add up to give the observed contour motion. If for small distances we assume the viewing ray through the contour sweeps out a planar region on the surfaces whose illuminations are generating the contour value, the changes in the illumination values of the surfaces along the viewing ray have to be equal and opposite for each position that the contour takes up. Figure 16.37 shows how two families of surfaces can be constructed to produce a particular accelerated movement in a contour line. If a contour moves with constant velocity this construction shows that only one surface is being viewed, as in the case shown in Figure 16.36, or one of the surfaces has a

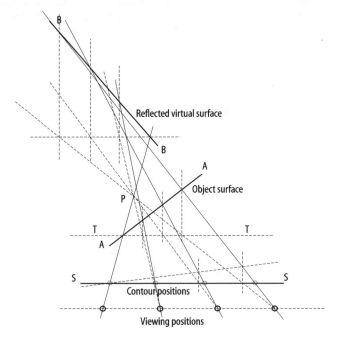

Figure 16.37 An accelerating contour line.

constant illumination value over the area swept out by the contour based viewing ray.

This approach is similar in nature to the shape from shading scheme based on cones of illumination, and suffers from a similar drawback. If the distance of one of the surfaces is known for one contour line, then its shape can be traced from contour line to contour line using this construct; however, it can be seen that there will be a cumulative quantization error built up if the process is taken too far from a safe datum point.

16.11 Screens, Virtual Contours and Surfaces

In Figure 16.29 gaps are shown where badly matched contours are pruned out and the surface cannot be constructed. Where this happens it is necessary to find a method which allows the gap to be filled in. Where multiple views are obtained from the same scene it is also necessary to integrate partial results to give a complete model.

There seems to be evidence that the human visual system can carry out this kind of operation, filling in missing pieces of a scene in various ways, the most direct example being where the optic nerve enters the eye. There seems to be an ability to generate virtual edges shown in optical illusion effects such as Kanizsa's triangle, illustrated in Figure 16.38. There are also other examples of virtual edges and surfaces that artists and designers become aware of during their work. There are many similarities in the effects experienced looking through transparent objects, looking in mirrors and looking at surfaces with a high specular reflection component. In each there are several depths that can be locked onto along the same direction of viewing. Sometimes the nearer surface is taken as the master surface, further surfaces becoming properties of this surface; sometimes it is further surfaces that take control. If the dependent surfaces are coherently structured they can be seen as images; where less so they can be perceived as a shine or surface gloss.

A personal observation of a strong virtual surface effect has been experienced viewing autostereograms. I usually find that it is hard to see an object in an autostereogram, but when I do it happens in two distinct stages. In the first stage a plane transparent surface appears on which some of the autostereogram's texture is

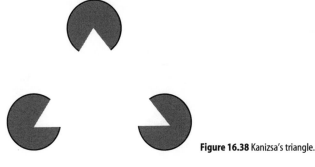

Figure 16.38 Kanizsa's triangle.

distributed, and in which a hole with very clearly defined edges indicate the presence of the object. In the second stage, by looking into the hole the object's smooth shape appears and the plane surface disappears. What is strange is the perception of a virtual, glass like surface that has no highlights or other shiny effects but which, for all that, appears to be solid but completely transparent, linking together pieces of textured pattern.

Interior designers use a possibly related but less powerful perceptual effect when they use frames and pierced screens to create enclosures and control the "flow of space" within buildings. It is amazing at times how little physical material is needed to create a visual barrier or virtual surface in an observer's sense of accessible space. In this context it is interesting that having learned the rules of perspective, the apprentice painter is often told to "feel" the space being created in a new picture as a means of controlling and fine tuning the use of color, texture and form rather than constructing it totally by "looking and measuring". It is this perception of multiple surfaces and depths that makes life drawing and painting a different skill from that of copying photographs and other pictures, and explains in part why the copyist can produce such "dead" images.

What was interesting about the concave–convex mirror effect in Figure 16.34 was the relationships between the objects and the images for the two types of mirror. For objects at reasonable distances from the curved reflectors the images would always be located *within* the convex envelope of the mirror (Figure 16.39). Only the shaving or vanity mirror use of a concave mirror, where the viewer was close to the mirror surface, would not exhibit this relationship. What this meant was that if the three-dimensional contour points were composed together into a surface represented by a hierarchy of convex hulls then the reflected elements would always be lower down the hierarchy than the reflecting surface. The motion behavior of the contours in many cases would allow this reflected image relationship to be

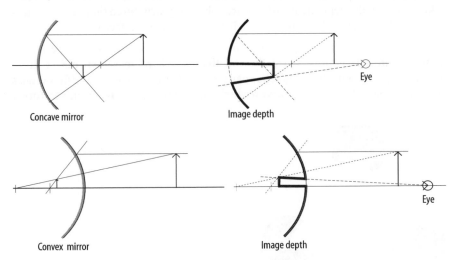

Figure 16.39 Reflected images within each mirror's convex envelope.

distinguished from a true indented surface and give the perception effect of a shiny or mirror like surface with reflections rather than a dented surface.

Several other methods could contribute to this quest to improve surface estimates in a passive vision system. One possibility, given cameras with focus and depth of field control, is to adjust the camera so that only a narrow depth range is in sharp focus, filter out the high-frequency elements in the display and use these in a stereo reconstruction process. Given the appropriate control, this could give a facility that would establish an original estimate that one of the methods outlined above could be used to improve on.

16.12 Conclusions

The system which is evolving in this work is a new interactive TV broadcasting system based on a passive, non-invasive machine vision system. Initially this vision system was being developed to capture object shapes and scene structures for CAD/CAM, robot navigation, and animated film and video applications. However, in the meantime active invasive vision systems have emerged which are probably better units to achieve some of the initial objectives, which were being sought. Laser scanning, as an example, gives results with high accuracy where object shape capture is required, though it tends to be carried out as an offline task; similarly, the Turing Institute's Stereo Capture system used to generate the images in Figure 16.30–16.32 requires special lighting in its current form.

There are two areas where the passive capture approach seems to offer a long-term advantage. The first is where the vision system is being used in what can be regarded as a predator–prey context. Where one's presence either as a predator or as potential prey needs to be kept secret, a non-invasive viewing system has permanent advantages over an invasive system. The second area of advantage is where multiple vision systems are likely to be active in the same space at the same time. At some level of use it can be expected that invasive systems will interfere with each other.

It is in the TV broadcasting industry that non-invasive, multiple capture systems appear to offer new possibilities. The real-time display capability has already been developed, down to the design of special-purpose integrated circuits. The capture system can already generate the kind of display model needed to drive this form of display system. Current work is improving the performance of the modeling system. Two aspects of this application make the next stage in development a viable task. Firstly, the requirements of a scene model as a three-dimensional projection screen make fewer demands on shape capture accuracy, perhaps, than other applications. Secondly, the studio end of this system can afford to be several orders of magnitude more expensive than the receiving hardware and still present a practical proposition. Finally, the success of this kind of system would make the broadcast for stereo viewing systems, particularly those that demand multiple image channels to support wide viewing angle parallax effects, less demanding on transmission bandwidths. The multiple channels could be set up locally in the receivers. Finally, if this work is successful it will bring together under one integrated approach the film, games, video, animation, computer-aided design, geometric modeling and TV communication industries, among others.

This chapter has been intentionally vague about the medium over which these displays are to be broadcast. The ideas presented here originated in "future application claims" made for a prototype display system developed between 1976 and 1978 as an SRC research project, when the possibilities that digital display technology offered were only beginning to emerge. The idea was that conventional TV broadcasts could transfer geometrical models of scenes rather than an electronic image sequence if the receivers were digital display processors. Work since then has served to refine these early fantasies into a more achievable set of goals, and the current targets have been aimed more at Internet broadcasting than at conventional TV. However, with the advent of digital television this may no longer be a necessary restriction.

The display list is made up of a sequence of independent packages, each able to generate part of the received display. This structure seems particularly suited to network communication in that retransmission of these packages is possible in any order. This makes the problem of applying error correction technology much simpler if a bad communication channel is encountered. There is a hierarchy of possible receiver designs, from one designed to handle a simple preprocessed subdivided display list, set up ready to feed directly into a panel refresh processor, to a full computer-based display system where a geometric model of the scene is processed locally and the viewing positions are selected by the system viewers. It is the latter system that offers extensions that are capable of supporting total surround viewing of the sort provided by virtual reality helmets or other stereo viewing systems. Bandwidth reduction will depend on the coherent structure and behavior of the scenes being transmitted; however, there seems to be plenty of scope to achieve it.

Acknowledgments

Ideas, discussion, criticism and help from members of the "Model Based Animation and Machine Vision" research group, School of Engineering, University of Sussex: A. Cavusoglu, H. Sarnel, H. Sue, G. Jones, U. Cevik, N. Papadopoulos, D. Joyce, C. Saunders, A. Lim, S. Zhang and B. Rey. The "Shape from Silhouette" study was carried out by M.J. Lavington, and the "Shape from Stereo" studies were carried out by Alan Lim.

Figures 16.28, 16.29 and 16.30 were produced by Dr Paul Sieberts from the Turing Institute, Glasgow University. Advice on projective geometry was obtained from Dr Hirschfeld in Sussex University. Discussions on contouring applications were carried out with Dr J. Patterson from Glasgow University and Professor P. Willis from Bath University.

SRC and SERC grants to develop the display processor hardware, initially as an LSI demonstrator, and then subsequently to investigate possible IC implementations of the same scheme.

Tector Ltd generated the simulator image at the bottom of Figure 16.5. This system implemented the simple modeling algorithm to give a real-time "target" as an inset into the display of a small pilot training simulator.

References

[1]   PG Comba (1968) A language for three-dimensional Geometry, *IBM Systems Journal*, 7(3,4).
[2]   A Guzman (1968) Computer recognition of three-dimensional objects in a visual scene, *PhD Dissertation*.
[3]   J Haugeland (1997) *MindDesign II*, The MIT Press, London.
[4]   BKP Horn (1975) Obtaining shape from shading information, in *The Psychology of Computer Vision* (ed. PH Winston), McGraw-Hill, New York, pp. 115–55.
[5]   JT Kajiya, IE Sutherland and Cheadle (1975) A random access video frame buffer, *Proc. IEEE Conference on Computer Graphics, Pattern Recognition and Data Structures*.
[6]   MJ Lavington (1986) Automatic data entry for simple volume models, *BSc Final-year Project Dissertation*, School of Engineering and Applied Sciences, University of Sussex.
[7]   AWT Lim (1997) Exploring vision mechanisms for constructing a CAD reconstruction and recognition system, *PhD Dissertation*, University of Sussex.
[8]   ME Newell, RG Newell and TL Sancha (1972) A new approach to the shaded picture problem, in *Proc. ACM National Conference*, pp. 443–50.
[9]   AAG Requicha and HB Voelcker (1982) Solid modeling: a historical summary and contemporary assessment, *IEEE Computer Graphics and Applications*.
[10] AL Thomas (1969) OBLIX: A two and three-dimensional mapping program for use with line plotters, *Abstracts*, Laboratory for Computer Graphics and Spatial Analysis, Graduate School of Design, Harvard University, V50.
[11] AL Thomas and TC Waugh (1970) *GIMMS: Geographic Information Management and Mapping System*, Manual, Leyland Systems, Boston.
[12] AL Thomas (1976) Spatial models in computer-based information systems, *PhD Dissertation*, University of Edinburgh.
[13] AL Thomas (1979) Hardware display processor, *Displays*, IPC Business Press Ltd, October.
[14] AL Thomas (1983) Geometric modeling and display primitives, towards special purpose hardware, *SIGGRAPH '83*, Detroit, pp. 299–310.
[15] AL Thomas (1984) Synthetic image generation, *University Computing Magazine*, August, 148–60.
[16] AL Thomas (1986) Overlap operations and raster graphics, *Computer Graphics Forum*, 5(1), 13–32.
[17] AL Thomas and AWT Lim (1996) Object reconstruction for CAD systems using constant illumination contours, *ICARCV '96, Fourth International Conference on Control, Automation, Robotics and Vision*, School of Engineering, Nanyang Technology University, Singapore, pp. 365–9.
[18] AL Thomas (1997) Speculation on virtual surfaces in machine vision systems, *IMVIP & AI '97, Irish Machine Vision and Image Processing Conference and Eight Ireland Conference on Artificial Intelligence*, School of Information and Software Engineering, Magee College, University of Ulster, pp. 53–60.
[19] D Vernon (1997) Removal of superimposed reflections from dynamic image sequences, *IMVIP & AI '97, Irish Machine Vision and Image Processing Conference and Eight Ireland Conference on Artificial Intelligence*, School of Information and Software Engineering, Magee College, University of Ulster.
[20] JE Warnock (1969) Hidden line problem and use of half-tone displays, in *Pertinent Concepts in Computer Graphics* (eds. M Fairman and J Nievergelt), University of Illinois.
[21] GS Watkins (1970) A real-time visible surface algorithm, *PhD Dissertation*, Computer Science Department, UTECH-CSc-70-101, University of Utah.

17

Semi-Automated Construction of Virtual Scenes from Cinematographic Data

P.R. Giaccone, D. Greenhill and G.A. Jones

Abstract

The aim of the present work is to demonstrate the benefit of integrating advanced computer vision techniques into a new generation of compositing tools for the post-production industry. The recent MPEG-4 image description standard supporting the overlay of multiple objects and sprites corresponds closely to the composition process and underpins our wider goal of creating the virtual post-production studio: collaborative creation of multimedia content between studios. Essential to this aim is the creation of efficient and robust compositing tools: in particular, rotoscoping and mosaicking functionality. Rotoscoping involves the separation of elements within a scene: an intensively manual procedure that we automate using active surfaces supported by edge chains. Mosaicking is a new and particularly exciting technique offering the post-production operator the opportunity to easily modify viewing trajectories, introduce computer-generated elements, stabilize jumpy action or positionally justify action in the viewport. Deriving a sophisticated three-dimensional motion model, an optical flow framework is used to facilitate the seamless merging of frames to create a larger virtual scene.

17.1 Introduction

The post-production industry is one of the most prolific generators of multimedia products for the cinematographic, broadcast, advertising and musical video industrial sectors. The research reported here is part of a wider effort aimed at demonstrating the integration of state-of-the-art computer vision techniques and recent MPEG-4 video-coding standards to create a new generation of post-production tools for broadcast content providers over cable, satellite and digital terrestrial media. The MPEG-4 coding standard not only matches perfectly the requirements of image and audio manipulation but is expected to scale well over a wide range of high-speed MAN architectures, facilitating collaborative content generation. The

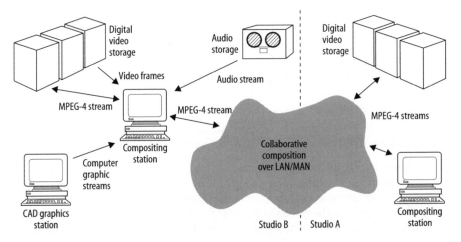

Figure 17.1 Integrated post-production studio.

goal of this research is to bring together computer vision, MPEG-4 and high-speed MAN technologies to develop post-production tools that enable:

- rapid generation of video and audio content from diverse sources (e.g. video, computer graphics or audio)
- collaborative content generation over local and metropolitan area networks (see Figure 17.1)
- encoding of textual content description for rapid retrieval and synchronization of elements
- encoding of textual, graphical or coded hearing disability information, e.g. VRML

In contrast to earlier standards, the recently proposed MPEG-4 and MPEG-7 standards have been description-oriented rather compression-oriented [17, 18]. In particular, the region-based coding scheme of MPEG-4 is ideally suited to the needs of the post-production industry, where the creation of video content is based largely on the compositing of multiple elements from a variety of sources such as film, video, computer graphics and sound [10]. In particular, the creation of special effects depends on the following functionality:

- segmenting foreground features from the background in a large number of frames to create a foreground and background sequence
- adding new static details into the background sequence
- combining different foreground and background sequences
- creating alternative camera trajectories

MPEG-4 employs a region-based approach to combining elements in a sequence. Each element is described by its spatial extent, texture, motion and depth, allowing multiple elements to move and overlap each other in an appropriate manner. In low bit rate videoconferencing applications, typical elements would include the background, torso, face and mouth of the talker each encoded at different bit rates. In post-production, elements include the background, each actor, computer graphical symbols and titles, etc. More specifically, the following MPEG-4 functionality is crucial to the creation of new types of special effect:

- creation of a single background sprite from a video sequence [11, 12, 22]
- separate description of foreground elements (once segmented from the background)
- depth coding of elements in composition
- Dynamic definition of image viewport dimensions (zoom) and motion (trajectory) independently of the motion of foreground and background elements

At the heart of any distributed multimedia content generation environment is the digital composition tool used for creating advanced digital effects using *rotoscoping*, *mosaicking* and *compositing* techniques (described in detail below). *Objects*, such as people in the scene, can be extracted and video-coded as separate data streams. In this work, these objects are detected and extracted from the original video data using *optical flow* and *active contour* techniques. Soundtracks and hand-signing (or instructions for home-based graphical generation) can be added as additional streams.

Rotoscoping is the process of extracting the boundaries of a visual object prior to its video coding. Many rotoscoping techniques do not use all available information to extract boundaries, relying instead on human operators to specify carefully and laboriously the object's boundary in each individual frame – an error-prone and time-consuming process. More advanced rotoscoping techniques employ *active contours, surfaces* [20, 8, 16] and edge tracking [19]. Active surface techniques can be used to align contour models iteratively to graylevel boundaries to recover an object's outline accurately. While still supervised by a human operator, these intelligent algorithms represent a dramatic improvement in productivity over manual boundary specification.

Mosaicking is a new and particularly exciting technique: the creation of a panoramic view of a whole scene [11, 12, 22]. This is produced by merging background elements of a sequence based on the visual motion within the scene. In even small sequences, this technique offers the post-production operator the opportunity to easily modify viewing trajectories, introduce computer-generated elements, and stabilize or positionally justify action in the viewport.

Compositing is the process of editing, combining and overlaying different sources of multimedia content, e.g. video, computer graphics, audio, subtitles and advertisements. These may be irreversibly merged into new elements or encoded separately by being multiplexed together with *composition rules* (MPEG-4 scene description) allowing both the regeneration of the intended sequence and other content providers to add their own elements. For the post-production studio market, this tool will prove invaluable for creating special effects quickly and easily: users describe how they would like the scene to appear, and the program then constructs the effect automatically. During distribution, other content generators may add advertisements appropriate to the market or country. In an MPEG-4 video-coded signal, these may be added both easily and in a highly creative manner.

Support for hearing disabilities normally takes the form of composited subtitles. This is simply another layer in the MPEG-4 encoding with the additional possibility of locally modifying the actual form of presentation, e.g. position, font and size of text. A more sophisticated approach is to include a separate hand-signing video stream within the MPEG-4 encoding. As with subtitles, multiple language versions may have to be contained within the signal. An alternative bandwidth-efficient method of supplying hand-signing and lip-motion data may be to encode instructions within the MPEG-4 stream for the home-based animation of a signing and talking avatar.

This chapter demonstrates how two sophisticated image analysis techniques (active contour segmentation and optical flow estimation – introduced below) can be combined to create a virtual scene: a seamless mosaic of frames from a video sequence. In the results section, an example of a special effect, a reconstructed panoramic view of a previously tightly zoomed sports shot, will be demonstrated.

Background Sprite Generation Using Optical Flow The visual motion between pairs of images has been traditionally recovered using optical flow [1, 4, 15]. Motion parameters of appropriate complexity (assuming a pan, tilt and zoom camera) can be used to fuse background images into a single virtual scene even where the motions are large [13], and the original foreground elements or new foreground elements replayed across this background mosaic. By defining new viewport dimensions and viewport trajectories, new shots including added zoom-in or zoom-out may be generated.

Semi-Automatic Object Segmentation Traditionally, object boundaries have been manually identified in each frame: a painstakingly slow and error-prone process. Enormous improvements in productivity can be achieved by employing active contours [20], in which crudely drawn contours iteratively mould to the boundary of the object [8]. Greater temporal stability can be obtained by extending the approach using active surfaces [16] that link together contours across multiple frames. Prototype boundaries are rapidly generated in key frames from edge chains and an elastic surface is stretched between these boundaries throughout the shot. Subsequent iterative fitting enables the surface to mould to the boundaries of the object in all frames simultaneously, subject to temporal as well as spatial elastic forces. User-selected edge data may be employed as a "scaffolding" to guide a crudely specified initial contour to its correct location. By matching edge chains, the scaffolding can be automatically located in future frames even when the object is moving.

17.2 Rotoscoping

Chroma-keying (otherwise known as *blue screening*) is an often used method of extracting objects and actors from the background so that they may then be super-imposed back onto other film elements, e.g. Superman flying through the clouds. More difficult is the situation where the objects need to be extracted from real scenes. In this case, the boundaries are tracked using rotoscoping techniques before they are composited [7]. Existing rotoscoping techniques do not currently use all the available information to extract boundaries. Instead, they make intensive use of human operators to carefully cut out objects from each individual frame in a shot. Moreover, the inability of a human operator to interpret local graylevel behavior in the same manner in each successive frames leads to *bubbling*: a particularly irritating artefact in which an object boundary vibrates. In this section we describe a tracker for extracting object boundaries that can operate on several frames simultaneously. Active surfaces are used to optimize the position of boundary contours based on information such as gray level or edge gradient, while ensuring temporal smoothness.

Active contours (or *snakes*) were devised by Kass *et al.* [20]. They operate as a connected set of vertices that move by an amount proportional to the force applied to them. These forces arise from two sources: internal forces cause the snake to be smooth, resisting bending, while the external forces guide the snake towards edges by climbing up the edge gradient. With each iteration the snake moves closer to the boundary until eventually it lies exactly on top of the boundary. The whole process is controlled by formulating the problem as the minimization of an energy functional. Special handling is required for *color* contours. Our tool processes color images by separately combining the edge gradients for the red, green and blue components of the image to guide the snake. The operator can give a higher weighting to those colors that are best suited to the problem (e.g. an actress in red against woodland) resulting in a more discriminating boundary tracker.

The following discussion is organized as follows: first the equations that govern the motion of active contours and surfaces are reviewed. Next, we describe how our tool can be used to generate the initial contours and surfaces using the edge data extracted from the images using a standard edge detector [5]. In particular, we show how the *scaffold-building* functionality can significantly decrease the amount of time required to construct an accurate boundary. Finally, chain matching [19] is used to propagate boundaries into the successive frames even in the presence of large visual motion.

17.2.1 Active Contours and Surfaces

An active surface model [6, 25] is used to generalize the series of contours generated within each image in the sequence. Active surfaces are a generalization of *snakes* (or active contours) pioneered by Kass [20]. They differ from active contours in that they take account of the boundaries within surrounding frames. The shape of a surface is controlled by internal forces that constrain the surface to be piecewise smooth and external forces that drive the surface to coincide with gradient edges throughout the image sequence. A spatio-temporal position on this surface S is represented parametrically as $\mathbf{x}(s,t) = (x(s,t),y(s,t),t)$, where t determines the temporal position of a point in the sequence, while s, the normalized contour path length, determines the spatial position of the surface within an image. The associated functional capturing the energy of the internal and external forces may be defined as

$$E(S) = E_{int}(S) + \alpha E_{ext}(S) \tag{17.1}$$

where α controls the relative influence of the internal continuity forces and the external image forces. The surface S is a projection of the 2D grid $\{s_i, t_j ; 1 \le i \le N, 1 \le j \le M\}$ into the spatio-temporal space. The vector $\mathbf{X}$ defines the subset of surface position coordinates where

$$
\begin{aligned}
\mathbf{X} = (& x(s_1,t_1), y(s_1,t_1), x(s_2,t_1), y(s_2,t_1), \ldots, x(s_N,t_1), y(s_N,t_1), \\
& x(s_1,t_2), y(s_1,t_2), x(s_2,t_2), y(s_2,t_2), \ldots, x(s_N,t_2), y(s_N,t_2), \ldots, \\
& x(s_1,t_M), y(s_1,t_M), x(s_2,t_M), y(s_2,t_M), \ldots, y(s_N,t_M))
\end{aligned} \tag{17.2}
$$

Spatio-temporal surface continuity is ensured using *tension* and *bending* forces. Using finite difference operators to approximate the partial derivatives, the above surface energy functional can be explicitly expressed as

$$
\begin{aligned}
E(\mathbf{X}) = \sum_i \sum_j \Bigg\{ & \omega_{10} \left\| \frac{\partial \mathbf{x}(s_i,t_j)}{\partial s} \right\|^2 + \omega_{10} \left\| \frac{\partial \mathbf{x}(s_i,t_j)}{\partial t} \right\|^2 + \\
& \omega_{20} \left\| \frac{\partial^2 \mathbf{x}(s_i,t_j)}{\partial s^2} \right\|^2 + 2\omega_{11} \left\| \frac{\partial^2 \mathbf{x}(s_i,t_j)}{\partial s \partial t} \right\|^2 + \\
& \omega_{02} \left\| \frac{\partial^2 \mathbf{x}(s_i,t_j)}{\partial t^2} \right\|^2 - \alpha \| \nabla I_{t_j}(\mathbf{x}(s_i,t_j)) \|^2 \Bigg\}
\end{aligned} \tag{17.3}
$$

where

$$
\begin{aligned}
\frac{\partial \mathbf{x}(s_i,t_j)}{\partial s} &= \mathbf{x}(s_i,t_j) - \mathbf{x}(s_{i-1},t_j) \\
\frac{\partial \mathbf{x}(s_i,t_j)}{\partial t} &= \mathbf{x}(s_i,t_j) - \mathbf{x}(s_i,t_{j-1}) \\
\frac{\partial^2 \mathbf{x}(s_i,t_j)}{\partial s^2} &= \mathbf{x}(s_{i+1},t_j) - 2\mathbf{x}(s_i,t_j) + \mathbf{x}(s_{i-1},t_j) \\
\frac{\partial^2 \mathbf{x}(s_i,t_j)}{\partial t^2} &= \mathbf{x}(s_i,t_{j+1}) - 2\mathbf{x}(s_i,t_j) + \mathbf{x}(s_i,t_{j-1}) \\
\frac{\partial^2 \mathbf{x}(s_i,t_j)}{\partial s \partial t} &= \mathbf{x}(s_i,t_j) + \mathbf{x}(s_{i-1},t_{j-1}) - \mathbf{x}(s_{i-1},t_j) - \mathbf{x}(s_i,t_{j-1})
\end{aligned} \tag{17.4}
$$

and where $\nabla I_{t_j}(\mathbf{x}(s_i,t_j))$ is the graylevel gradient at the pixel (x,y) in frame j. The relative influence of the continuity forces is controlled by the weights $\omega_{10}, \omega_{01}, \omega_{11}, \omega_{20}$ and ω_{02}.

A variety of algorithms have been developed to minimize this functional [6, 8]. As this function is non-convex and hence may contain many local minima, all necessarily iterative minimization schemes depend on the availability of an initial surface solution. The minimization process employed here uses a steepest gradient descent method to modify the spatial positions $x(s,t)$ and $y(s,t)$ of each point on the surface by an update step proportional to the partial derivatives of the above functional.

In the following section, we shall outline how an initial surface can be generated by a human operator to generate an initial solution X_0. Assuming this initial solution lies close to the correct minimum, the partial derivatives $\nabla E(X)$ of the above functional with respect to the spatial positions X is computed and used to update the surface points iteratively, i.e.

$$X_{i+1} = X_i - \delta \nabla E(X_i) \tag{17.5}$$

where δ is some suitably chosen step size, and

$$\nabla E(X) = \frac{\partial E(X)}{\partial X} = \left(\frac{\partial E(X)}{\partial x(s_1, t_1)}, \frac{\partial E(X)}{\partial y(s_1, t_1)}, \frac{\partial E(X)}{\partial x(s_2, t_1)}, \ldots, \frac{\partial E(X)}{\partial y(s_N, t_M)} \right) \tag{17.6}$$

17.2.2 Constructing the Initial Active Contour

In recovering an object boundary using an active contour, an initial contour is required as the first step. One method of obtaining such a contour is to allow the human operator to draw an initial boundary in roughly the correct location. A gradient magnitude frame is calculated to create the boundary ridges that the snake is able to climb (see Figure 17.2a). Pre-smoothing of the frame relaxes the accuracy with which the user must position the set of vertices to the true edge profile by

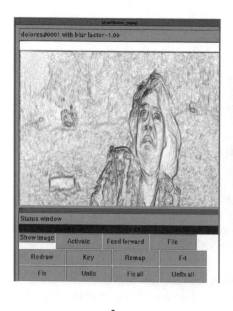

a

b

Figure 17.2 Generating initial snake contours. **a** Graylevel gradients; **b** initial contour.

widening the gradient magnitude ridge. The larger the blurring, however, the less accurate the final positioning of the minimized boundary will be. Interpolation between the user's points is employed to generate a highly sampled contour of initially equidistant points. The number of points will depend on the size of boundaries and the sharpness of the corners within the boundary. Figure 17.2b shows the generation of an initial contour in one frame.

Despite the improvement in productivity resulting from the use of snakes, the initialization process described above still results in the laborious task of individually specifying boundaries in many hundreds of images. Moreover, the level of graylevel blurring required to facilitate fast but approximate specification of initial contours leads to inaccurate final contours. Care must be taken to ensure that the initial contour does not lie close to large graylevel gradients that are not associated with the required boundary. The use of *edge* data [5] is a powerful method of allowing an operator to specify the intended gradient boundary. The edge detector recovers all edge chains from a *region of interest* defined by an operator. This data should include those chains that align with the majority of the required object. An example is shown in Figure 17.3a. Typically, the detector generates a large number of edge chains since the detection thresholds have been set deliberately low to maximize the likelihood of recovering the entire boundary of the target object. The user now selects those edges that best represent the perimeter of the object. These are blurred to create a gradient image that performs the same role as the $\|\nabla I_{t_j}(\mathbf{x}(s_i, t_j))\|$ image defined in Equation (17.4), i.e. guides the active contour to the object boundary (see Figure 17.3b). Once minimized, the smoothed edge map may be replaced with the original non-smoothed graylevel gradient image to refine the boundary location accurately.

a

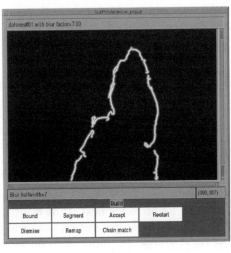

b

Figure 17.3 Edge support for active contours and services.

17.2.3 Constructing the Initial Active Surface

Establishing the initial active surface across an image sequence containing potentially fast-moving image structure is a non-trivial problem. Previous methods
involving medical image slices [6, 25] have tended to begin with a traditional 2D
active snake [20]. Once fitted to the first image in the sequence, this contour is
projected forward to form the initial solution for the active contour in the next
image. This *forward evolution* approach has the advantage of maintaining the
temporal correspondence of contour points necessary to compute the partial derivatives of Equation (17.4) efficiently. However, the approach is restricted to situations where the visual motion between successive frames is small, so that the prior
snake is a reasonable initial approximation to the next. While true for some medical
imagery, this assumption is not at all representative of cinematographic imagery.

An alternative *inbetweening* approach suited to our film effects application
employs the ability of the user to specify a 2D contour at both the beginning and
end of the image sequence. Initial solutions for each of the intermediate images
may be generated automatically by linear interpolation between contours placed at
the beginning, end and key intermediate frames. Note, however, that despite the
increased tolerance to large visual velocities, the approach is nonetheless restricted
to situations where the object evolves linearly. In general, therefore, additional
support is required to guide the surface close to the correct position before the full
surface minimization can be initiated. An obvious source of boundary data is the
edge segments generated by an edge detector [5]. As before, a subset of the automatically generated edge segments bordering the foreground object throughout
the sequence may be selected by the operator. These edge supports are used to
guide a linearly interpolated initial surface to the approximately correct location of
the set of object boundaries.

17.2.4 Chain Matching

The active surface tool described above significantly reduces the amount of time
required to locate object boundaries accurately, and consequently represents a
significant increase in the productivity of the composition process. Despite this, the
selection of edges from all or key frames throughout the sequence is still a laborious
and user-intensive activity. Having selected the set of object boundary chains in the
first frame, it would be attractive to invoke chain matching to help locate the corresponding edge boundaries in subsequent frames of a sequence.

Even in the presence of large visual velocities, object shape tends to vary slowly
from one frame to the next. Thus the matching of chains may be based on first
recovering suitable features on chains and then searching for correspondences
between features from different consecutive images [19]. The greater the similarity
between features, the more likely it is that the chains will match. The most basic
features are *corners* (points of high curvature), which may be attributed with local
edge orientation, curvature and graylevel. Rather than use curvature properties
recovered from the location of points on a chain, a graylevel corner detector [21] is

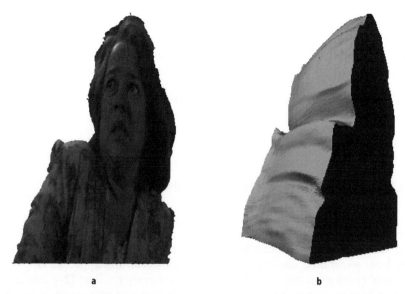

Figure 17.4 Result of rotoscoping based on edge-suppported active surfaces. **a** Rotoscope matte; **b** rendered active surface.

used where local curvature is generated for points on a chain from the local graylevel values. An initial match probability between any pair of corner features may be computed by comparing their attributes. If some information about the corner motions is available, the number of possible matches may be restricted to a *disparity bound*: a rectangular region in the one frame within which the correct match is expected to lie. Candidate chain matches are generated from the set of corner matches (i.e. there is a one-to-many relationship between chains and corners). These candidate matches are evaluated by comparing the shape of the chain using the corner locations as origins. The final set of matches is presented to the operator for correction if necessary. In this manner, the user may quickly generate the edge support for the whole surface by repeatedly projecting (and correcting) the set of selected edges throughout the shot.

Figure 17.4 presents the results of this edge-supported rotoscoping based on active surfaces. Figure 17.4a depicts the *matte* generated for the first frame in the *Cathy* sequence, while Figure 17.4b contains a rendered projection of the final active surface created from the first 15 frames. Notice that the surface is temporally smooth, i.e. the *bubbling* artefact has been suppressed by the temporal continuity of the active surface.

17.3 Generating Sequence Mosaics

Many image sequences are captured by cameras undergoing small rotational and zoom velocities with near zero translation. Under such conditions the projected view volume is free from perspective changes such as occlusions and parallax, and the image sequence may be merged to create a larger virtual image. This mosaic represents the union of all visited viewpoints and may be easily generated using any pixel interpolation algorithm given the set of visual motion fields between all pairs of consecutive images. These motion fields are computed by combining a suitable motion model with the optical flow constant brightness constraint [1, 15]. To ensure precise generation of the mosaic, highly accurate motion estimates are essential.

17.3.1 Global Motion Model for Uncalibrated Cameras

The most common approaches to generating dense optical flow fields use the *brightness constraint* but employ different sources of additional information to constrain the 2D visual motion fully at each pixel. These include regularization using *local smoothness* constraints [3]; the *multi-constraint* approach employing additional *constancies* such as color maps and intensity gradient [24]; and neighborhood-based *parametric motion models* [1]. In common with many other examples of the parametric type, the proposed algorithm uses motion models [2, 4, 9, 23] but differs both in the formulation of the motion estimator and in the process architecture of the algorithm.

This chapter presents a new generalized formulation of the motion model-based optical flow estimator. This formulation, described in Section 17.3.2, has the following advantages. First, given an initial estimate of the motion field the method can cope with arbitrarily large motions. Second, motion fields generated by other techniques such as *block matching* can be incorporated into the estimation process.

Many commonly used motion models, such as the two-parameter *uniform translation*, four-parameter *2D rotation and translation* and the six-parameter *affine* are not motivated by any three-dimensional concerns, but are nonetheless applied to moving three-dimensional scenes because of their computational simplicity. However, the accuracy of the motion field is extremely important when generating mosaics by merging frames: misalignment leads at best to blurring and at worst to severe distortions in topology. Consequently, in the following we have derived a linear motion model capable of modeling the visual motion of the rigid background scene in the image sequence. This depth-independent parametric model, defined in Equation (7.13), preserves the assumption that the camera motion is composed only of small rotational, translational and zoom velocities. The translational components should ideally be zero, as these are responsible for parallax distortions. Such a model is ideally suited to the panning cameras typically deployed in sporting events. Moreover, no camera calibration is required (assuming no significant spherical aberration).

This motion model is formulated by examining the three-dimensional motion of a point in the view volume. The point $\mathbf{X} = (X,Y,Z)^{\mathrm{T}}$ (measured in a camera coordinate system where the Z-axis is aligned along the optical axis) projects onto the 2D pixel position $\mathbf{x} = (x,y)^{\mathrm{T}}$ under a perspective transformation given the current focal length f. If $\mathbf{x}_0 = (x_0,y_0)^{\mathrm{T}}$ is the intersection point of the optical axis with the image plane, and α and β are the pixel dimensions, then x is related to the 3D position as follows:

$$\frac{X}{Z} = \frac{\alpha}{f}(x-x_0), \quad \frac{Y}{Z} = \frac{\beta}{f}(y-y_0) \tag{17.7}$$

Under a small rotational and translational motion, the point X in the view volume moves to the new position $X' = (X', Y', Z')^T$:

$$X' = R(\omega_x, \omega_y, \omega_z)X + T \tag{17.8}$$

where

$$R(\omega_x, \omega_y, \omega_z) = \begin{bmatrix} 1 & -\omega_z & \omega_y \\ \omega_z & 1 & -\omega_x \\ -\omega_y & \omega_x & 1 \end{bmatrix} \quad \text{and} \quad T = (T_x, T_y, T_z)^T \tag{17.9}$$

generating the following expressions for each component in terms of the original position X and the motion parameters:

$$\begin{aligned} X' &= X + (Z\omega_y - Y\omega_z) + T_x \\ Y' &= Y + (X\omega_z - Z\omega_x) + T_y \\ Z' &= Z + (Y\omega_x - X\omega_y) + T_z \end{aligned} \tag{17.10}$$

Under the perspective transformation, the new 2D pixel location of the point X' under the specified 3D motion and with the new focal length becomes

$$x' = x_0 + \frac{f'}{\alpha}\frac{X'}{Z'}, \quad y' = y_0 + \frac{f'}{\beta}\frac{Y'}{Z'} \tag{17.11}$$

We may assume that the depth of a point is much greater than its change in depth between frames, i.e. that in Equation (17.10), $\Delta Z = (Y\omega_x - X\omega_y) + T_z$ and $Z \gg \Delta Z$. Thus the approximation $(1 + \Delta Z / Z)^{-1} \approx (1 - \Delta Z / Z)$ can be used to rewrite Equation (17.11) in the following linear form:

$$\begin{aligned} x' &\approx x_0 + \frac{f}{\alpha}\left(1 + \frac{\Delta f}{f}\right)\left[\frac{X}{Z} + \left(\omega_y - \omega_z\frac{Y}{Z}\right) + \frac{T_x}{Z}\right]\left[1 - \left(\frac{Y}{Z}\omega_z - \frac{X}{Z}\omega_y\right) - \frac{T_z}{Z}\right] \\ y' &\approx y_0 + \frac{f}{\beta}\left(1 + \frac{\Delta f}{f}\right)\left[\frac{Y}{Z} + \left(\frac{X}{Z}\omega_z - \omega_x\right) + \frac{T_y}{Z}\right]\left[1 + \left(\frac{Y}{Z}\omega_z - \frac{X}{Z}\omega_y\right) - \frac{T_z}{Z}\right] \end{aligned} \tag{17.12}$$

where $\Delta f = f' - f$. The above expressions can be simplified enormously using the following assumptions. First, the assumption of small translation ensures that

$$\frac{T_x}{Z} \approx 0, \quad \frac{T_y}{Z} \approx 0, \quad \frac{T_z}{Z} \approx 0$$

and secondly, since $\omega_x, \omega_y, \omega_z$ and Δf are small, their products are negligible, i.e.

$$\omega_x\omega_y \approx 0, \quad \omega_y\omega_z \approx 0, \quad \omega_z\omega_x \approx 0, \quad \Delta f\omega_x \approx 0, \quad \Delta f\omega_y \approx 0, \quad \Delta f\omega_z \approx 0$$

By combining the above assumptions with the perspective expressions of Equation (17.7), Equation (17.12) may be expressed as a linear visual displacement model as a function of uncalibrated pixel coordinates

$$\Delta x(x, y) = a_0 x^2 + a_1 xy + a_2 x + a_3 y + a_4$$

$$\Delta y(x, y) = a_0 xy + a_1 y^2 + a_5 x + a_6 y + a_7 \tag{17.13}$$

where $\Delta x = x' - x$, $\Delta y = y' - y$, and the eight model parameters are given by

$$a_0 = \frac{\alpha}{f}\omega_y$$

$$a_1 = -\frac{\beta}{f}\omega_x$$

$$a_2 = \Delta f - \frac{\beta}{f}\omega_x y_0 - 2\frac{\alpha}{f}\omega_y x_0$$

$$a_3 = -\frac{\beta}{\alpha}\omega_z - \frac{\beta}{f}\omega_x x_0$$

$$a_4 = \frac{\beta}{f}\omega_x x_0 y_0 + \frac{\alpha}{f}\omega_y x_0^2 + \frac{\beta}{\alpha}\omega_z y_0 + \frac{f}{\alpha}\omega_y - \Delta f x_0 \tag{17.14}$$

$$a_5 = \frac{\alpha}{\beta}\omega_z - \frac{\alpha}{f}\omega_y y_0$$

$$a_6 = \Delta f - \frac{\alpha}{f}\omega_y x_0 + 2\frac{\beta}{f}\omega_x y_0$$

$$a_7 = \frac{\alpha}{f}\omega_y x_0 y_0 - \frac{\beta}{f}\omega_x y_0^2 - \frac{\alpha}{\beta}\omega_z x_0 - \frac{f}{\beta}\omega_x - \Delta f y_0$$

which may be expressed in the alternative vector matrix formulation

$$\Delta \mathbf{x}_t(\mathbf{x}) = \begin{bmatrix} \Delta x(x, y) \\ \Delta y(x, y) \end{bmatrix} = X(\mathbf{x})\mathbf{a}_t \tag{17.15}$$

where

$$X(\mathbf{x}) = \begin{bmatrix} x^2 & xy & x & y & 1 & 0 & 0 & 0 \\ xy & y^2 & 0 & 0 & 0 & x & y & 1 \end{bmatrix}, \quad \mathbf{a} = (a_0 \; a_1 \; a_2 \; a_3 \; a_4 \; a_5 \; a_6 \; a_7) \tag{17.16}$$

17.3.2 Generating an Optical Flow Estimator

The classical optical flow approach generates *motion fields* between successive images. Rather than motion, the generalized formulation presented here computes the *displacement field* $\Delta \mathbf{x}(\mathbf{x}, \mathbf{a}_t)$, which defines the change in position of a pixel $\mathbf{x} = (x, y)^T$ from frame t to the next frame at $t + 1$. Thus the position of a pixel $\mathbf{x}'$ at time $t + 1$ is given by

$$x' = x + \Delta x(x, a_t) \tag{17.17}$$

Assuming constant intensity over short sequences of images, the estimated displacement field should warp a pixel of a particular graylevel to one of the same graylevel in another image. The accuracy of this motion can be measured by an *error term* that compares the graylevel $I_t(x)$ at a point x in the image at time t with the graylevel of the image at time $t + 1$ at the displaced pixel location, i.e. the error term is defined as

$$e(x) = I_t(x) - I_{t+1}(x + \Delta x(x, a_t)) \tag{17.18}$$

As the above term is not sufficiently constrained to computet the displacement field at each pixel, a motion model defining motion over a local neighborhood of pixels is required to provide the additional constraint. The displacement field employed is the global motion model derived above and defined in Equation (17.13):

$$\Delta x(x, a_t) = X(x)a_t \tag{17.19}$$

where a_t are the motion parameters for the current image. Thus we can rewrite the error term as

$$e(x) = I_t(x) - I_{t+1}(x + X(x)a_t) \tag{17.20}$$

Combining this motion model expression with a first-order Taylor series expansion of the error term generates the usual optical flow constraint, which may be used to construct a *least squares functional* in terms of the motion parameters a:

$$e(x) \approx \Delta I_t(x) - \nabla I_{t+1}(x)^T X(x)a_t \tag{17.21}$$

where $\nabla I_{t+1}(x)$ represents the partial derivatives of frame $I_{t+1}(x)$, and the *frame difference* is given by $\Delta I_t(x) = I_t(x) - I_{t+1}(x)$.

17.3.2.1 *Iterative Estimation of Optic Flow*

A problem arises for all methods using the Taylor series expansion of the *intensity constancy* constraint: the magnitude of detectable changes in displacement is effectively restricted to the width of the spatial derivative operator ∇I. Larger motions are likely to be corrupted by aliasing. Typical methods of coping with this problem are based on the *multi-resolution* framework using a Laplacian pyramid [1, 23, 4]. Such an approach has the potential ability to capture large motions, reducing the likelihood of aliasing. Coarse motion estimates can be rapidly generated at lower resolutions and used to seed more accurate estimation as well as to guide segmentation at finer resolutions. In practice, relatively few layers are employed because of the considerable blurring of object structure and merging of regions containing multiple motion at lower resolutions in the hierarchy. A *multi-pass* pixel segmentation strategy is usually embedded within this framework using *robust-statistical* estimators [23, 4]. The motion parameters of the largest motion region are propagated and refined down through the hierarchy: moving regions are identified as *inliers* at the finest level. Recent work, however, has shown that a new iterative formulation of the *intensity constancy* constraint handles arbitrarily large motions [14, 13]. Given initial estimates of the optical flow, this approach, described in full below, can currently cope with remarkably large displacements provided the visual motions are not subject to large accelerations. In this context, the width of the spatial derivative operator acts only as a limit on the detectable *rate of change* of velocity.

17.3.2.2 Deriving a Least Squares Iterative Estimator

An iterative estimator utilizes a previous estimate of the motion to refine the final motion parameters. To generate this estimator, the error function of Equation (17.20) must be linearized around the current ith motion estimate $\mathbf{a}_{t,i}$:

$$e(\mathbf{x}, \mathbf{a}_{t,i+1}) \approx \Delta I_t(\mathbf{x}, \mathbf{a}_{t,i}) - \nabla I_{t+1}(\mathbf{x} + X(\mathbf{x})\mathbf{a}_{t,i})^T X(\mathbf{x})\Delta \mathbf{a}_t \qquad (17.22)$$

where $I_{t+1}(\mathbf{x} + X(\mathbf{x})\mathbf{a}_{t,i})$ is the *motion-compensated* frame $I_{t+1}(\mathbf{x})$ and $\Delta \mathbf{a}_t = \mathbf{a}_{t,i+1} - \mathbf{a}_{t,i}$ is the update to the current motion parameters. The *displaced frame difference* $\Delta I_t(\mathbf{x}, \mathbf{a}_{t,i})$ is given by

$$\Delta I_t(\mathbf{x}, \mathbf{a}_{t,i}) = I_t(\mathbf{x}) - I_{t+1}(\mathbf{x} + \Delta \mathbf{x}(\mathbf{x}, \mathbf{a}_{t,i}))$$

where $\Delta \mathbf{x}(\mathbf{x}, \mathbf{a}_{t,i})$ is the displacement field generated by the ith motion parameter $\mathbf{a}_{t,i}$ estimate using Equation (17.19). Any errors in the *motion-compensated frame* are compounded when computing its spatial derivatives. For this reason, we use the spatial derivatives $\nabla I_t(\mathbf{x})$ as a good approximation to $\nabla I_{t+1}(\mathbf{x} + X(\mathbf{x})\mathbf{a}_{t,i})$. With this, the error term may now be rewritten to relate the next estimate of the motion parameters $\mathbf{a}_{t,i+1}$ to the current estimate of the displacement field $\Delta \mathbf{x}(\mathbf{x}, \mathbf{a}_{t,i})$

$$e(\mathbf{x}, \mathbf{a}_{t,i+1}) \approx \Delta I_t(\mathbf{x}, \mathbf{a}_{t,i}) - \nabla I_t(\mathbf{x})^T \{X(\mathbf{x})\mathbf{a}_{t,i+1} - \Delta \mathbf{x}(\mathbf{x}, \mathbf{a}_{t,i})\} \qquad (17.23)$$

Such a formulation, relating motion parameters to the displacement field, enables accurate motion estimation, even in the presence of large velocities given an accurate initial estimate of the displacement field $\Delta \mathbf{x}_{t,0}(\mathbf{x})$ which may be generated using an alternative technique, e.g. *block matching*.

A least squares minimization problem may be formulated to locate the appropriate motion parameters that best fit the error term to the set of background pixels B_t in the frame $I_t(\mathbf{x})$. Using the error term of Equation (17.23), this error functional may be defined in terms of the current motion estimate $\mathbf{a}_{t,i+1}$ as follows:

$$\varepsilon(\mathbf{a}_{t,i+1}) = \sum_{\mathbf{x} \in B_t} e(\mathbf{x}, \mathbf{a}_{t,i+1})^2 \qquad (17.24)$$

Setting to zero the partial derivatives of the above functional with respect to $\mathbf{a}_{t,i+1}$ generates the following iterative estimator for $\mathbf{a}$:

$$\mathbf{a}_{t,i+1} = \left\{ \sum_{\mathbf{x} \in B_t} X(\mathbf{x})^T \nabla I_t(\mathbf{x}) \nabla I_t(\mathbf{x})^T X(\mathbf{x}) \right\}^{-1}$$

$$\times \left\{ \sum_{\mathbf{x} \in B_t} X(\mathbf{x})^T \nabla I_t(\mathbf{x}) [\Delta I_t(\mathbf{x}, \mathbf{a}_{t,i}) + \nabla I_t(\mathbf{x})^T \Delta \mathbf{x}_{t,0}(\mathbf{x})] \right\}$$

(17.25)

where the first parameter estimate $\mathbf{a}_{t,1}$ can be computed from the initial displacement field $\Delta \mathbf{x}_{t,0}(\mathbf{x})$, and subsequent parameter estimates are updated using

$$\mathbf{a}_{t,i+1} = \mathbf{a}_{t,i} + \left\{ \sum_{\mathbf{x} \in B_t} X(\mathbf{x})^T \nabla I_t(\mathbf{x}) \nabla I_t(\mathbf{x})^T X(\mathbf{x}) \right\}^{-1}$$

$$\times \left\{ \sum_{\mathbf{x} \in B_t} X(\mathbf{x})^T \nabla I_t(\mathbf{x}) \Delta I_t(\mathbf{x}, \mathbf{a}_{t,i}) \right\}$$

(17.26)

One immediate problem with the above estimator is that the set of pixels B_t to which the model is fitted must belong to the same moving region, i.e. the background. The inclusion in the estimation process of any pixels belonging to a foreground region will significantly corrupt the motion model, resulting in significant topological distortions to the generated mosaic. Empirical evidence has suggested that robust statistical M-estimators do not provide accurate solutions, even where the percentage of outliers is low. This is probably because the breakdown point for this eight-parameter fitting problem is very low. Currently it is necessary to extract the foreground features using the rotoscoping tool of Section 17.2.

17.3.3 Recovering Large Motions

The estimator developed in the last section can compute motion parameters even in the presence of large motions provided the initializing displacement field $\Delta \mathbf{x}_{t,0}(\mathbf{x})$ aligns the I_t and I_{t+1} frame to within the width of the smoothing ∇I operator. While a number of alternative methods could be used to generate a initial dense motion field, we demonstrate the robustness of using a block matching algorithm, which, despite its assumption of 2D translation, copes well with large motion. Since the complexity of the method is proportional to the square of the magnitude of the largest visual motion expected, we increase speed by performing block matching on a highly sub-sampled version of the frames.

The tolerance to large-scale motions is demonstrated using the image sequence shown in Figure 17.5. Here the moving camera is undergoing non-uniform pan, tilt and zoom velocities. For these 384×284 frames, the visual motion is approximately 30 pixels per frame. Note that in this example there were no objects moving independently within the scene. The spatial derivatives are computed after pre-smoothing using a Gaussian filter with standard deviation of 0.5 pixels. In Figure 17.6, the displaced frame differences, $I_t(\mathbf{x}) - I_{t+1}(\mathbf{x} + \Delta \mathbf{x}_t(\mathbf{x}))$, are shown to illustrate the quality of the results produced by the iterative estimator.

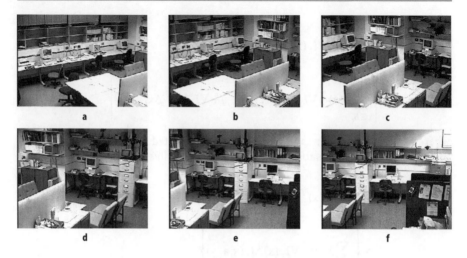

Figure 17.5 Research laboratory sequence. **a** Frame 00; **b** frame 06; **c** frame12; **d** frame 18; **e** frame 24; **f** frame 30.

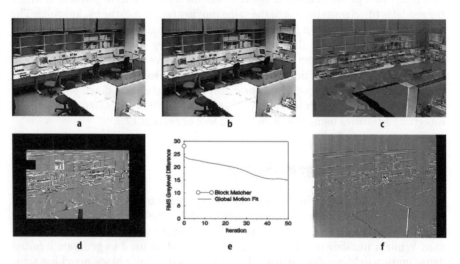

Figure 17.6 Recovering large motions. **a** Frame 00; **b** frame 01; **c** difference frame; **d** block match difference; **e** RMS errors; **f** displaced frame difference.

Figures 17.6a and b show the first and second frames in the sequence. The size of the motion is clearly evident in Figure 17.6c, the difference image between these two frames. This misalignment represents a serious problem for optical flow algorithms based on the Taylor's expansion of the brightness constraint, including approaches that use multi-resolution.

Our estimator, given by Equation (17.25), must be supplied with an initial displacement field: $\Delta \mathbf{x}_{t,0}(\mathbf{x})$. This is generated by a simple block matching scheme applied to subsampled versions of the previous and current frames. The highly approximate quality of the generated displacement fields may be appreciated by inspecting the displaced frame difference in Figure 17.6d generated using these crude motions. Although the block structure of the method is clearly evident in the result, and despite the large motion involved, the displacement fields do roughly align the two frames to a reasonable accuracy. (The outer dark border represents unmatched blocks whose search area falls outside the image.)

Having roughly aligned our images, the motion parameters may now be recovered iteratively using Equations (17.25) and (17.26). The RMS graylevel difference for the updated displaced frame difference at each iteration is presented in Figure 17.6e. The RMS graylevel difference using the displacements computed by block matching is presented in addition to the plot showing progressive refinement of the motion. Figure 17.6f shows the final displaced frame difference at convergence, and demonstrates the accuracy with which the visual motion has been modeled. A number of points about the results are worth mentioning. First, the motion model assumes zero translational velocities. Since the rotation axis of our panning camera does not contain the focal point of the camera, this assumption is clearly only approximate. The accuracy of the motion model remains high nonetheless. This is true even in the large zoom motion, which peaks mid-sequence. Second, despite the 2D visual translation assumption intrinsic to block matching, the initial alignments are sufficiently accurate to seed our iterative estimator. Third, the updating estimator of Equation (17.26) can be made extremely fast by noting that the expression

$$\left\{ \sum_{\mathbf{x} \in B_t} X(\mathbf{x})^{\mathrm{T}} \nabla I_t(\mathbf{x}) \nabla I_t(\mathbf{x})^{\mathrm{T}} X(\mathbf{x}) \right\}^{-1}$$

does not depend on the updated motion parameters and therefore need only be calculated once per frame. Thus, the speed of the estimator depends only on the time taken to create the displaced frame difference $\Delta I_t(\mathbf{x}, \mathbf{a}_{t,i})$.

17.3.4 Mosaicking by Merging Sequence Frames

A virtual scene may now be created using, say, the first frame as a reference image. The pixels in successive frames are moved to their appropriate position in this (enlarged) reference image (see Figure 17.7 for the mosaic created from the sequence shown in Figure 17.5). In practice, however, interesting sequences will typically be composed of one or more foreground elements, e.g. the car in Figure 17.8; see Figures 17.9 and 17.10. To create the background mosaic, the optical flow algorithm must correctly identify the visual motion of the background portion of the image irrespective of the size of the foreground element(s). While optical flow estimators based on *robust statistics* [4, 23] can be used to minimize the influence of the unwanted foreground element, some method of initializing the background motion will be required. We achieve this using the *rotoscoping* tool described in Section 17.2. A user outlines the foreground element in one image to create a mask identifying the required background pixels. The chain matching functionality of the tool facilitates the automatic generation of masks in subsequent frames. The

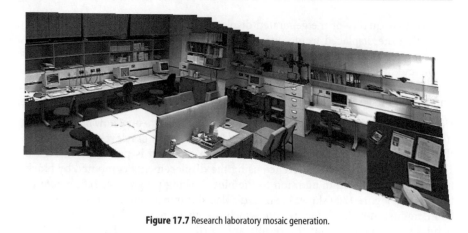

Figure 17.7 Research laboratory mosaic generation.

Figure 17.8 Rally car sequence. **a** Frame 000; **b** frame 080; **c** frame 158.

Figure 17.9 Rally car composition.

Figure 17.10 Rally car mosaic.

future use of robust-statistical estimators may ensure that even more crudely specified masks are sufficient to ensure accurate motion estimates.

17.4 Conclusions

As part of a wider collaborative post-production project, the work presented here aims to demonstrate the benefit of integrating advanced computer vision techniques into a new generation of compositing tools. Traditionally, this composition process has relied on the generation of *mattes*: image masks that identify which pixels are to be replaced by or composited over another frame. The recent MPEG-4 image-description standard, which supports the overlay of multiple *objects* and *sprites*, corresponds more closely to the composition process. The ability to create, transfer and composit MPEG-4-coded elements underpins our wider goal of creating the *virtual post-production studio*: the collaborative creation of multimedia content between users on a LAN or between studios on a MAN.

Essential to this aim is the creation of efficient and robust compositing tools, and in particular, *rotoscoping, motion segmentation* and *mosaicking* functionality. The use of *active surfaces* as presented in this work has a number of advantages. First, attraction forces based on graylevel gradients mean that a human operator need only specify the boundary approximately: a key feature that generates a significant increase in productivity. A subsequent surface-updating phase will locate the boundary accurately. Second, the temporal continuity of the surface will reduce the likelihood of *bubbling* by ensuring that the surface has a similar shape locally in each frame. Finally, the same temporal continuity property negates the need to specify an initial contour shape in every frame. Rather, where object shape evolves slowly, linear interpolation may be used to specify an initial surface. Where more complex shape evolutions or high visual motions are present, the operator can control the initial shape using attraction forces focused on selected edge chains.

Mosaicking is a new and particularly exciting technique offering the post-production operator the opportunity to easily modify viewing trajectories, introduce computer generated elements, stabilize jumpy action or positionally justify action in the viewport. Currently, the mosaicking process relies on assumptions about the motion of the camera (in our case negligible 3D translation) to derive a motion model capable of integration into an optical flow framework. The advantage is the seamless merging of frames to create a larger virtual scene without the need to calibrate either the intrinsic or the extrinsic camera parameters. Two important issues still require addressing: generalizing the method to arbitrary camera motions and coping with scenes containing independently moving elements.

A number of significant image analysis post-production problems still need to be tackled if a truly flexible and robust composition tool is to be created. These include reliable segmentation of hair; descriptive annotation of content for rapid retrieval and synchronization; and flexible tracking tools for both 2D and 3D features, e.g. lip and head orientation. In addition, the goal of a virtual studio requires urgent solutions to a number of networking issues including the transfer and repeated visualization of enormous volumes of data (since a typical working shot can comprise several gigabytes), and the need for cooperative composition between geographically distant studios.

References

[1] P Anandan, JR Bergen, KJ Hanna and R Hingorani (1993) Motion analysis and image sequence processing, in *Hierarchical Model-Based Motion Estimation* (eds. MI Sezan and RL Lagendijk), Kluwer Academic, Boston, pp. 1–22.

[2] S Ayer, P Schroeter and J Bigün (1994) Segmentation of moving objects by robust motion parameter estimation over multiple frame, in *Proc. European Conference on Computer Vision*, Stockholm, pp. 316–27.

[3] JL Barron, DJ Fleet and SS Beauchemin (1994) Performance of optical flow techniques, *International Journal of Computer Vision*, 12(1), 43–77.

[4] M Bober and J Kittler (1994) Robust motion analysis, in *Proc. IEEE Computer Soc. Conf. on Computer Vision and Pattern Recognition*, pp. 947–52.

[5] J Canny (1986) A computational approach to edge detection, *IEEE Transactions on Pattern Analysis and Machine Intelligence*, 6(6), 679–98.

[6] L Cohen and I Cohen (1993) finite-element methods for active contour models and balloons for 2D and 3D images, *IEEE Transactions on Pattern Analysis and Machine Intelligence*, 15(11), 1131–47.

[7] JM Corridoni, A Del Bimbo, D Lucarella and WX He (1996) Multi-perspective navigation of movies, *Journal of Visual Languages and Computing*, 7(4), 445–466.

[8] D Daneels, D Van Campenhout, W Niblack, W Equitz, R Barber, E Bellon and F Fierens (1993) Interactive outlining: an improved approach using active contours, in *Storage and Retrieval for Image and Video Databases*, Vol. 1908, pp. 226–33, Proceedings of the International Society of Optical Engineering.

[9] B Duc, P Schroeter and J Bigün (1995) Spatio-temporal robust motion estimation and segmentation, in *6th Int. Conf. Computer Analysis of Images and Patterns*, Prague, September, Springer-Verlag, p. 238–45.

[10] J Figue (1997) Nemesis project: advanced image analysis tools based on a new 3D wide sense object oriented data representation model for multimedia content creation and post-production applications, in *Workshop on Image Analysis for Multimedia Interactive Services*, Louvain-la-Neuve, Belgium, 24–25 June, pp. 117–26.

[11] E François (1997) Rigid layers reconstruction based on motion segmentation, in *Workshop on Image Analysis for Multimedia Interactive Services*, Louvain-la-Neuve, Belgium, 24–25 June, pp. 81–6.

[12] M Gelgon and P Bouthemy (1997) A hierarchical motion-based segmentation and tracking technique for video storyboard-like representation and content-based indexing, in *Workshop on Image Analysis for Multimedia Interactive Services*, Louvain-la-Neuve, Belgium, 24–25 June, pp. 93–8.

[13] PR Giaccone, D Greenhill and GA Jones (1997) Recovering very large visual motion fields, in *10th Scandinavian Conf. on Image Analysis*, Finland, June, pp. 917–22.

[14] PR Giaccone and GA Jones (1997) Feed forward estimation of optical flow, in *IEE Conf. on Image Processing and its Applications*, Dublin, July.

[15] PR Giaccone and GA Jones (1997) Spatio-temporal approaches to the computation of optical flow, in *Proc. British Machine Vision Conference*, Colchester, UK, September, pp. 420–9.

[16] D Greenhill and GA Jones (1997) Supervised segmentation of cinematographic sequences using active surfaces, in *Workshop on Image Analysis for Multimedia Interactive Services*, Louvain-la-Neuve, Belgium, 24–25 June, pp. 39–44.

[17] ISO (1994) Information technology – generic coding of moving pictures and associated audio information – Part 2: Video, *Dis 13818-2*, ISO/IEC.

[18] ISO (1997) Coding of moving pictures and audio: MPEG-7 applications document, N1735, ISO/IEC, *Stockholm MPEG Meeting*.

[19] GA Jones (1997) Matching corner features using edge contour data, *Technical Report KUCSES-97-02*, Computer Vision Research Group, Kingston University.

[20] M Kass, A Witkin and D Terzopoulos (1988) Snakes: active contour models, *International Journal of Computer Vision*, 1, 321–31.

[21] L Kitchen and A Rosenfeld (1982) Graylevel corner detection, *PRL*, 1, 95–102.

[22] J Kreyss, M Roper, P Alshuth, T Hermes and O Herzog (1997) Video retrieval by still image analysis with ImageMiner, in *Proc. International Society for Optical Engineering, Storage and Retrieval for Image and Video Databases*, San Jose, 13–14 February, pp. 36–44.

[23] E-P Ong and M Spann (1995) Robust computation of optical flow, in *Proc. British Machine Vision Conference*, Vol. 2, pp. 573–82, 1995.

[24] M Otte and H-H Nagel (1995) Estimation of optical flow based on higher-order spatiotemporal derivatives in interlaced and non-interlaced image sequences, *Artificial Intelligence*, 78, 5–43.

[25] J Porril and J Ivins (1994) A semiautomatic tool for 3D medical image analysis using active contour models, *Medical Informatics*, 19(1), 81–90.

18
Video Search and Retrieval: Current Practice and Future Evolution

Michele Re, Massimo Zallocco, Mariapia Monaldi and Giuliano Barsanti

Abstract

The broadcasting industry is currently in the process of embracing digital technology in the whole value chain, from the production and post-production phases, via storage and cataloguing, to delivery to the final user. As a consequence, the amount of video information made available online is globally increasing, and the use of the Internet is creating new services created by or addressed to broadcasters. This evolution requires standard and efficient search and retrieval tools on video databases, which do not exist today. This chapter addresses this issue, focusing on three main topics. First we describe the ATMAN ACTS project, where the new ORDBMS (object–relational database management system) technology has been used to develop a business-to-business service [1] trading AV objects through the Internet and ATM. Then we discuss the advantages of using the standard Z39.50 (search and retrieval) protocol, together with a suitable video profile, when searching and retrieving video metadata. Finally, we address the scope of MPEG-7 and how its definition could influence the future scenario; to this end, focusing on the objective of interoperability, we investigate the integration of MPEG-7 content descriptions with the Z39.50 search and retrieval protocol.

18.1 Introduction

Digital video is the promising new technology for applications dealing with electronic communications, such as VoD, Web Video Publishing and Video Banks. Currently it is characterized by a great variety of coding and compression tools (e.g. MPEG-2, MPEG-1, AVI, QuickTime). The cost for the equipment is decreasing rapidly and the demands for storage, network capacity and video memory are increasingly less relevant. Digital video is therefore going to be considered, even by end users, as a simple medium, at the same level as text or data.

Thanks to this evolution, the amount of video information available online is increasing very rapidly, in both local and wide area networks, inside companies and over the Internet. You can play, pause, fast forward, rewind or randomly access videos; you can also download, record and edit videos; and you can even protect the digital stream by scrambling and watermarking.

But how can you search for video content?

This question has become very important, especially because of the increased amount of video information that will be available on the Internet. People are used to searching for text information via search engines on the Internet and they would expect to apply exactly the same mechanisms when searching for video material.

Currently, the great majority of video search engines are based on free-text descriptions of the content which are manually inserted by human operators. Content producers need to create large numbers of free-text documents describing each single video shot or sequence, each description indicating the point at which the described shot happens.

Additionally, as existing video coding standards do not support search functionality, this expensive process produces information (actually meta-information, also called *metadata*) which is not standardized at all: the main consequence is that different video archives cannot interoperate.

Metadata standardization is therefore perceived as a strategic action that would reduce many barriers to the creation and use of video. This need is evidenced by the report on interoperability of broadband networks of the High Level Strategy Group (HLSG) for ICT standards. It is also confirmed by the creation of brand new standard activities: MPEG-7, carried out by ISO, and the MMI (Metadata for Multimedia Information) workshop, carried out by CEN/ISSS.

Even though research activities are being carried out in the areas of content-based video search and automatic feature extraction, in the following we will concentrate on the current practice for video search, and on how this practice will be changed by the introduction of MPEG-7.

FINSIEL, Italy's leading and one of Europe's major companies in information technology and consulting services, is particularly active in providing *new services for the information society*, an area where multimedia search and retrieval is a topical issue. As a result of this activity, over which a number of international projects are still running (e.g. ATMAN, HYPERMUSEUM, AQUARELLE), FINSIEL has developed Z-SUITE© a suite of products compliant with the Z39.50 search and retrieval protocol, which, as we will see in the following, can add powerful capabilities to distributed video databases.

18.2 The ATMAN Project and Object-Relational DBMSs

ATMAN (`http://drogo.cselt.stet.it/ufv/leonardo/atman.htm`) is a project in the ACTS (Advanced Communications Technologies and Services) program funded by the European Commission in partnership with a selected team of European and Japanese companies (FINSIEL, Italy; BBC, UK; BFL, France; CISAC, France; CSELT, Italy; and KDD, Japan). The objectives of this project are:

- to define, develop and test a new business-to-business service for trading and brokering digital audio-visual (AV) contents the service covers the entire supply/handling/delivery chain
- to show the new opportunity to the AV industry in order to promote awareness and consensus
- to produce a business plan that will be used by project partners to establish a commercial company

The technology adopted in the project is:

- Object–relational databases (ORDBMS, also named Universal Servers). This new technology provides the flexibility and richness of query languages typical of relational databases, together with the richness of data types managed by object-oriented databases.
- The Internet, the World Wide Web and its hypermedia-based paradigm are used as a world-wide shop window opportunity.
- World-wide ATM connectivity. This technology is used to transfer real-time MPEG-2 streams to the client (a PC or a workstation) at up to 155 Mbps. In ATMAN this happens when users browse AV content trailers, or when they download purchased AV content over their local area network.
- Digital satellites conveying ATM traffic. The project is developing an inexpensive and compact digital satellite news-gathering (SNG) system that will allow any content provider to immediately put on sale any content at the moment it is produced.
- Digital AV standards: MPEG-2, the Digital Audio-Visual Council (DAVIC) and ISAN. MPEG-2 [2, 3] allows the use of high-quality MPEG encoders and decoders with a full range of resolution profiles, resulting in TV or studio quality, depending on the compression factor; DAVIC [4] specifies tools that allow the provision of functionality required by typical applications such as TV distribution, (near) video on demand and tele-shopping; and ISAN is used to uniquely specify AV content via a standard identifier.
- DES encryption, electronic signatures and certificates, and other security mechanisms.

The above technology allows the implementation of the ATMAN scenario, as depicted in Figure 18.1.

The ATMAN DB shown in Figure 18.1 is the central database holding descriptions and catalogue information about all the AV content on sale. In our prototype this is a Unix workstation running an Object–Relational DB Management System (ORDBMS), namely Informix Universal Server (IUS version 9.10), together with the Verity DataBlade (version 1.10.UC1A3) text retrieval system.

The ATMAN DB is the access point for any service available to the user. Its software is implemented via typical Internet tools, mainly Perl modules (interfaced to the IUS via the DBD/DBI Perl interface), HTML and JavaScript. Almost every WWW

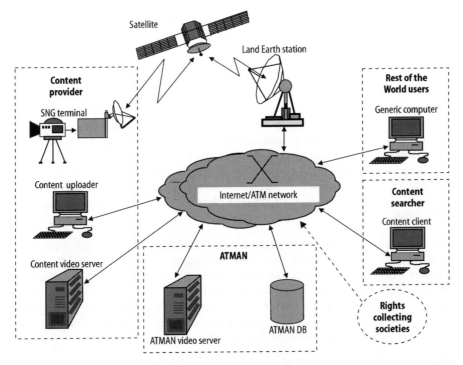

Figure 18.1 The ATMAN scenario.

page is dynamically created for the user according to the user's profile (supported profiles are guest, searcher, provider, company administrator and ATMAN administrator) and input parameters. The functionality provided by this module includes:

• entering the system and authentication of the user
• insertion/updating/deletion of videos and related metadata
• administration of users, companies, servers
• search and retrieval of AV objects via several search criteria
• browsing of collections of AV objects
• online viewing of high-quality video clips
• downloading of videos

As stated above, the ATMAN DB uses an ORDBMS [6], a concept of particular importance to video databases. An ORDBMS is an RDBMS [5] with the ability to access efficiently, via specialized functions, complex data types (e.g. images, 2D/3D graphics, video, text, music) and supporting extensible user-defined data types. By contrast, existing RDBMSs provide only limited support for complex data, which they store as binary large objects (BLOBs), which cannot be indexed, searched or manipulated within the server.

Most important of all, the ORDBMS adds extensibility to the RDBMS; for example, IUS can be extended to manage new kinds of data by means of dynamically loaded modules called DataBlades, each DataBlade defining new data structures together with the related and specific functions and access methods, which are the key to high performance.

In current RDBMSes the structure of the data is often concealed behind stored procedures (pre-compiled SQL command blocks with control-of-flow statements) that represent the only way to add application logic to the database server. ORDBMSes extend this concept by allowing functions written in a high-level language to occupy the same position as stored procedures do in an RDBMS. DataBlade developers can use functions to encapsulate the data, so applications only need to call functions performing data manipulation, rather than directly manipulating the data. Encapsulation reduces maintenance costs because it allows object designers to change an object's data structure without affecting the application.

The retrieval of AV objects in current video databases is usually performed via searches over a free-text field describing each single scene of the video; therefore there is a need to search very large text documents by means of an information retrieval (IR) system. However, the use of an IR system does not allow one to manage the complexity of a relational database, like the ATMAN DB, because the database schema has to be document-centered and queries must be limited to the maximum relationship between different tables.

Conversely, in the ATMAN DB, where the Verity DataBlade for text retrieval has been used, sophisticated video search services have been implemented. For example, users can combine searches by genre, year of production, original title, version title, standard identifier and country of origin (all of which are standard SQL data types) with free-text searches on very large text documents (which use the complex data type character large objects – CLOBs), relating as many different tables as needed.

The CLOB data type is used to store in the ATMAN DB the free-text description of each single scene of an AV object, and the VTS access method of the Verity Text DataBlade is used to make intelligent text searches on this field. Thus broadcasters can search for content containing scenes about "ancient fountains in Rome filmed on summer nights;" it is also possible to use a thesaurus utility to type search strings regardless of the language used for descriptions. An additional advantage of this technology is that it is very easy to switch from one information retrieval system to another. Our code in ATMAN can switch between different search engines: in addition to the Verity Datablade, we can in fact use the Excalibur or Fulcrum Datablades.

Figure 18.2 shows the E-R diagram of the ATMAN DB: boxes represent entities, while links represent relationships (1:1, 1:N, N:M) between entities.

In the following we provide two examples, taken form the ATMAN DB, of the kind of queries which are made possible with an ORDBMS; in these examples, the function `vts_contains` of the Verity DataBlade performs text searches with different operators on the specified column.

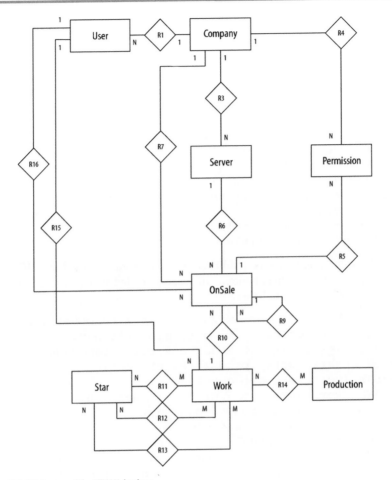

Figure 18.2 E-R diagram of the ATMAN database.

R1: each company has many users
R3: each company owns different servers
R4: each company has different permissions (to download AV content)
R5: each video content has different permissions (to companies to download its content)
R6: each server stores different video content
R7: each company is the owner of different video objects
R9: a video object consists of one or more episodes
R10: a work has different video versions
R11: a performer can play in different works; in a work different performers may play
R12: a director can direct different works; a work can be directed by different directors
R13: a crew member can be involved in different works; a work can involve different crew members
R14: a work is produced by different producers; a producer produces different works
R15: a work is uploaded by a user who is responsible for it
R16: a video object is uploaded by a user who is responsible for it

The following query selects published western movies released in 1997, and whose `full_description`, `version_title` or `original_title` fields contain the user-provided search strings:

```
SELECT DISTINCT work.work_num, work.thumbnail,
work.short_description, onsale.onsale_num,
onsale.version_title, onsale.version_language
FROM onsale, work
WHERE (work.work_num=onsale.work_num)
  AND (onsale.status = 'Published')
  AND (onsale.version_date = '1997')
  AND (work.genre = 'western')
  AND (vts_contains(work.full_description,
'UserString1, UserString2')
    OR vts_contains(work.original_title,
'UserString1, UserString2')
    OR vts_contains(onsale.version_title,
'UserString1, UserString2'))
ORDER BY version_title
```

The following query selects published videos produced by the BBC whose full_description field contains the user-provided string UserSearch1 at most five words away from UserString2:

```
SELECT DISTINCT work.work_num, work.thumbnail,
work.short_description, onsale.onsale_num,
onsale.version_title, onsale.version_language
FROM onsale, work, prod_work, production
WHERE (work.work_num=onsale.work_num)
  AND (work.work_num = prod_work.work_num)
  AND (prod_work.prod_company_num =
production.prod_company_num)
  AND (onsale.status = 'Published')
  AND (production.prod_company_name = 'BBC')
  AND (vts_contains(work.full_description,
'UserString1 <NEAR/5> UserString2'))
ORDER BY version_title
```

18.3 The Z39.50 Protocol

Z39.50 (ANSI Z39.50 – ISO 23950) [7, 8] is an open communications protocol standard for use in searching and retrieving electronic information over TCP/IP networks.

One of the major advantages of using Z39.50 is that it enables uniform access to a large number of diverse and heterogeneous information sources. It allows client applications to query databases on remote servers and to retrieve results regardless of the structure, the content and the DBMS in use. Z39.50 has been widely adopted to provide access to many classes of information, including but not limited to:

• bibliographic data
• government information resources (both nationally and internationally)

- scientific and technical data
- geospatial data
- digital library collections
- museum information

The Z39.50 standard, in addition to providing a rich set of search and retrieval tools, also includes some predefined views, called *profiles*, applicable to given application domains: a profile allows the implementation of servers which are open both in the access syntax and in the semantics of the contents. This feature, combined with multiplexing capabilities (Z-PROXY in Figure 18.7), allows the interconnection of multiple servers in a single virtual network. A Z39.50 server receiving a single query from the client can forward it towards multiple external servers (which are completely independent from the server which received the original query) and finally present the retrieved information as if it was contained in a single database. For these reasons Z39.50 is *the* search and retrieval standard in all those application domains where the relative profile has been defined, including digital libraries, museums, geospatial services, and government and Federal information locator services.

A Z39.50 session consists of an association between a client and a server where the following functions and facilities are supported (note that the version of the protocol referred in this document is Z39.50-1995, also called Z39.50 version 3, which is the latest version of the protocol approved by ANSI):

- *Session initialization*: the connection between client and server in Z39.50 is *statefull* in the sense that the session between the partners, and all the related information, remains active until the client explicitly terminates it. During the initialization phase, client and server agree on the service availability, transfer parameters etc.
- *Searching*: once the client has initialized the Z39.50 session, search requests can be issued toward one of the databases supported by the connected server. The search request parameters include the search profile used (e.g. BIB1, CIMI) and a query containing the logical combination of search criteria and specialized operators such as proximity and truncation.
- *Result sets management*: for each query issued by the client, the server builds a named result set containing the actual results (list of records) of the query. Clients can refer their own result sets in presentation and sorting requests.
- *Record presentation*: a presentation request (retrieval operation) can address specific entries of the result set or range of records (e.g. from the third to the fourteenth). Records may be presented in *brief summary* format (the distinguishing attributes only) or in *full record* format (all the user-accessible attributes). The client may indicate a preferred syntax for response records, for example, USMARC.
- *Sorting of results*: result sets may be sorted according to specific criteria.
- *Access control*: Z39.50 enables authentication on a per-session basis and authentication on a per-operation basis for cases where access to specific databases or records is controlled.
- *Index browsing*: the protocol provides a specific service (i.e. scan) to browse a window of index terms or specific fields within a database (e.g. title or author).

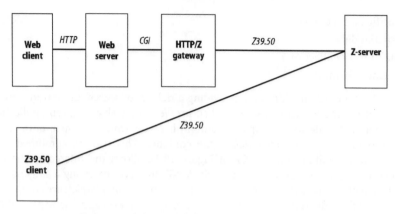

Figure 18.3 Z39.50 clients and Web clients can access a Z39.50 server.

According to this scenario, the client and the server communicate via the Z39.50 protocol; however, it is also possible, by means of an HTTP/Z39.50 gateway, to access Z39.50 servers via generic WWW clients (see Figure 18.3).

The objective of the HTTP/Z39.50 gateway is to convert the state-less nature of the HTTP sessions (each user request corresponds to a separate session) in the corresponding Z39.50 state-full interaction (a session does not terminate until the user explicitly closes it). The role of the gateway is fundamental in order to allow users to take advantage of the search results caching capability of the Z39.50 servers. To achieve its objectives the gateway behaves like a Z39.50 proxy with connection-restart capabilities.

Let us consider the example of bibliographic data, where the standard defines a special profile called *digital library profile*. Such a profile mainly builds on existing standard metadata definitions, such as USMARC, which, thanks to its field codes, supports field searches over usage-specific indexes (e.g. Author Index, Title Index, Subject Index).

On the basis of USMARC and similar metadata standards, the digital library profile specifies an attribute set, called Bib-1, which defines both the syntax and semantics of any field to be indexed and searched via Z39.50.

The use of structured data [9] is a substantial advantage with respect to dumb systems such as WebCrawler that, using flat indexes (i.e. a single index of all the words in all the documents of the database), do not understand context or relative importance (they do not know where to search, so they search everywhere, but they also miss information) and therefore waste bandwidth (they index everything, visit mirror sites and grab entire documents).

In the following paragraph we will introduce MPEG-7, a new proposal for structured multimedia metadata standardization. MPEG-7 is to video applications what USMARC is to bibliographic applications: as in the case with the digital library profile, a video profile specifying an attribute set for video applications based on MPEG-7 would provide the same benefits of standardized structured access to video databases. It is not the purpose of this paper to define such a video profile, especially because, as we will see in the following, such a definition should depend, in our opinion, on the MPEG-7 standard. However, on the hypothesis that such a standard video profile exists we can summarize the advantages of using Z39.50 for search and retrieval over video databases:

- Z39.50 is a standard search and retrieval protocol, suitable both for textual (catalogs, documents) and multimedia (images, videos etc.) databases, providing a commonly understood semantics for search and retrieval. This is a benefit for both the server and the client: they both understand the meaning of keywords like "Writer" or "Trailer" and this applies to any conforming server and client. Video archives can therefore interoperate, while clients do not need to know in advance the archive structure or fields.
- The use of standardized profiles provides a long-term availability of additional databases, possibly located in different sites, that could be easily added to the current system almost without effort.
- Z39.50 is session-oriented, i.e. it allows efficient queries to be performed based on the results previously obtained via other queries. In other words, Z39.50 maintains a "live" link (i.e. a state-full connection) allowing the user to do multiple and related search transactions with the database.
- Gateways with email, WWW, X.500 environments are available; this allows the user to use just a simple HTML browser (e.g. Netscape Navigator) for its operations, which in turns means a significant saving in implementation efforts.

18.4 MPEG-7

MPEG-7, formally called "Multimedia Content Description Interface," is the latest effort of the MPEG group within the ISO: it is expected to become a Draft International Standard by July 2000, and to reach International Standard (IS) status by November 2000. MPEG-7 people [10–12] are currently defining the scope of the standard and of requirements, and therefore the following text, based on the very first preliminary documentation available, could be subject to changes, when the standard definition will be more specific.

MPEG-7 will specify standardized descriptions of various types of multimedia information, including video, 3D models, audio and speech. This description (i.e. MPEG-7 data) may be physically located with the associated AV material, in the same data stream or on the same storage system, but could also live somewhere else in the world (some linking mechanism will be defined to this purpose). In any case, MPEG-7 data will be associated with the content itself in order to allow fast and efficient search and retrieval.

The specified content description will provide information at different levels of abstraction: in the case of video material, at the lowest level it will describe objective characteristics such as shape, size, color and position, while at the highest level it would provide semantic information. Depending on the level of abstraction, automatic extraction of features is possible in some cases, but when the level is higher, either semi-automatic or even completely manual feature extraction mechanisms

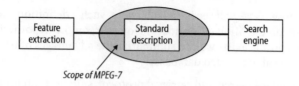

Figure 18.4 The MPEG-7 processing chain.

will be used; in any case, such feature extraction tools are outside the scope of MPEG-7 (see Figure 18.4).

MPEG-7 will not necessarily replace associated information such as free-text descriptions that, for some applications, cannot be derived in any way from the material itself (as an example, think of medical images having a therapy associated) and will therefore be supported by the standard.

As stated in the ISO documents, the standard will support the transparent retrieval of multimedia data in distributed databases, an issue of particular importance to this chapter; however, as shown in Figure 18.5, MPEG-7 does *not* specify the search engine, only the standard description. In the following we will show how, in our opinion, in order to satisfy the stated requirement of maximum interoperability, MPEG-7 should somehow be complemented by the specification of a standard interface to distributed search and retrieval.

MPEG-7 will address many application domains, including storage and retrieval of video databases. In the view of MPEG-7 people, as in ours, there is enormous potential in an international standard format for the storage and exchange of audio-visual descriptions, which could ensure:

• interoperability between video archive operators
• perennial relevance of the metadata
• wider diffusion of the data to the professional and to the general public

It is clear that, in order to satisfy these objectives, such an application requires "the ability to interoperate between different database schema, different thesauri, etc." In other words, it is necessary to have a standard interface to the MPEG-7 file format, allowing users to query, in a standard way, every DB containing MPEG-7 data.

Figure 18.5 shows our view of a system managing MPEG-7 data without such a standard interface. The figure shows an MPEG-7 file is managed by "MPEG-7 Indexing," i.e. a piece of software able to read an MPEG-7 file and to generate the appropriate indexed information on the user's database.

Then, in order to efficiently access MPEG-7 data, as with any other type of data, the only choice is to use a DB driver with one of its interfaces, such as ANSI SQL or

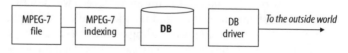

Figure 18.5 Non-interoperable scenario A: MPEG-7 data is accessed via a DBMS.

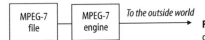

Figure 18.6 Non-interoperable scenario B: MPEG-7 data is accessed directly via specific MPEG-7 tools.

ODBC. As is known, these interfaces standardize only the syntax of the access, not the semantics. As a simple example, if you are looking for videos whose "Writer" is Alfred Hitchcock, then depending on the DB schema used, "Writer" may have different meanings or may not be present at all in the DB schema.

As an alternative to the scenario depicted above, one could think of accessing MPEG-7 data directly as a file, without using a DBMS. This is possible in theory, but we think that in order to achieve best performance, which is one of the objectives of the standard, MPEG-7 will generally need to be indexed by a DBMS/IRS. However, as shown in Figure 18.6, some standard interface to the outside world would be needed. In the example of the Hitchcock query, you should forward the search to the MPEG-7 engine, but since no syntax or semantics for a "Writer" have been standardized (at the level of the MPEG-7 engine) you will be able to perform your task only in a proprietary way. This, once again, would limit the potential of MPEG-7.

At this point, you should have clear in your mind why we think that, in order to achieve interoperability between video archive operators, MPEG-7 needs a standard interface to the outside world; this interface could probably be specified as a profile to access MPEG-7 data in distributed environments. In the following we propose a solution to this problem of interoperability.

In the previous section we explained that the Z39.50 protocol, used in conjunction with a suitable profile, provides a standard interface both to the syntax and to the semantics of database access.

Now imagine a Z39.50 profile defined for multimedia content and customized to the structure, fields and query types that will be defined by MPEG-7 (let us assume that Z-7 is the name of such a profile). Then, provided that MPEG-7 will specify a code for "Writer," the same "Writer" attribute will be included in the definition of the Z39.50 attribute set supported by Z-7. Therefore, the Hitchcock query would be very easily solved by any site supporting such a profile, whether on the WWW or on any other IP network.

Figure 18.7 shows the scenario just outlined. In the figure, any WWW user can perform a query on one or more sites providing a Z39.50 interface to the MPEG-7 data; the query is received by the Web server, which forwards it via CGI to the Z39.50 gateway (a component of Z39.50 products). Via a multiplexing module (Z-PROXY in Figure 18.7), the single user query can now also be dispatched to other Z39.50 servers (provided they are compliant with the standard), each server being connected to one or more drivers for each specific search engine used.

Similarly, any Z39.50 client, i.e. a client directly using the Z39.50 protocol to send queries and to retrieve results, can obtain the same flexibility and interoperability as the WWW user.

In order to implement the scenario depicted in Figure 18.7, one needs only the definition of a suitable Z39.50 profile based on the MPEG-7 content description. Such a

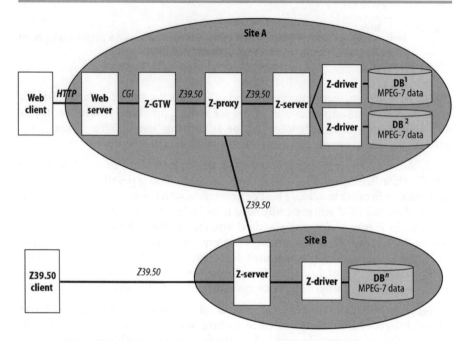

Figure 18.7 The interoperable scenario: MPEG-7 data is accessed via a standard Z39.50 interface.

definition is a rather simple task that, if accomplished, would provide the greatest interoperability potential to the MPEG-7 standard when used in distributed environments.

FINSIEL, which has already developed a complete set of Z39.50-compliant products called Z-SUITE©, will follow the process of MPEG-7 definition in order eventually to propose this approach to the standards bodies and to include its implementation in its products.

18.5 Conclusion

In summary, we have shown why video search and retrieval is an area where technology and standardization still have to provide efficient solutions to user's needs.

We have seen that emerging database technology, such as ORDBMS, addresses only part of the requirements, mainly providing the ability to efficiently search and relate, via SQL, relational databases which also contain free-text descriptions of video scenes. This solution leaves many open issues, some related to the requirement for remote access to video databases and others related to the need to have structured video metadata able to guarantee interoperability between video archives.

Z39.50, a standard protocol for networked search and retrieval, looks to be the best candidate to address the need for remote access to video databases, provided that a suitable Z39.50 video profile is defined. Such a profile could be defined on the basis of MPEG-7, a new ISO initiative for the specification of a structured syntax and semantics for multimedia and video metadata.

In the future, thanks to the combination of this technology, we can therefore expect to have better tools for video search and retrieval. Based on the specifications of MPEG-7, FINSIEL and other companies providing search and retrieval technology will have the opportunity to implement standard and interoperable tools for accessing video content in open and distributed environments. This new technology will surely reduce the existing barriers to the use and exchange of video as a communication medium, with consequent benefits to users and to the video industry.

References

[1]   M Re (1998) Business-to-business digital video mega-stores, *Advances in Information Technologies: the Business Challenge*, IOS Press.
[2]   ISO/IEC DIS 18818-1 to ISO/IEC DIS 18818-9, Information technology – generic coding of moving pictures and associated audio information.
[3]   D Le Gall (1991) MPEG: a video compression standard for multimedia applications, *Communications of the ACM*, 32(4).
[4]   L Chiariglione (1996) DAVIC: motivations and goals, *EBU Journal*, Vol. 1.
[5]   CJ Date (1995) *An Introduction to Database Systems*, Addison-Wesley Reading MA.
[6]   M Stonebraker and D Moore (1996) *Object–Relational DBMSs: the Next Great Wave*, Morgan Kaufmann Publishers.
[7]   C Lynch (1997) The Z39.50 information retrieval standard, Part I: A strategic view of its past, present and future, *D-Lib Magazine*, April.
[8]   P Evans (1997) Z39.50 Part 1 – an overview, *BiblioTech Review*, October.
[9]   R Denenberg (1996) Structuring and indexing the Internet, *Workshop on Earth Observation Catalogue Interoperability*, Ispra, Italy, 14–15 November.
[10] ISO/IEC JTC1/SC29/WG11 N1733 – MPEG-7: Context and Objectives (ver. 4)
[11] ISO/IEC JTC1/SC29/WG11 N1734 – MPEG-7 Requirements.
[12] ISO/IEC JTC1/SC29/WG11 N1735 – MPEG-7 Applications Document.

About the Authors

Michele Re, a computer scientist since 1984, has been working for more than 12 years in the fields of multimedia, computer graphics and animation, scientific visualization, networking and communications. He is currently engaged as a senior analyst at FINSIEL, where he is mainly involved in ATMAN, an ACTS project to advertise and trade audio-visual works through the Public European ATM Network and the Internet.

Massimo Zallocco has a degree in computer science, and is currently working as senior analyst in FINSIEL, where he is mainly involved in networking and communications projects. He is part of the FINSIEL Z-SUITE° development team.

Mariapia Monaldi graduated in computer science in 1987 and has focused her interest on object-oriented concepts and data analysis models, dealing with RDBMSes, ORDBMSes and text search and retrieval tools. She is currently senior analyst at FINSIEL, where she is involved in the design and implementation of network-enabled application services based on multimedia databases.

Giuliano Barsanti graduated in computer science in 1974 and has more then 20 years' experience in the fields of system and network management, multimedia, networking and communications. Currently working as a project leader in FINSIEL, he is mainly involved in networking and communications projects providing multimedia and interactive services.

19

Video Compression in MPEG-4

J. Jiang

Abstract

As information technology moves into a new phase of digital multimedia, MPEG-4 [1–3] is to be launched as an emerging world-wide standard to provide key technologies for efficient storage, transmission and manipulation of video data in multimedia environments. Unlike its predecessors, represented by MPEG-1 and MPEG-2, MPEG-4 will mainly emphasize interactive media services in the domain of compressed digital video data. To maintain this type of application, MPEG-4 adopts a content-based video compression technology as the main core of the development in its video compression. This is implemented by introducing new data structures for video data that are constructed by video objects and different layers inside each object. Hence data compression is designed in terms of video objects with arbitrary shapes rather than rectangular frames. As a result, the video compression technology in MPEG-4 can be classified into areas such as shape coding, texture coding, motion estimation and compensation enhanced predictive coding.

19.1 Introduction

Following the successful launch of MPEG-1 and MPEG-2, MPEG-4 is now under development to provide standardized core technologies for storage, transmission and interactive manipulation of video data to meet the ever-growing demand for digital media services in multimedia environments. To secure state-of-the-art technology development in this new standard, MPG-4 activities are organized into developing algorithms and tools for providing solutions to a number of key functionalities which are expected to be the important issues that need to be addressed in the MPEG-4 specifications. These typical functionalities include content-based efficient data compression, object scalability, spatial and temporal scalability, error resilience and interactivity. In this chapter we do not intend to explain MPEG-4 in terms of detailed syntax descriptions. Instead, we will emphasize those core technologies developed for video compression in MPEG-4 and how those technologies are integrated to provide solutions for those key functionalities. For details of MPEG-4 syntax and implementation of compatible encoders and decoders readers are referred to relevant MPEG-4 documents distributed over the World Wide Web [1, 2].

This section is arranged in such a way that previous MPEG video compression is reviewed first to lay the foundation for basic MPEG video compression techniques; MPEG-4 is then reviewed in that context. This arrangement should provide an appropriate environment for easy understanding of MPEG-4 and comparison with the familiar techniques in previous MPEG standards.

19.1.1 Review of Previous MPEG Video Compression

Video data compression in MPEG is mainly achieved by two basic techniques: transform-based texture coding and motion estimation and compensation enhanced prediction [5]. The former is designed to reduce spatial redundancy within each frame and the latter to reduce temporal redundancy involving neighboring frames in the video sequence. To apply these two techniques, a video sequence is divided into tree types of image frame. They are I-frames (intra frame), P-frames (predictive picture) and B-frames (interpolated picture), as shown in Figure 19.1.

I-frames are used to provide access points for random access, such as fast forward play in video playback operation. Hence they are standalone pictures without reference to any other frames in the sequence. The compression for these pictures is achieved through transform-based texture coding. P-frames are encoded with reference to a past frame that is either an I-frame or a P-frame. The prediction involved is referred to as forward prediction. Encoding of B-frames, in contrast, requires both past and future reference frames for prediction. In other words, both forward and backward prediction are required. Hence compression of both P-frames and B-frames is achieved by motion estimation and compensation-based prediction plus texture coding in the transform domain for those errors produced by the prediction. As a result, B-frames provide the highest amount of data compression while I-frames offer a modest amount of data compression. In addition, B-frames can never be used as references to predict other frames.

To reduce spatial redundancy, a frame is divided into blocks of 8×8 pixels and each block is transformed into 64 DCT coefficients via DCT operations. Each coefficient corresponds to a fixed size spatial area and a fixed frequency bandwidth.

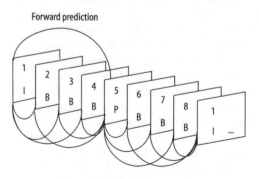

Figure 19.1 MPEG frames in a video.

Considering that DCT is an orthogonal transform, those coefficients are subject to further operations by an inter-coded scale quantizer. Orthogonality guarantees well-behaved quantization in sub-bands. Further research is often done at this stage to design various quantizers to adapt to the content of each block or frame for improved compression performance. As a simple example, for those blocks with smooth gradients, where any slight inaccuracy could be rendered as a visible blocking effect, the quantizer step should be designed to be smaller. Hence the quantizer can be designed on a block-by-block basis to provide a smooth adaptation to a particular bit rate and human visual system. Following the scale quantization, Huffman or arithmetic coding is often applied to complete a so-called entropy coding operation to further compress the output of the quantizer on a lossless basis.

Temporal redundancy is reduced in MPEG by motion estimation and compensation-based prediction. The prediction, both causal (pure prediction) and non-causal (interpolation), is conducted in terms of a so-called macroblock with a size of 16×16 pixels. Specifically, motion estimation is implemented by a block matching optimization process. In principle, the motion vector for each macroblock is obtained by minimizing a cost function measuring the mismatch between a macroblock and each predictor candidates. Let M_i be a macroblock in the current frame I_c, mv the motion vector with respect to the reference picture, and $D(.)$ the cost function; then the optimal motion vector can be estimated by the following equation:

$$\overline{mv}_i = \min^{-1} \sum_{x \in M_i} D\{I_c(\bar{x}) - I_r(\bar{x} + \overline{mv})\} \qquad (19.1)$$

where $\bar{x}$ is the coordinate of the pixel concerned.

Based on the optimal motion vector estimated, motion compensation-enhanced prediction can then be described by Table 19.1, in which forward prediction requires macroblocks in frame $I_1(x)$ to predict the blocks in the current frame $I_2(x)$, and backward prediction requires frame $I_3(x)$ to predict the current frame $I_2(x)$. In Table 19.1, mv_{12} stands for the motion vector relative to reference frame I_1 and mv_{32} for the motion vector relative to reference frame I_3. Both vectors are optimized and obtained from motion estimation. The notation used in Table 19.1 is considered on the ground that if we use frame I_i to predict the frame I_j, I_i is then referred to as the reference frame and I_j as the the current frame. This is also illustrated in Figure 19.1.

As mentioned earlier, the predicted errors are further compressed by quantization in the DCT domain plus entropy coding. The quantizer, however, is different from

Table 19.1. Motion compensation-based prediction

Macroblock type	Predictor	Prediction error
Forward predicted	$I_2(\bar{x}) = I_1(\bar{x} + \overline{mv}_{12})$	$I_2(\bar{x}) - I_2(\bar{x})$
Backward predicted	$I_2(\bar{x}) = I_3(\bar{x} + \overline{mv}_{32})$	$I_2(\bar{x}) - I_2(\bar{x})$
Interpolation	$I_2(\bar{x}) = \frac{1}{2}\{I_1(\bar{x} + \overline{mv}_{12}) + I_3(\bar{x} + \overline{mv}_{32})\}$	$I_2(\bar{x}) - I_2(\bar{x})$

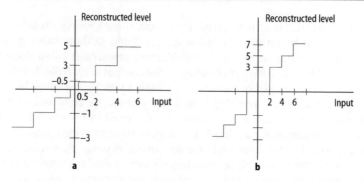

Figure 19.2 a A quantizer for intra-coded blocks; **b** a quantizer for predictive coded blocks.

those used for intra-coded frames. Typical examples of these quantizers are illustrated in Figure 19.2.

By taking the two techniques in reducing spatial redundancy and temporal redundancy into consideration together, the overall MPEG video encoder and decoder can be summarized in Figures 19.3 and 19.4.

To facilitate applications of MPEG video compression and ensure bit stream compatibility, the MPEG video sequence is actually divided into the following data structure:

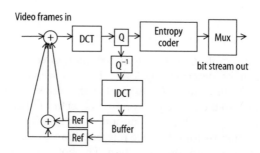

Figure 19.3 Overall video encoder.

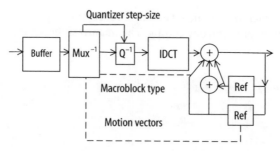

Figure 19.4 Overall video decoder.

Sequence layer:	random access unit
Group of pictures layer:	random access unit
Frame layer:	primary coding unit
Slice layer:	resynchronization unit
Macroblock:	motion compensation unit
Block layer:	DCT unit

MPEG-2 has a slightly different data structure due to the fact that the interlaced video format needs to be supported for applications of digital broadcasting.

19.1.2 Overview of MPEG-4 Video Compression

To enable a wide range of functionalities, developments in MPEG-4 video compression are dominated by fulfilling the following four features:

1. Content-based data representation
2. Interactivity
3. Scalability
4. Robustness in error-prone environments

With content-based data representation, audio-visual content is structured by a basic unit of so-called AVO (audio/visual object). For visual information, an image frame is represented by a composition of video objects with a number of intrinsic properties including shape, motion and texture. Examples of such video objects are a 2D fixed background, a picture of a talking person or a moving vehicle. Video compression in MPEG-4 has the flexibility that data compression can be operated on both conventional frames and extracted objects with arbitrary shapes. Correspondingly, the data structure for MPEG-4 video is more complicated than that of its predecessors. This is illustrated in Figure 19.5, in which a video session is a collection of one or more video objects. Each object is then divided into a number of object layers to allow for spatial and temporal scalabilities. Under each object layer there is an ordered sequence of snapshots in time that are referred to as video object planes. This is also the basic unit at which MPEG-4 video compression is applied and described. From this data structure it can be seen that information access is

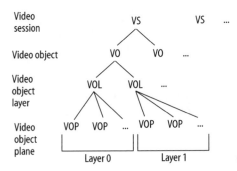

Figure 19.5 Video data structure in MPEG-4.

made through video object planes, and hence content-based interactivity and scalability become possible.

Because MPEG-4 provides standard ways to compose AVOs to create compound audio-visual scenes, interactivity in MPEG-4 can be established on two sides: the encoding side and the decoding side, corresponding to service suppliers and end users. On the encoding side, authors will have the flexibility to construct complex scenes with those objects, yet on the decoding side consumers can manipulate these objects by constructing the scene differently. Typical manipulations supported by MPEG-4 include: (a) place AVOs anywhere in a given coordinate system; (b) group some AVOs to form compound AVOs; (c) interactively change the user's viewing and listening points anywhere in the scene; and (d) modify the attributes of AVOs to alter the scene construction. If a back channel is supported, the server side interaction can be made responsive to end users.

MPEG-4 transmits the composition information that is necessary to form the scenes together with the AV objects. The scene description information is encoded independently of those AVO bit streams and contains information about (a) how objects are grouped together and (b) how objects are positioned in space and time. Since AVOs in MPEG-4 have both spatial and temporal extent, AVOs in a scene are organized into a tree structure as shown in Figure 19.6, in which each node has a local coordinate system for that particular AV object, serving as a handle for manipulating the AVO in space and time. The local coordinate system at each parent node is also referred to as a global coordinate system with respect to all its child nodes. Hence AVOs are positioned in a scene by specifying a coordinate transformation from their local coordinate system into their parent global coordinate system.

Scalability is provided in the form of content-based scalability and spatial, temporal and quality scalability. This enables MPEG-4 to fit in with a wide range of bit rates, from a very low bit rate at 5–64 kbps with a frame rate of up to 15 Hz, to a high bit rate at 64 kbps to 4 Mbps. The content-based scalability allows users to choose some key objects and discard those less interesting objects. While temporal scalability allows for choice of frame rate, spatial and quality scalability allow for the variable resolution and quality of scenes for the whole video sequence.

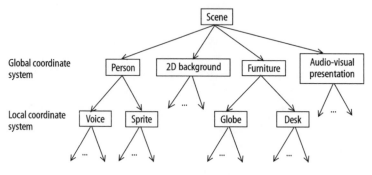

Figure 19.6 Description of scenes.

Therefore MPEG-4 videos can be decoded at virtually any bit rate, depending on the complexity of the decoder and the capacity of the channel.

The main techniques adopted by MPEG-4 to implement robustness in error-prone environments such as wireless networks at a bit rate of less than 64 kbps include (i) resynchronization, (ii) data recovery and (iii) error concealment.

Resynchronization in MPEG-4 is implemented via a packet approach, in which the length of video packets is determined by a predefined threshold for the total number of bits contained inside each packet, and all the information encoded with prediction is confined within the same video packet in order to prevent error propagation. The resynchronization markers for each VOP are inserted only at legally fixed interval locations in the bitstream. This helps to avoid the problem that errors occurring in a bit stream could emulate a VOP resynchronization marker.

For data recovery, a so-called reversible variable length code is used with which the codes can be read in both the forward and reverse directions. Examples of such codes are 1111 and 1001.

Error concealment is designed to recover the lost data from that which is most similar to the lost data. The simplest form of concealment is to copy blocks from the neighboring frames. In fact, MPEG-4 partitions the data into motion and texture. Assuming the texture information is lost, the motion information can then be used to compensate the previously decoded VOP to conceal the errors. This requires that a second resynchronization be inserted between texture and motion information.

Accordingly, the error robustness is implemented such that the data between the synchronization point prior to the error and the first point where synchronization is re-established is discarded. After that, the data is recovered either by reading in the reverse direction for those reversible variable length codes or using the error concealment technique.

Finally, MPEG-4 does not specify how video objects are obtained from video sequences. This allows maximum flexibility for different manufacturers and implementations. Different techniques used in obtaining the video objects, however, do affect the compression performance of those MPEG-4 encoders. This leaves good potential for further research by applying those techniques in areas such as texture analysis, feature recognition, contour analysis and edge detection. In summary, MPEG-4 video compression can be illustrated in Figure 19.7.

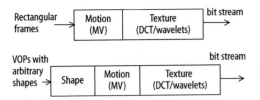

Figure 19.7 MPEG-4 video compression overview.

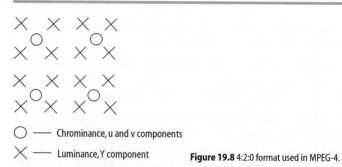

◯ —— Chrominance, u and v components

✕ —— Luminance, Y component   **Figure 19.8** 4:2:0 format used in MPEG-4.

19.2 Shape Coding

Content-based video compression requires shape representation for each object extracted from scenes. This problem is usually investigated in the areas of image processing, computer vision and graphics. As a result, two types of shape information, binary shape and gray-scale shape, are considered by the MPEG-4 video verification model. With the binary shape, shape information is given by a matrix with the same size as that of the bounding rectangle of a video object plane. Each element of such a matrix only has two possible values giving the definition whether the pixel is inside or outside the video object. The two possible values are "0" (completely transparent) and "255" (completely opaque). The gray-scale shape corresponds to a similar structure, with the difference that every element of the matrix can have a range of values from "0" to "255" to represent the degree of transparency of that pixel. In this way, the representation of binary shape and gray-scale shape is referred to as an alpha plane.

The coding of alpha planes takes a number of important factors into consideration such as I-VOP, B-VOP, P-VOP, luminance alpha plane, and chrominance alpha plane. MPEG-4 supports a so-called 4:2:0 format in which the phase between the luminance and chrominance samples is arranged as illustrated in Figure 19.8. Therefore, after each input VOP color image in a VOP sequence has been partitioned into non-overlapping macroblocks of 16×16 pixels, each macroblock actually contains four luminance blocks and two chrominance blocks (u, v components) all with a size of 8×8 pixels. To form a binary alpha plane, the associated chroma alpha pixel is set to 255 if any of the four luminance alpha pixels is equal to 255 for each 2×2 luminance alpha pixel block. To form a gray scale alpha plane, the associated chrome pixel is set to the rounded average of the four luminance alpha pixels. Hence the complete shape information can be represented by an alpha plane. In a way, the shape coding is primarily designed in MPEG-4 as motion compensated. This is because, even for those intra-coded binary alpha planes, the block of all "0"s or all "255"s can be used for motion-compensated prediction.

19.2.1 Binary Shape Coding

Binary shape coding consists of two main techniques. One is motion estimation and compensation-enhanced prediction and the other is context-based arithmetic coding (CAC for short). Since the shape information is represented by a bounding rectangle which contains multiples of 16×16 macroblocks, shape coding is conducted with the macroblock as the basic unit. In binary shape coding, the macroblock is referred to as a binary alpha block or BAB for short.

To encode each BAB, motion estimation is carried out to locate those motion-compensated reference blocks for prediction of the current BAB. As a result, context-based arithmetic coding can be determined either as an inter-coded mode or as an intra-coded mode. The comparisons involved in making such decisions are carried out in terms of a so-called BAB accepted quality. In other words, the BAB accepted quality is used as a criterion for all the comparisons carried out in the prediction. Specifically, if a current binary alpha block, BAB, is predicted by a reference block $\overline{BAB}$, the quality of such a prediction is measured by $ACQ(\overline{BAB})$, the BAB accepted quality function. Its definition is given below:

$$ACQ(\overline{BAB}) = \text{Min}(acq_1, acq_2, ..., acq_{16}) \qquad (19.2)$$

where acq_i is the accepted quality value for the ith pixel block with a size of 4×4 pixels inside the binary alpha block. Hence the BAB prediction quality is actually measured through the accepted quality values of its 16 pixel blocks of 4×4 pixels.

To define each acq_i value, a threshold is required to act as the quality measurement that is represented as $alpha\_th$ in the MPEG-4 draft documents. $alph\_th$ can have values of {0, 16, 32, 64, ..., 256}, representing different quality standards in which $alpha\_th = 0$ corresponds to lossless and 256 to a maximum distortion with which any incorrect value prediction will be regarded as acceptable quality. The acq_i can be specifically calculated by:

$$acq_i = \begin{cases} 0 & \text{if } SAD\_PB_i > 16 \times alpha\_th \\ 1 & \text{else} \end{cases} \qquad (19.3)$$

where $SAD\_PB_i(BAB, \overline{BAB})$ is defined as the sum of absolute differences for PB_i. The definition is constructed from the consideration that each pixel block (PB_i) consists of 16 pixels (4×4 block).

It can be seen from the definition that a value "1" of acq_i corresponds to high quality, and from Equation (19.2) that the macroblock BAB would not have an accepted quality for prediction until the minimum value of all 16 $acqs$ is equal to 1. This is essential for understanding shape coding based on binary alpha planes.

In principle, MPEG-4 shape coding supports altogether four major coding modes, which can be summarized below:

1. not coded
2. all_0 (all elements inside the current BAB are "0")
3. all_255 (all elements inside the current BAB are "255")
4. coded (intra-CAC or inter-CAC coded)

The decision about selecting the above coding modes can be summarized in Figure 19.9.

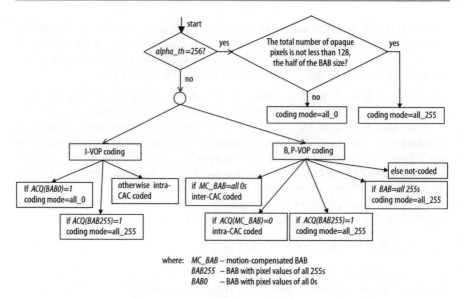

where: MC_BAB – motion-compensated BAB
         BAB255 – BAB with pixel values of all 255s
         BAB0   – BAB with pixel values of all 0s

Figure 19.9 Decision-making structure for coding modes.

In Figure 19.9, the threshold value *alpha_th* = 256 is used to detect the case that all pixels inside the current BAB can be predicted by any completely incorrect values. In this circumstance, the coding mode can be selected as either *all_0* or *all_255* depending on whether or not the total number of opaque pixels is over half of the macroblock size. Otherwise, binary shape coding can be further classified into I-VOP coding and B,P-VOP coding, corresponding to intra-coded mode and inter-coded mode. For I-VOP coding, BABs with all 0 elements or 255 elements are also used to predict the current BAB. If the prediction quality is acceptable, coding modes of *all_0* or *all_255* are selected. Otherwise, intra-coded CAC has to be used to compress the BAB on a lossless basis. Inter-coded mode selection for B,P-VOP is mainly carried out by using the motion-compensated reference block, MC_BAB, to predict the current BAB. The motion-compensated reference block is obtained by simple motion vector displacement and bordering of 1 pixel around the block. If the displaced position is outside the binary alpha map, then these pixels are set to be zero. This is similar to the bordering of current blocks, as illustrated in Figure 19.10.

Context-based arithmetic coding is designed similar to Q-coders [8, 9]. The basic idea involves constructing a context from a number of previously encoded bits and estimating the probability conditioned by the context to drive the arithmetic coder. In order to build up contexts, each current BAB to be encoded is actually bordered by two pixels from its neighboring BABs. This bordered BAB can be illustrated in Figure 19.10, where the pixels in the shaded area are the bordering pixels. These pixels are obtained from previously encoded and reconstructed BABs except for those marked "0," which are unknown to the decoder at decoding time.

For intra-coded BABs, the context is built up from its neighboring 10 bits according to the illustration in Figure 19.11a. The context for inter-coded BABs, however, is

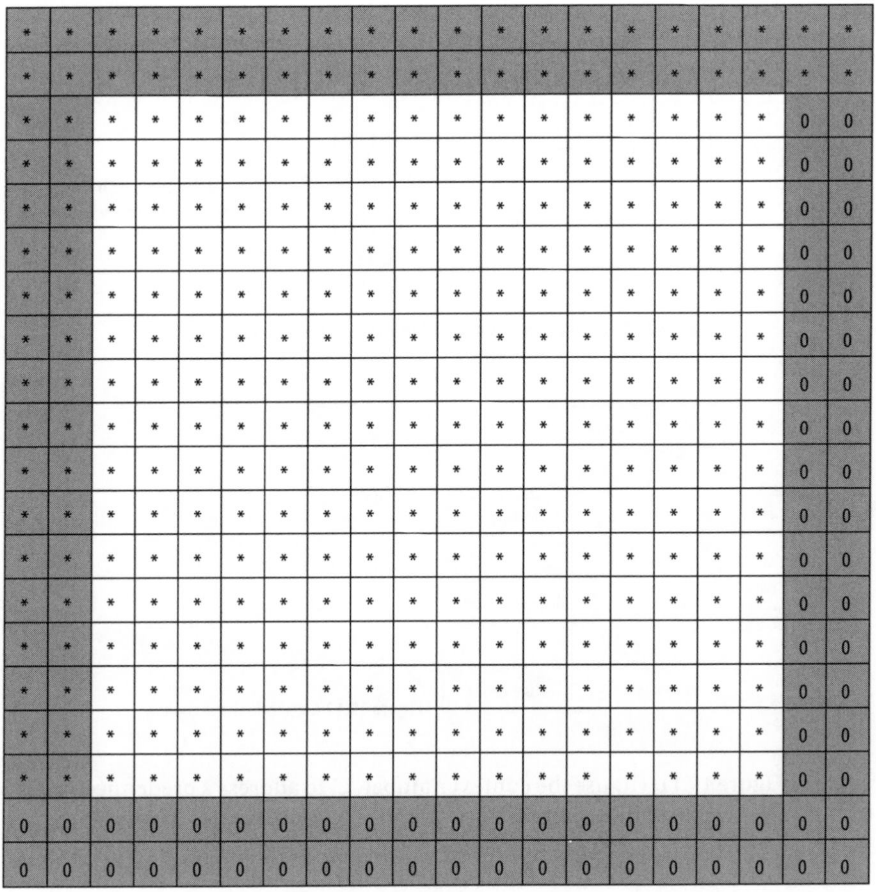

Figure 19.10 Bordered current BAB to be encoded.

constructed from both the current BAB and the motion-compensated reference blocks, as shown in Figure 19.11b. If any pixel outside the bounding rectangle of the current VOP is involved in the construction of contexts, it will simply be set to be zero. In practice, building a context may involve some pixels that are not known at the decoding end at that particular time, as illustrated in Figure 19.10. In this case, the following rules are used to overcome this problem.

For intra-coded contexts:

1. If (C_7 is unknown) $C_7 = C_8$
2. If (C_3 is unknown) $C_3 = C_4$
3. If (C_2 is unknown) $C_2 = C_3$

For the inter-coded context: if (C_1 is unknown) $C_1 = C_2$.

In summary, the complete CAC coding process can be described in three operational steps: (i) compute a context number: $C = \Sigma_k C_k \times 2^k$, where C_k is the kth bit

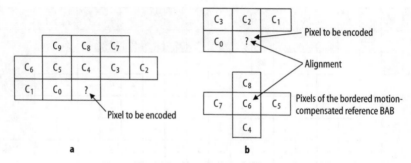

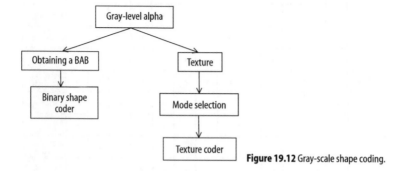

Figure 19.11 a Intra-coded context construction and **b** inter-coded context.

Figure 19.12 Gray-scale shape coding.

value in Figure 19.11; (ii) use the context number, C, to address a predefined probability table; (iii) drive the arithmetic coder with the probabilities so produced.

19.2.2 Gray-Scale Shape Coding

MPEG-4 encodes the gray-scale shape information in a similar way to DCT-based texture coding plus the binary shape coding techniques described above. Specifically, each gray-scale alpha plane is converted into a binary alpha block and a texture block with the same size. The corresponding binary alpha plane is simply obtained by comparing the alpha value inside the gray-scale alpha plane with 0, and any value greater than 0 is replaced by 255. The residues of those alpha values are then encoded by a texture encoder described in Section 19.4. The overall gray-scale alpha plane coding structure can be described in Figure 19.12.

19.3 Motion Estimation and Compensation

19.3.1 Padding Techniques

Motion estimation and compensation techniques developed in MPEG-4 are basically extended from those block matching techniques in previous standards, such

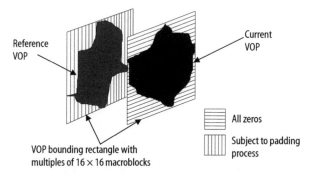

Reference VOP

Current VOP

All zeros

Subject to padding process

VOP bounding rectangle with multiples of 16 × 16 macroblocks

Figure 19.13 Motion estimation and compensation for arbitrarily shaped VOPs.

as MPEG-1/2 or H.261/3, towards image sequences of VOPs with arbitrary shapes. To enable the prediction of arbitrarily shaped VOPs, a padding process technique is designed to define the values of those luminance and chrominance samples outside the reference VOP as shown in Figure 19.13, i.e. the padding process only applies to those reference VOPs.

With luminance components, macroblocks on the VOP boundary are padded by replicating the boundary samples of the VOP towards the exterior via the process of horizontal padding and vertical padding. Macroblocks which are completely outside the VOP are padded with a so-called extended padding.

Let $d[y][x]$ be the decoded reference macroblock and $s[y][x]$ be its corresponding shape block; the horizontally padded block $hor\_pad[y][x]$ and its padded shape block $s'[y][x]$ can be generated by the following pseudocode:

```
for (x=0; x<N; x++){
   if (s[y][x]==1){
      hor_pad[y][x]=d[y][x];
      s'[y][x]=1;
   }
   else if (s[y][x']==1 && s[y][x'']==1){
      hor_pad[y][x]=(d[y][x']+d[y][x''])/2;
      s'[y][x]=1;
   }
   else if (s[y][x']==1){
      hor_pad[y][x]=d[y][x'];
      s'[y][x]=1;
   }
   else if (s[y][x'']==1){
      hor_pad[y][x]=d[y][x''];
      s'[y][x]=1;
   }
}
```

where x' is the location of the nearest valid sample (corresponds to $s[y][x']=1$) at the VOP boundary to the left of the current location x, x'' is the location of the nearest boundary sample to the right, and N is the total number of samples in a row.

After the macroblock d[y][x] is horizontally padded into hor_pad[y][x], vertical padding can be further applied to pad hor_pad[y][x] into the block hv_pad[y][x]. The following pseudocode can be used to describe the procedure:

```
for (y=0; y<M; y++){
  if(s'[y][x]==1)
    hv_pad[y][x]=hor_pad[y][x];
  else if (s'[y'][x]==1 && s'[y''][x]==1)
    hv_pad[y][x]=(hor_pad[y'][x]+hor_pad[y'][x])/2;
  else if (s'[y'][x]==1)
    hv_pad[y][x]=hor_pad[y'][x];
  else if (s'[y''][x]==1)
    hv_pad[y][x]=hor_pad[y''][x];
}
```

where y'' is the location of the nearest valid sample corresponding to s'[y'][x]=1 above the current location y at the boundary of hv_pad, y'' is the location of the nearest boundary sample below y, and M is the total number of samples in a column. The basic principle is to use those nearest boundary samples to fill in the positions outside the VOP shape.

Macroblocks completely outside the VOP can be classified into two types: those blocks immediately next to boundary blocks and those not located next to any boundary macroblocks. The former are padded by the border samples of the boundary macroblock having the largest priority number, and the latter are padded with a fixed value 128. The priority number for those boundary macroblocks is allocated according to Figure 19.14.

Macroblocks of chrominance components are padded in terms of 8×8 blocks.

With regard to the current macroblock, which also refers to the block to be encoded throughout this chapter, a polygon-matching technique is designed in which all the sample values outside the VOP are simply set to be zeros. This can be seen in Figures 19.13 and 19.15.

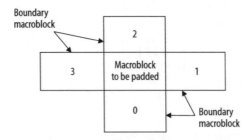

Figure 19.14 Priority number allocation for extended padding.

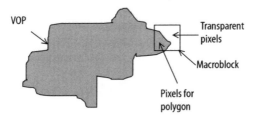

Figure 19.15 Polygon-matching techniques.

19.3.2 Basic Motion Estimation and Compensation Techniques

Motion estimation is a process to search for the best matching macroblock inside the previously reconstructed VOP for the current macroblock to be encoded. The search is carried out for both 8×8 blocks and 16×16 blocks. The best of the two is selected to generate the motion vector. With 16×16 blocks a full search is carried out around the position of the current macroblock by integer pixel displacement. The 8×8 block search, however, is centered on the 16×16 motion vector produced from the search in 16×16 blocks. The search window is of ±2 pixels around the vector. The actual comparison is completed in terms of $SAD_{16}(x,y)$, the sum of absolute differences for 16×16 blocks and $SAD_8(x,y)$, the sum of absolute differences for 8×8 blocks; (x,y) stands for the location of the blocks in the frame coordinate system (global). $SAD_N(x,y)$ is calculated from the following equation:

$$SAD_N(x, y) = \sum_{i=1,j=1}^{N,N} |current - previous| \quad \text{with} \quad Alpha_{current} \neq 0 \qquad (19.4)$$

$Alpha_{current} \neq 0$ means that the equation is run only for those pixels whose corresponding alpha values are not zeros.

The pair (x,y) corresponding to the lowest SAD_{16} is taken as the 16×16 integer pixel motion vector, which is then used to define the window for 8×8 block search.

To enable the comparison between SAD_{16} and SAD_8, a $SAD_{k×8} = \Sigma_1^k SAD_8(x, y)$ is defined, where $0 < k \leq 4$ stands for the number of 8×8 blocks that are not located outside the VOP shape. Therefore the final SAD_{inter} representing the quality of motion estimation is selected from below:

$$SAD_{inter} = Min(SAD_{16}(x, y), SAD_{k×8}) \qquad (19.5)$$

The value of SAD_{inter} is then used to make a decision about whether the current macroblock should be encoded in intra or inter mode. The basic idea is to use a mean value of all the pixels inside the macroblock to do the prediction and see whether such a prediction is better than the SAD_{inter}. The detail can be described as follows:

$$MB\_mean = \sum_{i=1,j=1}^{N_c} current / N_{VOP} \qquad (19.6)$$

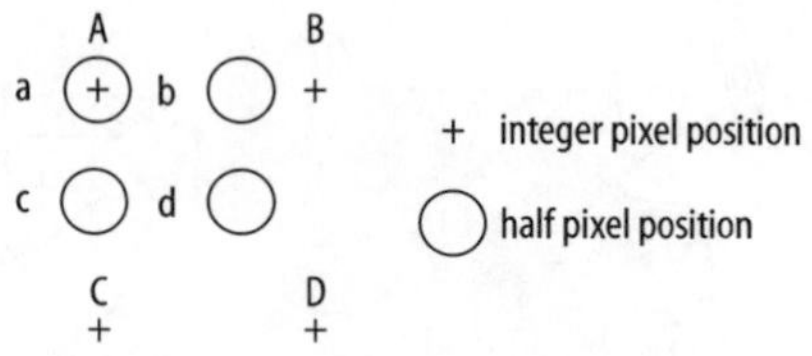

Where interpolation is defined as:
a=A;
b=(A+B+1−rounding_control)/2;
c=(A+C+1−rounding_control)/2;
d=(A+B+C+D+2−rounding_control)/4

Figure 19.16 Half sample search interpolation.

where N_{VOP} represents the number of pixels inside the VOP.

$$A = \sum_{i=1,j=1}^{16,16} |current - MB\_mean| \quad \text{with } alpha_{current} \neq 0 \tag{19.7}$$

$$\text{Coding mode} = \begin{cases} \text{intra} & \text{if } A < (SAD_{inter} - 2 \times N_B) \\ & \text{and } N_B = N_{VOP} \times 2^{(bits\_per\_pixel-8)} \\ \text{inter} & \text{otherwise} \end{cases} \tag{19.8}$$

The motion estimation will terminate if the intra coding mode is selected. If inter mode is selected, however, further search is supported in MPEG-4 at half sample precision to optimize the motion estimation. The comparison involved will be similar to the above, but pixel values attending the operation will be drawn by interpolation at those half pixel positions. This is illustrated in Figure 19.6.

The motion vector, $MV = (MV_x, MV_y)$, is obtained from the best match in the half sample search for both 16×16 blocks and 8×8 blocks. Whether the final prediction is conducted in 16×16 blocks or 8×8 blocks is decided by the following rule:

$$\text{Mode} = \begin{cases} 8 \times 8 \text{ block based} & \text{if } SAD_{k \times 8} < SAD_{16} - (N_B / 2 + 1) \\ 16 \times 16 \text{ block based} & \text{otherwise} \end{cases} \tag{19.9}$$

Motion vectors are encoded by further prediction or so-called differential coding plus entropy coding with variable length codes. In other words, the variable length codes produced represent the motion vector difference (MVD_x, MVD_y) rather than the vector itself. (MVD_x, MVD_y) is obtained from the following equations:

$$\begin{aligned} MVD_x &= MV_x - P_x \\ MVD_y &= MV_y - P_y \end{aligned} \tag{19.10}$$

and

$$\begin{aligned} P_x &= \text{Median}(MV1_x, MV2_x, MV3_x) \\ P_y &= \text{Median}(MV1_y, MV2_y, MV3_y) \end{aligned} \tag{19.11}$$

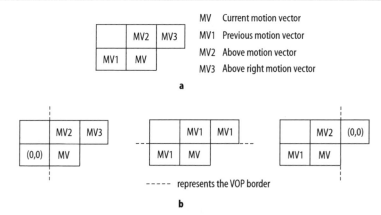

Figure 19.17 a Motion vector prediction; b predictor replacement scheme.

The location of predictor vectors $MV1$, $MV2$, $MV3$ is illustrated in Figure 19.17a.

If any macroblock referred to by the predictor vector is outside the VOP, a replacement scheme is carried out according to Figure 19.17b.

MPEG-4 also supports other motion estimation and compensation techniques such as advanced prediction modes, interlaced video prediction and unrestricted motion compensation etc. Further details can be referred to the MPEG-4 draft documents.

19.4 Texture Coding

19.4.1 DCT-Based Texture Coding

MPEG-4 applies texture coding to compress both intra VOPs and error VOPs after the motion-compensated prediction. DCT-based texture coding is generally similar to that used in H.263 and previous MPEG standards. The differences cover the content-based coding characteristics of MPEG-4, in which VOPs with arbitrary shapes are the basic units of operations to achieve video data compression. To use the conventional 8×8 DCT scheme, those boundary blocks need to be padded to define pixel values for those outside the VOP shape. For those blocks completely inside the VOP, however, the 8×8 block DCT can be directly applied without any change.

Padding for intra boundary blocks is carried out by a so-called low pass extrapolation process, which uses the pixels inside the object region to define the pixel values for those outside the region. Let $f(i,j)$ be the pixel outside the object region R, and N the total number of pixels inside the object region in an intra 8×8 block. Then the specific padding process can be described in three steps:

1. Calculate a mean value m of all block pixels that are inside the object region:

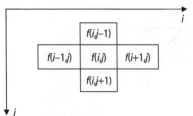

Figure 19.18 Filtering process.

$$m = \frac{1}{N} \sum_{(i,j)\in R} F(i,j) \tag{19.12}$$

2. Assign m to each pixel outside region R:

$$f(i,j) = m \qquad \forall(i,j) \notin R \tag{19.13}$$

3. Starting from the top left corner of the 8×8 block and move along the normal zigzag direction, each pixel outside the region R is further filtered by the following equation (see Figure 19.18):

$$f(i,j) = \frac{f(i,j-1) + f(i-1,j) + f(i,j+1) + f(i+1,j)}{4} \tag{19.14}$$

where division is done by rounding the result into the nearest integer.

In the filtering process, those pixels outside the 8×8 block will not be included, and the value of the denominator in Equation (19.13) is also adjusted correspondingly.

Apart from the padding technique, MPEG-4 also proposes a so-called shape adaptive DCT which applies the DCT transform only to those pixels inside the object region. The complete SA-DCT scheme can be described in Figure 19.19. The arbitrary shape represented by the shaded area in Figure 19.19a is rearranged first by shifting all columns vertically to the top of the 8×8 block, as shown in Figure 19.19b. Following that, vertical DCT is applied to each column vector in which the length of the vector is variable (see Figure 19.19c). Similarly, all rows inside the block generated from the vertical DCT are shifted left to align with the left border of the 8×8 block prior to the horizontal DCT. It can be seen from Figure 19.19d that the length of each row vector is also variable. After the horizontal DCT, the complete 2D SAD-DCT coefficients can be obtained as shown in Figure 19.19f. Similar techniques (such as quantization and entropy coding) to those used in H.263 and previous MPEGs are also used to complete the texture coding.

19.4.2 Zero Tree Wavelet-Based Texture Coding

Wavelet-based texture coding is supported in MPEG-4 mainly for still image compression to achieve high coding efficiency and scalabilities at both spatial level and SNR (signal-to-noise ratio) level. The main advantage of using wavelets is its multi-resolution analysis feature. This provides a signal representation in which

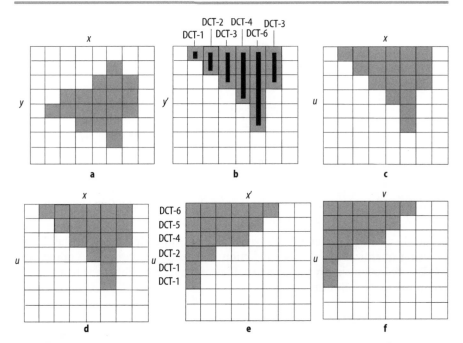

Figure 19.19 Description of SA-DCT. **a** Original VOP block; **b** column vectors; **c** after the vertical; **d** pixel location prior to horizontal DCT; **e** row vectors shifted; **f** location of 2D SA-DCT coefficients.

information about all different textures can be made available at all scales; hence wavelets shows promise at extremely low bit rate coding. In contrast, DCT decomposes images into a signal representation in which each coefficient corresponds to a fixed size spatial area and a fixed frequency bandwidth. Hence the bandwidth and spatial area are virtually same for all coefficients in the DCT domain. Since the information about those short data lags corresponds to a wide band of high frequency range, such as edges, and such content of images will disperse in the DCT domain, more non-zero coefficients are required for the data representation in order to maintain a good reconstructed quality. Therefore the major difference between wavelets and DCT techniques is that wavelet-based data compression spreads the loss of information at a number of scales, yet DCT-based data compression spreads the loss of information at one scale.

From a wide range of wavelet filter designs and research on their assessment [10], MPEG-4 uses Daubechies (9,3) tap bi-orthogonal filters (9 taps for low-pass filter and 3 taps for high-pass filters) to decompose still image textures. The overall structure of such a decomposition can be seen in Figure 19.20.

At each decomposition scale, four sub-bands are generated, represented as LL (low–low), LH (low–high), HL (high–low), HH (high–high). As the sub-band LL is subject to further decomposition, all sub-bands are represented in terms of their scales as well, such as LL_1, the lowest sub-band at decomposition scale 1, and so on. As we move from decomposition scale 1 to scale n, it is also referred to as moving from the finest scale to the coarsest scale. From Figure 19.20 it can be seen that each

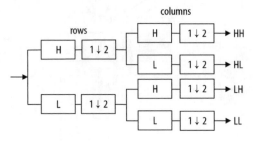

Figure 19.20 Wavelet transform structure.

wavelet coefficient actually represents a spatial area corresponding approximately to a 2×2 area of the original image.

MPEG-4 encodes the coarsest sub-band LL_n independently from other sub-bands by using quantization, DPCM prediction and adaptive arithmetic coding. The DPCM prediction simply picks one coefficient from its neighbors as its predictor according to the following rule:

$$if\ (|w_A - w_B| < |w_A - w_C| \overline{w}_x = w_C;)$$

$$else \overline{w}_x = w_A;$$

$$w_x = w_x - \overline{w}_x;$$

where w_x represents the coefficient to be encoded and $\overline{w}_x$ its predictor, and w_A, w_B and w_C are neighboring coefficients, as shown in Figure 19.21.

The rest of the sub-bands are encoded via a so-called zero tree data structure originated from reference [7] plus adaptive arithmetic entropy coding. The zero tree is developed from the hypothesis that if a wavelet coefficient at a coarse scale is insignificant with respect to a given threshold T, then all wavelet coefficients of the same orientation in the same spatial location at finer scales are likely to be insignificant too. This is because the wavelet transform decomposes the image into different scales and the corresponding sub-bands from different scales are actually related to each other, such as $HH_2 - HH_1$, $LH_2 - LH_1$ and $HL_2 - HL_1$ as shown in Figures 19.20 and 19.22. In terms of spatial position, each coefficient at a coarse scale corresponds to four coefficients at its next finer scale. Therefore a tree structure can be constructed such that coefficients at one scale can be viewed as children of those coefficients at their next coarser scale, i.e. each coefficient at one scale has four children in the corresponding sub-band at the next finer scale. The root of the tree is defined to be the lowest sub-band at the coarsest scale that has three children within

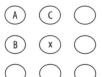

Figure 19.21 Prediction for LL_n coefficients.

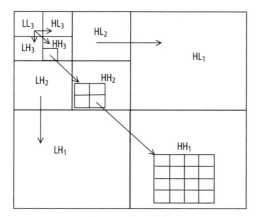

Figure 19.22 Zero tree formation.

the same scale. This is illustrated in Figure 19.22. If we use a threshold T (this is defined as zero in MPEG-4) to classify all coefficients, those greater than T can then be taken as significant and those less than T can be taken as insignificant. Therefore the tree structure can be used to represent a so-called significance map to encode the position of each coefficient, and the value of each coefficient can be further encoded by entropy coding. Such a tree structure is referred to as a zero tree.

To construct the zero tree, all the coefficients are scanned in order from the coarsest scale to the finest scale, and, within each scale, from left to right and from top to bottom. Specific procedures are summarized in the flow chart given in Figure 19.23.

Three types of node are identified by zero tree scanning. Both *zero-tree-root* and *valued-zero-tree-root* represent the coefficients with which all their children coefficients are insignificant. The difference between these two nodes is that the *zero-tree-root* coefficients are themselves insignificant (zero amplitude), yet the *valued-zero-tree-root* coefficients are significant (non-zero amplitude). In both cases, no child coefficients need to be further scanned. Any other coefficients are classified as

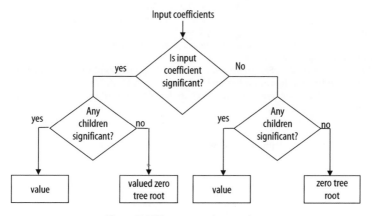

Figure 19.23 Zero tree scanning procedure.

value with either zero amplitude or non-zero amplitude. The symbols and quantized coefficients are then encoded by adaptive arithmetic coder [6, 11].

Other variations exist around zero tree wavelet scanning by identifying different types of symbol and bi-level quantization rather than using adaptive arithmetic entropy coding. Further details are given in references [1, 2, 7].

19.5 Conclusions

In this chapter we have described some of the core techniques proposed and tested in MPEG-4 video compression. The mainstream is still along the major development successfully launched in previous MPEG standards. Other variations are extended around the feature that MPEG-4 is content-based and video compression needs to be adaptive to those video objects with arbitrary shapes. Therefore we can summarize all the core techniques in MPEG-4 video compression in three main categories: (i) bitmap-based shape coding; (ii) DCT and zero tree wavelet-based texture coding and (iii) arithmetic coding-based entropy coding.

Apart from video compression, other techniques are also designed to support a number of functionalities which are relevant to video data compression. These functionalities include scalability, error robustness and interactivity. For a detailed description, refer to the MPEG-4 draft documents [1–4].

References

[1] MPEG-4 working draft (1997) Coding of moving pictures and audio, *ISO/IEC JTC1/SC29/WG11*, Stockholm; http://www/cselt.stet.it/mpeg/standards/mpeg-4.htm.
[2] T Ebrahimi (ed.) (1997) MPEG-4 video verification model-version 8.0, *MPEG97/N1796*.
[3] T Silkora (1997) The MPEG-4 video standard verification model, *IEEE Trans. On Circuits & Systems for Video Technology*, 7(11), 19–29.
[4] T Ebrahimi (1996) MPEG-4 video verification model: a video encoding/decoding algorithm based on content representation, *Image Communication, Special Issue on MPEG-4*.
[5] Information technology – coding of moving pictures and associated audio for digital storage media at up to about 1.5 Mbits/s. Part 2: Video, *ISO/IEC 11172-2*.
[6] J Jiang (1995) A novel design of arithmetic coding for data compression, *IEE Proceedings-E: Computer and Digital Techniques*, 142(6), 419–24.
[7] JM Shapiro (1993) Embedded image coding using zero trees of wavelet coefficients, *IEEE Trans. on Signal Processing*, 41(12), 3445–62.
[8] WB Pennebaker *et al.* (1988) An overview of the basic principles of the Q-coder adaptive binary arithmetic coder, *IBM Journal of Research & Development*, 32(6), 775–95.
[9] J Jiang (1996) A novel parallel design of a codec for black and white image compression, *Image Communication*, 8, 465–74.
[10] JD Villasenor *et al.* (1995) Wavelet filter evaluation for image compression, *IEEE Trans. on Image Processing*, 4(8), 1053–60.
[11] IH Witten *et al.* (1987) Arithmetic coding for data compression, *Commun. ACM*, 30, 520–40.

20
Implications of Television Over the Internet

Nikolaos Kotsis, Robert B. Lambert and Douglas R. McGregor

Abstract

The enormous expansion of the Internet has brought a new dimension to the Information Age, allowing ever-greater quantities of information to be distributed to an ever-growing number of people. More than 50 million users world-wide now have Net access and there are at least 300 000 Internet servers (July 1996). With the growth of the Internet has come an expansion of the underlying communications infrastructure, allowing ever-greater quantities of information to be accessed as bandwidth is increased. As a result of this rapid and widespread growth, expectations have risen about the possibility of transmitting television over the Internet. TV, as a medium, offers high-quality video, stereo sound and a wide range of entertaining and informative productions. The Internet, on the other hand, is a different medium with an enormous capacity for information propagation and interactivity rather than providing the quality of entertainment and broadcasts delivered by TV. In developing a hybrid successor to these two technologies, a number of challenges must be overcome. Significant technical innovations are now becoming available. These include improved video compression, higher bandwidth communication links and improved data delivery methods. These alone will not be sufficient. Further advances are needed in controlling network traffic, possibly by pricing mechanisms. Finally, the technical advances are revealing that further major agreements must be reached on social and other issues of access.

20.1 Introduction

The enormous expansion of the Internet has brought a new dimension to the Information Age, allowing ever-greater quantities of information to be distributed to an ever-growing number of people. More than 50 million users world-wide now have Net access, and that number continues to grow as the services provided via the Internet become increasingly popular and sophisticated. The World Wide Web offers the most powerful and wide-reaching new publishing medium since television and may well surpass all previous media in its scope and importance. The

313

Internet promises to enhance digital media by making it increasingly available and practical.

Digital audio is one of the most important components of TV transmission. Real-time audio implementations [1] are now available over the Internet. Experience in the area of audio compression [2] has shown that high-quality audio transmission is practicable over the current Internet infrastructure. With the availability of audio over the Internet has come the expectation of Internet TV. Conventional TV, as a medium, offers high-quality video, stereo sound and a wide range of entertaining and informative productions. The Internet, on the other hand, conveys most information in the form of text, still graphics and simple animations. Little use has so far been made of high-quality video material. However, audio requires only a fraction of the bandwidth required to encode video. The step from audio-only to full TV over the Internet is not a simple step.

The great attraction of the Internet is its interactivity. Users have access to more information via their computers than they could absorb in their lifetimes. Users must select the information they wish to view. Combining TV with the Internet to give interactive, high-quality, entertaining and informative productions seems an attractive proposition. However, before expending considerable resources to make Internet TV a reality, it is necessary to consider not just the technical issues but also the social and political implications.

20.2 The Internet

The Internet can be defined as a world-wide system of computer networks. It was conceived by the Advanced Research Projects Agency (ARPA) of the US government as a network that would continue to function even if large portions were destroyed. The Internet is now a public, self-sustaining facility accessible to tens of millions of people worldwide.

The underlying infrastructure that makes the Internet possible is the international public telecommunications network. Using a combination of dedicated digital and standard voice links, the Internet provides a mechanism whereby data can be exchanged between any pair of connected computers. This is achieved via a set of protocols, principally TCP/IP (Transmission Control Protocol/Internet Protocol), and by assigning every connected machine a unique IP address. In effect, the TCP/IP protocols mainly in use today implement *point-to-point* communication.

The services provided by the Internet (for example email, telnet, ftp, news, World Wide Web etc) all rely on the basic Internet protocols and communications infrastructure. All these services are thus limited by the physical bandwidth of the communications path. Figure 20.1 shows a schematic view of the Internet and its communication infrastructure.

In many cases it is necessary to provide a one-to-many data service; e.g. for videoconferencing. The Internet provides the mechanisms for both one-to-one (unicast), and one-to-many (multicast and broadcast) by allowing the routers to

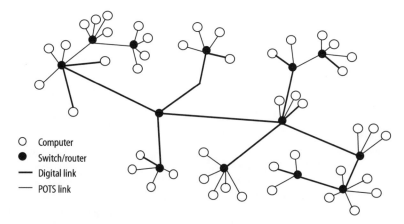

Figure 20.1 Simplistic view of the Internet communications infrastructure.

send the same data down multiple links. Each block of data transmitted via the Internet contains information on the computer or computers that should receive the data. The routers ensure that the data, originating at a single source, is directed to all recipients requesting the information. This process is termed "multicast," as the originator must have a list of recipients. This process is quite distinct from broadcasting, in which data is propagated to an arbitrary set of recipients with no duplication of information.

The Internet is practically limited by the underlying communications infrastructure. With its growth has come an expansion of the communications networks, allowing ever-greater quantities of information to be propagated. However, this expansion has failed to match the increase in the load generated by an ever-increasing number of users accessing ever-greater quantities of information. The principal bottlenecks are the link from the home to a service provider, the switches routing the information across the Internet, and (most important) the bandwidth of the Internet backbone which must support many simultaneous users. The portion of the telecommunications network that connects users to the switches (the so-called "last mile") is still dominated by twisted-pair copper wire. There are over 560 million twisted-pair copper connections worldwide [3]. The UK alone has around 27 million copper access connections. It is estimated that it will cost over £11 billion to replace this with optical fibers. Such an investment can only be made over a period of years. The Internet itself uses a wide range of communications technologies, providing a wide range of bandwidths. Table 20.1 lists some of the current and forthcoming technologies.

A number of technologies are emerging which tackle this last mile. In particular, the Digital Subscriber Loop (DSL) aims to deliver high bandwidth over existing copper wires, making high-speed data channels available to any user with a standard copper telephone line. As such technologies are applied to the telephone network, so the bandwidth constraints between the user and the switch will relax.

A key bottleneck is the user's connection to the system. For example, the technologies applicable to the "last mile" include Asynchronous Digital Subscriber Loop

Table 20.1. Technologies used to support the Internet infrastructure

Technology	Bandwidth	Physical medium
Regular telephone service (POTS)	14.4–56 kbps	Twisted-pair copper wire
Dedicated 56kbps on Frame Relay	56 kbps	Various
ISDN	64 kbps–1.544 Mbps	BRI: Twisted-pair
		PRI: T-1 line
IDSL	128 kbps	Twisted-pair
Digital satellite	400 kbps	Airwaves
Frame Relay	56 kbps–1.544 Mbps	Twisted-pair coaxial cable
T-1,T-2	1.544–6.312 Mbps	Twisted-pair optical fiber
T-1C (DS1C)	3.512 Mbps	Twisted-pair optical fiber
T-3 (DS3)	45 Mbps	Coaxial cable
T-3D (DS3D)	135 Mbps	Optical fiber
E1,E2,E3 (DS1)	2.048–34.368 Mbps	Twisted-pair or optical fiber
E4,E5	139.264–565.148 Mbps	Optical fiber
ADSL	1.544–8 Mbps	Twisted-pair
VADSL	1.544–51 Mbps	Hybrid copper fiber
Cable modem	512 kbps–52 Mbps	Coaxial cable (Ethernet)
Ethernet	10 Mbps	Twisted-pair coaxial optical fiber
Fast Ethernet	100 Mbps	Twisted-pair coaxial optical fiber
Gigabit Ethernet	1 Gbps	Optical fiber copper
FDDI	100 Mbps	Optical fiber
OC-1, OC-3	51.84–155.52 Mbps	Optical fiber
OC-12, OC-24	622.08 Mbps–1.244 Gbps	Optical fiber
OC-48, OC-256	2.488–13.271 Gbps	Optical fiber
SciNet	2.325 Gbps (15 OC-3 lines)	Optical fiber
STM-64	10 Gbps	Optical fiber

(ADSL), and VADSL. ADSL can provide bandwidth of up to 8 Mbps to the users over a single copper loop. In addition to the simplex downstream channel, an ADSL system will transport a return or control channel (C) for user-to-network signaling. The most promised of all is the very high rate (with up to 51 Mbps downstream) digital subscriber loop or VADSL. VASDL is a hybrid fiber/copper access network that uses the same transmission techniques developed for ADSL. Upstream data rates are mainly focused in the range 500 kbps to around 2 Mbps.

The main Internet backbone is also crucial. Telecommunications companies expect over the next five years that the Internet backbone bandwidth will increase to over 100 Gbps [4].

20.3 Digital Video

A single analogue TV picture or frame is built up from a sequence of horizontal scan lines, where each scan line encodes the picture detail for a single horizontal slice of the original scene. This picture detail specifies the intensity of the red, green and blue phosphors in a CRT, which, when combined, allow any desired color to be generated for each point on the screen.

A digital TV frame is a digitized sampling of an analogue TV picture. It is composed of a two-dimensional array of *picture elements* (pels) where the number of rows in the array corresponds to the number of scan lines used to encode the TV picture and the number of columns corresponds to the number of discrete samples across each scan line. Each sample consists of a color triple giving the respective intensities of the red, green and blue primaries. The depth of each primary color, or the number of quantization levels, determines the total colors that can be generated by the digital encoding.

For most applications, 256 quantization levels are used to encode the intensity of each primary color, giving a total of 24 bits per pel (8 bits for each component where 8 bits represent the range 0 to 255), allowing 2^{24} colors to be encoded. However, the human eye is more sensitive to luminance than it is to color [5]. Thus the RGB color space is not an efficient representation for real-world images, as each color primary has the same depth and display resolution. For this reason, many image coding standards and broadcast systems encode color as luminance (Y) and two chrominance, or color differences, (U and V).

YUV color-coding is the basic format used by the PAL, NTSC and SECAM composite color TV standards. The Y component represents the luminance (or black and white) information, while the U and V components allow color to be added to the basic black and white picture. The YUV coding of color is more efficient than RGB, as the chrominance components can be spatially sub-sampled without adversely affecting the image quality [5].

The CCIR R-601 standard defines how the YUV components should be sampled and quantized to create a digital representation of a TV signal. Table 20.2 summarizes the main sampling formats for the active region of a digital television frame as defined in CCIR R-601. Note that the standard specifies 8-bit precision for the luminance and chrominance samples.

Even at smaller frame sizes, digital video requires ultra-high bandwidth communications links. A frame size a quarter of the area used by broadcast TV is sufficient to give a picture quality comparable to VHS. Even with this reduction in size and 4:1:1 or 4:2:0 sampling, 31 Mbps of data will be generated. Without data compression, it is clearly impracticable to store and transmit anything other than very short sequences of digital TV.

Table 20.2. Standard YUV sampling as defined in CCIR R-601.

YUV sampling format	Luminance plane	Chrominance plane	Bits per YUV frame (Mbit)	Data rate at 25 frames/s (Mbps)
4:2:2	720×576	360×576	6.6	166
4:1:1	720×576	180×576	5.0	124
4:2:0	720×576	360×288	5.0	124

20.3.1 Compression of Digital Video

Video compression relies on spatial and temporal redundancies in the video information. Within a frame, neighboring pels will tend to represent similar colors. Similarly, as each new frame is captured, the temporal change in each pel will tend to be small, reflecting small changes in the detail between captured frames.

Video codecs (coder/decoder) targeting high compression are based primarily on *predictive encoding*, where frames are compressed by encoding the differences between frames rather than directly encoding the spatial detail. The two most popular predictive encoding techniques are:

- Motion estimation [6], which involves comparing the detail in the source frame with detail in one or more decoded frames taken from the encoding of frames earlier or later in the sequence. This technique relies on temporal similarities to achieve high compression.
- Encoding pel differences with the Discrete Cosine Transform (DCT). This maps spatial differences into the DCT domain [7, 8] which de-correlates the pel differences, concentrating the entropy into a few DCT coefficients. These coefficients can be more efficiently encoded, typically with quantization and variable length coding, than the original pel differences. DCT encoding relies on spatial similarities to achieve high compression rates.

The compression of a TV signal implies audio in addition to video. All the audio-visual codec standards define algorithms and integration processes for audio and visual coding. In practice, the compressed audio stream normally requires only a small fraction of the bandwidth required by the compressed video.

20.3.2 The ITU Video Standards

The International Telecommunications Union (ITU) is a global intergovernmental treaty organization within which governments and the private sector cooperate to develop recommendations that guide telecommunication service providers and manufacturers of telecommunication equipment to ensure interoperability. The Telecommunications Standardization Sector (ITU-T) was created by the ITU to facilitate the elaboration, distribution and follow-up of recommendations (non-binding standards) in order to standardize telecommunications on a world-wide basis.

An objective of the ITU-T was the standardization of audio-visual services over $p \times$ ISDN, POTS and mobile radio bandwidths. This led to a set of standards, the principal ones being H.320 for teleconferencing applications at ISDN bandwidths and H.324 for multimedia communications at POTS and mobile radio bandwidths. Both H.320 and H.324 specify component standards for the compression of video. These are:

- H.261: Coding of video for $p \times$ ISDN
  The H.261 codec operates by dividing the luminance and chrominance planes into non-overlapping blocks. Motion estimation (optional in H.261) is used to locate

similar detail from the last encoded frame and to build an approximation to the source frame. The pel by pel difference between this approximation and the source frame is calculated for each block and transformed to the DCT domain. The DCT coefficients are then quantized and variable-length encoded.

The complete encoding of the frame consists of the motion vector for each block (if motion estimation is enabled) and the encoded DCT coefficients.

- H.263: Video codec for low bit rate communication
  H.263 was designed to code video at data rates less than 64 kbps. In practice, H.263 covers a wide bandwidth range, from 2 Mbps down to 10 kbps. It uses the same basic coding algorithm as used by H.261, with a number of extensions. These include a better representation of motion including half-pel motion vectors, bidirectional motion (builds detail from last and next encoded frame), and more efficient encoding of the DCT coefficients.

These extensions to the basic H.261 algorithm give a substantial improvement in coding performance for the same bandwidths, but at the expense of algorithmic complexity.

20.3.3 The MPEG Video Standards

The International Organization for Standardization (ISO) is a federation of approximately 100 national standards bodies. Recognized world-wide, the ISO is a nongovernmental organization with a mission to promote the development of standardization with a view to facilitating the international exchange of products and services, and to encourage cooperation in the spheres of intellectual, scientific, technological and economic activity. The ISO facilitates international agreements, which are published as international standards.

Its technical committees, subcommittees and working groups carry out the technical work of the ISO. These committees consist of representatives from industry, academia, research institutes, governments, consumer bodies and international organizations from around the world which come together as equal partners in the resolution of global standardization. Working groups are established by these committees to consider, and evolve through consensus, standards addressing key areas of technology.

Working group ISO/IECJTCI/SC2/WG11, better known as the Motion Picture Experts Group (MPEG), was established to develop standards for the coding of audio-visual information. The MPEG work is organized into separate projects, which are summarized as follows:

- MPEG-1: Coding of moving pictures and associated audio for digital storage media
  Developed for storage media such as compact disc, digital audiotape and magnetic hard disks, MPEG-1 is targeted to provide audio-visual coding and playback at data rates up to 1.5 Mbps.

The MPEG-1 video coding standard was developed to provide VHS picture quality similar to that provided by ITU-T H.261. The compression scheme used is similar to that of H.261 with the main differences being that MPEG-1 allows bidirectional interpolation of frames and the optional use of half-pel motion vectors.

- MPEG-2: Generic coding of moving pictures and associated audio information
  MPEG-2 has been designed for a wide range of audio-visual applications, including storage/retrieval, broadcast TV (contribution and distribution), satellite TV transmission and high-definition TV. The video coding of MPEG-2 is similar to MPEG-1, with the same basic techniques used to encode video. The principal difference is that MPEG-2 is optimized to encode interlaced video, which is not practicable with MPEG-1.

20.3.4 Codec Application and Complexity

The ITU and ISO video codecs have been widely adopted for a variety of applications. A summary of the target bandwidth, application(s) and frame sizes for each is shown in Table 20.3. Note that the target bandwidths include audio and video coding.

MPEG-2 is directed at high-quality digital broadcasting. It provides algorithmic tools for efficiently coding interlaced video, supports a wide range of bit rates (4–20 Mbps) and provides for multi-channel surround sound coding. While the very high bandwidth links that form the backbone of the Internet are capable of supporting MPEG-2, wide area networks, which make up a large portion of the Internet infrastructure, are severely limited by the large number of users requiring concurrent access to information.

Employing higher compression of the audio and video with MPEG-1 (1.5 Mbps) will increase the video streams that the backbone can support. However, MPEG-1 does little to address the current bandwidth constraints of wide area networks, and delivers below broadcast quality. Using H.324 with H.263 could, by targeting very low bandwidths, provide video and audio with little expansion of the communications infrastructure. However, the quality of the material delivered is unlikely to be acceptable to viewers used to current TV quality.

Table 20.3. Target bandwidths and applications of the ITU and ISO video codecs

Standard	H.261	H.263	MPEG-1	MPEG-2
Nominal bit rate	56 kbps–1963 kbps	Low bit rate	1.5 Mbps	4 Mbps–20 Mbps
Applications	Videophone	Videophone	VCR	Broadcast TV contribution
	Videoconferencing	Videoconferencing	CD	
	Interactive audio-visual services	Over PSTN and mobile networks	Hard disk	Distribution
			Storage and retrieval	DBS
				HDTV
				DVD
Frame sizes	176 × 144	176 × 144	CCIR R-601	CCIR R-601
	352 × 288	352 × 288		HDTV
		704 × 576		

The compression standards provide a means of substantially reducing the bandwidth required to transmit digital video. The algorithm, frame size, YUV sampling, frame rate and bandwidth will all determine the quality of the video material when decompressed and displayed. What has not been considered is the complexity of the video codecs, which will determine the eventual cost of both compression and decompression engines for digital TV.

Perceptual quality, bandwidth and algorithmic complexity can be considered as three key parameters that describe the performance of a codec. For the ITU and ISO video codecs, quality is proportional to the bandwidth and the complexity. Reduce the bandwidth and/or the complexity and the quality will drop. This is a key consideration in providing digital TV over low bandwidth links, since the only way to improve quality at low bandwidths is to increase algorithmic complexity and hence the cost of the hardware necessary to implement the coders and decoders.

New compression technologies [9, 10] are being developed that have significantly lower algorithmic complexity, especially for decoding, than the traditional DCT-based codecs. The advantage of such systems is their implementability in software running on general-purpose processors. By implementing the decoder in languages such as Java, digital video can be viewed by anyone with an Internet browser, independent of their hardware platform.

Perhaps the most important criterion is perceptual quality. The viewing public has come to expect high-quality audio and video from terrestrial, cable and satellite TV. Will the same public accept, and pay for, poorer quality over the Internet?

20.4 Internet TV

The availability of full-screen full-motion video to home users via the Internet is optimistically supported by a number of advocates. However, as the Internet continues to expand, applications that require high bandwidth may experience "digital brownouts and blackouts." The tremendous population of users on the Internet who want simultaneous access to video data may result in network congestion.

The feasibility of TV on the Internet goes beyond the engineering of video servers, communications infrastructures and data transfer protocols. Before TV material is widely available on the Internet, a number of issues must be considered:

- Video server technology
- Backbone capacity
- Pricing of services
- Social and political implications

20.4.1 Video Server Limitation

Given the current normally used point-to-point interactive protocols, server throughput is a critical limitation to their wider use for video. Several companies

[11, 12] in server technology are able to support multiple channels of MPEG-2 quality transmission [13]. The key specifications for the Server according [14] are the following:

• Client data rate
• Number of streams
• Price per stream
• Data format: MPEG-1, MPEG-2, JPEG, TIFF etc.
• Client interactivity and response latency
• Program storage requirements
• Software support for operations, administration

For a given disk technology and required channel data rate, servers are limited in the number of users they can simultaneously interact with. Hence for Internet use, client data rate and the number of parallel streams are the main video server restrictions. For example, if a video server is to support 1000 viewers, each needing 6 Mbps of data, then the disk bandwidth required is 6 Gbps. To overcome these problems, distributed hierarchical server architectures are employed.

Such technology is suited to intranet video on demand given the constrained nature of the network and user population. But in an open environment, such as the Internet, problems arise due to the unpredictability and variability in demand, and care must be taken in the server design. For example, consider a major event such as NASA's Pathfinder spacecraft providing a video feed from Mars. Merely providing images caused significant network delays and disruption last year as servers and communications technologies were pushed to their limits by the Internet community. Video would substantially increase the volume of data, and potentially the number of users wishing access.

Supplying TV material with MPEG-2 quality, to compare with the quality of conventional broadcast services, under high-demand scenarios where potentially millions of people want access to the same video feed, could impose impossible demands on current video server technology.

20.4.2 Backbone Limitations

The bandwidth of the backbone, while apparently high, provides a very limited bandwidth to each individual user as a consequence of the size of the user population. Telecommunication companies have announced that, within the next several years, the backbone will support a bandwidth of more than 100 Gbps. Such increases do little to address the number of potential users requiring simultaneous access to resources. In reality, the effective bandwidth is increasingly restricted as the user population continues to grow.

Consider the scenario where a small percentage of the current Internet population world-wide, say one million (just 2%), simultaneously accesses disparate video materials. The limitation is no longer the video servers, but rather the bandwidth of the backbone. For MPEG-2 video, over 6 Tbps (6×10^{12} bps) of data will have to be conveyed. Clearly the transmission of such volumes of data is impracticable with current communications technologies.

Programs available world-wide via the Internet are likely to create severe communication bottlenecks if they become popular with the Internet viewing population.

20.4.3 Push Technology

Considering the high degree of variability in demand on the Internet due to its interactive nature, it becomes clear that, for high bandwidth applications, the interactive request–response (pull-based) method of data delivery cannot be supported by current network technology.

An alternative approach to data delivery, which seeks to reduce the peaks in network traffic, is push technology. In push-based data delivery, the servers send information to a user population in advance of any specific request. With data push, the transmission of data is initiated without requiring the user's explicit request. A possible scenario could involve push in combination with one-to-many delivery mechanisms such as multicast and broadcast. The push and pull approaches are shown in Figure 20.2, where the information brokers can be considered equivalent to the ISPs.

With push technology, some of the problems arising from the request–response method can be solved, as users do not have to poll servers for new and updated data,

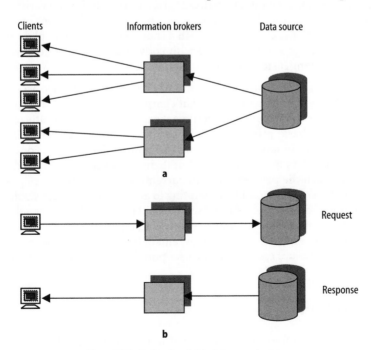

Figure 20.2 a Push vs. **b** pull data delivery mechanisms.

reducing the peaks in network traffic [15]. Note, however, that push technology in its ideal implementation does not actually differ from the conventional passive TV, where the viewer receives particular programs without initiating the delivery of the content.

20.4.4 Pricing

In many ways one of the most attractive features of today's Internet is that from the user's viewpoint, data transfer is "free" at the time of use. The costs of data transfer are reflected only remotely in the Internet Service Provider's (ISP's) charges. This would not matter if users always imposed the same constant load on the system. However, this is far from being the case. Users' traffic demands are extremely non-uniform, both in time and location. The time constant for a drastic change in traffic is of the order of seconds, whereas the time constant for changing the network's capacity is of the order of months or even years. It is important to the stability of the network that users find it in their "enlightened self-interest" to make more economical use of resources which are currently limited and insufficient to meet the unconstrained demand.

The present Internet has only the crude inherent control mechanism that when demand is excessive the users are discouraged by unbearable response times. This is very unsatisfactory, as it allows activities which (even as perceived by their perpetrators) are of marginal value, while effectively prohibiting high-value applications. Pricing of data transfer [16] is clearly one possible solution. It does, however, impose considerable accounting overheads given the flexibility and variety of data transfer on the Internet, and the overheads may be high as well as being psychologically unattractive to the average user. Such a charging policy would place Internet TV at a disadvantage when compared with conventional TV services which are provided free, relying instead on advertising revenue.

In the long term, such pricing mechanisms may be necessary if video access in not to cripple the Internet. Issues of copyright charges and even possibly the imposition of a bit tax to support general government expenditure could be utilized. In the shorter term, the basic principle should be implemented that users should be encouraged to work in ways which benefit the community of users. For example, information providers might stamp each of their pages with a guaranteed "sell by date" before which the page will remain current. Browsers, proxies etc. can thus recognize that there is no point in attempting to access a more recent version from the originating site. The effect of this would be that users and browsers adhering to the convention will impose a lower network load and will be rewarded by more rapid response times. If the Internet is to remain free, then encouraging cooperative behavior by users is essential as the user population continues to grow.

20.4.5 Social Factors

There are very big differences in the social impact of Internet-like and TV-like systems. Conventional TV systems are relatively easily controlled by governments and other agents of society. This gives rise to censorship or broadcasting standards, depending on the circumstances and one's viewpoint. The general viewing of popular programs can give rise to shared common social attitudes and expectations, and may indeed be an important element in creating a cohesive society.

Internet-like systems, on the other hand, handle information at a much smaller level of granularity. Few users access the same streams of pages, and these pages in themselves may come from a wide set of Web sites around the world, and may be the responsibilities of an even larger set of authors. Increasingly, governments are becoming aware of the inherent difficulties of controlling the content and access of information. In effect, information is available to individuals that may be deemed immoral or subversive by their society. It also gives individual citizens an unrivaled opportunity to make their views known. As has been known from time immemorial, however, not all views are equally valid. How is the Internet to develop mechanisms for selection of important topics if users are not to drown in electronic rubbish? It has not hitherto been generally recognized that the addition of a page on a user's own Web site imposes a cost on all other users. This page, too, now belongs to the universe of Web information demanding attention. As the information content on the Internet increases, where is the line drawn between filtering the information to remove inappropriate or redundant information and the rights of the individuals to make known their ideas.

It is likely that before TV can be generally distributed on the Internet, an international consensus or even agreement will be needed to govern acceptable standards and program content. As has been demonstrated in recent years with the media drawing the public's attention to the easy access to pornography on the Internet, access to unregulated material can result in a conflict of interests between users, ISPs and governments world-wide. Within a single community, arriving at a consensus on what is acceptable has proven to be difficult enough. Finding an international consensus is all the more difficult with a potential conflict between fundamental attitudes and beliefs.

20.5 Conclusion

The great attraction of the Internet is its interactivity. Combining TV with the Internet to give fully interactive, high-quality productions may be attractive, but it presents significant challenges. If Internet TV is to compete with conventional terrestrial, cable and satellite TV, it must provide not only the functionality associated with the Internet, but also the quality of broadcast material in terms of both production and visual acuity that the viewing public have come to expect.

Digital TV requires significant bandwidth, even with compression. As communications and server technologies develop, so the underlying bandwidth, both to the home and the backbone, will increase. However, any increases are likely to be negated by both the increase in the user population and the increasing demand for audio-visual content. The loading imposed by video data can be reduced with improved video coding, but not eliminated.

The underlying technology is available for Internet TV, but substantial investment is needed for it to become a reality. Recouping this investment and making a profit raises the issue of financing. Generally program production is financed by some combination of advertising, licensing, and subscription. Each pricing mechanism has pros and cons when applied to the Internet, which currently operates on a subscription basis, although increasing use is being made of advertising. In an interactive environment the user has the choice of what to watch and when to watch it. Advertisers may have to expend substantial resources to produce highly entertaining adverts which users are likely to view. The possible need to charge for information as the Internet grows is an issue that must be addressed. Viewers are unlikely to pay for programs on the Internet that are available cheaper via conventional broadcasting.

Solving the technical and pricing problems of Internet TV may prove simpler than its regulation. Without international consensus on standards for Internet TV, national governments are likely to impose constraints on Internet service which may stall its development. Regulation, implementation and pricing are all simpler without interactivity, but all this leaves is another TV service. The challenge of the next few years is to achieve the necessary degree of consensus, which will allow the development of services with the desirable properties of both Internet and TV technologies.

References

[1] RealNetworks, Inc., http://www.real.com/.

[2] JS Solari (1997) *Digital Video and Audio Compression*, McGraw-Hill, New York.

[3] NG Gole, G Young, NJ Lynch-Aird *et al.* (1992) A low-complexity, high-speed digital subscriber loop tranceiver, *British Telecommunications Technical Journal*, 10(1), 72–9.

[4] British Telecom, http://www.labs.bt.com/library/online/.

[5] WN Sproson (1983) *Color Science in Television and Display Systems*, Heyden and Son, Philadelphia PA.

[6] MI Sezan and RL Lagendijk (1993) Motion Analysis and Image Processing, Kluwer Academic, Hingham MA.

[7] N Ahmed, T Natarajan and KR Rao (1974) Discrete cosine transform, *IEEE Transactions on Computers*, C-23:90–3.

[8] KR Rao and P Yip (1990) *Discrete Cosine Transform: Algorithms, Advantages, Applications*, Academic Press, New York.

[9] RB Lambert, RJ Fryer, WP Cockshott *et al.* (1996) A comparison of variable dimension vector quantization techniques for image compression, in *European Conference on Multimedia Applications, Services and Techniques*, Louvain-la-Neuve, Belgium, May, pp. 655–70.

[10] RB Lambert, RJ Fryer, WP Cockshott *et al.* (1996) Low bandwidth video compression with variable dimension vector quantization, in *Advanced Digital Video Compression Engineering*, Cambridge, UK, July, pp. 53–8.

[11] Hewlett-Packard, http://www.hp.com/.

[12] Sun Microsystems, http://www.sun.com/servers/smc_external.html.

[13] S Christodoulakis (1997) Multimedia databases, in *International Conference in Very Large Databases*, Athens, Greece.

[14] A Kovalick and P Sampson (1995) Next decade television production tools, *EBU Technical Seminar*, Hewlett-Packard.

[15] M Franklin and S Zdonik (1997) A framework for scalable dissemination-based systems, in *ACM SIGPLAN '97*, Vol. 32.

[16] N Negreponte (1995) *Being Digital*, Coronet, London.

21

The Implementation of PANIVE: a PC-Based Architecture for Networked Interactive Virtual Environments

Karin Coninx, Frank Van Reeth, Marc Flerackers and Eddy Flerackers

Abstract

Microcomputers are increasingly becoming capable of supporting high-end multimedia applications. The multimedia extensions in current central processing units, together with the supplementary functionality of audio, graphics and networking plug-in boards, make it possible to realize applications that a very few years ago still needed supercomputer capabilities. As today's off-the-shelf graphics plug-in boards are able to render fully textured 3D scenes at ever-increasing frame rates and resolutions, it becomes possible to implement 3D Networked Virtual Environments (NVEs) using networks of PCs. This chapter reports on our implementation of PANIVE, a PC-based architecture for networked virtual environments.

Various aspects of PANIVE will be highlighted in this chapter:

- the client–server architecture
- the interaction primitives
- audio support (of utmost importance in the realization of NVEs)
  - ambient sound that can be given a location in 3D space
  - sound that can be attached to any (potentially moving) object
- the transparent communication layer, enabling various kinds of modular grouping functionality at the application level

Our current results and the application of the architecture in the EC ESPRIT HPCN project VISTA (Virtual Interactive Studios for TV Applications) will also be described.

21.1 Introduction

Networked Virtual Environments (NVEs), allowing many people to interact over networks using 3D computer graphics interfaces, are increasingly gaining interest. The objective of this interaction is to realize collaboration between several people sharing the same 3D Virtual Environment, either for business or for entertainment purposes. As these kinds of NVE require a substantial amount of graphics computing power, they are conventionally implemented on networks of high-end graphics workstations. With the increasing capabilities of modern PCs to process multimedia data in general and 3D computer graphics in particular, it has become feasible to implement NVEs on networked PCs that are equipped with graphics plug-in boards. This paper describes our efforts in realizing such a system, which we term PANIVE: a PC-based Architecture for Networked Interactive Virtual Environments.

Apart from the ever-increasing performance issue, a number of additional motivations can be given for going in this direction:

• High-end PCs are much more widespread (because they are less expensive) than high-end graphics workstations. Consequently the potential set of users is higher on the one hand, so that it becomes feasible to implement and test applications in which a large number (more than, say, three to five) of simultaneous participants is involved.

• Development tools are more advanced on PC-based platforms, implying a reduced system development time as well as a more advanced and easy-to-use GUI.

• The number of available "plug-ins" and reusable (software and object) components is much larger in the PC domain, hence increasing available functionality considerably, without making recourse to additional implementation resources.

In this chapter we focus on the implementation issues of PANIVE as an NVE architecture, while putting less emphasis on applications that can be realized on top of it.

Various NVE systems have been reported upon in the literature, most of which run on high-end graphics workstations. Examples of such systems are described in [1], where NVEs exploiting high-end SGIs on ATM networks are the topic and [2], where the emphasis is put on human representation in NVEs.

NPSNET is another high-level NVE that is mainly used in battlefield simulation. In [3], large-scale simulations using NVEs have been described.

Some commercial systems for developing VEs exist as well – dVS (by Division) and WorldToolkit (by Sense8 Corporation) are typical examples – but they are not primarily designed for NVE applications in which a dynamically changing number of simultaneous participants are interacting.

Section 21.2 describes the overall system architecture, while the interaction primitives and scripting functionality are discussed in Section 21.3. Section 21.4 describes a prototype application in context which ran the EC ESPRIT project VISTA and gives network measurement results.

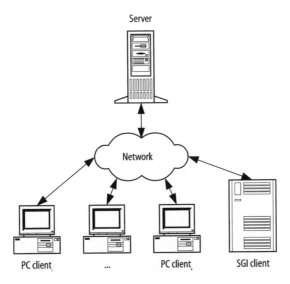

Figure 21.1 Client–server architecture.

21.2 System Architecture

21.2.1 The Overall Client–Server Architecture

The basic structure of the PANIVE infrastructure is implemented as a client–server architecture, which is schematically depicted in Figure 21.1. In the most common configuration, the architecture has only (Windows 95/Windows NT) PCs in its network (cf. Section 21.2.2 for SGI client inclusion). We have currently implemented the system on a single server, but the system is extensible towards multiple servers, following approaches like the ones followed in NetEffect [4].

More detailed views of the components of the PC clients and the server are given in Figures 21.2 and 21.3 respectively.

21.2.1.1 PC Client

A PC client consists of three main components, all of which are implemented using the DirectX suite of libraries:

• The 3D/2D/video component is implemented using the Direct3D and DirectDraw libraries. The 3D graphics are implemented in the DirectX Retained mode in which real-time Gouraud shaded, texture mapped (with linear to tri-linear or Mip-Mapped filtering), alpha-blended, z-buffered triangles can be rendered if state-of-the-art (though low-cost, i.e. less that $300) graphics cards are utilized. In an overlay buffer, 2D static images as well as video sequences can be displayed (various decompression routines are available).

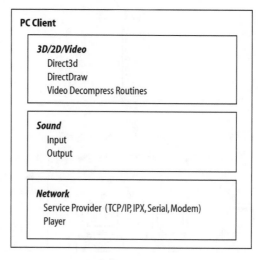

Figure 21.2 PC client components.

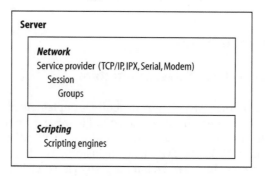

Figure 21.3 Server components.

- The sound component is implemented using the DirectSound library. Using a 3D sound engine, sounds located at fixed as well as moving positions are integrated in the PANIVE architecture. Although the current implementation includes mainly sound output functionality, we are currently adding sound input functionality as well (using the DirectSound library).
- The network component is implemented using the DirectPlay library. This part of the client obviously takes care of the client–server and event/command handling.

21.2.1.2 Server

Whenever users (players) join an application that is currently running they are categorized within a so-called "group." A group is a collection of online users who share the same "world" within the currently running networked virtual environment – a "session." A session can consist of many worlds. The server is continuously updated with the position of all the users in their various worlds. Whenever a certain event (cf. Section 22.3.2) is triggered by a user, the server is notified and will start sending corresponding commands to all users in the current group (or session) that is affected by the command. For example, when a user triggers an "OnLClick" event, e.g. by clicking on a doorknob, all the clients of users that are located in the same world receive animation commands to open the door at issue.

The server has two main components:

- As with the client part of the architecture, the network component (again implemented using DirectPlay) takes care of the server part of the event/command handling.
- The second main part of the server consists of the scripting component: for each world that is active (i.e. contains at least one user) within a session, a so-called ScriptEngine is running. A ScriptEngine is one of the COM objects (COM = Component Object Model) that Microsoft ships with its Internet Explorer. By integrating it into the PANIVE architecture, each world can be given a script that enables objects in the virtual environment to be given more advanced (i.e. "programmed") behavior, depending on user interaction. Section 22.3.3 includes some examples regarding the Scripting functionality.

21.2.2   Inclusion of a High-End Graphics Workstation as Client

As mentioned before, modern PCs are becoming extremely powerful. However, for some high-end applications (e.g. broadcast applications needing full-screen real-time anti-aliasing) their graphics computational power might not suffice. For these kinds of application we extended the PANIVE architecture with functionality to also include high-end graphics workstations; in this case, high-end SGI computers are used as clients.

As mentioned before, the networking protocol (on top of IP) of the purely PC-based PANIVE architecture is implemented using DirectPlay. This solution is currently not available for SGIs running the IRIX Operating System, so alternative approaches have to be pursued. In PANIVE, we solved this issue by providing for each SGI in the network a normal PC on which an extended PC client with "gateway" functionality is implemented. This permits events and commands to be relayed to a TCP/IP socket that connects to the network in which the SGI at issue is present. Only commands coming in from the server that can be executed by the SGIs are relayed; these are all graphics and most animation commands, but commands related to 3D sound, for example, are not relayed to the SGI (i.e. the 3D sound is played on the corresponding PC client).

21.2.3   PANIVE Data and Programming Model

PANIVE is implemented under Windows 95 (and Windows NT) in C++ using the Microsoft Foundation Classes. Given this object-oriented programming approach, the PANIVE data model is inherently object-oriented as well. Most of the internal structures are build around COM – the Component Object Model. The following list gives a brief overview of the four COM objects we created at the foundation of PANIVE:

- D3D: hosting all the functionality regarding the 3D world (3D objects, frames, meshes, lights, backgrounds, textures, etc., all of which are also implemented as COM objects).
- DS: covering all aspects with respect to 3D sounds.
- DP: dealing with all the networking issues, creation/destruction of users etc.
- System: supporting Windows-related functionality, such as creating a message box or executing program files.

Scenery with meshes, lights, 3D sounds, etc. can be accessed directly by scripts through the ScriptEngine or by the network.

The scenery is copied to each client and is synchronized by the server by means of the event/command structure. For user-related data, a so-called "shared memory" technique (a feature of DirectPlay), that acts as a synchronization mechanism for remote data and messaging is used. The protocol takes care of synchronizing the value of variables across the network each time they are adjusted.

Hierarchical motion can be given to objects by scripting or by using predefined motion paths (linear as well as spline-based) which can be included in the geometry files. These paths can be imported from commercial modeling/animation packages like Lightwave or 3D Studio MAX.

21.3 Interaction Primitives and Scripting Functionality

21.3.1 Interaction in Virtual Environments

Interaction with virtual environments has often been regarded as the "ultimate user interface." This statement emphasizes the desire of virtual environments to make the interaction with the virtual world as natural and intuitive as possible. Looking at VR systems in general, there are different interpretations of the concept "natural and intuitive user interface," as indicated by the following examples. Some researchers argue that the interface should be invisible [5]. The principles of natural interaction and presence are translated by some authors to full body immersion [6]. Their argument is that tracking the whole body is necessary to interact naturally (similar to interaction in the physical world) with the virtual environment. Most contemporary VEs limit body tracking to head tracking and tracking of one or two hands. Some researchers advocate the use of a glove as an interaction device because this device is an immediate extension of the user's hand. Others argue for the use of intermediate objects ("virtual tools") because humans tend to use tools for a number of tasks in the physical world [7, 8]. In general, a direct manipulation interaction style is used in VEs, with the user's hand or an intermediate input device as an interaction device.

We believe that the interpretation of a "natural and intuitive user interface" depends on the chosen platform and on the application in question. The decision to use PCs as well as high-end graphics workstation clients in the PANIVE network has implications for the adopted interaction style (being the way in which users communicate or interact with computer systems). The "look-and-feel" of the Windows interface is integrated with the interaction with the 3D virtual world. Even if stereo viewing could be supported, non-immersive viewing on the PC is straightforward in the PANIVE architecture. So are mouse and keyboard-based interaction, although interactive devices supporting six degrees of freedom (6DOF) are supported.

The following section describes the basic PANIVE interaction primitives for 3D navigation and event triggering (picking or collision based). More advanced object behavior and interaction based on scripting are described in Section 21.3.3.

21.3.2 Interaction Primitives

Current interaction with the PANIVE system takes place within the point-and-click metaphor of a Windows interface. Navigation through the 3D world is achieved using the keyboard, mouse or joystick (internally, a full 6DOF navigation is available). We currently focus on non-immersive navigation and interaction.

By clicking on certain objects in the 3D world and by colliding with objects – or by approaching objects – events are triggered on the client. Using the network, the server is informed and each user in the world (and sometimes, users in other worlds as well) is affected by the behavior induced by the corresponding command. Interaction can also be invoked via commands that are induced through events that are triggered by the system itself.

Another important factor on the interaction level involves 3D sound. We have currently implemented this functionality for 3D sounds on the output level, meaning that sounds (e.g. stored in a .WAV file) can be positioned on fixed or moving 3D locations within the 3D world. We are currently finishing sound input, which will allow networked vocal human-to-human interaction within the 3D world.

21.3.3 Scripting Functionality

Scripting is a powerful technique used in various VE and animation systems for realizing more advanced behavior. DIVE [9] uses Tcl commands to invoke scripts in the behavior of its entities, whereas SPLINE [10] uses Scheme (planning to move to Java) as its scripting language. PANIVE can utilize whatever scripting language is provided through Microsoft's ScriptEngine. We focused on providing Visual Basic as well as JavaScript as the current PANIVE scripting languages. The remainder of this section contains some example scripts.

21.3.3.1 Example 1: Script Activated When a User Clicks on the Object DoorHandle

```
...
function D3D_OnLClick (PlayerId, GroupId, ObjectName)
// triggers if user clicks with left mouse button
{
if (ObjectName=="DoorHandle")
  // if user clicks on doorhandle
  {
    D3D.Animation_Play (2, GroupId, "Frame_Door",
                        "Animation_OpenDoor", 0 );
  }
}
...
```

`D3D.Animation_Play (...)` is a routine which executes an animation using the parameters specified:

- first parameter: targeted users (1: send to entire session; 2: send to the entire group; 3: send to an individual user)
- second parameter: 0 in case of session; otherwise: Id of Group/User targeted
- third parameter: name of object to be animated
- fourth parameter: name of the animation file containing the animation keys
- fifth parameter: animation repetition (0: play once; 1: loop until stopped by user; 2: oscillate animation forward and backward)

21.3.3.2 Example 2: Script Activated When a Collision Is Detected Between a User and the Object IRBeam

```
...
function D3D_OnCollide ( PlayerId, GroupId,
Object1Name, Object2Name )
{
  if ( Object1Name=="UserXYZ" )
  { // if UserXYZ walks through the Infra Red beam
    // the above test must be omitted if each user
    // has to trigger the explosion
    if ( Object2Name =="IRBeam" )
    { // show explosion animation
      D3D.Animation_Play (2, GroupId, "Frame_Bomb",
                          "Animation_Explosion", 0);
      // each player of the group needs to hear the
      // sound of the explosion
      DS.StaticSoundBuffer_Play ( 2, GroupId,
                              "Sound_Explosion" );
```

```
        // send every player to the world
        // "HighInTheSky"
        for ( i=0; i<DP.GetPlayerCount (GroupId); i++ )
        {
            KillPlayer ( DP.GetPlayerId (GroupId, i) );
        }
    }
  }
}
...


...
KillPlayer ( PlayerId )
{
  DP.ChangeGroup ( PlayerId, "HighInTheSky" );
}
...
```

Scripts may also contain Windows-related commands, enabling the invocation of Windows-related functionality. For example, the command

```
System.ShellExecute ( 3, PlayerId, 1, "http://
www.cocacola.com", "", 3);
```

will activate the default Internet browser with the indicated URL, whereas the command

```
System.MessageBox ( 1, 0, "This is an important
announcement" );
```

will alert all the users in the current session with the message given in the third parameter.

21.4 Preliminary Applications and Results

21.4.1 Prototype Applications for VISTA

Part of the infrastructure described will be applied in the European ESPRIT HPCN research project VISTA, in which the realization of Virtual Interactive Studios for TV Applications is the central theme. The applications envisaged in this project allow users on PC clients, which are connected to the Internet (or a studio LAN), to interact in real time with a shared 3D virtual environment of which a television program is being produced/broadcast. In this context a set of 3D worlds – with associated 3D objects and scripts – have been realized. A set of screenshots is shown in Figure 21.4.

For this particular kind of application, some blocky representations were chosen to represent the users within the world (Figure 21.5). Notice also that inanimate characters can be part of the world's scenery (for example, the dog-like object can be

Figure 21.4 Some screenshots.

provided with a script so that it follows always its owner). Recent results in other contexts of more advanced user representations in NVEs can be found in [11, 12].

21.4.2 Network Measurements

In order to assess the load on the network, several tests have been performed over different networks. In particular, we measured the time needed to send and receive certain types of data which are applicable to the application that we envisage. The following data are measured:

Figure 21.5 Screenshot containing "blocky" character representations.

- Event/command: the client sends a certain event (e.g. clicking on a hotspot), and receives back a command from the server (e.g. playback of a sound clip); this will be used for distributing local events to all other participants in the 3D world.
- Shared memory: clients can share a global chunk of "shared memory" via the server; changes in this shared memory are propagated by the server when it detects this change.

Table 21.1 summarizes the average timings (in milliseconds) observed in these different cases. The measurements were performed while using different access methods:

- a local dial-up connection via a 28.8 kbps modem line to the dial-in server of the LUC-EDM
- a dial-up connection via a 28.8 kbps modem to a dial-in server of an ISP (Ping, a subsidiary of Eunet Belgium)

Table 21.1. Network measurements for different types of network.

Test	Dial-up	ISP	LAN (TCP/IP)	LAN (IPX)
10 events/commands (first command arriving)	417	1873	10	10
10 events/commands (last command arriving)	621	8938	20	15
5 events/commands (first command arriving)	125	1006	10	10
5 events/commands (last command arriving)	264	2191	12	10
1 event/command (command arriving)	114	930	5	4
Shared memory: 32 bytes changed	130	828	10	4
Shared memory: 64 bytes changed	155	628	10	5
Shared memory: 256 bytes changed	182	812	10	6

- the LUC-EDM LAN (using two different protocols: TCP/IP and IPX)

Note that the ISP connection is quite slow compared with the local dial-up line. This is due to the route that is followed over the Internet between Ping and Belnet (the Belgian research network to which the LUC-EDM is connected). The connection between Belnet and the Ping dial-up server goes via various other networks (e.g. Unisource and Eunet) and apparently the delay is quite large at the interconnection between these two networks. The fact that sometimes relatively less time is spent than could be expected from extrapolating the amounts of data transmitted is due to the potential gain by invoking compression in the modems. Table 21.1 shows that the delays over a direct dial-up line are well within reasonable limits, while the connection via an ISP can be quite slow. As a consequence, the application will need to incorporate methods such as extrapolation to cope with these delays.

21.5 Conclusions and Future Work

This chapter described the implementation aspects of PANIVE, a PC-based architecture for networked virtual environments. The object-oriented paradigm in the program and data model has been discussed and the underlying client–server structure has been detailed. Given the ever-increasing performance of modern PCs (enhanced with powerful – though cheap – graphics boards), architectures like PANIVE offer functionality previously only encountered on high-end graphics computers like SGI. For applications needing still more performance than can be delivered on even the highest level PCs, a hybrid PC/SGI fallback solutions has also been described.

Future work could manifest itself in many dimensions:

- Finishing our current efforts regarding input of sound and its broadcast to all the participants in the 3D virtual environment that are near enough to the origin of the sound.
- Inclusion of advanced lighting (e.g. pre-calculated radiosity maps) and rendering techniques (e.g. lens flares).
- Having finished the basic architecture, future work will naturally also involve the implementation of various applications on top of it.
- With respect to the networking issues, research on the level of compression and other speed-up techniques can/will also be tackled.

Acknowledgments

Part of this work is funded by the Commission of the European Community, the European Fund for Regional Development and the Flemish government. The implementational as well as creative help of the people at ANDROME NV is greatly appreciated.

References

[1] W Lamotte, E Flerackers, F Van Reeth et al. (1997) VISINET: collaborative 3D visualization and VR over ATM networks, *IEEE Computer Graphics and Applications*, 17(2), 66–75.

[2] I Pandzic, T Capin, N Magnenat-Thalmann et al. (1995) VLNET: a networked multimedia 3D environment with virtual humans, *Proc. Multi-Media Modeling (MMM '95)*, Singapore, pp. 21–32.

[3] M Macedonia, MJ Zyda, DR Pratt et al. (1994) NPSNET: a network software for large-scale virtual environments, *Presence: Teleoperators and Virtual Environments*, 3(4), 265–87.

[4] TK Dias, G Singh, A Mitchell et al. (1997) NetEffect: a network architecture for large-scale multiuser virtual worlds, *Proc. ACM VRST '97*, pp. 157–63.

[5] S Bryson (1994) Virtual reality and its applications, *Virtual Reality and its Applications*, British Computer Society, Leeds, UK, 7 June.

[6] M Slater and M Usoh (1995) Modelling in immersive virtual environments: a case for the science of VR, in *Virtual Reality Applications* (eds. RA Earnshaw, JA Vince and H Jones), Academic Press, London, pp. 53–70.

[7] MM Wloka and E Greenfield (1995) The virtual tricorder: a uniform interface for virtual reality, *Proc. UIST_95 (ACM Symposium on User Interface Software and Technology)*, Pittsburgh PA, 14–17 November, pp. 39–40.

[8] M Ferneau and J Humphries (1995) A gloveless interface for interaction in scientific visualization virtual environments, *Proc. SPIE Stereoscopic Displays and Virtual Reality Systems*, Vol. 2409, pp. 268–93.

[9] O Hagsand (1996) Interactive multiuser VEs in the DIVE system, *IEEE Multimedia*, 3(1), 30–9.

[10] RC Waters, DB Anderson, JW Barrus et al. (1997) Diamond Park and SPLINE: social virtual reality with 3D animation, spoken animation and runtime extendability, *Presence: Teleoperators and Virtual Environments*, 6(4), 461–81.

[11] T Capin (1998) Virtual human representation in networked virtual environments, *PhD Dissertation*, EPFL, Switzerland.

[12] I Pandzic (1998) Facial communication in networked virtual environments, *PhD Dissertation*, University of Geneva, Switzerland.

About the Authors

Karin Coninx is currently a post-doctoral researcher at the Limburg University Center in Diepenbeek (Belgium). She obtained her Master's degree in 1987 at the University of Antwerp and her PhD in 1997 at the Limburg University Center. Her research interests at the Expertise Center for Digital Media (a research institute at LUC) include Human Computer Interaction, virtual reality and networked multimedia. She is a member of the IEEE Computer Society and the Virtual Reality Society.

Frank Van Reeth is currently full professor of computer science at the Limburg University Center in Diepenbeek (Belgium). His research interests at the Expertise Center for Digital Media (a research institute at LUC) include computer graphics, VR, computer animation, multimedia technology and telematics. He is project leader of various industrial projects as well as European research projects. He is a cofounder of three spin-off companies working in the multimedia and computer graphics fields. He is a member of ACM, IEEE, the Computer Graphics Society, Eurographics and the Virtual Reality Society.

Marc Flerackers is currently research student at the Free University of Brussels, finishing his MSc in networked multimedia in collaboration with the Expertise Center for Digital Media (at LUC) and ANDROME NV. His research interests include computer graphics, computer animation and networked multimedia.

Eddy Flerackers is currently full professor of computer science at the Limburg University Center in Diepenbeek (Belgium). He is chairman of the Informatics Department at the Limburg University Center and also director of the Expertise Center for Digital Media (a LUC Research Center). He is a consultant to government and industry and has refereed a number of European research projects. He is also project leader of a large number of industrial research projects. He is a cofounder of three spin-off companies who are working in the multimedia and computer graphics fielda. He is executive editor of the *Virtual Reality Journal*, a member of ACM, IEEE, the Computer Graphics Society and Eurographics, and Fellow of the Virtual Reality Society. His research activities are in the area of computer graphics, computer animation, virtual reality, multimedia and telematics.

22

Applications for 3-, 4- and 5-Sided CAVES

J.L. Encarnação, C. Knöpfle, S. Müller and M. Unbescheiden

Abstract

In November 1996, a three-sided CAVE [2] (two walls and a floor with screen dimensions of 2.4 m × 2.4 m) was installed at Fraunhofer-IGD. The goal of this installation was to transfer the technology of the most exciting VR output device into an industrial scenario; to elaborate its usage in sectors where traditional output devices were insufficient; and to integrate it in innovative application areas. Based on the experience with this installation, a five-sided CAVE (three walls, floor and ceiling with sizes 2.4 m × 2.4 m) was constructed and installed in our new institute building in October 1997. In this chapter some CAVE application examples will be presented: design review (architecture, construction and planning), digital prototyping (assembly/disassembly in car and ship construction), and edutainment (virtual oceanarium for EXPO '98). The advantages and technological drawbacks of CAVE technology will also be discussed.

Figure 22.1 Three- and 5-sided CAVE installation at Fraunhofer-IGD.

22.1 Introduction

In 1997 the time of people asking "What is virtual reality and what are the applications?" was almost over. Today, VR describes an established market with applications in several industrial sectors, and awareness of its use is also very high in other potential application areas. Since VR is established as a technology, the current challenge is how to overcome various technological drawbacks and to find solutions to industrial problems and make VR an integrated and useful tool. To bridge this gap, Fraunhofer-IGD established a new VR-Technology Lab in addition to its VR demonstration center. One of the most important devices in this lab is a 5-sided CAVE installation [2], which is unique in the world. Before describing this installation and its applications in detail, a short review of other VR output devices is given in the next section.

22.1.1 Comparison of the Different VR Display Technologies

One of the best known VR output devices is the head-mounted display (HMD). Such devices are used today for assembly/disassembly tasks, flight simulation and ergonomic studies, but they are less and less important as they suffer from several technological drawbacks: limited field of view, low resolution, poor ergonomics and single-user immersion. Handheld devices (e.g. BOOM) are very similar and provide better resolution, but restrict the user's working envelope. One of the main disadvantages of these immersive displays is the missing sense of presence. The virtual body of the user has to be represented as an avatar, requiring complex human movement simulations which lack realism.

In fact, immersive projection technologies overcome most of these drawbacks and have found increasing interest in several VR applications. Large screen projections, combined with active shutter or passive polarization techniques, provide very high image quality, brightness and color saturation. This kind of image quality plays a key role in the area of design and styling using virtual prototypes. The size of the projection system enables a large audience to be immersed in a "cinema-like" setup. The viewpoint remains fixed in relation to the screen, with the best stereo effect located at the center of the room.

The position and orientation of the user can also be tracked in front of a stereo screen, displaying the images depending on the perspective view of one user. This kind of display provides an image impression which can be compared with a hologram. The first example of this device is the so-called workbench or virtual table, which is very useful for applications where a desk metaphor can be used for interacting with the virtual environment. The ultimate extension of this technology is a CAVE, which combines high resolution, high image quality, large screen projection and therefore a large field-of-view with a fully immersive output technology. In addition, a CAVE provides a true sense of presence, since users observe the VR scenario in relation to their physical bodies. A CAVE can also support the navigation of virtual environments and interaction with virtual objects on a 1:1 scale.

Table 22.1. Comparison of different stereo display technologies.

	Screen	HMD	Boom	Large screen	Workbench	CAVE
Immersion	no	yes	yes	maybe	yes	yes
Presence	no	no	no	no	maybe	yes
Tracked viewpoint	no	yes	yes	no	yes	yes
Large audience	no	no	no	yes	no (max. 3)	no (max. 5)
Resolution	good	bad-good	good	good	good	good
Field of view	bad	bad	good	good	medium	very good
Ease to use	good	very bad	bad	good	good	good
Price	low	low–high	high	medium–high	medium–high	high

Today, 3- or 4-sided CAVEs are used with front, left, right and bottom walls. These CAVEs satisfy most of the requirements, but because of the top projection for the floor a shadow appears around the user and destroys the holographic impression. Only a 5-sided CAVE with rear projection for all surfaces creates a shadow-free environment with an unrestricted field-of-view.

Table 22.1 offers a comparison of the various stereo display technologies.

22.1.2 VR Technology Lab

The goal of this lab is to present and demonstrate high-end VR technology; to elaborate its usability for industrial requirements; and to transfer innovative technology into existing and potential application areas by integrating hardware and software tools into a full VR process cycle.

The VR Technology Lab used to house a 3-sided CAVE consisting of three perpendicular stereo projection screens (two walls and a floor with dimensions of 2.4 m × 2.4 m). However, a 5-sided CAVE (three walls, floor and ceiling) has now replaced this. The whole construction is mainly made of wood to avoid any electromagnetic distortion for the tracking system. To provide rear projection for the floor, the CAVE is raised about 2 m above ground level. The floor consists of a 30 mm thick "paraglass" plate – a special acrylic glass that is strong enough to carry 10 people – and has excellent optical characteristics. The wall screens consist of special plastic material and are carefully blended along the edges to guarantee shadow-free projection. The projectors are five modified Electrohome Marquee 7500 projectors with an image resolution of 1024 × 1024 pixels operating at 120 Hz. The images are generated by a 3-pipe SGI ONYX Infinite Reality with six CPUs (R10000). In addition, there is a 3D sound system with four speakers and several 3D tracking devices.

Apart from the CAVE, other innovative I/O devices are installed in the VR Technology Lab. A motion platform (SIMTEC) combined with motion rendering enables the user to get haptic feedback from forces due to accelerations. This is used as a therapy simulator to treat people with fear of flying. The PHANToM (SensAble Devices) and a ThermoPad (developed by IGD) provide the possibility to stimulate other important human senses such as thermal and haptic sensations in combination with force feedback. All devices mentioned above are already supported by the VR system "Virtual Design II" of IGD [1].

To date, there are three CAVE installations at industrial sites in Germany (VW, Daimler Benz and Opel), and from the very beginning they have received positive feedback from users in industry and academia. The reason why the car industry is very interested in this kind of technology is described in the following section.

22.2 Digital Prototyping

A very important reason for using virtual reality, especially in the construction industry, is to avoid having to make physical mock-ups, thus minimizing development time and reducing time-to-market for innovative products. The idea is to exploit a 3D model (including product information and process data) through the whole product life cycle: design, styling, construction, assembly/disassembly, training, sales, recycling etc. The challenge is to provide tools that enable the design or construction engineer to operate with a digital prototype (also called a digital mock-up) in an efficient manner. In addition, digital prototypes provide the ideal platform for supporting concurrent engineering.

A CAVE projection system provides the optimal output device for digital prototypes, especially if intuitive two-hand interactions, full-body freedom, space perception of 1:1 scale and communication with other engineers are needed. Therefore most CAVE projects have been realized in the scope of digital prototypes in cooperation with companies from the car industry [3], ship construction, plant design, aircraft construction and architecture.

22.2.1 Design Review

A very exciting and photorealistic model of a VW Sharan, modeled and prepared by Volkswagen AG, was presented in our CAVE (Figure 22.2). This very complex model is well suited to design review purposes and ergonomic studies.

The benefit of a CAVE presentation in comparison with other presentation techniques for this task is the perception of space and the possibility of discussion and communication with other engineers during the review process. A CAVE can also support very high-quality graphics that are essential for assessing design and styling issues. Furthermore, to aid the sense of realism shadows and reflections are included in the rendering process.

On the other hand, the display systems must also satisfy the requirements of color saturation and brightness. The main problem here is that the projected luminance levels on large screens are insufficient and need improving. Another difficult problem is the light inter-reflection between the screens of the perpendicular walls – especially for very bright scenes – which give rise to unwanted visual artefacts.

Figure 22.2 Design review of a VW Sharan (by courtesy of Volkswagen AG).

22.2.2 Assembly/Disassembly

A very important issue for digital prototypes in the car industry is the verification of assembly/disassembly processes. The problems here are to make sure that constructed components fit together (packaging), that available tools are sufficient for the task and that the assembly/disassembly path of each component is optimized.

Based on a digital prototype, a scenario for assembly and disassembly studies of a car door was presented in the CAVE in cooperation with BMW (Figure 22.3). Users interact with the computer using speech recognition and a data glove. They can point at objects, display important product information, grab objects and tools, design the assembly path and verify the task for different components.

Real-time collision detection is very important for evaluating assembly paths, and the CAVE has proved to be a very powerful tool for this type of application. Because there are no haptic and force-feedback output devices, the missing force-feedback cues (e.g. grabbing components, collisions between objects, etc.) need to be replaced by other interaction paradigms.

22.2.3 Plant Design

In plant design, customers' needs are making design reviews of new construction projects based on a digital prototype more and more important. As an example, a real-time walk-through was developed and presented in a CAVE using a data set provided by Lurgi (Figure 22.4). A virtual trainer, implemented as an autonomous

Figure 22.3 Assembly/disassembly of a car door (by courtesy of BMW AG).

Figure 22.4 Design review of a plant including particle simulation (by courtesy of Lurgi).

object, is able to find its way through the factory without any user intervention and is guiding the user for training purposes. In addition, real-time simulation of particle clouds enables the visualization of hazardous environments, which is very important for training applications.

22.2.4 Ship Construction

Another construction and assembly project was demonstrated for ship and machinery construction. A complex data set from Bloom & Voss, representing parts of a ship, was imported into the VR system by converting ACIS data files (SAT) from Applicon's CAD system BRAVO (Figure 22.5).

Figure 22.5 Ship construction and piping (by courtesy of Bloom & Voss).

In a prototype construction scenario, users were able to virtually lay out pipe and component structures with their hands. This presentation opened up new opportunities for engineers: instead of constructing components with 3D coordinates, they are able to put pre-constructed components together with their hands. Because of the enhanced sensation of presence, this interaction paradigm (*composing* instead of *constructing*) proved to be a very important CAVE feature.

22.2.5 Virtual Airport

Architecture was one of the first application areas for VR. Based on a digital scene description (digital prototype), a customer is able to navigate through the building and evaluate alternative routes.

In cooperation with Lufthansa AG, an immersive walk-through of the new Terminal 1 building at Frankfurt airport has been shown in the CAVE (Figure 22.6). The reconstruction of the old terminal was planned and carried out by several architects. The goal of the VR presentation was to visualize the construction for non-experts and to show new components in the context of their environment (e.g. a new counter in the entrance hall). The benefit of the CAVE presentation was the perception of space, which is very important in the field of architecture. The enhanced level of presence proved to be an important sensation in the CAVE, and allowed users to observe the new environment relative to their own physical bodies.

In addition, a radiosity simulation was calculated for the scene to improve depth perception and visual realism. Due to the scene's complexity (150 000 polygons), the renderer had to use a progressive and hierarchical radiosity technique. The resulting patch structure created a complexity of approximately 500 000 polygons. For real-time display, level-of-detail and radiosity texture maps were applied.

Figure 22.6 Terminal 1 at Frankfurt airport (by courtesy of Lufthansa AG).

22.2.6 Functional Analysis and Ergonomic Studies

BMW provided a virtual car interior so that the CAVE could be used to investigate the accessibility and functionality of cockpit components in combination with new interaction and visualization techniques (e.g. real-time visualization of airflow in the interior of the car). The user was able to control the accessibility of components within the car's interior and examine important ergonomic issues. A special feature enabled the evaluation of the air circulation, where particle sources were connected to the user's fingertips and used to visualize the wind field in pseudo-colors (Figure 22.7).

Figure 22.7 Real-time visualization of air circulation (by courtesy of BMW AG).

22.3 Edutainment

Edutainment combines education and entertainment and is an important application area for VR. Because VR is used for marketing purposes, the CAVE is potentially a very exciting output device.

22.3.1 Virtual Oceanarium

The tradition and history of Portugal is strongly linked with the ocean. The main building of the world exhibition EXPO '98 is one of the biggest oceanariums in the world, consisting of five water tanks of approximately 7 m height, with more than 30 000 plants and fish, including sharks.

In cooperation with EXPO '98, Centro de Computação Gráfica (CCG, Coimbra) and Fraunhofer-IGD, a virtual oceanarium was developed (Figure 22.8). In contrast to the real oceanarium, the visitor is enabled to explore the exciting scenario and to interact with its population like a virtual diver. Hundreds of fish are simulated in real time (e.g. school behavior, attacking other fishes, feeding etc.) using artificial intelligence techniques. Virtual actors guide the virtual diver through various scenarios and explain important facts about the oceans.

The virtual oceanarium was presented during EXPO '98 at a special auditorium on a stereo screen projection. It was also presented at some important fairs before the EXPO in Germany, Portugal and USA for marketing purposes. After EXPO '98 it will be used as an edutainment installation, rather like a planetarium.

This virtual underwater world was also presented in the CAVE and the interaction between the diver and the fish was a fascinating experience (especially when sharks are swimming through the CAVE). Unfortunately, the "throughput" of a CAVE is too low for events such as an EXPO. A stereo projection is better suited for hundreds of visitors per hour. On the other hand, the CAVE is very practical for long-term installations where smaller groups of people are attracted.

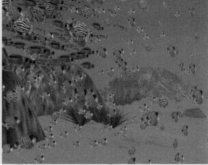

Figure 22.8 The Oceanarium of EXPO '98 and a snapshot of the underwater world, by courtesy of EXPO '98 and CCG.

22.4 Conclusion

In 1996 a 3-sided CAVE was built to gain experience with this very exciting type of display device and to present this technology in combination with industrial applications. The CAVE proved to be a very important technology, since it supports features that are missing in other VR output devices. It also provides presence of the user's body, very good space perception and the possibility of discussion and communication with other observers. Based on the very good industrial feedback from this project, a 5-sided CAVE was installed in 1997, which proved to overcome most of the technological problems associated with a 3-sided CAVE.

However, a few disadvantages of such a projection system still need to be addressed. In the context of digital prototyping, applications still suffer from missing haptic and force-feedback devices, especially in a CAVE. Therefore a combination of such a device with a CAVE would be the ultimate installation for this application area. In addition, better tracking techniques need to be developed which deliver accurate tracking results without latency and cables. The projection technology still needs improvements in brightness and color saturation, especially for design and styling applications.

References

[1] P Astheimer, W Felger and S Müller (1993) Virtual Design: a generic VR system for industrial applications, *Computers & Graphics*, 17(6), 671–7.

[2] C Cruz-Neira, D Sandin and T DeFanti (1993) Surround-screen projection-based virtual reality: the design and implementation of the CAVE, *Computer Graphics (SIGGRAPH '93 Proceedings)*, pp. 135–42.

[3] F Dai, W Felger, T Frühauf, M Göbel *et al.* (1996) Virtual prototyping examples for automotive industries, *Proc. Virtual Reality World*, Stuttgart, February.

[4] N Magnenat-Thalmann and D Thalmann (eds.) (1994) *Realism in Virtual Reality*, John Wiley & Sons, Chichester, pp. 189–210.

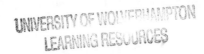
UNIVERSITY OF WOLVERHAMPTON
LEARNING RESOURCES

Author Index